ICELAND
FROM PAST TO PRESENT

ICELAND

FROM PAST TO PRESENT

by
ESBJÖRN ROSENBLAD
&
RAKEL SIGURÐARDÓTTIR-ROSENBLAD

translated by
ALAN CROZIER

Mál og menning
Reykjavík 1993

Original title: *Island i saga och nutid*, published by Norstedts, Stockholm

Text © Esbjörn Rosenblad and Rakel Sigurðardóttir-Rosenblad 1993
Translation © Alan Crozier 1993
Foreword © Vigdís Finnbogadóttir 1993

Colour photos © Andrés Arnalds (26, 27, 28), Björn Hróarsson (10, 11, 12, 15, 18, 19, 25), Jóhannes S. Kjarval (31, 34), Kristján Pétur Guðnason (29, 30, 32, 33, 36), Landmælingar Íslands (3), Páll Stefánsson (23), Ragnar Axelsson (8), Sigurður S. Jónsson (13), Snorri Snorrason (2, 4, 5, 6, 7, 14, 17, 20, 21, 22), Veðurstofa Íslands (24)
Black and white photos © Skrifstofa forseta Íslands (p. xiv), Kristján P. Arngrímsson (p. 7), Þjóðminjasafn Íslands (p. 33), Kristinn Ingvarsson (p. 41), Landsbókasafn Íslands (p. 145), Kristján Pétur Guðnason (p. 171), Ævar Jóhannesson (p. 241), Þjóðskjalasafn Íslands (p. 353)

Printed in Iceland by Prentsmiðjan Oddi hf.

ISBN: 9979-3-0502-9

❧ Iceland ❧

What good fortune for mankind,
Iceland of the seas, that you exist.
Iceland of the silent snow and the fervent waters,
Iceland of the night arched
over waking and dreams.
Island of the white day that returns,
youthful and mortal as Baldur.
Cold rose, secret island,
that became the memory of Germania
and rescued for us
its quenched, buried mythology,
the ring begetting nine rings,
the tall wolves in forests of iron
swallowing moon and sun,
the ship built by Someone or Something
from the nails of the dead.
Iceland of the waiting craters
and the calm flocks of sheep,
Iceland of the static evenings
and men of strength
who are now sailors, fishermen, and parsons
and yesterday discovered a continent.
Island of the horses with long manes
multiplying in meadows and lava fields,
island with a lake full of coins
and unfulfilled hope.
Iceland of the sword and the rune,
Iceland of the great concave memory
that is not nostalgia.

Jorge Luis Borges, Islandia
From *Historia de la Noche* 1977
Translated by Bernard Scudder

❧ Contents ❧

⊰ Foreword ⊱

From the 'Ultima Thule' of the ancients to the 'Land of Ice and Fire' of the modern tourist trade, the names used to describe Iceland have always suggested extremity and distance, a remote and isolated place. We ourselves see it not as somewhere far away but as the centre of our world, closely connected with everything happening around us and also with the past that has made us what we are today. This island is home to a people who are highly conscious of their identity and their role among the nations of the world. A people who have preserved their ancient Nordic language and have definite goals for their future.

We Icelanders always welcome the publication of books which can make other people interested in who we are, because we think it is worth the effort of learning how a people can have survived for 1,100 years in a country which made life for our ancestors so hard for many centuries, but which recent generations have transformed into a near and dear friend. Through memories dating right back to the settlement of our country and the origin of our nation, we feel that the Icelanders, past and present, form a single family to which it is a great privilege to belong, and we wish to cultivate our friendship with other nations in the spirit of the old maxim in *Hávamál:*

Ungur var eg forðum,	Once I was young
fór eg einn saman,	I travelled alone,
þá varð eg villur vega;	then I lost my way.
auðigur þóttumk	Rich I thought myself
er eg annan fann	when I met someone else
maður er manns gaman.	— man is man's delight.

⊰{ Preface }⊱

THIS BOOK IS NOT A DIPLOMATIC report to the Swedish Ministry for Foreign Affairs. Nor is it a book of memoirs, a travelogue, or an easily digested newspaper report. It is a declaration of love for Iceland.

The aim of our book is to give some insight and to spread knowledge about Iceland yesterday and today. Great emphasis is laid on history and culture in a broad sense (Chapters 1–4). This is followed by an account of the transition to modern Icelandic society (Chapter 5). After a look at various aspects of contemporary Iceland (Chapters 6–9) there is a concluding survey (Chapter 10). It is our hope that this book will arouse the reader's interest in this island of poetry and saga. Indeed, every traveller to Iceland is enchanted by the uniquely colourful landscape. Against a backdrop of crystal-clear skies, the land displays tempestuous waterfalls and geysers, steaming hot springs and black fields of lava, flowering meadows, massive glaciers, the hazy blue of distant mountains and fiords. Iceland is worth a visit.

A brief statement of our background is relevant.

Esbjörn Rosenblad MA, LL D: I am a doctor of international law. I have behind me thirty-eight years of work as a diplomat in the Swedish foreign service. I was bewitched by Iceland immediately on arrival in 1977. Since then I have lived in Iceland, where I served between 1977 and 1986 at the Royal Swedish Embassy in Reykjavík.

Rakel Sigurðardóttir-Rosenblad: I am an Icelander by descent and culture. I am a qualified tourist guide in English and French and a member of the Iceland Travel Guides' Association. I am married to Esbjörn Rosenblad. I have assisted him and been his guide.

Had it not been for our cooperation, this book would never have appeared. It is the fruit of inspiring conversations and long daily strolls along the shore to an old whitewashed lighthouse. It stands on Grótta, a narrow neck of land which can be reached only when the tide is low.

Readers should not be put off by any initial difficulty they may feel in coping with the exotic look of Icelandic names. We assume that anyone who is interested enough to read a book about Iceland is also willing to learn a little about the Icelandic language.

The lesson can suitably begin with a look at the Icelandic alphabet, which has two letters—*ð* and *þ*—not found in English, although they represent familiar consonant sounds. The letter *Ð, ð* is called *eð* and pronounced like English *th* in *mother* (which in Icelandic is *móðir*). It comes after *d* in the Icelandic alphabet. The letter *Þ, þ* is called *þorn* and pronounced like English *th* in *thorn*. It comes after *z* in the alphabet. When Icelandic characters are not available, foreign printers usually replace the letter *ð* by *d* and *þ* by *th*. In this book, however, they are retained.

Icelandic has two vowel characters not found in English. They come at the end of the alphabet. The vowel *ö* is like the sound in German *hören* or French *peur.* The ligature *æ* represents a sound like that in *eye*. The vowels *a, e, i, o, u, y* can all be written with an acute accent: *á, é, í, ó, ú, ý.* The accent does not indicate stress (all Icelandic words are stressed on the first syllable); it denoted length in Old Icelandic, but now the accented vowels differ greatly in quality from the unaccented ones and are often alphabetized separately. They have the following pronunciation: *á* sounds roughly like *ow* in *cow*; *é* is pronounced like *ye* in *yes*; *í* and *ý* are both like *ee* in *see*; *ó* is a diphthong [ou] like the pronunciation of *o* in many varieties of British English; *ú* is like *oo* in *school*.

The order of the Icelandic alphabet, as seen in a telephone directory, a modern dictionary, or the index to this book, is as follows:

aáb(c)dðeéfghiíjklmnoóp(q)rstuúvxyý(z)þæö

Icelandic is a highly inflected language with a full range of endings for verb conjugations in present and past, and noun declensions in four cases. The equivalents of the English Christian names Eric and Anne, for example, are declined as follows in the nominative, accusative, dative, and genitive: Eiríkur, Eirík, Eiríki, Eiríks; Anna, Önnu, Önnu, Önnu. Only the nominative forms are used in this book.

In English books dealing with Viking history and in translations of the Icelandic sagas there is fluctuating practice in the treatment of proper names. Let us once again take the name Eiríkur, which was borne by the Viking who discovered and named Greenland. Some books use the Old Icelandic form *Eiríkr,* others drop the nominative ending and the accent to leave *Eirik,* and others anglicize the name as *Eric.* Any of these approaches may be appropriate for Old Icelandic names, but it would be unacceptable to treat, say, the modern Icelandic artist Eiríkur Smith in this way. To avoid inconsistency, we use only the modern Icelandic forms of all proper names, where necessary giving well-known English equivalents in parentheses. Thus the discoverer of Greenland is referred to here as 'Eiríkur rauði (Eric the Red)'. The only exceptions to this rule are four names from Norse mythology—the familiar Odin, Thor, Valhalla, and Valkyrie are used for Icelandic Óðinn, Þór, Valhöll, and Valkyrja—and the name of the Icelandic parliament, which is rendered here as the Althing (Icelandic Alþingi).

In this book the term 'Vikings' refers to the participants in the Scandinavian voyages of 793–1066, whether they were peaceful or militant. The Icelanders, however, employ this term solely to denote ravaging plunderers of the period.

We extend our warmest thanks to all those who have been generous with their assistance and encouragement during the writing of this book. Our gratitude goes first to some of our old friends: Aðalsteinn Davíðsson and Heimir Pálsson, both experts on Icelandic literature and history; Þór Magnússon, the State Antiquary of Iceland; Professor Jónas Kristjánsson, Director of the Arnamagnæan Institute in Iceland; Sveinn Einarsson, historian of the theatre, author, and producer; Halldóra Ásgrímsdóttir-Rocksén, employed at the Royal Swedish Embassy; Hallfreður Örn Eiríksson and Stefán Karlsson, both researchers at the Arnamagnæan Institute; and Håkan Jansson, the former Swedish lector at the University of Iceland. The same circle of friends includes Hjálmar Hannesson, Icelandic ambassador to Germany, and scholars such as Professor Baldur Jónsson, the archaeologist Helena Forshell, the marine biologist Jóhann Sigurjónsson, Dr Guðmundur Pálmason, and the meteorologist Dr Þór Jakobsson. We also appreciate the contributions on specialist topics kindly provided by Professor Gunnar

Karlsson (history), Dr Páll Imsland (geology), Guðmundur Sigvaldason, Director of the Nordic Volcanological Institute (volcanoes), Gunnar Gunnarsson (security policy), Dr Ágúst Valfells (nuclear engineering), Director of Shipping Magnús Jóhannesson (shipping), Professor Gunnar G. Schram (constitutional and environmental law), and Eyjólfur Konráð Jónsson, Member of the Althing (the law of the sea).

We honour the memory of Per Olof Forshell, the late Swedish Ambassador to Iceland.

We extend profound thanks to Dr Jóhannes Nordal, Governor of the Central Bank of Iceland, and members of his staff, including Finnur Sveinbjörnsson (economist), Ólafur Pálmason, and Gyða Helgadóttir.

The manuscript of the Swedish original was scrutinized by Professor Karl-Ivar Hildeman and Professor Göran Frostell. Our old friend Jacques de Wærn, of the National Archives in Stockholm, has generously shared his extensive knowledge of Norse mythology with us. He is the author of the Appendix on the subject of the Indo-European roots of Norse mythology. He is also responsible for the heraldic drawing which adorns the book.

Other Swedes who deserve our thanks for their encouragement are Dr Wilhelm Odelberg, former chief librarian, and Jan Prawitz, formerly of the Ministry of Defence.

A number of photographs, maps, and slides have been kindly made available by Björn Th. Björnsson, the Central Bank of Iceland (including an extract from a map of Iceland drawn in Amsterdam around 1680), the Arnamagnæan Institute in Iceland, the National Museum of Iceland, the National Library, and the Icelandic Meteorological Office (satellite photograph).

The statistics have been checked and brought up to date as per 1 December 1991 by Dr Magnús S. Magnússon. We are particularly indebted to Magnús, who has been attached to the Statistical Bureau of Iceland since 1985.

The publication of the Swedish original of this book would not have been possible without a munificent donation of 500,000 Icelandic krónur from the Central Bank of Iceland. We also extend our thanks for support from the following cultural funds in Sweden: Konung Gustaf VI Adolfs fond för svensk kultur, Clara Lachmanns fond, Letterstedtska föreningen, and Längmanska kulturfonden.

This translation of the Swedish original, *Island i saga och nutid* (Stockholm: Norstedts, 1990) allows us to make the work available to a much wider audience. For this purpose the text has been thoroughly revised and updated. The English translation is the work of Alan Crozier, who took his doctorate in Germanic Philology at Cambridge in 1980. Born in Northern Ireland, he now lives in Sweden, where he works as a full-time translator.

Here in Iceland we have also enjoyed the cooperation of Peter Kidson Karlsson from Yorkshire, former British diplomat and international translator, now an Icelandic citizen.

We are also much obliged to three other experts on English. They are Professor Desmond Slay of the University College of Wales, Aberystwyth, Professor Robert Cook of the University of Iceland, and Bernard Scudder. Bernard has provided us with the masterly rendering into English of the introductory poem on Iceland by Jorge Luis Borges, as well as translations in Chapter 4 of poems by three Icelandic poets, Hannes Sigfússon, Sigurður Pálsson, and Gyrðir Elíasson.

This book has been written for different kinds of reader. It is intended both for reading at a stretch and for use as a handbook. For the latter purpose it is often practical to repeat the same facts in different contexts. This approach has therefore been employed deliberately.

We hope that this book will give pleasure and enlightenment, spreading an interest in Iceland over the globe.

Esbjörn Rosenblad   *Rakel Sigurðardóttir-Rosenblad*

❧ Chapter 1 ❧

Historical and Cultural Background

Discovery and Settlement (*c*.870–930)

Ingólfur . . . made his home at the spot
where his high-seat pillars had been
washed ashore, and lived at Reykjavík.

Landnámabók

ICELAND LONG REMAINED undiscovered, a *terra incognita*. The main reason for this is its geographical position in the middle of the North Atlantic, at a great distance from continental Europe. On the other hand, we have an unusually extensive knowledge of the early history of Iceland, from the time when it finally was discovered, and we have a rich and captivating store of Old Icelandic literature in the Eddic and skaldic poems and the sagas.

The Icelandic word *saga* means not only 'story' but also 'history'. Its original meaning is something that is said, regardless of whether the tale that is told is based on reality or is a product of the imagination.

Iceland was the last country in Europe to be peopled. According to *Landnámabók* (The Book of Settlements), the first colonizers were the families of Norwegian chieftains who could not tolerate the autocratic rule of King Haraldur hárfagri (Harald Fairhair, 860–940?). In the second half of the ninth century, they began to settle in Iceland, where they found refuge from tyranny. They built their houses and farms by the deep fiords and in the green valleys of the virgin island, and the embryo of a new society began to grow.

The settlement of Iceland was part of the remarkable wave of emigration from Scandinavia which goes under the name of the Viking Age (c.800–1060). The Vikings steered their ships to east and west alike, not only pillaging and harrying but also trading peacefully. Their western travels brought them all the way to North America, the Vinland of the sagas, while the eastern route took them as far as Constantinople, which they called Mikligarður ('Great City'). They took their ships down the mighty rivers of Russia. They sailed the Volga all the way to the Caspian Sea, where they traded with the Arabs. The Swedish Vikings who ventured eastwards were called 'Rus' by the Slavs who lived there, and it is they who have given their name to Russia.

There are two explanations for the ability of the Vikings to undertake such long voyages; they were skilled sailors, and they had discovered the art of building swift vessels which were more seaworthy than earlier craft. The design of the Viking ships can be studied thanks to finds of ships in Norway, such as those from Gokstad, Oseberg, and Tune. They had a single mast which bore a large, square sail. They were also equipped with oars. Viking ships had high, pointed prows and small raised half-decks. All the biggest vessels, longships like King Ólafur Tryggvason's *Long Serpent*, were steered with a rudder, which was attached near the stern on the right side (facing forward)— hence the Icelandic *stjórnborði* and English *starboard* 'steer-board'. The helmsman consequently had to turn his back to the left side, hence the Icelandic name *bakborði*, which the French have borrowed from the Normans as *bâbord* 'port'. Small vessels were completely open, but this evidently did not deter the Vikings from putting to sea in stormy weather.

Historians generally agree that the main causes of the Viking Age migrations were overpopulation, crop failures, and starvation in Scandinavia, combined with the reluctance of defiant chieftains to submit to the growing power of the king. A thirst for adventure and a desire for change were no doubt added incentives. The Vikings were bold warriors. Their success was made easier by the general unease and dissolution that affected much of Europe after the death of Charlemagne in 814. Vikings from Norway and elsewhere in Scandinavia who could manage the voyage to the Faroe Islands and Iceland found another advantage there—they could land on virtually uninhabited islands.

Before the Vikings came to Iceland, the island had been discovered by Irish monks and anchorites, known in Icelandic as *papar*. It is not known when they first came to Iceland, but a possible date is around AD 800. Some scholars suggest a date a little earlier or later. All this is, however, mere speculation. In a geographical work from 825, the Irish scholar Dicuil equated the Ultima Thule of classical antiquity with an island in the northern ocean, just south of a frozen sea. The island was later given the name Iceland. According to Dicuil's statement, the *papar* had sailed there and witnessed the midnight sun. They settled down in a number of places on the south-east corner of the island. One of their sites is an island which still bears their name— Papey. There are other place-names testifying to the presence of these Christians, such as Papós (where *ós* means 'estuary') and Papafell (where *fell* means 'mountain').[1]

The Irish monks left Iceland in a hurry as soon as the Vikings landed on the island. This story is told by the Icelandic priest Ari fróði (Ari the Learned, 1067–1148) in his *Íslendingabók* (The Book of the Icelanders),[2] and a similar account can be read in *Landnámabók*. The *papar* sailed away because they did not want to share the island with pagans. They left behind them Irish books, bells, and crosiers.

Ari fróði then goes on to tell how Iceland and Greenland were discovered and colonized by Norse settlers. He puts these events in a Christian chronology. His *Íslendingabók*, which was originally written on calfskin, can still be easily understood by modern Icelanders. It is almost a miracle that this work has been preserved for posterity. The oldest manuscript was destroyed in the great fire of Copenhagen in 1728, when a great deal of Árni Magnússon's collection fell victim to the flames; luckily, however, it had been copied by an Icelandic priest before it was removed from Iceland.

A more detailed narrative of the settlement of Iceland is preserved in *Landnámabók*.[3] This specifically states that some of the emigrants from Scandinavia were Vikings. We also learn that many of them came to Iceland via the British Isles.

The original version of *Landnámabók* was edited at the start of the twelfth century by Ari fróði and his collaborator Kolskeggur hinn vitri (Kolskegg the Wise). They amassed their information by talking to the descendants of Iceland's first settlers. Their history is thus based on oral tradition. It was not put down on parchment until some two hundred years after the events it describes. In view of the defects of human memory and the long line of oral transmission, how are we to judge its value as a historical source?

The same question arises in the source criticism of, say, the Homeric epics and the medieval chronicles, such as those of the rise of the Ottoman Empire, since these are also based on a long oral tradition—which as a rule is regarded as unreliable. It is also easy to point out sources of error. It can be difficult, for example, to distinguish fact from fantasy. Accounts handed down via a long chain of transmission may have been altered, distorted, or deliberately embellished with legendary material.

Sources of this kind nevertheless often contain an element of truth, corroborated in some cases by archaeological finds. A famous example is the excavation of Troy, where the Homeric enthusiast Heinrich Schliemann was inspired by his faith that the *Iliad* could at least have a partial historical foundation.

It has also been shown that some genealogies have been well preserved because they constitute 'natural systems', uniform complexes which can be preserved in the memory more easily than isolated details. A genealogy forms a natural framework on which the epic material can be hung.[4] Scholars have observed that the genealogies in *Landnámabók* could have functioned in this way. The historical reliability of the book is generally considered to be high.[5]

The issue of the value of the Icelandic sagas as historical sources has been examined in a broader context by Jónas Kristjánsson, director of the Arnamagnæan Institute in Reykjavík.[6] He draws no general conclusions on the matter; instead his working hypothesis is to let each group of sagas speak for itself a priori. He also summarizes the findings of previous scholars.

Many of the Icelandic sagas are permeated with a belief in destiny (such as *Laxdæla saga*) or superstition (such as *Grettis saga*), while some early sagas aim chiefly at recording historical events. A relevant feature here is the distance between the historical event and the time when it was recorded in writing. How was this gap bridged? In the earliest sagas the gap was not at all big: the heroine of *Laxdæla saga*, Guðrún Ósvífursdóttir, was the great-grandmother of Ari fróði, so the saga characters and those who recorded the stories were separated by only eighty to a hundred years. Moreover, the oldest sagas have in common the scene of the events (mostly Icelandic settlements), a virtually unchanged language, and conversations recorded in direct speech. A comparison between the oral tradition in two sagas which describe the same events—*Grænlendinga saga* and *Eiríks saga rauða*—shows many points of striking similarity. According to Jónas,[7] then, the comparison supports the belief that these sagas have a significant core of truth as regards the voyages to Vinland.

Jónas mentions that in his youth he liked to listen to what his grandfather (1860–1945) and aunt (1878–1979) told him of his ancestors. His grandparents were masters of the storyteller's art. They could tell of people going back as far as 120 years. Jónas later studied the parish registers and found that his grandparents had been correct in every detail.

Jónas Kristjánsson concludes that the Icelanders could well have preserved historical truth through the oral tradition for at least 120 years. After this the accuracy declines. Jónas also found that the oldest sagas 'give an embellished but complete picture of a distant age. Small details in the narratives and descriptions are unhistorical. But the main events, such as the killings of the leading characters, are faithfully rendered, as are in large measure the genealogies. The sagas thus convey a great deal of truth about the tenth and eleventh centuries.'[8]

The pithy language of *Landnámabók* gives a fascinating record of the colonists of Iceland. Many of them came from western Norway (especially the districts of Sogn, Fjordane, and Hordaland), while others came from southern Sweden and Denmark. They sailed from one group of islands to the next: to the Shetlands, the Orkneys, the Hebrides, the Faroes, and on to Iceland. Their voyages also took them to Ireland, the Isle of Man, Scotland, and England.

Landnámabók tells us that the Norwegian Viking Naddoddur was on his way from Norway to the Faroe Islands when he was driven off course by the wind and ended up in Iceland. He called it Snæland or

'Snowland', since it was snowing heavily on the mountains when he left it to return to the Faroes in the autumn.

Later, the Swedish seafarer Garðar Svavarsson came in search of Snæland, following the directions of his second-sighted mother. He landed on the east coast and then sailed all round the country, thus ascertaining that it was an island. He called it after himself, Garðars-hólmur or 'Garðar's Isle'. Garðar spent the winter and built a house at a place in northern Iceland which he called Húsavík—'House Bay'— and which still bears this name. After his winter at Húsavík, Garðar prepared to sail for Norway. When he had put to sea, a boat drifted away from his ship with a man called Náttfari aboard, along with a slave and a bondwoman. Náttfari settled by a nearby bay to the west, Náttfaravík. But Garðar sailed for Norway. There he praised the new-found island very highly. At that time it was wooded between the mountains and the coast.

The next traveller to Iceland was the Norwegian Flóki Vilgerðarson, 'a great Viking'. He sailed without a compass, but he had with him three ravens. When he released the first one it flew back towards Norway. The second returned to the ship, but the third flew off in the direction of Iceland. This tale has its counterpart in the book of Genesis, where Noah did reconnaissance from the top of Mount Ararat by releasing a bird three times, first a raven, then a dove which returned since it found no resting place, and then after another seven days the dove again; this time it returned to the ark with a fresh olive branch in its beak.

Like Garðar, Flóki spent a winter in Iceland. He noted the huge waterfalls, the rich fishing banks, and the occurrence of whales. In the west he sailed into Breiðafjörður as far as Vatnsfjörður at Barðaströnd. That winter all his cattle died because of a shortage of hay. The spring was cold too. Then Flóki climbed up a high mountain, from where he could see a fiord full of drift-ice to the north: this was the reason he and his men called the country Ísland or 'Iceland'.

So much for the laconic account in *Landnámabók*. We may surmise that the chilly name was an expression of Flóki's disappointment over the Icelandic climate that year. Flóki's fellow traveller Þórólfur gained a much more favourable impression of the new country, where he said

The Norwegian Ingólfur Arnarson, the first settler in Iceland, as sculptured by Einar Jónsson (see p. 181). Einar's rather romantic bronze sculpture has been raised at Arnarhóll in central Reykjavík, just in front of the topmodern building of concrete, housing the Central Bank of Iceland. — This contrasting constellation may be said to underline the main theme of our book. It is to give some insight about Iceland yesterday and today — Iceland from Past to Present.

that butter dripped from every blade of grass. This exaggeration earned him the nickname Þórólfur smjör (Thorolf Butter).

When did the Northmen discover Iceland? It has been claimed that it was around 870. This date, although uncertain, is a reasonable assumption. Archaeological finds at burial sites under layers of volcanic ash, together with geological, linguistic, and toponymic evidence, all point in the same direction: Vikings sailed to Iceland in the latter half of the ninth century and settled there.

The first Northman to settle permanently in Iceland was the Norwegian Ingólfur Arnarson. According to *Landnámabók*, he landed there around 874. Both Ingólfur and his foster-brother Hjörleifur are described as Vikings. They had been together on pillaging trips before. Hjörleifur had also harried 'in the west', that is, in Ireland, where he had captured ten Celtic thralls. The foster-brothers sailed to the south coast of Iceland in separate ships. Hjörleifur settled on the promontory that bears his name, Hjörleifshöfði, but he was treacherously murdered by his Irish slaves. After the murder the slaves fled to some islands further to the west, which are still called after these 'Westmen', Vest-mannaeyjar. When Ingólfur sighted Iceland and neared the south coast, by a promontory which was later called Ingólfshöfði, he threw the pillars of his high-seat overboard and said that he would settle where they drifted ashore. Later he sent two slaves west to search for them. It took them a long time to find the pillars, which had drifted with the currents and floated ashore at Arnarhvál in Reykjavík. Ingólfur built his house there, and 'the high-seat pillars still stand in the hall (*í eldhúsi*) there', according to *Landnámabók*.

This may sound like a fantastic tale, but excavations in Reykjavík, south of Aðalstræti, have uncovered remains of dwellings in the neigh-bourhood of Arnarhvál. These suggest that this place was occupied a short time before 900.[9]

The year 930 was a milestone in the history of Iceland, since it is reckoned as the date when the Icelandic commonwealth was born. In the high summer of that year, all the most eminent men of Iceland assembled at Þingvellir, about 50 kilometres from the present capital of Reykjavík. The venue for this open-air gathering—the Althing—has been sculpted by volcanic eruptions and earthquakes, with a prominent rock, the law-rock (*lögberg*), from where speakers could address the assembly. The year 930 is also accepted as the date of the foundation of one of the oldest surviving parliamentary traditions.

Ingólfur Arnarson's grandson, Þorkell máni, was law-speaker of the Icelandic commonwealth. *Landnámabók* tells us that he was 'civi-lized' (*siðaður*); although a pagan, he acted with such a pure heart that he could have been a Christian. As he lay on his deathbed he asked to be carried out into the sunshine. There he entrusted himself to the hands of the god who had created the sun.

After Ingólfur Arnarson, Northmen came to Iceland in a steady stream. Initially the population grew rapidly—from roughly 23,000 in 930 to 30,000 in 1000 and 77,000 in 1095. The first two figures are rough guesses, while the latter figure is estimated on the basis of a census conducted by Bishop Gizur Ísleifsson.[10]

From *Íslendingabók* and *Landnámabók* we learn that the majority of the immigrants probably came from Scandinavia, especially from the three districts of western Norway mentioned above: Sogn, Fjordane, and Hordaland. This is borne out by the well-known similarities between Icelandic and the dialects spoken there.[11]

At the same time, it is obvious that there is a strong Celtic strain in the Icelandic people. Evidence from physical anthropology and comparisons of blood groups point in the same direction. Previous studies of this kind were unambiguous in their conclusions that the Celtic element was greater than one might suspect from the written historical sources. However, these conclusions have been challenged in a more recent study. Not surprisingly, the question of the size of the Celtic element is a subject of heated controversy.

Many Scandinavian Vikings, before they arrived in Iceland, had settled in the British Isles. Not only was their Nordic blood intermingled with Celtic, but they also brought with them many Celtic servants and slaves, who were later freed. Some of the most celebrated heroes of the Icelandic sagas—such as Melkorka, Kormákur, Njáll, Kjartan—bear Gaelic names. Furthermore, some Icelandic place-names are of Gaelic origin; examples are Papey and Dímon.[12]

Scholars are not in agreement about the degree and the significance of this admixture of Celtic elements. It is clear, however, that there has been mutual influence between the Scandinavian and Celtic groups. Icelanders and Irishmen share a keen interest in poetry and song, literature and history.[13]

Historians have claimed that this unique mixture, the Icelanders, derives from the character of the settlers from Scandinavia—they were often members of chieftain clans, adventurous freebooters and rampant individualists—and the colourful Gaelic dash. Soon after their arrival in the melting pot of the new country, the colonizers were blended into a distinctive people. They developed their own laws and customs, and an extraordinarily rich culture.[14]

On their remote island, the settlers were probably united by the new language variant which was already emerging in the tenth century, similar to the old Norwegian dialects. A factor which later helped to weld them together was the literature that was written in Icelandic in the Middle Ages. Their form of government, together with their shared historical background, their laws and customs, their language and literature, all combined to create a sense of togetherness, a feeling of belonging to a distinct nation.

The Vikings Westwards Seen in Icelandic Sagas and Research

Bitter is the wind tonight,
White the tresses of the sea;
I have no fear the Viking hordes
Will sail the sea on such a night.

Irish stanza from the ninth century

This stanza, scribbled one stormy night by an Irish monk in the margin of his manuscript, reflects his terror of the Vikings.[15] But the storm did not last forever. In 795 Norwegian Viking ships sailing from the Hebrides turned up in the Irish Sea, not far from Dublin, plundering a monastery. After some fifty years of devastating raids recorded in Irish annals, the violence died down. The Vikings realized that they had a great deal in common with the Irish. Ultimately, they were looking for land and for trade. Numerous Irish place-names—such as Waterford (*Vatnsfjörður*), Wexford (*Veigsfjörður*), Wicklow (*Víkingaló*), and Limerick (*Hlymrekur*)—remind us of the Norse presence; so does Leixlip, meaning 'salmon-jump' (*Laxhlaup*). As settlers the Vikings built houses, traded, farmed, and married Irish women.

As evidenced in archaeological finds, some Northmen stubbornly kept their swords and continued to wear Thor's hammer round their necks. Others assimilated more quickly to Irish culture. Perhaps they could not resist playing chess. Soon they were all baptized. In 997, when the Norse king Sigtryggur Silk-Beard, ruler of Dublin, struck the first Irish silver coins, they were stamped with the Christian cross. Sigtryggur went on a pilgrimage to Rome. In the heart of the old Dublin he started the construction of Christ Church Cathedral.

Our knowledge of the Vikings—their ships, weapons, ornaments, coins, tools, sacrifices, and runic inscriptions—has grown as a result of archaeological finds in various corners of the world. In 1989 Reykjavík was proud to host an exhibition of a representative selection of finds from York, the Viking town of Jórvík, where there have been extensive excavations in recent decades. According to the saga, Egill

Skalla-Grímsson once saved his life when he sat there as a prisoner of King Eiríkur blóðöx (Eric Bloodaxe) by composing an encomium in honour of the king; he called the poem his 'Head-Ransom' (*Höfuð-lausn*).[16]

What sort of everyday life did the Vikings lead? The exhibits from York and the detailed catalogue lucidly convey a concrete reality, perhaps replacing many of the vague images formerly conjured up by reading the Icelandic sagas.

It also gives pause for thought to compare how different development was for the Vikings who settled in the uninhabited Iceland and those who sailed to England. In Iceland, as we have seen, the settlers blended quickly into a distinctive people. England, however, had already been peopled with successive waves of Britons, Romans, and Anglo-Saxons, and amidst this heritage the rule of the Vikings was short-lived. They were quickly converted to Christianity, as we see from their stone crosses, which they nevertheless decorated with scenes from tales of the pagan gods. The Northmen were absorbed by the native population, adopting their way of life and their language. Yet they did not entirely forget their origins.

The Vikings speak to us through their runic inscriptions, often hewn into stone in snaking or dragon-like coils. Both on the memorial stones raised to dead kinsmen and in the Icelandic sagas, the Northmen see themselves as heroes. So they were, in their own way. But the monks in their devastated monasteries and the ravished Christian population usually saw the Vikings in a different light. The German medieval historian Adam of Bremen describes them as 'pirates'.[17]

They themselves used the term Viking (*víkingur*). According to one etymology, this derives from *vík* 'bay', from their habit of frequenting inlets and fiords. Concrete evidence of their presence in England still survives in numerous everyday features of the English language. These include grammatical forms like *they are* (Icelandic *þeir eru*), and phonological features such as words beginning with *sk-* (*sky, skill, skirt, skin*, and so on). Other Norse loan-words include *call, die, egg, husband, knife, law, outlaw, take, thrall, tidings,* and *window*. Northern England, in particular Yorkshire, has many place-names of Viking origin, such as those ending in *by* 'settlement, village' (Grimsby, Sewerby, Whitby), *dale* (Swaledale), or *thorpe* 'outlying settlement'

(Gristhorpe), and English surnames ending in *son* (like Stevenson) are also based on Scandinavian naming practices.[18]

Almost all these Old Norse loan-words in English have counterparts in modern Icelandic, the language that has remained almost unchanged as regards vocabulary and morphology since the Viking Age.

In Normandy, the province in northern France established by invading Vikings, evidence of Norse presence is preserved in place-names such as Honfleur, Le Havre, and Yvetot, and in maritime and nautical loan-words, such as *étrave* ('stem of a ship', from *stafn*), *guinder* ('to hoist', from *vinda*), *homard* ('lobster', from *humar*), and *marsouin* ('porpoise', from *marsvín*).

Theories about the Date of the Earliest Settlement of Iceland

In September 1989 Margrét Hermanns-Auðardóttir, an Icelandic archaeologist, presented her doctoral thesis at the University of Umeå in Sweden.[19] The study was based on excavations of remains of farms at Herjólfsdalur on Vestmannaeyjar, conducted between 1971 and 1983. She contests the traditional view that the Northmen began to colonize a previously uninhabited land in the second half of the ninth century, at the time when King Haraldur hárfagri was enforcing his lordship over the local Norwegian chieftains. She argues that this dating is based on secondary sources, chiefly *Landnámabók*, and on the dating of two layers of volcanic ash, especially the 'settlement layer' (*landnámslag*) which geologists have dated to 898. She rejects this view with her claim that colonization and settlement began as far back as Merovingian times, during the seventh century. Her conclusions are in large part based on radiocarbon (C14) analyses of charcoal.

Margrét writes that 'archaeological and internationally accepted methods of dating have almost been considered superfluous in Iceland'.[20] This statement has been challenged, since such dating methods have been used by Icelandic scholars, for example, the geologist and geographer Sigurður Þórarinsson and the archaeologist Kristján Eldjárn (President of Iceland 1968–80). The latter achieved fame for his many excavations, such as those at the episcopal site of Skálholt and on the island of Papey, east of the mainland.[21]

Margrét asserts that several C14 datings, 'including some from Reykjavík, show that much of Iceland was settled at the same time as Herjólfsdalur, that is, already in the Merovingian era'.[22] Other Icelandic scholars point out that this conclusion does not agree with the findings published by the Swedish archaeologist, Else Nordahl, about a year before Margrét presented her thesis. Nordahl gives an exhaustive account of her excavations in Reykjavík, which she led between 1971 and 1975. She dug four sites in the old centre of the town, near the parliament, the cathedral, and the lake (Tjörnin). She found that the oldest settlement there began at the end of the ninth century. Nordahl bases her conclusions both on C14 datings and on geological datings of the *landnámslag*. She also mentions that the C14 datings obtained for the samples from Herjólfsdalur, according to an expert in Uppsala (Professor Ingrid U. Olsson), can be due to contamination by old carbon dioxide in the sea water and volcanic activity.[23]

Summing up her discussion of dating, Nordahl mentions that four Roman coins from the third century AD have been found in Iceland.[24] These are exceptional: all other archaeological finds, such as graves and farm foundations, are from the Viking Age or later. The earliest attested settlement in Iceland is the place where Reykjavík is located.[25]

When dating the earliest settlement of Iceland, archaeologists have thus drawn divergent conclusions. The source material is scanty. It does not allow complete certainty. Future excavations may shed more light on the subject. Ari fróði's *Íslendingabók* has been described as an unreliable source, but many scholars have been struck by the way this remarkable account often proves to be essentially correct. At any rate, it is thought-provoking that the oldest antiquities found in Reykjavík come from just beside Tjörnin—not far from the shore in the old town centre where, according to *Landnámabók*, the pillars of Ingólfur Arnarson's high-seat floated ashore.

The study of the settlement of the Faroe Islands provokes interesting comparisons, on the basis of *Færeyinga saga*,[26] place-names, and the sparse archaeological evidence. The Faroese archaeologist Símun V. Arge adheres to the traditional view about the date of the colonization of Iceland.[27]

Iceland as a Free Commonwealth (930–1262)

Cattle die,
and kinsmen die,
and so one dies one's self;
but a noble name
will never die
if good renown one gets.

Hávamál

The history of the Icelandic commonwealth can be roughly divided into the following four phases:

- the age of the sagas, 930–1030
- the age of peace, 1030–1120
- the age of literature, 1120–1220
- the age of the Sturlungs, 1220–1262

This division into phases is antiquated and has been criticized by historians. It can nevertheless be useful to bear it in mind, even though the periods are far from being watertight compartments. In many respects—as regards politics, economics, culture, law, and religion—the periods may overlap.

The following survey concentrates instead on some main features of development. It examines the continued geographical discoveries of the Northmen after the colonization of Iceland, the form of government, the conversion to Christianity, and the relentless family feuds that were the main cause of the decline and fall of the Icelandic commonwealth. An agreement with the Norwegian king in 1262 brought the end of Iceland as an independent state.

The Discovery of Greenland and North America

The insatiable roving spirit of the Vikings persisted in the blood of the early settlers in Iceland. Nothing could prevent them from setting out to sea—as long as they remained free and had their own ships.

The Vikings sailed without fear. They lacked the technical aids available in later times: charts, compasses, and other nautical instruments. According to *Landnámabók*, the Vikings who discovered Iceland had no guiding *leiðarsteinn* (lodestone). They probably had no instruments for determining their bearings. They navigated with the aid of landmarks such as high mountains or glaciers, and they judged their position by observing the sun and the stars.[28] They sailed only during the summer half of the year, thus avoiding the hazardous winter storms. They normally calculated the distance they had covered on the basis of a standard day's sailing, adjusted to take account of winds and ocean currents. Favourite destinations of the Icelanders were Ireland and Scandinavia. Ireland attracted them with promises of booty in the form of wealthy monasteries and comely women. In Scandinavia they visited kinsmen and friends, or acquired new ships and weapons. They often paid their respects to kings, especially at the Norwegian court, where they declaimed their poems of praise.

Through these journeys they maintained lively but irregular connections with the surrounding world for about four centuries. Towards the end of the tenth century their travels brought them—by accident—first to Greenland and a few years later to North America. These discoveries are recounted in a number of sagas, particularly in *Eiríks saga rauða* and *Grœnlendinga saga*. According to these sources, a Norwegian settler in Iceland, Eiríkur rauði (Eric the Red), found a huge ice-covered island to the west of Iceland, around 985. He named it *Greenland*, 'for he said that people would be much more tempted to go there if it had an attractive name.'[29]

Archaeological finds show that Icelandic settlement in Greenland for a time comprised nearly 4,000 people. They made their living by animal husbandry, hunting, and fishing. Excavations have uncovered the ruins of no less than nineteen churches, two monasteries, and about three hundred farms built of turf and stone. These colonies were destroyed some time during the fifteenth century. The cause is unknown. One significant factor may have been the deterioration in climate that occurred, according to some scholars, in the second half of the thirteenth century. This also affected Iceland. Other contributory causes were presumably the Black Death, soil erosion by grazing animals, and possibly attacks by Eskimos or pirates.[30]

According to *Grœnlendinga saga*, Leifur Eiríksson (Leif Ericsson),

son of Eiríkur rauði, came to North America around the year 1000. He sailed from Brattahlíð in western Greenland, where his father had settled. The crossing of Leifur and his companions is vividly described in the saga. The lucid account is full of closely observed detail.

First, we are told, they cast anchor and rowed in a small boat to the deserted shore. They could see no grass. Massive glaciers stretched across the horizon, and the terrain between these glaciers and the sea was like an inhospitable slab of rock, to which they gave the name *Helluland*. Their next anchorage was off a land that was flat and wooded, with wide expanses of white sand and a gentle slope down to the sea; this they called *Markland*. After two more days' sail in a northeasterly wind they sighted land again. They came to an island where they landed and looked about them. The weather was fine. There was dew on the grass. The first thing they did was to dip their hands in the dew and put it to their lips. They thought they had never tasted anything sweeter.

Finally, they rowed up a river to a lake where they cast anchor. They carried their belongings ashore and decided to build houses and spend the winter there. Both the river and the lake were full of salmon, bigger than any they had ever seen before. Tyrkir, a German member of the crew, and Leifur's foster-father since his childhood, also found 'vines

This type of Viking ship, a so-called knörr, *had great carrying capacity and was suitable for long ocean voyages. The settlers and the merchants during the first centuries of the settlement used the* knörr. *It was navigated with only one sail, but it was too heavy for rowing.*

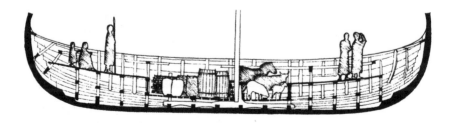

and grapes' (*vínviður og vínber*). 'Is that true, foster-father?'[31] asked Leifur. 'Of course it is true,' Tyrkir replied. 'Where I was born there were plenty of vines and grapes.' When spring came, they made ready and left this land, which Leifur the Lucky named for its vines, *Vínland*. They put out to sea, and a favourable wind brought them back 'until they sighted Greenland and its mountains beneath the glaciers'.

The account in *Grænlendinga saga* is supplemented by the details in *Eiríks saga rauða*. The two sagas together give a full picture of the Vinland voyages. Leifur himself appears to have made two trips to North America. The coast of this new land had already been sighted in 986 by Bjarni Herjólfsson, who had been driven off course by the wind while sailing from Iceland to Greenland. Unlike Leifur, he did not land on the unknown shore. It is therefore Leifur and not Bjarni who is generally credited with the discovery of North America. Later travellers to Vinland included Leifur's brother Þorvaldur and sister Freydís, and Þorfinnur karlsefni. The latter is known for his attempt to colonize North America; he sailed there with three ships carrying 160 people, both men and women. During their stay in Vinland, Þorfinnur and his wife Guðríður Eiríksdóttir had a son, Snorri—the first European to be born in North America.

According to some scholars, there is evidence that the Vinland of the Vikings should be located on the island of Newfoundland off the east coast of Canada. Yet is it conceivable that vines could have grown wild so far north? Although there is no certain answer, some light may have been shed on this riddle by recent research.

To begin with, the first syllable of Vinland need not originally have been *vín* 'wine' but could come from *vin* 'meadow'. The mention of vines and grapes in *Grænlendinga saga* would thus be the result of a linguistic distortion or misunderstanding.[32]

Another hypothesis supported by plausible arguments is that the words *vínviður* and *vínber* actually refer to currant bushes related to those which grow in northern Europe, like the *ribsber* and *sólber* of Iceland or our black currants and red currants. The latter are known as *vinbär* in Swedish (Old Swedish *vinbær*), and it is possible that this word was applied to currants in the Viking Age, when a common Norse language was spoken throughout Scandinavia. The etymology can be explained by the suggestion that currants were used like grapes for making wine. Vitamin-rich currants grow wild in Newfoundland. In 'Vinland the Good' they would have been relished by Leifur and his companions after their long voyage, when they had no doubt lived on such a vitamin-deficient diet as dried or salted meat or fish washed down with water, mead, or beer.

The misinterpretation as grapes may have arisen if the person who wrote down the saga was unaware of the existence of wild red currants; none such were found in Iceland or Greenland. The Vikings—men like Egill Skalla-Grímsson—drank mead or beer; it was only after the introduction of Christianity that, like Leifur's German 'foster-father', they began to acquire a taste for wine in the strict sense of a drink made of fermented grape-juice.

Another possibility, however, is that Leifur Eiríksson—following the example of his father—simply wanted to give the new land an attractive name. Like today's tour operators, the Vikings probably knew how to advertise.

Secondly, the Norwegian archaeologist Anne Stine Ingstad, when excavating at L'Anse aux Meadows on the northern tip of Newfoundland in the 1960s with her husband, Helge Ingstad, discovered the remains of a Viking camp. They concluded that it dated from the start of the eleventh century. In other words, Viking settlement in Newfoundland cannot be disputed. The overgrown foundations—of houses and boat sheds of the same Viking Age type as those found in Iceland and Scandinavia—were surrounded by a flat area of grass and heather. The abundant grasslands around this bay are, according to Anne Stine Ingstad, so typical of the area that they have given the place its present name, L'Anse aux Meadows, 'meadow cove'.[33]

Thirdly, Helge and Anne Stine Ingstad have also drawn attention to a number of other factors, including a map from the end of the sixteenth century, drawn by Sigurður Stefánsson, headmaster of the school at the episcopal see of Skálholt in southern Iceland.

Leifur Eiríksson's discovery, as we have seen, was a stimulus to further voyages to Vinland. It is evident that the Vikings tried for a short time to establish a permanent settlement in North America. Why did they fail? The main reason seems to have been surprise attacks by Indians, whom the Vikings called *Skrælingjar*. As well as being numerically superior, the Indians were in a better position to make new weapons locally.[34]

At L'Anse aux Meadows the archaeologists have not found any skeletal remains which can be identified as Nordic. One interpretation of this is that the Northmen took the remains of their relatives with them when they left North America. This theory is uncertain, however. Other finds suggest that the Norse sojourn in North America was short-lived—an estimated three to thirty years.

The Vinland Map, known since the end of the 1950s, has been scathingly criticized.[35] It is most likely a forgery. Nevertheless, both the finds excavated in Newfoundland and the details in the Icelandic sagas about the household belongings and weapons of the Indians unequivocally indicate the same thing: Leifur Eiríksson discovered North America around the year 1000.

South of Newfoundland the archaeologists do not appear so far to have found anything of relevance. Is it nevertheless possible that Leifur Eiríksson travelled further south—perhaps all the way to Maine, just south of the US–Canadian border? This question remains to be answered.[36]

In any case, it appears clear that Leifur Eiríksson—an Icelander with a Norwegian father—sailed to North America almost five hundred years before the two Italian mariners Christopher Columbus and Amerigo Vespucci (from whom America has received its name). It should be borne in mind that Columbus and Vespucci were sailing in bigger ships than the Vikings. In addition, they had the compass, a nautical instrument first used in the thirteenth century. These circumstances only serve to emphasize the skill of Leifur Eiríksson as a navigator and the magnificence of his bold achievement.

Leifur Eiríksson departed from Brattahlíð in Greenland, where his father had settled. The longship in which Leifur sailed to America had been built in Norway. For Icelanders and Norwegians it was therefore natural to join in the millennial celebration of the discovery of Vinland by repeating the voyage. This was done in the *Gaia*, which was built in Norway on the model of the old longships. She sailed across the Atlantic—with stops in the Orkneys, the Shetlands, the Faroes, Iceland, and Greenland—to L'Anse aux Meadows in Newfoundland. The ship cast anchor in Washington on 9 October 1991, which is celebrated there as Leif Ericsson Day. The guests of honour included the two presidents, George Bush and Vigdís Finnbogadóttir, Queen Sonja of Norway, and the Norwegian explorer Thor Heyerdahl.

Form of Government

When the men of Iceland assembled at Þingvellir in the summer of 930, they adopted a law for the entire country. This was probably modelled on the laws of western and central Norway, adapted to Icelandic conditions. These laws were not written down until the twelfth century. They are generally known as *Grágás* (Greylag Goose), although this was originally the name of a manuscript of the Norwegian law of Frostathing. *Grágás* is of considerable interest, partly because it is the main source for our knowledge of the form of government of the Icelandic commonwealth.[37]

Legislative power was exercised by a body known as *lögrétta*, which met at the Althing during its two-week-long annual gathering. A strict procedure was followed, and the members of the court sat in fixed places in a ring. The settlers—like latter-day Icelanders—attached great importance to legal matters, particularly the procedural rules to be followed in court. The chairman of the *lögrétta* was a law-speaker (*lögsögumaður*), while the other members were a number of prominent priest-chieftains whose title was *goði* (plural *goðar*)—a word derived from *goð* '(pagan) god'. The area ruled by each of these chieftains was called a *goðorð*, where he presided over a pagan temple, *(goða)hof*. The law-speaker recited the law by heart, so that it was transmitted orally for many generations.

Judicial power was exercised during the sessions of the Althing by four courts, one for each quarter of the country. Later a fifth court was established as a higher court of appeal. On the local level, spring and autumn assemblies—things (*þing*)—were held by the chieftains in their own *goðorð*.

The Althing thus had legislative and judicial powers. The assembly also functioned as an important meeting-place for the entire people, a place for spreading news, telling stories, and meeting kinsmen and friends.

As regards executive power, however, the commonwealth had no national government. The *goðar* and other prominent farmers would not submit to any superior power. They ignored or circumvented every attempt by the Icelandic church to exact obedience at the local and national level, for example, by excommunication and imposing tithes (following the law on tithes of 1096). In other words, as long as the commonwealth lasted, there was never any generally recognized executive or administrative power. The Icelanders thus lacked the preconditions for achieving a satisfactory separation of the powers in the spirit of Montesquieu.[38]

This lack of a strong central government was to have fateful consequences. In many lawsuits it meant that the parties themselves exacted justice. This tendency to take the law into one's own hands led to blood vengeance, feuds between kindreds, and divisive power struggles between leading chieftains; in the age of the Sturlungs some of these men sought help from the king of Norway.

Despite this deficiency in their form of government and the growing risk of intervention by the Norwegian king or the archbishop of Niðarós (now Trondheim), the Icelandic commonwealth lasted for over three hundred years. This society of farmers was held together by the Althing, with its law-speaker and its courts to settle disputes. The farmers ascribed great value to a knowledge of the law and the ability to achieve reconciliations. This explains the respect shown to the eponymous hero of *Njáls saga*, Njáll Þorgeirsson of Bergþórshvoll, a man well versed in the laws, famous for his good counsel and uprightness.[39]

The Æsir and the White Christ

The Middle Ages are generally reckoned as beginning around the year 400—five years after the division of the Roman Empire between the two sons of Theodosius. Moreover, it was around this time (*c.*375) that the great migrations of the Germans began, under the pressure of the Huns, with the result that one Germanic nation after the other settled on Roman territory.

In Scandinavia, however, the Middle Ages are reckoned to have begun some seven centuries later, around 1060, when the Viking Age began to peter out.

Both these ways of determining the start of the Middle Ages are based on the same milestone in history—the victory of Christianity over paganism. They differ in the form of the confrontation between cultures with divergent world-views, as incompatible as fire and water.

It was only after centuries of merciless persecution of the Christians that the Roman Empire adopted Christianity, at the command of Constantine the Great. He moved the imperial capital to the old Greek city of Byzantium on the Bosphorus, which he named Constantinople after himself; it is now known as Istanbul. When Constantine succeeded his father as emperor in 306, the empire was predominantly pagan. According to tradition, Constantine had a dream in 312 on the eve of a decisive battle in Italy. The dream prophesied that he would defeat his opponents if his soldiers bore a cross engraved on their shields. The following day, the soldiers saw the sign of the cross in the sky with the words *in hoc signo vinces* (by this sign you will conquer). And they did win the battle. The Roman Empire became Christian.

In Iceland, by contrast, the conversion to Christianity involved no bloodshed.[40] It was the result of a decision made at the Althing around the year 1000. The men who assembled before the law-rock that midsummer were divided into two roughly equal parties, pagans and Christians. Both were heavily armed. Yet a bloody confrontation was averted by a few days' rational deliberation. The decision was more a political settlement than anything else. It came about as part of a compromise, according to which, in the words of the saga, 'all men in Iceland should be baptized and believe in one God, but as to the exposure of children, and eating of horse-flesh, the old law should hold. People should be allowed to continue heathen sacrifices in secret, if they wished, but they would be outlawed if witnesses came forward against them'.[41]

The advocate of this Solomonic solution was the law-speaker, Þorgeir Ljósvetningagoði, who was still a pagan and who had been appointed arbitrator by the Althing. He took his time. Brooding under a cloak, he lay in his tent at Þingvellir for a whole day.[42] In this state he probably appeared to be in a deep sleep, as if away from this world. This matter has been studied in a doctoral thesis by Jón Hnefill Aðalsteinsson. According to him, there are other narratives, both Old Norse and Lappish, of people who seem to be relaxing in a way similar to Þorgeir's, while they are actually working magic or appearing in a different form. Is there perhaps a link between the shamanism of the Lapps and *seiður*, the magic of the pagan Northmen? The conclusion of the thesis is that Þorgeir was not lying under the cloak merely to ruminate; he was conducting an ancient divinatory ritual to see into the future.[43]

Perhaps Þorgeir was doing both.

On the morning of the second day, Þorgeir rose and summoned everyone to the law rock, from where he proclaimed his solution. He justified it as follows: Although both the pagans and the Christians had good grounds for their views, 'let us all have one law and one faith. For this saying shall be proved true, if the constitution be broken the peace will also be broken'.[44]

Þorgeir in his wisdom has been compared with the Athenian legislator Solon. Þorgeir set a good example by personally implementing the decision of the Althing. On returning to his farm at Ljósavatn (south of Húsavík), he removed the idols from his temple and threw them into a nearby waterfall. Since then it has been known as Goðafoss.[45]

For those who want to familiarize themselves with the background to the decision of the Althing, *Landnámabók* is recommended reading. We learn from it that some of the first settlers—such as the female chieftain Auður djúpúðga, ancestress of several famous heroes in *Laxdæla saga* and *Njáls saga*—were Christians. Many of the early settlers had come into contact with Christianity in the British Isles. Yet some of the baptized settlers were perhaps not so whole-hearted in their faith. Of Helgi the Lean, for example, we read that his 'faith was very much mixed: he believed in Christ but invoked Thor when it came to voyages and difficult times.'[46] The pagans blamed bad weather and poor crops on the White Christ.

The Northmen had a view of life which included a strong loyalty to one's kin, the demand that the honour of the kin must be asserted—if necessary by blood vengeance—when wrongs have been suffered, and the belief that life is largely predestined. In the Icelandic sagas a dream or other form of premonition is often an expression of this belief that a person's life is guided by an inexorable fate—personified in the three

Norns of mythology: Urður, Verðandi, and Skuld (Past, Present, and Future).

This deterministic view of life was occasionally relieved by the hope that the supposedly mighty gods—the Æsir (Odin, Thor, and others)—could be persuaded to change the course of destiny for the better. The ancient Swedes at least believed that the gods could be propitiated by sacrifice.

The gods were no paragons of virtue. They had their faults and weaknesses. Like the Greek gods on Olympus, the Norse gods in Ásgarður were ethically indifferent. They did not require people to lead lives of purity.

The existence of these traditional beliefs no doubt helps to explain why it took so long for Christianity, with its good tidings of love and its ten commandments, to conquer the minds of the Northmen. Their scepticism about the Christian doctrine had deep roots. When Örvar-Oddur agreed to be converted, he said, 'I'll take your faith, but keep my old habits.'[47]

Before the decision in 1000 by which the Icelanders collectively embraced Christianity, a man came running to Þingvellir, according to the account in *Kristni saga*. He reported that a flow of lava had broken out further south at Ölfus. The pagans interpreted this as a sign that the gods disapproved of this new-fangled Christianity. But Snorri, one of the chieftains, was not short of an answer: 'What were the gods wroth over then, when the lava on which we are now standing was burning here?'[48]

At any earlier volcanic eruptions Iceland had been uninhabited.

Following the decision of the Althing, all the men at the assembly had to be baptized. For this they chose to ride from Þingvellir to hot springs nearby, since they were reluctant to be baptized in the ice-cold waters of the nearby lake, Þingvallavatn. When the priest-chieftain Runólfur was baptized, one of the thing-men commented, 'We are now teaching the old chieftains how to pull faces in the salt.'

The compromise at the Althing meant that, for once, there was a bridge of tolerance between pagan and Christian, between the traditional beliefs in the Æsir and the new teachings about the White Christ. This gave a peaceful foundation for a national Icelandic church with a native clergy who were not blind to the value of the ancient cultural heritage.

The first churches were soon built on the sites of the pagan temples. In 1056 the Althing elected a bishop for the country; he was installed at Skálholt in southern Iceland. A second episcopal see was established in 1106 at Hólar in northern Iceland. Nine monasteries in all were founded, and two convents. Monastic schools were also established; Latin was quickly replaced by the vernacular as the language of instruction. These monasteries and monastic schools were to become flourishing centres of culture and learning, and Icelandic students also sought an education at European universities.

The first Icelandic monastery in a strict sense, that is, under the direction of an abbot, was founded in 1133 at Þingeyrar in Húnaþing (northern Iceland). However, it is clear that a century earlier there had already been monastic life in some form at Bær in Borgarfjörður (western Iceland). An Anglo-Saxon missionary bishop, Hróðólfur, thought to be a kinsman of King Edmund, apparently served there in 1030–49. When he left, three monks remained. The monastic life at Bær probably lasted until about 1100, and it has been thought that it was from there that the Benedictine monastery at Þingeyrar was founded. Furthermore, it has been said that Hróðólfur founded the first school in Iceland at Bær. This must be considered doubtful, however. Rather, Hróðólfur may have introduced some kind of rudimentary teaching, including instruction in the alphabet instead of the runes. There is undeniably some indication of a possible Anglo-Saxon origin of the Þingeyrar monastery. One may even go so far as to mention southern England, and especially the interesting Cathedral Priory of Winchester. The Þingeyrar monastery might, on the other hand, have been the mother-monastery of the Benedictine Order in Iceland.[49]

The year 2000 will be celebrated as the millenary of the conversion of Iceland, and the present-day Althing is preparing concrete manifestations of its links with the former parliament at Þingvellir. The patriotic Icelanders are already looking forward eagerly to this jubilee.

The Age of the Sturlungs (*c*.1220–1262)

A boatless man is bound.

Faroese proverb

The closing phase of the Icelandic commonwealth appears as an age of great contradictions.[50] It was a time of strife at the same time as it was a golden age of literature. It has therefore been described as 'a semi-tragedy' (*hálfgerð sorgarsaga*), since this time of great sorrow had a silver lining. Culture, especially literature, blossomed with extraordinary vigour. Yet it blossomed against a dark background. Conditions in Iceland were chaotic: civil conflict combined with social and moral decay. Added to this there were overpopulation, deforestation, devastation of the soil through over-grazing, and an incipient shortage of food. There was no central executive authority to maintain peace in the country. The Althing could not enforce its laws and judgements. The domestic church lacked political influence, if not nominally then in practice.

Power was divided among a few chieftains. Since the territory of a chieftain could be inherited, given away, or sold, it was possible through time for one chieftain to acquire power over several *goðorð*. The result of this development was that half a dozen chieftains' families contested for power. Most prominent among these was the famous Sturla clan, the Sturlungs after whom the period is named, but they were weakened by internal divisions. There were brutal assaults, treacherous ambushes, and veritable pitched battles—the battle of Örlygsstaðir in 1238 was fought by a thousand men on either side. The warring factions also ravaged each other's territory by fire and pillage.[51]

The Icelanders were also ill-fated in that they lacked ocean-going ships, owing to a shortage of money and timber. A people without its own merchants and ships bears the seeds of its own destruction. It is doomed to lose its independence.[52] The difficulty of being without boats is encapsulated in the Faroese proverb, 'Bundin er bátleysur maður', which we have chosen as the epigraph to this section. Yet the social and moral dissolution that gnawed at thirteenth-century Iceland was even more serious. Throughout this time of great unrest the country was Christian, but only on the surface. It was a Catholic country, but the Christian commandments had still not penetrated to any depth. If this was not true of the people, then it certainly applied to their leaders. In a letter of 1180, Archbishop Eysteinn of Niðarós reproved the chieftains for 'living like cattle', a life of debauchery, deceit, and disloyalty, of robbery, brigandage, and murder.[53] The chieftains themselves think that they are independent. But they are not. It is an illusion. The king of Norway has all the power in his hands. He holds all the strings. The rival chieftains blindly tumble in his presence. He looks on them as puppets lacking a will of their own.

During these civil wars the leading Icelandic magnates occasionally visited the Norwegian king, Hákon Hákonarson the Old, and his earl (*jarl*), whose name was Skúli. They were usually received hospitably and treated to ships, weapons, and other magnificent gifts. In return they pledged allegiance to the king. They would rather entrust themselves to him than to their hated rivals for power in Iceland.

In this way the decisive power over the outcome of the internal Icelandic wranglings gradually slipped into the hands of the king of Norway. At the same time, the archbishop of Niðarós was appointing Norwegians as bishops in Iceland. This immediately gave the church greater influence. The king began to intervene in internal Icelandic matters. He finally succeeded in bringing Iceland under his rule, and he also added Greenland to his kingdom in 1261.

In 1262 the Icelanders signed a treaty with the Norwegian king, in which they swore him allegiance. As part of this treaty (known as *gamli sáttmáli* 'the old pact', and later invoked by the Icelanders as a sort of Magna Charta guaranteeing their rights) the king pledged to respect Icelandic law and to ensure that necessary produce was transported to Iceland every year, initially on six vessels from Norway the two following summers.

The Icelanders were guaranteed reassuring freedoms and rights—on paper. But the Icelandic commonwealth ceased to exist as an independent state. Iceland came under foreign sway, first Norway and then Denmark (after the unification of the two kingdoms in 1387). Over 650 years would elapse before Iceland regained her independence.

The circumstances in which the commonwealth fell are reminiscent of the political dissolution of Greece in the fourth century BC. The small city states of Athens, Sparta, Thebes, and so on spent their force in internal strife. This continued despite the Athenian orator Demosthenes, who warned of foreign intervention. In 338 BC Philip of Macedon made himself lord of the Greeks.

It would be going too far to dwell on the details of events in the Age of the Sturlungs. They are recorded in a collection of sagas known as *Sturlunga saga*.[54] The longest narrative, *Íslendinga saga*, was written by Sturla Þórðarson (1214–84), nephew of Snorri Sturluson. In other words, Sturla was a close kinsman of one of the main actors in the power struggle, as well as being involved in the fighting. In spite of this, his account is remarkably objective, although biased in places. For example, he describes Snorri as a miser, but he scarcely mentions his writings; Sturla records his uncle's faults, but appears to forget his merits. Ever since the days of Ari fróði, about a century earlier, Icelandic historians had been aware of the need for original research and objectivity. Sturla Þórðarson cherished this tradition. So too did Snorri Sturluson (1179–1241), Iceland's greatest historian and something of a Renaissance man. Both men belonged to the Sturla clan.

The highly talented Snorri was brought up on the farm Oddi by a chieftain named Jón Loftsson, a learned and refined man with such scholarly interests as history and law, poetry and Latin. Snorri derived great value from his early years in this intellectually stimulating home, with its great collection of manuscripts. This became obvious when he later entered the political arena, and in his work as a law-speaker and author. He was a skilful negotiator. On the other hand, he could also be calculating, ambitious, stingy, and his lack of courage bordered on cowardice.

Thanks to cleverly calculated marriages and intrigues, Snorri became one of the richest and most powerful chieftains in Iceland in his twenties. For two periods (1215–18 and 1222–31) he occupied the position of law-speaker at the Althing. For a few years in between he visited the king of Norway, Hákon Hákonarson, swearing allegiance to him. At this time he also visited Sweden, meeting Eskil, the law-speaker of Västergötland, also known for his codification in 1220 of the oldest Swedish provincial law.

In the summer of 1220 Snorri returned to Iceland. Before his return he warded off the threat of a Norwegian invasion of Iceland by promising the king that he would act to have Iceland united with Norway. He never kept this promise, however, and the king's distrust of him grew into disfavour when Snorri was defamed by his opponents in Iceland. One of these was his son-in-law, Gizur Þorvaldsson, who later became liegeman and earl to the Norwegian king (1258–68).

During a second visit to Norway in 1237–39, Snorri tried to improve his relations with King Hákon. The king was cold to Snorri and expressly forbade his return to Iceland. Snorri nevertheless defied the prohibition, with the frequently cited words *Út vil ek,* 'I will go out (to Iceland)'.[55]

From that moment, King Hákon regarded Snorri as a traitor. As such his fate was sealed. He had so many enemies in Iceland too, including close relatives like Gizur Þorvaldsson. For a while he regained his position of power, but a few years later he was the victim of a surprise attack on his home at Reykholt. Outnumbered by his enemies under the leadership of Gizur, he was put to death at his kinsman's command.

Snorri Sturluson met his downfall in his old age, rather like Marcus Tullius Cicero, the great Roman with whom he has been compared. Both Snorri and Cicero began by enjoying a socially privileged position in life. Both belonged to distinguished families. They were given a good education, with a deep understanding of the humanities and the law. In young years they reached the highest offices of the state. Both were endowed with unusually rich and versatile talents: as orators, pleading and negotiating with a sense of elegance, and as captivating writers. Yet both of them met a violent death. In times of ruthless power struggles they were—each in his own way—sometimes incautious, thoughtless, and at bottom timorous. Cicero was also, it has been said, vain and boastful. At the same time, he was undoubtedly an extremely profound and interesting philosopher, thoroughly familiar with Plato, Aristotle, and other Greek thinkers. Moreover, he had an exquisite command of language and style.

Snorri's intellectual greatness and creative fantasy are similarly revealed in his literary works. His setbacks in the tragic final phase of his life in no way diminish the magnificence of his writings. These comprise his *Edda* and *Heimskringla* and, according to Sigurður Nordal and other scholars, following studies in statistical linguistics, perhaps also *Egils saga Skalla-Grímssonar*.[56] He is said to have written these works during his second period as law-speaker, no doubt having been influenced by the studies of his youth and his travels to Norway and Sweden.

Heimskringla takes its name from the first two words, 'Kringla heimsins', the orb of the world, *orbis terrarum*. We may mention in passing that medieval maps of the known world (Europe, Asia, and Africa) depict it as a round disc. Jerusalem was the centre, with the Mediterranean Sea just to the west of centre. In Snorri's words, this round was 'much indented' with bays.[57]

Heimskringla is a history of the kings of Norway from the earliest times to 1177. It reveals Snorri to be a first-rate pragmatic historian, with a well-arranged presentation of the course of events and lucid analysis of cause and effect. He combined this ability with an understanding of human psychology and an elegant style. He was a master of prose.

It has also been maintained that, through his writings, Snorri helped to preserve a cultural heritage that would otherwise have been lost. Without *Egils saga Skalla-Grímssonar* and *Heimskringla*, posterity would have been poorer. The same can be said of Snorri's *Edda*. As Njörður P. Njarðvík has pointed out, Norse mythology, teeming with its gods, goddesses, giants, and dwarfs, would probably have been a closed world to us children of later times, had not Snorri immortalized it in his *Edda*. He blows life into the gods. He lets us see them as if they were imperfect human beings. The gods try to solve problems that arise, in much the same way as we try to handle the atomic bomb. Yet their clumsy solutions only give the gods greater problems.[58]

During his various visits to Iceland, the late King Olav V of Norway praised Snorri for similar reasons. He last did so on a sunny September day in 1988, during an excursion to Reykholt, where the wild landscape was afire with the brilliant flowers of autumn. It was at Reykholt that Snorri wrote his *Heimskringla*, the work which Norwegians, ever since the revival of national consciousness in the early nineteenth century, have read with delight, and which has inspired so many Norwegian poets and artists. 'For us Norwegians, the knowledge of our origin would have been scant without Snorri,' said the king. For this reason Norwegians feel a particularly close bond with Reykholt. The king presented a national gift from Norway, a million Norwegian kroner, to be used to erect a cultural centre, dedicated to Snorri, at Reykholt. It will be called Snorrastofa.

In his speech of thanks to King Olav, the headmaster of Reykholt quoted some words from Gunnar of Hlíðarendi, spoken to Njáll, who had brought food and hay to Hlíðarendi after a bad crop: 'Your gifts are good, but I value your friendship even more highly.'[59]

Under Foreign Monarchs (1262–1944)

Reformation and Cod Wars

During the many centuries when Iceland was ruled by foreign monarchs, first Norwegian kings and then Danish, the Icelandic people lived in strained circumstances. The population shrank. The hardships of the Icelanders culminated in the seventeenth and eighteenth centuries, when they were subjected to a merciless Danish monopoly on trade (1602–1787), combined with the worst smallpox epidemics, volcanic eruptions, and earthquakes in the history of the country. The nineteenth century saw the start of an economic upswing, and with it a single-minded struggle for independence. This continued in stages until the Republic of Iceland was proclaimed at Þingvellir on 17 June 1944.

In the period before the Danish trade monopoly, political and economic power was initially concentrated in the Icelandic church, which came into possession of about half of all the landed property. On the whole the Icelanders themselves disposed of the country's natural resources, but there were exceptions. One such was the Danish king's sole right to the extraction of sulphur and the catching of falcons (Icelandic *fálki* or *valur*). The sulphur was used to make gunpowder, while the falcons were kept in a house on a hill in the present-day town of Seltjarnarnes near Reykjavík, which still bears the name Valhúsa-hæð.

In the fifteenth century the farmers were still in a position to defend themselves against unjust treatment by their superiors—just like the barons in England, with their resistance to the King John successfully leading to the Magna Charta of 1215. Although this was really a feudal charter of privilege, it was later to be perceived as a guarantee of freedom for the entire people, as the very foundation of England's free form of government.

On one occasion the Icelanders took a hated bishop of Skálholt called Jón Gerreksson and drowned him in a bag in a nearby river. They could not bear to be under the domination of a foreign bishop and his foreign henchmen, these 'unruly barbarians who dwell apart'. This Bishop Jón, alias Johannes Gerrechini, of Danish origin, had a far from honourable past. In 1420 he had been deposed from the archbishopric of Uppsala in Sweden, according to malicious gossip because of an affair with a rich widow. A few years later he was granted the bishopric of Skálholt by Erik of Pomerania, king of the united Scandinavia.[60]

There were, however, bright spots in the picture. Towards the end of the Middle Ages, the monasteries—such as the one on Viðey—retained their position as centres of learning, as bearers of the European cultural heritage, and as places of refuge for pious Christians. One such was the Icelandic Augustinian friar Eysteinn Ásgrímsson (died in Niðarós in 1361). His sonorous poem *Lilja* (The Lily), written in Norway during the Black Death, is an exquisite collection of songs of praise and fervent prayers to Mary, the Mother of God.[61]

After the implementation of the Reformation in Denmark and Norway in the 1530s, the new doctrine was combated in Iceland by the last Catholic bishops, Ögmundur Pálsson of Skálholt and Jón Arason of Hólar. They both met cruel fates. In 1541, when Ögmundur was old and completely blind, his property was confiscated. He was treacherously taken on board a Danish warship and brought captive to Denmark.

For many years after Ögmundur's removal, Jón Arason continued to defend the Catholic cause in Iceland. In the spring of 1550 he rode to the Althing at the head of a force of four hundred men. He conquered the Danish commander and put him to flight, after which he was left as the true ruler of Iceland. In the autumn of that year, however, he ran into an unexpected attack, following which he was captured in a church where he had sought sanctuary. The Protestants scarcely knew what to do with such a dangerous opponent. They chose to put Jón Arason to death. On 7 November 1550 he was beheaded along with

Mary, the Mother of God. Medieval wooden sculpture, presumably dating from the 10th or 11th century. Photo kindly made available by the National Museum of Iceland.

two of his sons outside the cathedral of Skálholt. Nearby, a stone has been raised in honour of Bishop Jón and what he stood for.

Jón Arason has been hailed as one of Iceland's greatest national heroes and freedom fighters. His struggle was also a political one. He founded the first printing press in Iceland, and was also renowned for his poetry.

The execution of Jón Arason marked a turning-point in the history of Iceland. After his death there was no obstacle to the Reformation, no impediment to the power of the king. The treasures and lands of the church and the monasteries were confiscated by the crown. Danish noblemen were put in charge of the administration. They resided in Denmark, usually visiting Iceland only in the summer. Penalties for many crimes were increased. The Supreme Court in Copenhagen became the highest court of appeal for the Icelanders, while the Althing lost its importance. In practice the country was treated like a Danish colony.

Iceland's political decline from the fourteenth century was exacerbated by a series of violent volcanic eruptions (chiefly Hekla) and epidemics, combined with growing famine and drastically diminished communications with the outside world. The Icelanders often complained about the lack of shipments from Norway which had been promised in the treaty of 1262. Perhaps most serious of all was the Black Death, which harried Europe in the mid-fourteenth century. The date of its arrival in Iceland is disputed, but the worst plague years were 1402–4. The Icelandic sources describe a terrible epidemic, which claimed about a third of the population.

Before this, the population growth during the commonwealth had led to unchecked grazing and deforestation. This abuse of natural resources, combined with cold winters, rain, and poisonous emissions from volcanic eruptions, created the conditions for extensive denudation, with the loosened vegetation cover being blown away by the wind (hence the Icelandic term *uppblástur*). By 1800 around half of the woodland and grassland that had existed at the time of the settlement had been transformed into barren desert.[62]

One way to eke out the diet was to fish in rivers and lakes, in fiords and the ocean. Fishing is mentioned in Icelandic sagas from the thirteenth and fourteenth centuries. Prices rose for fish, especially dried fish, which became an important and lucrative export item. For the Englishmen of the late Middle Ages, the name Iceland conjured up stockfish and little else:[63]

> Of Yseland to wryte is lytill nede
> Save of stokfische.

Fishing grew in importance for coastal farmers in Iceland. They generally had nothing but open rowing-boats in which they fished near the shore, but some also had slightly bigger sailing-vessels in which they could venture further out to sea. Whales were considered too big a prey, since the boats were too small and the Icelanders did not have the necessary equipment to catch them. Stranded whales, however, were used for food.

The Icelandic fishing banks also attracted foreign fishermen. Foreign fishing vessels were not excluded from these until 1975, when Iceland proclaimed an exclusive economic zone of 200 nautical miles.

In the fifteenth and sixteenth centuries the majority of the fishing vessels came from the Hanseatic League (mainly Hamburg) and England. A report from the English parliament in 1415 said that English vessels had been sailing to the Icelandic fishing grounds for six or seven years. According to the author of the report, the English fishermen could therefore claim a traditional title to this fishery.[64]

The rivalry of the English and Hanseatic fishermen lasted for many years. They fought five wars over the right to fish off Iceland. The fifth cod war ended with setbacks for the English; in the sixteenth century they turned their attention to the rich fishing grounds recently discovered off the coast of Newfoundland.

It was in this era that Christian II of Denmark found himself in financial difficulties. Just before his fall in 1523, he offered Iceland to Amsterdam as a mortgage for a loan of 20,000–30,000 guilders. Christian II then made a similar offer to Henry VIII of England; had he been interested he could have obtained Iceland for between 50,000 and 100,000 florins.

Trade Monopoly and Natural Disasters

It is no secret that Icelanders in their
thousands have suffered death by
famine.

*From a letter to Landfógeti Skúli
Magnússon*

There was no deal between Christian II and Henry VIII. Nor did anything come of a similar proposal from Hamburg to Christian IV of Denmark during the Danish war with Sweden and the Netherlands in 1643–5.[65] It was evidently this kind of bargaining which Halldór Laxness had in mind when he wrote his novel *Íslandsklukkan* (Iceland's Bell).[66] It takes place in Iceland and Copenhagen at the end of the seventeenth century and the start of the eighteenth. The opening scene is dramatic. One of the main characters, the farmer and *rímur*-singer Jón Hreggviðsson, is accused of theft without sufficient grounds. He is forced by the executioner at Þingvellir to take an axe and chop off the rope of the bell that hangs on the gable of the courthouse by the river Öxará. The bell is very old and cracked. It symbolizes Iceland's freedom, which is gradually being lost. But this bell is destined to ring again. This happens on 17 June 1944, when it rings in the free Republic of Iceland, at exactly the same spot, the thousand-year-old meeting-place at Þingvellir, in the crystal-clear air, accompanied by the surging waters of the river Öxará.

Another major character in the novel is the cultured humanist and man of the world, Arnas Arnæus, who is based on the manuscript collector Árni Magnússon (1663–1730), professor at the University of Copenhagen and one of the king's most trusted officials. Out of the mouldy hay in the bed of Jón Hreggviðsson's mother Arnas pulls some wrinkled scraps of leather, which turn out to be sheets of parchment with a manuscript from the fourteenth century. He is delighted with the valuable find, since 'the soul of the Nordic peoples is concealed in Icelandic books'.

By good luck, some important manuscripts had been copied in Iceland before the originals were taken to Copenhagen. Other manuscripts had found their way to Sweden; manuscripts of works such as Snorri's *Edda* and *Heimskringla* are still preserved in libraries in Stockholm and Uppsala.

One purpose of Laxness's novel was to describe the consequences for the Icelandic people of the Danish trade monopoly under the absolute rule of the king. Frederik III assumed absolute powers in 1660, and in Iceland this was confirmed at an assembly in Kópavogur in 1662. Trade with Iceland came into the hands of a few Danish merchants. They could set arbitrary prices on goods to obtain the highest possible profits. The English, Germans, and other foreigners were forbidden to fish and hunt whale within a zone of some 32 nautical miles.

With the introduction of absolutism, the monopoly which had been in force for sixty years was enforced with greater severity. Iceland was divided into a number of commercial districts. Icelanders were prohibited from selling fish and other goods from one district to another. Breaches of the law were punished with confiscation of the goods and life imprisonment in Denmark.

How did the Icelanders themselves view the Danish trade monopoly? This is illustrated by the following extract from a letter from the prefect (*stiftamtmaður*) Magnús Gíslason to Skúli Magnússon, the official in charge of administrative affairs (*landfógeti*). It dates from the middle of the eighteenth century.[67]

> From the point of view of the Icelandic population, Icelandic trade can scarcely be called trade, since everyone is forced to hand over his most important goods at a price which the king or the merchant is pleased to establish. All profit from the trade has gone to the merchants, whereas the Icelanders have had to bear all the losses. They have had to work like slaves for their food, but their position has been much worse than that of slaves, in that they have not obtained any food. Nowhere do we hear of any slaves who have been allowed to starve to death. But it is no secret that Icelanders in their thousands have suffered death by famine.

There is no doubt that the Danish trade monopoly dealt harshly with the starving, defenceless people of Iceland, while favouring Danish commercial interests in a rather one-sided way. It is hardly surprising that the Danish trade monopoly is still a controversial issue in Iceland. While repression can never be excused, it can be explained. In this case it should be seen against the background of contemporary conditions in Denmark and the rest of Europe. Research in recent years has shown that the main features of the monopoly were in keeping with the mercantile system that prevailed in Europe in the seventeenth and eighteenth centuries. The powers in Copenhagen—an absolute monarch surrounded by his officials—probably did not treat the Icelanders much worse than they did their native population. The great distance and poor communications between Denmark and its overseas possessions, however, certainly exacerbated the material destitution and the absence of rights in Iceland. The plundering of the Icelandic people by the Danish merchants may also have been facilitated by the passivity of government officials.

The situation was made worse by the 'little ice age', with its onset around 1600. The colder climate made it impossible to grow grain and difficult to fish. Some severe winters were so cold that the ice covered not only the rivers but also the water round the coast—despite the Gulf Stream.

On top of this, the Icelanders had to endure repeated epidemics of smallpox and volcanic eruptions. One of the most violent and destructive eruptions in historical times was in 1783, when Laki, south-west of Vatnajökull, erupted. A 25 kilometre long fissure in the earth's crust

(Lakagígar) spewed forth enormous flows of lava. Volcanic fires blazed over the glaciers, their glare being visible far out to sea. Fluorine-rich dust fell over virtually the whole island, followed by a haze of sulphur dioxide, which the winds carried over Europe and all the way to Siberia.

The following year there was an earthquake of record force. It destroyed settlement in large areas. At the old episcopal see of Skálholt, for instance, all the buildings except the cathedral were demolished. Both the bishopric and the Latin School were moved. The new Latin School was established first in Reykjavík and then in the old governor's residence of Bessastaðir (now the president's residence). Until 1846 it was the only seat of higher education in the country. The bishopric was moved to Reykjavík. In 1786 this became a staple town (with about 300 inhabitants), capital, and two years later also the seat of the court which had been held at Þingvellir ever since the commonwealth era. In 1800 the Althing was closed. In 1787 the trade monopoly was abolished, but until the 1870s the real power over trade still lay almost entirely with the Danish merchants.

The famine years of 1783 and 1784, with the poisonous volcanic haze, were truly terrible. 'The famine of the mist' (*móðuharðindi*) was a time of unfathomable poverty, starvation, disease, and epidemic.[68] People froze in their wretched dwellings. The situation was so serious that a commission in Copenhagen—according to one disputed source—even considered moving some of the Icelanders to Denmark (Jutland) or northern Norway (Finnmarken).[69] This drastic measure was opposed by Skúli Magnússon and other Icelanders.

This unparalleled nadir in the history of Iceland is also reflected in the demographic statistics. In the twelfth century the population may have been about 70,000, but in the eighteenth century it fell at some critical dates to 34,000–40,000.

What kept the Icelanders alive in these dark years was their mental resilience and their strong religious faith, their will to survive and their hopes of regaining independence. They had the incitement of their living cultural heritage, a vigorous native language, the old sagas and the rhyming ballads known as *rímur*, which they knew by heart. Long winter evenings were spent with recitations of the sagas, chess, and other parlour games. The Swedish traveller Uno von Troil mentions other pastimes: singing and music-making, board-games and card-games, Icelandic wrestling (*glíma*), a ball game played on ice (*knattleikur*), and horse-racing. The Icelandic love of chess and other board-games is of great antiquity. Boards, counters, and dice found in graves show that a predecessor of chess, known as *tafl* 'tables', was played in Scandinavia in ancient times. In the Eddic poem *Völuspá* (The Sibyl's Prophecy) the Æsir are described as 'cheerfully playing at tables in the enclosure', but after Ragnarök their 'golden pieces will be found in the grass'.[70]

It is not certain when the Icelanders began to play true chess. It may have been learned by Vikings who travelled to Mediterranean countries, or by Icelanders who had studied at English or Irish monasteries. It is likely, however, that Snorri Sturluson and his contemporaries knew the game. The word *chess* (Icelandic *skák*), which is similar in many European languages, originates from the Persian word *shah*, the king on the chessboard.[71] The origin of the game is unknown. According to an Arabian tale, it was invented in India by a wise man; he described it as 'a battle without bloodshed'. This battle rapidly achieved great popularity. Among Icelanders it became the best-loved of all the noble sports.

On Sundays and holy days the people went to church, where the clergy preached in Icelandic. During and after the Reformation, Icelanders were inspired by a number of highly talented priests and other learned men with scholarly interests. One of the most prominent was Oddur Gottskálksson, son of the second last Catholic bishop of Hólar, the Norwegian Gottskalk Nicolausson. Oddur translated the New Testament into Icelandic. He did the work in secret in the cowshed of the bishop's residence. According to an anecdote, he said: 'My saviour Jesus was laid in an ass's manger. Now I am translating his word into my mother tongue in a cowshed.'[72]

In Oddur's footsteps followed the Bishop of Hólar, Guðbrandur Þorláksson, who also translated parts of the Bible. With the aid of the Swedish printer Johan Matthiasson, Bishop Guðbrandur printed and published a magnificent Icelandic edition of the Bible in 1584. 'The Guðbrandur Bible' is adorned with lovely woodcuts, some of them, according to tradition, carved by the bishop himself.

These translations of the Bible with their pithy language—together with Hallgrímur Pétursson's well-loved hymns, the sermons of Jón Vídalín, Bishop of Skálholt, the sagas, and the *rímur*—all helped to strengthen the bonds between the spoken language and the literary language. In this way the Icelandic tongue was preserved as a living language, spoken and written by everyone.

Another celebrated prelate was Brynjólfur Sveinsson (1605–75), bishop of Skálholt. Like Árni Magnússon, he was a humanist and antiquarian, and a collector of manuscripts. Bishop Brynjólfur was an immensely educated man and something of a prince of the church. But the end of his life was darkened by a family tragedy, partly self-in-flicted. Brynjólfur forced his daughter Ragnheiður to swear that she was a virgin, so that she could clear herself of a rumour concerning her and her teacher, Pastor Daði Halldórsson. Nearly forty weeks after the oath, she gave birth to a child. Had she perjured herself? Brynjólfur and Ragnheiður are the leading characters in Guðmundur Kamban's novel *Skálholt* and in his play of the same name. He portrays them both as unbending in their pride. Deep in her heart, Ragnheiður loved Daði. According to Kamban's version, she did not sleep with Daði until the night after the oath. She was driven to this deed not only by love but also by an urge to defy her father.[73]

The leprous poet-priest Hallgrímur Pétursson (1614–74) wrote his *Passíusálmar* (Passion Hymns), which are still sung and read during Lent. Hallgrímskirkja in Reykjavík is named after him; the largest church in Iceland, it was begun just after World War II but was not consecrated until 1986.

A special place in Icelandic history is occupied by Skúli Magnússon (1711–94), who managed to have the trade monopoly lifted. He furthered the interests of his people in every way. In Reykjavík, a statue has been raised to Skúli Magnússon, near the Althing and an old house from his time, now restored as a restaurant and known to tourists as 'Fógetinn'. Skúli's official residence was on the nearby island of Viðey. Built in a simplified Rococo style in 1755, the first stone house in Iceland, this has recently been restored. Examples of a similar architectural style are the residence at Bessastaðir, the newly restored cathedral at Hólar (northern Iceland), and Nesstofa, the splendid stone house at Seltjarnarnes near Reykjavík, which was once the residence of Iceland's first national physician, Bjarni Pálsson (1719–79); it also

The full moon, hanging just over the top of the mountain Esja, like a Chinese lantern of pure glistening gold, illuminates the isle of Viðey with the Viðeyjarstofa of 1755. It was the first stone house in Iceland and the official residence of Skúli Magnússon.

housed the first pharmacy. Bjarni was an enterprising man. He co-authored a detailed account of travels in Iceland in the mid-eighteenth century.[74] Bjarni was son-in-law to Skúli Magnússon. Perhaps Skúli wanted his daughter and her husband to have as magnificent a dwelling as his own on Viðey.

The National Museum, in collaboration with pharmacists and doctors, has restored Nesstofa. Two adjacent buildings will house museums. The idea is that one of them will present a picture of a bygone pharmacy, with old pillboxes and bottles, while the other one will illustrate the history of medicine starting from the days of Bjarni Pálsson, with his catheters and other instruments.

Archaeological finds show that Viðey was settled as early as the tenth century. The island is of historical interest, with sights that include a dimunitive church consecrated in 1774 and the foundations of an Augustinian friary established in 1226. Most of this beautiful island was bought by the town of Reykjavík, and the remainder was donated by the state to the town in 1986, when Reykjavík celebrated its bicentennial.

On 18 August 1988, a day when the sun lit up the brightly coloured houses of Reykjavík and glistened in the mirror of Faxaflói bay, Viðey was inaugurated by the town of Reykjavík, with speeches by the president, the mayor of Reykjavík, Davíð Oddsson, and the former Dean of Reykjavík Cathedral, Þórir Stephensen. The latter is the fifth-generation descendant of the members of the Stephensen family who owned the island for over a century after the death of Skúli Magnússon in 1794. Skúli's residence, and beside it the graceful little eighteenth-century stone church with room for 50–60 people, have both been faithfully restored. They will not stand empty. It is planned to use them for social occasions and divine service. At a wedding held a few days after the inauguration, people took their pews in the church, in the same way as in bygone days: the women sat on the left and the men on the right.

Iceland now had a new attraction. Viðey is open for visitors. There is also a conference centre on the island.

In his letters from Iceland of 1777, the Swedish traveller Uno von Troil records many interesting impressions from a visit in 1772, when he accompanied Sir Joseph Banks on his exploration of Iceland. He was struck by the way every Icelander appeared to know the history of his own country. The Icelanders had 'an indescribable love of their birthplace'. They had a thirst for knowledge, but they were also superstitious. On the subject of their fear of God, he made the following observation: 'An Icelander never passes a river, or any other dangerous place, without previously taking off his hat and imploring divine protection; and he is always thankful for the protection of God, when he has passed the danger in security.'[75]

It was probably the memory of outrages committed on Vestmanna-eyjar by North African pirates in 1627,[76] along with the isolation imposed on the Icelanders by the Danish trade monopoly, which made the people afraid of foreigners. They showed this fear when the ex-plorers' ship was cruising in towards the coast at Bessastaðir and needed a pilot. Here is von Troil's account:[77]

> We were therefore quite glad to see a boat with three men coming out from the shore, but we were disappointed when we saw them take another course to fish, notwithstanding our calls to them. There was nothing else to do then but to send out a boat to talk to them, but scarcely did they see the boat before they hurried away. We finally met them, and

when we had appeased them with tobacco, they accompanied us on board. They said that they had been afraid that it was an enemy ship coming to conquer the country, so they feared to fall into our hands.

The Struggle for Independence (*c*.1830–1944)

Never give way.
Jón Sigurðsson's motto

The External Framework

In the 1830s, inspired by the ideas of German romanticism, the emergence of nationalism, the July Revolution of 1830, and an incipient economic upswing, a group of Icelanders in Copenhagen—linguists and antiquarians, poets and politicians—began an uncompromising struggle for independence and democracy. In 1845 the Althing was re-established as a consultative body. In 1874 it was also granted limited powers over taxation and legislation within the framework of Iceland's first constitution. Other milestones in the struggle were the introduction of free trade, freedom of the press, gradually extended suffrage, and in 1904 the appointment of a Minister for Icelandic Affairs, responsible to the Althing and with his seat in Reykjavík. The final stage was the Act of Union with Denmark in 1918. This remained in force until the Republic of Iceland was proclaimed in 1944, on 17 June, the birthday of the national hero Jón Sigurðsson. In just over a hundred years, an exploited colony had become independent, an internationally recognized sovereign state.

The liberation of the Icelandic people was to some extent a product of the gradual democratization of Denmark. The February Revolution in Paris in 1848, the first war over the duchies of Schleswig and Holstein, and the abolition of the Danish king's absolute power in 1849 gave Jón Sigurðsson good arguments. The breakthrough of parliamentarism in Copenhagen in 1901 preceded a comparable change of system in Reykjavík, by which the politician and poet Hannes Hafstein became Minister for Iceland.

Military events affecting Denmark were also of significance for development. The Napoleonic wars brought military defeats for Denmark: the British attack on Copenhagen and the capture of the Danish fleet in 1807, and the Treaty of Kiel in 1814, which led to the loss of Norway. Fifty years later another blow was struck against Denmark as a multinational state—the loss of Schleswig and Holstein in the second war of 1864.

The Napoleonic wars had meant that Iceland, far away in the North Atlantic, was even more isolated from Denmark. Instead, this defence-less island felt the impact of Britannia's rule over the waves. Iceland's contacts with the outside world were totally in the control of British warships and trading ships. Cargoes of grain from Britain saved the Icelandic people from starvation. In 1803, for example, about 450 people nevertheless died of hunger. Ever since his exploratory journey to Iceland in 1772, Sir Joseph Banks had nourished plans to invade the island. Although he met no active response from the British govern-ment, they did not wish to see any other state than Denmark controlling the islands in the North Atlantic.[78]

A British emissary was present at the peace negotiations in Kiel. According to an Icelandic historian,[79] he declared that Iceland, Green-land, and the Faroes were to be regarded as under British protection. Under no circumstances were they to come under Swedish rule. It is not unlikely that the British did indeed adopt this position. Yet it did not conflict with essential Swedish interests. The newly elected crown prince of Sweden, Karl Johan Bernadotte—formerly one of Napo-leon's marshals—seeking compensation for the loss of Finland to Russia, demanded only Norway. The old 'vassal states' of the Norwe-gian empire, however, were not necessary for the natural boundaries which Sweden aspired to under the leadership of Karl Johan. The result was that, under the Treaty of Kiel, Denmark ceded Norway but not Iceland, Greenland, and the Faroes.

Thus these aims of British and Swedish foreign policy convincingly explain the outcome in Kiel. Most probably it was not, as has been asserted, caused by insufficient knowledge of Nordic history, nor by 'a strange misunderstanding'.[80]

The Beginnings

When the Danes shall have stripped
off our shirts, the English will clothe
us anew.

The epigraph is taken from a book by Sir George Steuart Mackenzie,
who visited Iceland in the summer of 1810.[81] Before his tempestuous
journey back, Sir George was seized with compassion 'for the calami-
tous situation of an innocent and amiable people, at that critical period
when oppression or neglect may overwhelm them in misery'. He
concludes:

> I must not be understood as intending to convey any insinuation against
> the government of Denmark, which has done everything that was pos-
> sible to encourage the trade with Iceland. But in doing so, with the best
> intentions, the people have been neglected, and the Danish merchants
> alone regarded. Whatever good the regulations of Denmark might have
> been calculated to effect, the prohibition against trading with other
> nations has left the Icelanders nearly in the same state they were in,
> when subjected to the monopoly of a company.

Iceland's isolation from Denmark during the Napoleonic wars
meant that in some years no ships arrived with necessities such as
grain, salt, iron, coal, and timber.

The famine that arose has been described by an Icelandic historian.
The Icelanders had to live on a diet of seaweed, kelp, roots, leather,
bone-brawn (*bruðningur*), and similar food to which people turn in
times of starvation. They ate only twice a day. Breakfast could consist
of whipped milk with a porridge made of lichen. The Icelanders
nevertheless thanked God and man for these wretched meals. They
would rather die in God's name than eat horse-flesh. Potatoes were
popular but rare. They could seldom be grown, owing to a shortage of
seed potatoes.[82]

The Scottish clergyman Ebenezer Henderson, who visited Iceland
early in the nineteenth century on behalf of the British and Foreign
Bible Society, described his impressions of the state of the country and
the people.[83] They were starving to death, but there was widespread
literacy. Most children aged nine or ten could read and write Icelandic
without difficulty. They mainly assimilated Icelandic culture in the

The magnificent panorama of Reykjavík around 1836, which at that time counted no more than 650 inhabitants. To the right we see, close to the shore of a lake (Tjörnin), the diminutive Cathedral, consecrated in 1796. The horizon is dominated by the mountain Esja, covered with snow. Sailing ships have, quoting the lyrical description of Albert Engström, 'cast anchor on the world's most beautiful roadstead.' — Drawing by the French painter Auguste Mayer.

home, when the family gathered at twilight for the 'evening vigil' (*kvöldvaka*) to read aloud, sew, and do handicrafts. There were scarcely any primary schools in the country, but the clergy monitored the reading skills of their young parishioners in the catechetical examinations held before confirmation. Books were in extremely limited supply, but people freely lent books and transcripts of books, particularly those concerning Icelandic history and the sagas. Henderson was constantly impressed by the Icelanders as people. Besides being patriotic and interested in reading, they were hard-working, content with

their lot, and honest. Despite their abject poverty, they could tell stories and compose poems.

Similar accounts have been left by other travellers to Iceland during the same period, such as the Frenchman Paul Gaimard and the Irish Lord Dufferin.[84]

Talented young people had relatively good opportunities for further education through private tuition. Aspiring clergymen, for example, could obtain their entire grammar school education from a relative or the minister of their own parish. The famous philologist and statesman Jón Sigurðsson (1811–79) was brought up by his parents at Arnar-fjörður in the Vestfirðir, where his father was minister. At the age of twelve, Jón had already learned Latin and Greek from his father. He never visited a school until he privately obtained his higher certificate at the age of seventeen from the Dean of Reykjavík Cathedral.

The Latin School at Bessastaðir was generally known as the Learned School (*Lærði skólinn*). Between 1805 and 1845 this was the only institute of secondary education in Iceland. It was housed in inferior premises, and the teachers were badly paid, but tuition and study were of high quality. One of the teachers and later headmaster of the school was Sveinbjörn Egilsson (1791–1852). He knew his classics, translating into Icelandic such works as the *Iliad*, the *Odyssey*, and some works of Plato. He compiled a dictionary of the Old Icelandic poetic language, *Lexicon Poeticum*. As a result of his fine linguistic sensibility and his aspiration to maintain ties with the living folk-speech, he was of great significance for the Icelandic written language. A number of gifted students from Bessastaðir—such as the national poet Jónas Hallgrímsson (1807–45)—later continued their academic studies at the University of Copenhagen. In Denmark they founded journals with a variety of special interests—philology, literature, and culture—which were to be significant for the independence struggle that was soon to begin.

During the early years there was no instruction in Icelandic at the Latin School in Bessastaðir. In the eighteenth century this had been partly displaced by Danish as the language of officialdom. In the interior of the country the people still spoke pure Icelandic; no one understood a word of Danish. In Reykjavík and the other commercial towns along the coast, however, the important position of the Danish merchants meant that many people spoke a mixture of Icelandic and Danish. Did this involve a threat to the Icelandic language in the long term? Opinions differ on this issue.

One person who observed what was happening to the Icelandic language at this time was the Danish philologist Rasmus Christian Rask (1787–1832), who spent two years in Iceland in the early years of his short but eventful life. One of his major achievements was the foundation of an Icelandic literary society, Hið íslenzka bókmennta-félag, with the aim of preserving Icelandic language and literature. The society's journal Skírnir, called after the god Freyr's servant, is still being published today.[85]

Another scholar from the same period who was of significance for Iceland was the Danish antiquarian Carl Christian Rafn (1795–1864). He also founded a literary society and started the National Library of

Iceland (Landsbókasafn). In earlier periods of Icelandic history there had been few Danes who had made themselves popular among the Icelanders. Rask and Rafn, however, were genuinely admired.

A new age dawned. It came with the German romantics. They were impassioned by folk culture and manifestations of distinct national character. They took a keen interest in the tales and legends, the ballads and customs of their own people, the history, language, and literature of their forefathers. It was these ideas which inspired the Icelandic students in Copenhagen, like a breath of spring air. They discussed, studied, researched, and wrote. They vied with each other to compose lyrical nature poetry and patriotic poems. For them romanticism and national feeling pointed in the same direction. They were united by an awareness of the magnificent past of their bewitchingly beautiful homeland and the dream of an independent Iceland.

One of these avant-garde students was the romantic poet Jónas Hallgrímsson, who praised the commonwealth era and the legendary heroes in melancholy, nostalgic verse. Jónas and three of his companions—known as Fjölnir's men—started the journal *Fjölnir* (called after one of Odin's names). During the relatively brief life of the journal (1835–47) it was a brilliant mouthpiece for the four young men and their ideas.

Around 1840 Jón Sigurðsson made his political debut on the stage in Copenhagen. He and his fellows started to issue the annual *Ný félagsrit*. After a few years it replaced *Fjölnir* as the organ of the independence movement. By virtue of his charismatic personality, Jón Sigurðsson quickly established himself as the undisputed leader of the movement.

The snowball started to roll, particularly under the influence of the July Revolution in Paris in 1830. This signalled the start of the Icelandic independence movement.

To create safe channels for the unease brought on by the July Revolution, the autocratic Danish king decided to establish four advisory assemblies in his multinational kingdom. One of them was to have its seat in Roskilde, and it was suggested that Iceland should be represented there. This was unacceptable to the Icelanders, however. They maintained that, ever since the commonwealth, they had belonged to a separate nation with its own language, a rich literary heritage, and distinct national customs. Moreover, they lived in a land far removed from the Danish islands.

Fjölnir's men wanted instead to re-establish the Althing at its ancient site of Þingvellir. This was a romantically inspired notion. Jón Sigurðsson, showing wisdom and a spirit of cooperation, respected their arguments. He appreciated that in the initial phase of the independence struggle it might be meaningful to gather, as before, at Þingvellir. Yet Jón was also a clear-sighted realist. He pointed out practical reasons that made it more suitable to locate the future Icelandic parliament in Reykjavík, the new capital. There it could plead forcefully for home rule and free trade, as well as improvements in matters like education and medical care.

The Danish king finally agreed to re-establish the Althing as a *consultative* body in Reykjavík, with twenty-six representatives, twenty to be elected by the people and six appointed by the king. Suffrage was granted only to men over 25 with a certain amount of property; this meant that only about 5 per cent of the people were entitled to vote.[86]

The re-established Althing had its first meeting in the summer of 1845 in the Latin School, which was completed by then in Reykjavík. Jón Sigurðsson was elected to represent his native district of Vestfirðir, as he did until his death in 1879.

The Althing and the Danish Government: A Trial of Strength (1845–1904)

After the February Revolution in France in 1848, the absolute power of the Danish king was abolished, after nearly two centuries, to be replaced by a constitutional monarchy in accordance with the constitution of 1849.

In this state of affairs Jón Sigurðsson pleaded for home rule for Iceland, citing historical arguments. He referred first to the 1262 treaty (*gamli sáttmáli*) in which the Icelanders pledged their loyalty to the king of Norway. The treaty was thus an agreement between them and the Norwegian king. This did not mean that Iceland had been incorporated in Norway.

In the same way, the Icelanders had recognized the absolute power of the Danish king in 1662, but, he emphasized, they had never submitted to Danish sovereignty. Iceland never belonged to Denmark. In legal terms, Iceland had merely shared a monarch, first with Norway and then with Denmark.

Jón Sigurðsson's conclusion was that the Icelandic–Danish connection, now that absolutism had been abolished in Denmark, should be regulated within the framework of a personal union, where both nations had a joint king. Iceland should have a parliament (the Althing) with independent power to impose taxes and introduce legislation, with a government in Reykjavík responsible to the Althing.

This was, in outline, Jón Sigurðsson's programme for the independence struggle. It was far-sighted and well thought out, although he did not foresee that only a century would elapse before the Republic of Iceland was proclaimed. Important milestones on the way were the constitution of 1874, the granting of limited home rule in 1904, and personal union with Denmark in 1918.

For the rest of the nineteenth century this struggle for national independence and parliamentarism was to be an obdurate trial of strength between the Althing and the Danish government.

In the summer of 1851 it led to a direct confrontation between the two sides. In the years before this, the Icelanders formulated far-reaching demands for self-determination at meetings at Þingvellir and in the Althing. The Danish government, led by the prefect Count Jørgen Trampe, was not prepared to accede to these demands. The Danish government had a totally different overall view of developments. They were increasingly concerned about the German nationalist movement in Schleswig-Holstein. Although a corresponding movement in far-off Iceland did not worry the Danes as much, they feared that a showdown with Iceland—whether it led to independence or not—could lead to political complications in the delicate relations with Schleswig-Holstein.

In a Danish bill concerning the position of Iceland within the kingdom of Denmark, Iceland was equated with a Danish county and the Althing with a county assembly. The Danish constitution was to apply also to Iceland, which was regarded as an indivisible part of Denmark. Since the bill was diametrically opposed to the aspirations of the Icelanders, the Althing repeated the demands previously articulated in 1851.

The prefect waited for a few days before reacting. When he did respond, he used the language of power. He posted a number of soldiers near the Althing. He then entered the chamber. In a sharply worded speech he criticized the Althing's proposal and then declared the meeting closed. Jón Sigurðsson asked to speak but was silenced. He then protested. He complained of the lawless behaviour of the prefect. As the prefect was leaving the chamber, most of the members of the Althing rose from their seats and cried in chorus: 'We all protest. Long live our king, Frederik VII!'

The prefect had been too hasty. Jón Sigurðsson, on the other hand, had the law on his side. He was the moral victor in the duel.

This remarkable occurrence has been portrayed in the eye-catching historical painting by the artist Gunnlaugur Blöndal, which hangs in the entrance hall of the Althing. Jón Sigurðsson's portrait adorns the wall beside the rostrum in the present session chamber of the parliament.

It should be emphasized that Jón Sigurðsson's protest was directed at the abuse of power by the Danish government, not at Denmark as a nation and a kingdom. King Christian IX's monogram, the letters C IX surmounted by a crown, can still be seen on the façade of the Althing. It faces a square called Austurvöllur, where a statue was raised to Jón Sigurðsson in 1931. Opposite Lækjartorg, another square in the centre of Reykjavík, lies Government House (Stjórnarráðshúsið). Two statues stand before this building: on the right Hannes Hafstein, the first native minister, and on the left Christian IX holding the constitution of Iceland in his hand.

A period of almost seven centuries under the rule of foreign monarchs is and will remain a part of Iceland's history.

After this strained meeting, the parties were long deadlocked. In 1871 the Danish king ratified a status act (*stöðulög*) which began by declaring that 'Iceland is an indivisible part of the Kingdom of Denmark with special national rights'. The Althing rejected this act because it had come about without its participation.

Jón Sigurðsson did not yield. He maintained Iceland's demands in all their essentials. His motto was 'Never give way'—*Eigi víkja*. It was a source of strength for the Icelandic people to have him as their spokesman for forty years. Not for nothing is he Iceland's national hero. He was not just brilliantly talented. He had a fixed purpose and a steadfast character, yet his manner was always calm, pleasant, and winning. He was one with the independence movement. In short, he had all the qualities that characterize a great leader and statesman.[87]

Jón Sigurðsson was speaker of the Althing for many years. In his old age he received an honorary salary from the Althing. He and his wife Ingibjörg, however, spent the major part of their lives in Copenhagen, where they lived in a large house shaped like a smoothing iron, at number 8 Østervoldgade, near Kongens Nytorv. Their home was always open to Icelanders.

The building now belongs to the Icelandic state. Known as 'Hús Jóns Sigurðssonar', it houses a library, a guest flat for holders of Icelandic scholarships, the offices of the Icelandic Association in Copenhagen, and a meeting place for Icelanders in the Danish capital. It also contains a memorial museum to Jón Sigurðsson in the flat where he lived.

After the confrontation of 1851 and the status act of 1871, the independence movement appeared to have reached an impasse. For many years the Icelanders were in a dismal economic and social state. Although Iceland had been granted the right to free trade with all the states of the world in 1854, this long remained a right on paper only. The Icelanders still lacked the resources required to build, equip, and operate ocean-going trading vessels. Danish commercial houses still handled the majority of Iceland's foreign trade. Imports to Iceland in 1863 were transported by ships of the following countries:

    84% by Danish ships
    3% by Icelandic ships
    5% by Norwegian ships
    8% by ships of other nations[88]

The Icelanders lived in very difficult social circumstances. There was still widespread poverty, high infant mortality, diseases like leprosy, a shortage of doctors and hospitals, of schools, harbours, roads, and bridges. Despite the lack of schools, however, there was general literacy. Housing was very poor. The inhabitants of Reykjavík (around 1,500 in 1860) lived in turf houses with grass roofs and windows of dried animal cauls and transparent skins. On top of everything, there were once again volcanic eruptions and earthquakes, an inexorable part of the Icelandic people's destiny. Volcanic ash contaminated the soil with fluorine, bringing crop failures, as in the famine years of 1783–4.

For many people the solution was to emigrate. The 1870s saw the beginning of a major wave of emigration from Iceland to North America (chiefly the mid-west of Canada and the USA), with a small number of people also leaving for Brazil.[89]

People at this time were also leaving Ireland, and the reasons behind the emigration from Iceland were similar: poverty, crop failure (mostly because of bitter cold and volcanic eruptions), cramped living conditions, and discontent with foreign domination. Dissatisfaction was expressed in 1873 when a black flag was hoisted over the governor's residence, bearing the words 'Down with the governor'. The demonstration was probably the work of pupils of the Latin School. Half-starving farmers read enticing letters from America. They longed for a more meaningful existence with more prosperity and greater freedom.

Things became brighter in the summer of 1874, the year when the Icelanders celebrated the thousandth anniversary of the first settlement of the country. That year the Rev. Matthías Jochumsson (1835–1920)—the inspired poet who translated some of Shakespeare's plays into Icelandic—composed the Icelandic national anthem. It begins with the words 'Ó Guð vors lands' (O God of our land) and is sung to a tune by Sveinbjörn Sveinbjörnsson (1847–1927). Sveinbjörn spent most of his life in Edinburgh, where he worked as a piano teacher and a composer. The national anthem is inspired by Psalm 90, about the eternal nature of God and the transitory existence of man; the same psalm is the source of the English hymn 'O God our help in ages past'. In Matthías's anthem, however, this message is linked to the nation's history, to Iceland's first millennium. Many thousands of Icelanders sang this anthem at Þingvellir. They sang out their undisguised joy in the presence of representatives of the Faroe Islands, Denmark, the united kingdom of Sweden-Norway, and the United States. One who was not present was Jón Sigurðsson; although he should have been a self-evident participant, he was not invited.

The city of Copenhagen donated a bronze cast of a statue of the famous sculptor Bertel Thorvaldsen, whose father was an Icelander. It now stands in a little park in the centre of Reykjavík, not far from the residences of the British, French, Norwegian, Swedish, and American ambassadors, by the glittering waters of the bird-lake Tjörnin—which reflects lovely wooden houses from the start of the twentieth century and a newly built (and, in the opinion of many, misplaced) town hall of concrete. This self-portrait of Thorvaldsen shows him in full figure. In his right hand he holds a hammer and in his left a chisel; the left arm is resting on a statue called Hope.

The guests at the millennial celebrations included King Christian IX, the first Danish monarch to visit Iceland. He brought with him as a gift a constitution for the country. He had issued it 'of his own free authority' but without prior consultation with the Althing. It was thus a Danish offer from a position of power. For the Icelanders it nevertheless meant progress, since it increased the scope of the Althing's powers.

The constitution of 1874 was based on a tripartite division of power in the spirit of Montesquieu. Legislative power was to be exercised by the Althing, with certain restrictions; the Althing also had the power of imposing taxes. Judicial power was to be exercised by Icelandic courts, with the Danish Supreme Court as the highest court of appeal. Executive power was to be in the hands of a Governor-General (*landshöfðingi*), responsible to the Danish government, not to the Althing.

According to this constitution, the Althing was to consist of two chambers. The upper chamber was to have twelve members, six elected and six appointed by the king. The lower chamber was to have twenty-four elected members. Suffrage was still restricted to men aged 25 and over with a certain minimum income or occupying certain offices. The constitution also included provisions concerning basic human rights such as freedom of religion, freedom of assembly, and freedom of association.[90]

The king's approval was required for a law to come into force. Moreover, the king's representatives in the upper chamber could have a bill thrown out. The king, in other words, had the power to prevent the passing of any legislation which he disliked.

The king often used this veto in the subsequent period (1874–1904) when Iceland was under a Governor-General. Although the new constitution was initially greeted by Icelanders with joy and anticipation, this later turned to disappointment and bitterness. The Icelanders gradually became discontented and resigned. They realized that they were powerless, although they were inspired by the Norwegian nationalist movement, especially Johan Sverdrup's successful struggle for parliamentary government.

An incident in this period has recently been the subject of a literary debut—which surprised many people—by Ragnar Arnalds, who represents the People's Alliance in the Althing. His play *Uppreisn á Ísafirði* (Revolt in Ísafjörður) had a long run in the Icelandic National Theatre, 1986–7. The plot is based on a study of an Icelandic legal scandal from the 1890s, the Skúli case. This occurred in the small town of Ísafjörður, where the sheriff, a radical member of the Althing, Skúli Thoroddsen, was dismissed from his post in 1892 in a sensational manner by the Governor-General, Magnús Stephensen, his political opponent. Skúli obtained redress from the Supreme Court in 1895, and then continued to sit in the Althing until 1915.[91]

The play is set against a broad, at times rich and colourful, backdrop where the scene switches between Ísafjörður, Reykjavík, and the royal court in Copenhagen. It shows in no uncertain terms that a popular leader of the calibre of Skúli Thoroddsen will not let himself be suppressed. In this respect he is reminiscent of many freedom fighters all over the world, but Skúli Thoroddsen, like Jón Sigurðsson, waged his struggle with words, not with the sword.

Limited Self-Government (1904–1918)

While Iceland was under a Governor-General, Denmark had been ruled by conservative governments, first under the leadership of the landowner Jacob Estrup, who was prime minister for nearly twenty years. Estrup was opposed by a majority in the Danish parliament, and when they refused to grant money to the government, he issued provisional financial laws. He also rejected various proposals for reform in Iceland.

Iceland's constitution was modernized after a general election in Denmark in 1901, which forced a change of power in Copenhagen. The new left-wing government enjoyed the support of a parliamentary majority. Since the left had struggled for parliamentarism for so long and had finally achieved their goal, they could hardly do anything but accept parliamentary government in Iceland as well. The Althing unanimously ratified a Danish act to this effect, which came into force on 1 February 1904. It meant that Iceland received her own minister, who was to reside in Reykjavík and be responsible to the Althing.

Iceland's autonomy, however, was curtailed in various ways. It was still considered an indivisible part of the Danish realm. The Minister for Iceland was still formally a member of the Danish government. He was obliged to obtain approval for important measures and laws from the Danish privy council. Moreover, certain areas—chiefly foreign policy, defence, protection of territorial waters, fishing limits, and the functions of the supreme court—were still the preserve of Copenhagen. Iceland's situation can therefore be described as limited self-government.

The first occupant of the attractive post of Minister for Iceland was the poet, lawyer, and member of the Althing, Hannes Hafstein (1861–1922), whose poems are still read today. This elegant man of the world was widely admired. He had a reputation for being a practical man of action, with the ability to set wheels turning. This was badly needed. During his periods as Minister (1904–9 and 1912–14) he also succeeded in implementing a large number of reforms.

This reforming work, which had begun gradually during the preceding decades and continued to grow at an increasing pace, was absolutely vital. It should be seen against the background of the medieval structure of Icelandic society which still prevailed in the middle of the nineteenth century. We have seen some of the wretched conditions: appalling housing, rampant infectious diseases, and a shortage of almost everything: secondary schools, hospitals, roads, bridges. Families had many children. Population growth was nevertheless checked by high infant mortality, epidemics, and emigration (which did not stagnate until around 1912). In 1901 the population was roughly 78,000, which we may compare with the 1992 figure of 260,000.

Iceland gradually became more modern. As they became more independent, the Icelandic people acquired up-to-date farming methods along with producers' cooperatives, decked fishing vessels, and a growing fleet of trawlers. Competing with foreign trawlers, the fishermen harvested the rich fishing grounds off the coast of Iceland. In addition, they could benefit at times from the profitable herring fishery and whaling, although this was mainly pursued by Norwegians. Other stimuli came from the growth of banks and the formation of shipping companies, such as the steamship company Eimskip, whose first proud possession was called the *Gullfoss*. New communications came with the building of roads, bridges, harbours, lighthouses, telephone connections, and—around 1914—a single railway line. It was short. It was used for transporting stone and other material during the construction of Reykjavík's old harbour (the new one is called Sundahöfn). It would have been too expensive to build any more railways in Iceland, with its mountains and its fickle climate. The Icelanders therefore took the step directly from horses to aeroplanes. At the same time, they built hospitals and institutes of vocational education, teaching agricultural and domestic science, and training seamen, clergy, and doctors.

This leap into the present was incredibly swift. Heimir Pálsson, known for his quick wit, says that the Middle Ages ended when the telephone cable reached the town of Seyðisfjörður on the east coast. Yet decades were to pass before Iceland began to take on the outline of a modern Nordic welfare state. It was not until 1936 that a law on social security was passed. This has since been broadened in scope, with much better benefits for the citizens.

Development culminated on 17 June 1911, the centenary of Jón Sigurðsson's birth, when the University of Iceland, with four faculties, was opened.

Hannes Hafstein was self-confident. He wanted to make a lasting contribution on behalf of his country, to be remembered in the future for repealing the hated status act of 1871. To this end, after the visit of Frederik VIII in 1907, he collaborated with the Danes to draw up a bill concerning links between Iceland and Denmark within the framework

1 *To the left: the Icelandic national coat of arms from 1918 to 1944. — To the right: the present coat of arms. See p. 62.*

2 *Þingvellir (see p. 8) on a clear autumn day.*

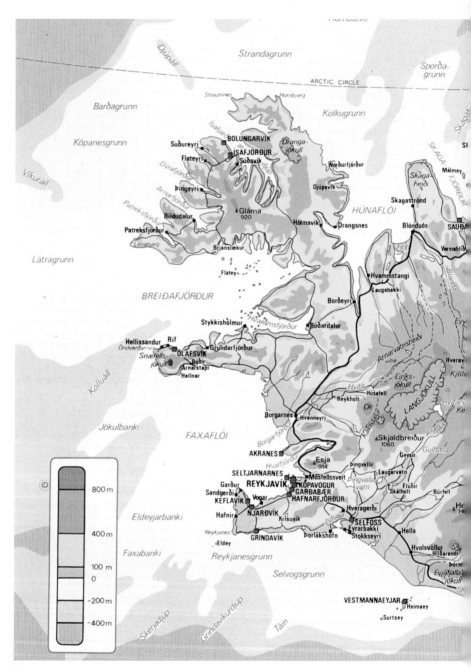

3

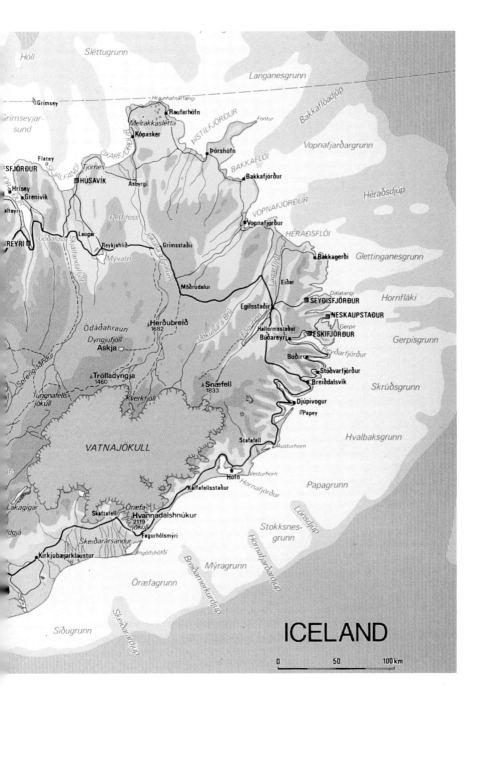

ICELAND

0   50   100 km

4 *Gullfoss is considered one of the most beautiful waterfalls in Iceland.*

5 *Geysir is one of the most famous hot springs in the world. In many languages, its name is used as a collective term for hot springs of this type.* *See p. 381.*

6 *The cathedral at Skálholt. For 700 years, Skálholt was an important centre for cultural and religious life.*

7 *A summer day in Laugarvatn, southern Iceland.*

8 *Reagan and Gorbachev meet in Höfði in Reykjavík in 1986 (see pp. 318-20).*

9 *The Nordic House in Reykjavík, designed by the Finnish architect Alvar Aalto (see p. 209).*

10 *Þingvellir, site of the world's oldest parliament (see p. 8).*

11 *Sheep in Galtalækjarskógur, near Hekla. The mountain in the background is Búrfell. See p. 387.*

12 *The hot spring Bláhver at Hveravellir, between the glaciers Langjökull and Hofsjökull in central Iceland.*

13 *Breiðamerkurlón in south-eastern Iceland.* *See p. 243.*

14 *The hostel of the Icelandic Travel Association (Ferðafélag Íslands) at Þórsmörk. The mountain in the background is Tindfjallajökull.*

15 *A quiet evening at Reykjavík harbour. The mountain Esja in the background.*

16 *Vestmannaeyjar in 1973: the eruption threatens the deserted town. See pp. 371-2.*

17 *A fishing vessel leaving harbour in a squall.*

18 *A bird's eye-view of the summit of Snæfellsjökull. See pp. 368-9.*

19 *Lake Askja in central Iceland was formed in an eruption in 1875. See p. 370.*

20 *Hekla is one of the most active volcanoes in Iceland. See p. 370.*

21 *Öræfajökull is both a glacier and a volcano. Its peak, Hvannadalshnúkur, is Iceland's highest point (2,119 m). See p. 370.*

22 *The beauty of Mývatn. See pp. 273-5.*

23 *An Icelandic mare with a foal. See pp. 233-6.*

of a union. The bill, with some modifications, was to serve as a model for the Act of Union of 1918.

According to the bill, Iceland was to be 'a free, autonomous, and independent country'. It would be united to Denmark through a joint king and some common concerns (foreign policy, military defence, etc.). After twenty-five years each party could reconsider the arrangement, and after an interval of ten years it was permitted unilaterally to revoke the clauses about the common concerns. However, the clauses about the king's civil list, foreign policy, and defence were irrevocable.[92]

It was not long before this revocation clause was devastatingly criticized by the old member of the Althing, Skúli Thoroddsen, the freedom fighter whom we met in the previous section. He pointed out that, according to the concluding words of this clause, Iceland could in theory never become independent. The bill became the main issue in the 1908 election to the Althing. The election was a defeat for Hannes Hafstein, who had only nine members on his side against twenty-five for the opposition. This led to his fall in 1909, after a vote of no confidence in the Althing.

There followed a period with a few reforms (such as the 1915 act which allowed women to vote and to be elected to the Althing) but it was mostly marred by a series of disputes on domestic policy. These became less heated, however, after the outbreak of the Great War. The three biggest parties formed a coalition government in 1917.

The 'hunger blockade' of Germany, the German submarine war against Britain, Iceland's isolation from Denmark, and the shortage of food and fuel gave the Icelanders other things to think about than petty internal issues and personality clashes which had previously led to political squabbles. Once again—as during the Napoleonic wars—Iceland noticed how dependent she was on Britain, the leading sea power.

During the war years Iceland never ceased to demand a *national flag,* as Norway had done while under Swedish rule. The poet Einar Benediktsson (1864–1940) had proposed a white cross on a blue background. At the Stockholm Olympic Games in 1912, however, the Danish government had prohibited the Icelandic athletes from parading into the stadium under an Icelandic flag.

Another famous flag incident occurred the following year. When an Icelander hoisted the blue and white flag on his small rowing-boat in Reykjavík harbour, it was confiscated by a Danish warship which happened to be in the harbour in conjunction with coastguard operations. The captain sent the flag to the sheriff of Reykjavík with a message that it was forbidden for vessels to fly the blue and white emblem within the realm of Denmark.

The seizure of the flag stirred national feelings in Iceland. It was like putting a light to a powder keg. The news of the confiscation spread like wildfire among the inhabitants of the little town. They started making blue and white flags at once. After a few hours the blue and white flag was flying all over Reykjavík—from windows, roofs, and flagpoles. That evening a protest meeting was arranged. The flag issue was soon brought up in the Althing, where the demand for an Icelandic flag was reiterated.

The flag dispute dragged on for some time. The Danes yielded, but only slowly and in stages. In 1915 they were resolutely opposed to Einar Benediktsson's idea of a white cross on a blue field since, they claimed, it would be too similar to the flag of the king of Greece. Finland had not yet received her flag, which is described in the law of 29 May 1918 as a rectangular flag with an ultramarine cross on a white field.

There was a temporary solution to the dispute in 1915, when a Danish resolution declared that a red cross should be inserted in the white cross, with the background still being blue. This became the national flag of Iceland, which is described in technical terminology as a blue flag with a red cross fimbriated in white. This flag was not to be flown outside Iceland's territorial waters. Between 1914 and 1918 Icelandic vessels therefore sailed—reluctantly—under the red and white Danish flag.[93]

The flag dispute continued. In the summer of 1918 it resulted in negotiations on a higher level. The parties concluded an agreement on the union of Iceland and Denmark, which came into force on 1 December 1918. The Danes showed that they were willing to make concessions. Explanations of this have referred to the critical international situation, the consideration for the vigorous growth of nationalist movements throughout Europe, and especially Denmark's desire to regain the Danish-speaking part of Schleswig from Germany.

According to a recent textbook in Icelandic history, the Icelandic flag of 1918 was at first received without enthusiasm, because of the red cross which had been forcibly added in 1915. 'Many people were aggrieved that they had not been given the flag for which patriotic Icelanders had struggled.' Einar Benediktsson never gave up his personal idea for the Icelandic flag. At his burial at Þingvellir in 1940—close to the grave of Jónas Hallgrímsson—his coffin was draped with the blue and white flag.[94]

Now, over seventy years after the Danish flag decree, the Icelanders are well accustomed to their flag. They have come to appreciate it. They would not change it for anything. It has become one with their dreams. For them it is like a vision of the Icelandic landscape.

Of the three colours on the flag, the background—the fundamental element—is painted with the deep blue of the ocean and the iridescent tones of the firmament. This makes an effective contrast to the white and red in the flag. The gleaming expanses of ice and snow on glaciers and mountains unite in symphony with the sparkling scarlet flames of the volcanic magma flowing from the bowels of the earth.

The cross on the flag, with its upright slightly towards the hoist, also appears on the flags of the other Nordic countries (with the exception of Greenland's). The cross symbolizes the Christian faith, which the Nordic people have shared for over a millennium. In the sign of the cross, the colours of the Icelandic flag unite in a harmonious triad.

Reflections about Independence Day, 1 December 1918

The winter of 1918 was the coldest within living memory (−25°C in Reykjavík, −33°C in Akureyri). The extreme cold was exacerbated by a shortage of fuel. This was followed in October 1918 by the eruption of the ice-covered volcano Katla. This caused massive glacial outbursts (*jökulhlaup*), where the glacier rivers flooded adjacent areas with meltwater, boulders, sand, and ice. The series of natural disasters culminated in November with a death-dealing influenza epidemic, the Spanish flu.

It was in these exceptionally grim circumstances that the union with Denmark came into force. It was nevertheless celebrated in duly dignified forms in front of Government House in Reykjavík on 1 December 1918. That day was then commemorated as Independence Day until the coming of the republic in 1944. On the same day Iceland received a new *national coat of arms*, which was used until 1944. It consisted of the Royal Danish Crown and a Shield supported by four heraldic figures in the form of a dragon, a bird of prey, a bull, and a giant. They are the *landvættir*, as described in Chapter 3, 'Folk Belief and Folk Tales'.[95]

The heraldic emblem in the coat of arms has changed from time to time. In the period 1904–18 a falcon coloured silver was shown against a blue shield background. Earlier, as in the fourteenth century, the coat of arms consisted of a crowned, headless and flattened cod. The origin of this national coat of arms has not been fully investigated.

The oldest source for the cod emblem is an illustration in a vellum manuscript from about 1360, now preserved in the Royal Library in Stockholm. It is similar to the heraldic drawing in this book in black and white by Jacques de Wærn of the National Archives in Stockholm.

The use of the cod emblem undoubtedly has its roots in the Icelandic dried fish (stockfish), which was for centuries an important export item. Foreign sources in the fifteenth and sixteenth centuries show this crowned cod. The same emblem appears on the reverse of the title-page in Bishop Guðbrandur's psalm-book, which was published at Hólar in 1589.[96]

The following descriptions of the programme for the first Independence Day show how differently two discerning people can recall the same occasion.[97]

Ágúst H. Bjarnason, professor of philosophy, recorded this version of the event:

> On 1 December last year, Iceland became a free and independent state. It was a solemn, glorious moment when our national flag was hoisted over Government House. The Danes behaved towards us with exceptional grace; the soldiers on the coastguard vessel saluted the flag, and the commanding officer made a fine, sincere speech.

Sixty years later, however, Halldór Laxness recalled the same event in a different light:

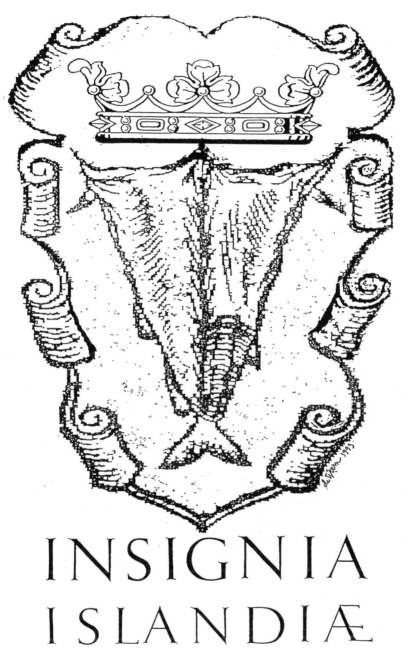

INSIGNIA
ISLANDIÆ

Reference has just been made to the use of the ancient cod emblem. It is similiar to this heraldic drawing in black and white by Jacques de Wærn of the National Archives of Stockholm.

It happened in the bitter cold of the late autumn, before a thaw. I remember mud and slippery ground under a sky with low-hanging clouds. In this raw chill, people—all those who were not dead—met to rejoice over independence in Bakarabrekka and Lækjargata and to look at Government House. Horn music was played. A senior Danish officer commanded a small troop of marines. In his hand he held an Icelandic flag, which he hoisted over our Government House as a sign that the Danes hereby handed this diabolical country over to us Icelanders. He then saluted and marched on board the ship with his soldiers.

Disputes still occasionally arise in Iceland about whether the country really did achieve independence on 1 December 1918, when the union came into force. During the period up to the proclamation of the republic in 1944, many people appear to have believed that this was the case. The first section of the Act of Union states that 'Denmark and Iceland are free and sovereign states, united through a joint king and through the agreement which is incorporated in this act of union'. The Kingdom of Iceland existed *de facto* and *de jure* within the framework of a constitution which came into force in 1920.

On the other hand, Denmark was to take care of Iceland's foreign policy, if not also the orientation of her foreign policy. For this purpose an Icelandic emissary (Sveinn Björnsson) had been accredited to Copenhagen since 1920, and Iceland—unlike Denmark—never became a member of the League of Nations.[98] In addition, Denmark acted as coastguard in Iceland's territorial waters (three nautical miles since 1872), although the Icelanders soon assisted in this, and in providing a supreme court until Iceland established her own in 1920. The parties were to have the same rights to each other's fishing waters.

With reference to these restrictions of sovereignty—especially the clauses concerning the head of state, foreign policy, and coastguard operations—one may ask with the former prime minister, Ólafur Jóhannesson, whether the Kingdom of Iceland really was a sovereign state in terms of international law. When discussing this matter we are justified in employing current definitions of the concepts 'state' and 'sovereignty'.

For a country to be a *state* it must have an organized power with institutions which directly represent the state. The state must have an associated territory containing a people, that is, persons who belong to the state in the capacity of citizens. A state is *sovereign* when it has no higher power above it; it is represented solely by its own institutions in international connections.

The Kingdom of Iceland obviously met only some of these criteria of international law. A Swedish international lawyer has argued that Denmark-Iceland formed a real union in the period 1918–1940, like Sweden-Norway 1814–1905 and Austria-Hungary 1867–1918.[99] This may be true. But its head of state was a Dane, and foreign policy and coastguard operations were in principle handled by Denmark.

There can only be one conclusion. Iceland did not become fully sovereign until 17 June 1944. She then received her own head of state, her own foreign representation in the form of Icelandic embassies, consulates, and delegations, and her own coastguard.

Personal Union with Denmark (The Kingdom of Iceland, 1918–44)

Icelanders love history, so they relish historical celebrations. These give them cause to go to Þingvellir, the most magnificent of all places of assembly in Iceland, with its law-rock majestically situated for addressing the crowds. They meet for speeches, pomp, singing, and a sense of community. In this place the winds of history bring them pride, the memories of past greatness, patriotism, a sense of festivity.

One such memorable day in the history of Iceland occurred in the high summer of 1930. About 40,000 Icelanders made the pilgrimage to Þingvellir, there to celebrate for three days the millenary of the foundation of the Althing. Among the guests of honour was the popular King Christian X of Denmark, who also visited Iceland in 1921, 1926, and 1936, and the Swedish Crown Prince Gustaf Adolf.[100]

As a gift to the Icelandic people the United States Congress marked the occasion by donating an imposing statue of Leifur Eiríksson, discoverer of America. It stands on a rise in the centre of Reykjavík.

The celebrations in 1930 were completely carefree, as if the Icelanders little suspected that they were on the eve of the worst economic crisis in modern history. The Wall Street crash on 24 October 1929 (Black Thursday), which has been ascribed to over-production, speculation, and unrealistically inflated stock rates, had serious repercussions because of the vital importance of the USA and the dollar in world trade. The crash triggered an international crisis of nightmare proportions. Disaster followed like a chain reaction: prices fell, consumption dropped, production declined, resulting in decreased international trade and a wave of bankruptcies and mass unemployment.

Iceland was one of the countries which suffered most from the global depression. Between 1930 and 1939 it led to a record number of bankruptcies, prolonged high unemployment, widespread poverty, labour disputes, and strikes. There were tendencies to class strife, sometimes in violent forms. The flight from the countryside was accentuated at the same time, when ruined farmers poured into the towns, as they had done earlier in the twentieth century. The Icelanders found it hard to pull themselves out of the crisis. This did not happen until the demand for Icelandic goods and services increased in conjunction with the occupation of Iceland—first by the British, then the Americans—in World War II.

The devastating effects of the international crisis nevertheless do not detract from the total picture of social development between 1918 and 1944. In this period the winds of change blew with increasing strength over Iceland. The country gradually took on the features of a modern society. The Icelandic people retained their identity—their language, their customs, their thousand-year culture—but they were subject to relentless influence from outside. For centuries they had lived in isolation, but now they began to develop links with the surrounding world, especially countries like Norway, Germany, and Britain. At the same time, they grew less dependent on Denmark.

Iceland—like Finland after her independence in 1917—also began to be involved in Nordic cooperation. This had previously been Scandinavian, encompassing only Denmark, Norway, and Sweden, but after World War I it was extended to comprise the whole of 'Norden'. The Icelandic association for Nordic cooperation, Norræna félagið, was founded in 1922, followed by a corresponding Finnish association in 1924.

As the towns grew, the rural population declined. Agricultural production nevertheless increased its yield in most of the areas which are suitable for Iceland at her latitude and with her natural resources: milk, butter, cheese, eggs, animal fodder, and—thanks to the geothermally heated greenhouses—garden produce. Fish yields also grew, although the increase for fish and fish products was not so palpable until World War II, and especially after 1945, when the Althing decided to grant some of its currency reserves for the purchase of thirty-three new trawlers. Everything expanded: the fishing fleet, foreign trade, the road network in a country which had once been virtually without roads, and industries such as herring factories and cold storage.

More and more schools were built: primary schools, secondary schools, vocational schools. Later a chain of boarding schools was established in the rural municipalities. They still exist, and are used in the summer as cheap tourist hotels.

It is clear, however, that these rapid changes in society and living conditions brought countless new worries: economic, social, and mental problems. The old values were no longer sufficient. Most Icelanders were forced to seek new occupations, new jobs, new schools for themselves and their children. The newcomers to the towns also needed somewhere to live. First, however, they had to crowd in small homes (often in damp basements) or build new houses, all depending on their income. For those who remained on their ancestral farms, circumstances were often difficult.

Looking back, we see that the Icelandic people made the leap from the draught horse to the jet plane in record time. Iceland developed from a poor, traditional farming country of medieval character to a prosperous, high-technology welfare state, with the population concentrated in towns. In particular, there was a movement towards the densely populated area in the south-western corner of the island, around the capital Reykjavík.

The Icelandic state church has found it difficult to adjust in tune with the changes. So have the Icelanders. It has been a source of strength to them, however, that they have maintained their firm bonds with the past, preserving their living cultural heritage—the Icelandic sagas. Although most Icelanders no longer bother to attend church except on special occasions, it appears that deep down they have retained their faith in God.

A Monarchy Becomes a Republic (1939–44)

In bygone times, when Iceland was still a Danish colony, it could appear exotic or beautiful, but scarcely of strategic importance. It was found exotic by the imaginative Jules Verne, who let his *Journey to the Centre of the Earth* begin from the extinct volcanic crater of Snæfellsjökull in western Iceland. The Swedish writer Albert Engström found Iceland 'the most beautiful thing I have ever experienced'.[101] Strategically, however, this distant island with its tiny population of poor farmers and fishermen had been of no interest.

During World War II, however, the Icelanders were shocked to discover that their country was no longer outside the interest of belligerent states. The technical achievements of the twentieth century— chiefly the development of shipping and aeronautics—had broken Iceland's isolation. New arms technology (remote-controlled submarines) meant that Iceland with her geographical position in the middle of the North Atlantic was deemed to be of considerable strategic importance by the general staffs of the great powers. Control of Iceland gave the power to protect, or prevent, transports over this busy ocean, one of the vital arteries in world trade. A base in Iceland was therefore suitable for combating submarines, monitoring communications, transporting troops, and convoying ships.

The German geopolitician Karl Haushofer (1869–1946) maintained that the country which controlled Iceland had a revolver firmly pointed at England, America, and Canada. Winston Churchill was one of those who cited Haushofer's words.[102] The truth of the statement has been repeatedly confirmed. When war broke out in 1939, this was perfectly clear to Britain and the USA.

Ever since 1935 the incorporation of Iceland in the Third Reich had been the goal of the SS leader, Heinrich Himmler. The SS officer Paul Burkert, Himmler's representative and 'knight' in Iceland, travelled around the country trying to capture in his net influential Icelanders, including the prime minister, Hermann Jónasson. Himmler sought to win his friendship, inviting him to the Olympic Games in Berlin. Hermann delayed before sending his reply, and at the last minute he politely declined the invitation. Meanwhile, Himmler sent a research expedition to Iceland, consisting of men from the SS and Gestapo, organizations later notorious for their infiltration, espionage, and mass murders. Plans were also made to build German industries in Iceland and to train Icelandic Nazis with the SS.[103]

It may be mentioned in passing that in Iceland, as in the other Nordic countries, a Nazi party was formed. They arranged noisy demonstrations but attracted few members. The highest vote for the party was 2.8 per cent, in the municipal elections in Reykjavík in 1934.[104]

The Icelandic state was not particularly flattered by this attention from the German Nazis. In 1918 it had proclaimed its permanent neutrality under section 19 of the Act of Union. Many sceptics wondered what this neutrality was worth now. They pointed out what had happened to Belgium, whose eternal neutrality had been ceremoniously guaranteed by the great powers in 1830. 'Just for a scrap of paper,' said a German general in 1914, after the German invasion of Belgium, when he heard that Britain was going to war to defend Belgium's neutrality.

In moments of danger, people close the ranks. In April 1939, facing the threat of war, Hermann Jónasson formed a coalition government. He was the leader of the Progressive Party, an agrarian party founded in 1916, with close links with the cooperative movement (he was also father of the equally famous politician from the same party, Steingrímur Hermannsson, prime minister 1983–7 and 1988–91). The partners in this government were representatives of the Labour Party (also founded in 1916) and the Independence Party, Iceland's largest party, formed in 1929 as an amalgamation of the Conservative and Liberal Parties. Hermann Jónasson's coalition government was in power until 1942, when it fell on account of compulsory legislation to combat spiralling prices and wages. While it sat, this coalition government had a broad base which made it well prepared for all eventualities. But Iceland was a small, defenceless country.

In retrospect, we know that the 'Phoney War' in the autumn of 1939, after the collapse of Poland and the enforced pacts of the Baltic states with the Soviet Union, was a calm before the storm. The attention of the Western powers was directed to the Nordic countries by the Finno-Soviet Winter War of 1939–40 and the shipments of Swedish ore to Germany. The Western powers, however, were too late in planning a military expedition to northern Scandinavia. The British mining of Norwegian territorial waters at three places on 7–8 April was also without major effect. The following day, Hitler launched lightning attacks on Denmark and Norway. These invasions had been in preparation for some time, and at a more intensive speed after the *Altmark*, a German auxiliary cruiser sailing in Norwegian territorial waters, was captured in February 1940 by a British destroyer which rescued nearly three hundred British prisoners of war.

Denmark capitulated immediately. The war in Norway lasted for two months. King Håkon VII and his government fled to London on 7 June, after a brave but unequal battle against superior forces. On 9 April 1940, the same day as Hitler launched his blitzkrieg against Denmark and Norway, Iceland became another Nordic pawn in the game played by the great powers.

From April 1940 Iceland is mentioned here and there in Winston Churchill's great work on World War II. His assessments of the state of affairs changed quickly in pace with the development of the war in Norway. On 9 April the Franco-British Supreme War Council agreed at a meeting in London that 'suitable measures were to be taken to occupy the Faroe Islands, and assurances of protection would be given to Iceland'.[105]

That same day, the British Consul General in Reykjavík handed over a note to the Icelandic government, pointing out the fate just suffered by Denmark and Norway. Iceland was invited to join the war as an ally. Two days later the Icelandic government declined the request, invoking Iceland's unswerving and permanent neutrality. They also said that, since Iceland had no military defence, she neither could nor should take part in military alliances.

On 28 April—just nineteen days later but now in the light of the German military successes along the Norwegian coast—Churchill, who was still First Lord of the Admiralty (he did not become Prime Minister until May), saw that the situation demanded more radical action. He thought it 'indispensable that we have a base in Iceland for our flying-boats and for oiling the ships on the Northern Patrol. Let a case be prepared for submission to the Foreign Office. The sooner we let the Icelanders know that this is what we require the better.'[106]

Undeterred by the negative Icelandic response, the British occupied

Iceland on the night of 10 May 1940, just before the evacuation from Dunkirk. One of their first moves was to proceed straight from Reykjavík harbour to the home of the German consul, Dr Werner Gerlach in Túngata, where he and his family were busy burning papers in the bath. Shortly before this, the British had also occupied the Faroe Islands.[107]

The Icelandic government immediately lodged a vehement protest. The same evening, however, the prime minister spoke to the citizens of Iceland on the radio. He asked them to regard the British soldiers as guests from a friendly country and to treat them as such.

On 5 June there were rumours of a German landing in Iceland, but they soon proved to be false.[108]

On one occasion the British military police arrested some striking workers. They had been handing out leaflets to the soldiers, urging them not to do the work of the strikers. The military police later arrested three journalists from the socialist newspaper *Þjóðviljinn* for what they had written about the incident; they were deported to London. Apart from these incidents, relations with the British were generally good. The same friendly relations continued with the American soldiers who relieved the British on 7 July 1941, by agreement with the Icelandic government.

The occupation obviously had both positive and negative sides. The very fact that there were large numbers of soldiers spread all over the country made them a disruptive element among the small Icelandic population, which was only about 121,000 in 1940.[109] Icelandic men were irritated by the sight of well-paid soldiers having shallow fun with Icelandic women. Or as the English used to say about the Americans, 'They are overfed, oversexed, and over here.' According to an Icelandic police report from 1941, there was widespread prostitution in Reykjavík.

Amusing pictures of life in Reykjavík during the allied occupation have been painted by Kjartan Ragnarsson in his musical *Land míns föður* (Land of My Father), with music by Atli Heimir Sveinsson. This popular musical played to full houses at the Iðnó theatre for about a year.

The allied presence influenced Iceland in many ways. Their extensive construction projects—including the airfields at Reykjavík and Keflavík, an oil terminal in Hvalfjörður, roads, communication facilities, and military barracks—brought instant full employment and considerable earnings in foreign currency. Another source of income was the shipments of fresh and frozen fish to a Britain short of food. The submarine war, air attacks, and mined waters made this traffic deadly dangerous. Iceland's losses on the seas in World War II were proportionately as great as the number of soldiers lost by the United States.

The influx of currency was welcome. It had its negative effects, however: high inflation, which has been the scourge of Iceland since the last war.[110]

Iceland's union with Denmark came to an end *de facto* on 9 April 1940, when Denmark was occupied by Germany. Iceland assumed responsibility for her own foreign policy, the coastguard, and other duties reserved for Denmark in the Act of Union. The union was formally revoked by Iceland in the spring of 1941. Between 1941 and 1944, the regent who exercised the functions of the king was the diplomat Sveinn Björnsson (1881–1952). He was elected president in 1944. The election was preceded by a referendum in the spring of 1944, where the turnout was an all-time high—98.6 per cent. No less than 97.4 per cent voted for a dissolution of the union and 95.1 per cent for the proposal to introduce a republic.[111] This was proclaimed at Þingvellir on 17 June—Jón Sigurðsson's birthday—which has since been celebrated as Iceland's national day.

Those who were there that day at Þingvellir will never forget it. Despite the cold and rainy weather, the participants had made their way there, over Mosfellsheiði, from the south and from Borgarfjörður, by all conceivable means of transport: cars, buses, and horses. Some had arrived the day before and pitched their tents in the rain. On the law-rock, just east of the Almannagjá chasm, the prime minister Björn Þórðarson opened the ceremony at 1.30 p.m. The Althing then held a session, in which the chairman announced that the constitution of the Republic of Iceland had come into force. At exactly 2.00 p.m. there was a peal of bells from the church at Þingvellir. A minute's silence followed. One-fifth of the population of Iceland, about 25,000 people, bowed their heads reverently and heard the storm whipping the ropes against the flagpoles and stretching the rain-drenched flags.

The members of the Althing elected as president the regent Sveinn Björnsson. The national celebrations then continued with many short speeches. The greatest interest was captured by the prime minister when he asked for silence to read a telegram which had arrived from King Christian X. It ran:[112]

> While regretting that the separation between myself and the Icelandic people has been implemented under the prevailing circumstances, I wish to express my best wishes for the future of the Icelandic nation and my hope for a strengthening of the bonds between Iceland and the other Nordic countries.
> Christian R.

The struggle for Icelandic independence was over.

Notes to Chapter 1

1   Jón Jóhannesson, *A History of the Old Icelandic Commonwealth: Íslendinga Saga*, trans. Haraldur Bessason (Winnipeg: University of Manitoba Press, 1974), pp. 3–7; Björn Þorsteinsson, *Island,* Politikens Danmarkshistorie (Copenhagen: Politiken, 1985), pp. 13–14.

2   *The Book of the Icelanders (Íslendingabók) by Ari Þorgilsson*, trans. Halldór Hermannsson (Ithaca: Cornell University Press, 1930).

3   *The Book of Settlements: Landnámabók*, trans. Hermann Pálsson and Paul Edwards (Winnipeg: University of Manitoba Press, 1972).

4   Cf. Guðni Jónsson, *Íslendinga sögur* (Reykjavík: Íslendingasagnaútgáfan, 1953), preface to vol. 1, on the source value of the Icelandic sagas.

5   *The Book of Settlements*, p. 6.

6   Jónas Kristjánsson, 'Sannfræði fornsagnanna', *Skírnir* 161 (1987), pp. 233–69.

7   An Icelander is always referred to and addressed by his first name. According to the Icelandic name system, Jónas Kristjánsson *is called* merely Jónas, while he *is* Kristjánsson; in other words, his father was called Kristján. In the same way, the name of the President of Iceland is simply Vigdís. She *is* Finnbogadóttir, daughter of Finnbogi. See Chapter 6, 'The Icelanders and Their Language'.

8   Jónas Kristjánsson, 'Sannfræði fornsagnanna', p. 268.

9   Páll Líndal, *Reykjavík 200 ára* (Reykjavík, 1986), p. 14.

10   Ágúst Valfells, *Iceland 2000: Production, Population and Prosperity* (Reykjavík: Landsvirkjun, 1979), p. 7.

11   Kenneth G. Chapman, *Icelandic-Norwegian Linguistic Relationships, Norsk Tidsskrift for Sprogvidenskap*, Suppl. VII (Oslo: Universitetsforlaget, 1962); Jónas Kristjánsson, *Icelandic Sagas and Manuscripts* (Reykjavík: Iceland Review, 1980), p. 8.

12   Sigurður A. Magnússon, *Northern Sphinx: Iceland and the Icelanders from the Settlement to the Present* (London: Hurst, 1977), p. 8; Páll Líndal, *Reykjavík*

200 *ára*, p. 36; *Iceland 1986: Handbook Published by the Central Bank of Iceland* (Reykjavík, 1987), p. 56.

13   See Gísli Sigurðsson, *Gaelic Influence in Iceland: Historical and Literary Contacts: A Survey of Research* (Reykjavík: Bókaútgáfa Menningarsjóðs, 1988).

14   Jónas Kristjánsson, 'Icelandic Sagas and Manuscripts', pp. 8–9.

15   The Irish stanza is quoted from Magnus Magnusson, *Vikings!* (London: Bodley Head, 1980), p. 152. Of the many other books on the Vikings we may mention Peter Brent, *The Viking Saga* (London: Weidenfeld and Nicolson, 1975); Gwyn Jones, *A History of the Vikings*, revised edition (Oxford: Oxford University Press, 1984); T. D. Kendrick, *A History of the Vikings* (London: Methuen, 1930); Magnus Magnusson, *Viking Expansion Westwards* (London: Bodley Head, 1973); Alexander Fenton and Hermann Pálsson, eds., *The Northern and Western Isles in the Viking World* (Edinburgh: John Donald, 1984).

16   *Egil's Saga*, trans. Hermann Pálsson and Paul Edwards (Harmondsworth: Penguin, 1976), ch. 60.

17   Adam of Bremen, *History of the Archbishops of Hamburg-Bremen*, trans. Francis J. Tschan (New York: Columbia University Press, 1959), p. 37.

18   Albert C. Baugh and Thomas Cable, *A History of the English Language*, 3rd ed. (London: Routledge & Kegan Paul, 1978), pp. 90–106; John Geipel, *The Viking Legacy: The Scandinavian Influence on the English and Gaelic Languages* (Newton Abbot: David & Charles, 1971); Mary S. Serjeantsson, *A History of Foreign Words in English* (London: Kegan Paul & Co., 1935), pp. 61–103.

19   Margrét Hermanns-Auðardóttir, *Islands tidiga bosättning: Studier med utgångspunkt i merovingertida-vikingatida gårdslämningar i Herjólfsdalur, Vestmannaeyjar, Island*, Studia Archaeologica Universitatis Umensis 1 (Umeå, 1989).

20   Ibid., p. 165.

21   The report from the Papey excavations has been published in the 1988 yearbook of the Icelandic archaeological society (*Árbok hins íslenzka fornleifafélags*), where C14 datings are repeatedly mentioned.

22   Margrét Hermanns-Auðardóttir, *Islands tidiga bosättning*, p. 144.

23   Else Nordahl, *Reykjavík from the Archaeological Point of View*, Aun 12 (Uppsala, 1988), pp. 113–14. Many other experts have publicly rejected Margrét's conclusions.

24   The State Antiquary in Iceland, Þór Magnússon, has pointed out that the Roman coins could have been brought to Iceland during the Viking Age as souvenirs of visits to the British Isles.

25   Nordahl, *Reykjavík from the Archaeological Point of View*, pp. 7, 114.

26   *The Faroese Saga*, trans. G. V. C. Young and Cynthia R. Clewer (Belfast, 1973).

27   Símun V. Arge, 'Om landnamet på Færøerne', In *Nordatlantisk arkeologi — vikingetid og middelalder*, Hikuin 15 (Moesgård: Hikuin, 1989), pp. 103–28.

28   Jón Jóhannesson, *A History of the Old Icelandic Commonwealth*, pp. 106–9.

29 *The Vinland Sagas: The Norse Discovery of America: Grænlendinga Saga and Eirik's Saga*, trans. Magnus Magnusson and Hermann Pálsson (Harmondsworth: Penguin, 1965), p. 50.

30 Anne Stine Ingstad, *The Discovery of a Norse Settlement in America: Excavations of L'Anse aux Meadows, Newfoundland 1961–1968* (Oslo: Universitetsforlaget, 1977), pp. 11–12 and 242. Cf. Sigurður A. Magnússon, *Northern Sphinx*, p. 26; Erik Wahlgren, *The Vikings and America* (London: Thames and Hudson, 1986); Gwyn Jones, *The Norse Atlantic Saga*, revised edition (Oxford: Oxford University Press, 1986).

31 *Grænlendinga saga*, ch. 4. Leifur uses the epithet *fóstri* (foster-father), although according to the account in *Grænlendinga saga*, Tyrkir was more of an adviser and tutor to Leifur. He has features reminiscent of the Mentor who advised Odysseus' son Telemachos when Odysseus left Ithaca to fight at Troy. However, Old Icelandic *fóstri* may also denote a close friend.

32 Ingstad, *Discovery of a Norse Settlement*, p. 12. Wahlgren, in *The Vikings and America*, and other scholars have contested this interpretation.

33 Ingstad, *Discovery of a Norse Settlement*, p. 239.

34 Ibid., p. 244.

35 R. A. Skelton, Thomas E. Marston, and George D. Painter, *The Vinland Map and the Tartar Relation* (New Haven and London: Yale University Press, 1965), preface, pp. 167–9, 208–13, 233–9; W. P. Cumming, R. A. Skelton, and D. B. Quinn, *The Discovery of North America* (London: Elek, 1971), pp. 34, 42–51, 295. Cf. Haraldur Sigurðsson, 'Vínlandskortið: Aldur þess og uppruni', *Saga* 5 (1967), pp. 329–49.

36 Ingstad, *Discovery of a Norse Settlement*, p. 233; Sigurður A. Magnússon, *Northern Sphinx*, pp. 26–29; Wahlgren, *The Vikings and America*.

37 *Iceland 1986*, pp. 99–100; Sigurður A. Magnússon, *Northern Sphinx*, pp. 11–15; Jón Jóhannesson, *A History of the Old Icelandic Commonwealth*.

38 Charles de Montesquieu, *De l'esprit des lois* (1748).

39 *Njal's Saga*, trans. Magnus Magnusson and Hermann Pálsson (Harmondsworth: Penguin, 1960), ch. 20.

40 Jón Jóhannesson, *A History of the Old Icelandic Commonwealth*, pp. 125–38.

41 *Kristni saga*, edited and translated by Gudbrand Vigfusson and F. York Powell in *Origines Islandicae: A Collection of the More Important Sagas and Other Native Writings Relating to the Settlement and Early History of Iceland* (Oxford: Clarendon Press, 1905), ch. 11. The permission to expose infants, to eat horse-flesh, and to sacrifice in secret was abolished after a few years.

42 Ibid., ch. 11. Cf. *Njal's Saga*, ch. 105.

43 Jón Hnefill Aðalsteinsson, *Under the Cloak: The Acceptance of Christianity in Iceland with Particular Reference to the Religious Attitudes Prevailing at the Time* (Uppsala, 1978), p. 142.

44 *Kristni saga*, ch. 11. See also Peter Hallberg, *The Icelandic Saga*, trans. Paul Schach (Lincoln: University of Nebraska Press, 1962), p. 13.

45 For this folktale see Sigurður Nordal, *Íslenzk menning* (Reykjavík, 1942), p. 231.

46   *The Book of Settlements*, p. 97.

47   *Arrow-Odd*, in *Seven Viking Romances*, trans. Hermann Pálsson and Paul Edwards (Penguin: Harmondsworth, 1985), p. 72.

48   *Kristni saga*, ch. 11.

49   Þórir Stephensen, 'Menntasetur að Viðeyjarklaustri', treatise (Faculty of Theology, University of Iceland, 1992), pp. 37–8; the account of Hróðólfur comes from *Landnámabók*. Cf. Janus Jónsson, *Um klaustrin á Íslandi* (Reykjavík: Ljósprentun úr Tímariti Hins íslenska bókmenntafélags, 8. árgangi, 1887).

50   Einar Ól. Sveinsson, *The Age of the Sturlungs: Icelandic Civilization in the Thirteenth Century,* Islandica 36 (Ithaca: Cornell University Press, 1953).

51   Björn Þorsteinsson, *Island*, pp. 79–93; *Iceland 874–1974*, pp. 39–40; Ágúst Valfells, *Iceland 2000*, pp. 8–10; Hallberg, *The Icelandic Saga*, pp. 18–23.

52   Ásgeir Jakobsson, *Þórður kakali* (Reykjavík: Skuggsjá, 1988), p. 30. Þórður kakali and Sturla Þórðarson were cousins, both nephews of Snorri Sturluson.

53   *Diplomatarium Islandicum: Íslenzkt fornbréfasafn*, published by the Icelandic Literary Society (Copenhagen, 1857–76), vol. 1, p. 262. Cf. Guðrún Nordal's doctoral thesis entitled 'Ethics and Action in Thirteenth Century Iceland: An Examination of Motivation and Social Obligation in Iceland, as Represented in *Sturlunga saga*' (Oxford, 1987).

54   *Sturlunga Saga*, trans. Julia H. McGrew and R. George Thomas, Library of Scandinavian Literature 9–10 (New York: Twayne, 1970–4).

55   Long after the colonization, Icelanders continued to talk of Iceland as being 'out'. To go home to Iceland from Norway was to sail *út* 'out', and to visit Norway was to go *utan* 'from outside'.

56   Sigurður A. Magnússon, *Northern Sphinx*, pp. 35, 39. Although the hypothesis that Snorri is the author of *Egils saga* is not undisputed, good arguments have been advanced in its favour; see Hallberg, *The Icelandic Saga*, pp. 69, 131.

57   Snorri Sturluson, *Heimskringla: History of the Kings of Norway*, trans. Lee M. Hollander (Austin: University of Texas Press, 1964).

58   Njörður P. Njarðvík, interview in *Morgunblaðið*, 16 June 1987, in connection with his play *Hvar er hamarinn?* (Where's the Hammer?), about the disappearance of Thor's hammer, based on the Eddic poem *Þrymskviða*.

59   *Njal's Saga*, ch. 47.

60   Björn Þorsteinsson, *Island*, pp. 124–5.

61   Eysteinn Ásgrímsson, *Lilja (The Lily): An Icelandic Religious Poem of the Fourteenth Century*, ed. and trans. Eiríkr Magnússon (London, 1870).

62   Ágúst Valfells, *Iceland 2000*, p. 10.

63   *The Libelle of Englyshe Polycye: A Poem on the Use of Sea-Power, 1436*, ed. Sir George Warner (Oxford: Clarendon Press, 1926), p. 41.

64   This—together with several other English documents—is quoted in *Helztu sáttmálar, tilskipanir og samþykktir konunga og Íslendinga um réttindi þeirra og stöðu Íslands innan norska og dansk-norska ríkisins 1020–1551.* ed. Björn Þorsteinsson (Reykjavík: Hið íslenzka bókmenntafélag, 1972), pp. 24–5. See

also E. M. Carus-Wilson, *Medieval Merchant Venturers* (London: Methuen, 1954), ch. 11, 'The Iceland Venture'.

65   Björn Þorsteinsson, *Island*, p. 138, 165.

66   Halldór Laxness, *Íslandsklukkan* (Reykjavík: Helgafell, 1943). This book has been translated into some sixteen languages but not, for some reason, into English.

67   Quotation from Einar Fors Bergström, p. 15 of his introduction to the learned, interesting, and witty letters on Iceland written by Uno von Troil, *Brev om Island*, Skrifter utgivna av Samfundet Sverige–Island 3 (Stockholm: Höker-berg, 1933). Uno von Troil's book was later translated into several languages, thus greatly supplementing the previously scanty knowledge about a distant island at 66° north. For the English version see note 75.

68   Vilhjálmur Bjarnar, 'The Laki Eruptions and "the Famine of the Mist" ', in *Scandinavian Studies: Essays Presented to Dr Henry Goddard Leach*, ed. Carl F. Bayerschmidt and Erik J. Friis (Seattle: University of Washington Press, 1965), pp. 410–20.

69   Björn Þorsteinsson, *Island*, p. 191.

70   English translations often render these terms loosely as 'chess' and 'chessmen': see, for example, *Poems of the Vikings: The Elder Edda*, trans. Patricia Terry (Indianapolis: Bobbs-Merrill, 1969), pp. 4, 11; or as 'draughtsmen': see Jacqueline Simpson, *The Northmen Talk: A Choice of Tales from Iceland* (London: Phoenix House, 1965), pp. 21.

71   On the derivation of *chess* and *check(mate)* from Persian *shah* see *The Oxford English Dictionary* (Oxford: Clarendon Press, 1933), s.v. *check*. On the origin of the game see Chapter 4, 'Chess'.

72   Sigurbjörn Einarsson, 'Islands tusen år', in *Våra nordiska syskonkyrkor* (Stockholm: Proprius, 1985), p. 80.

73   Guðmundur Kamban, *The Virgin of Skalholt*, trans. Evelyn Ramsden (London: Nicholson & Watson, 1936).

74   *Travels in Iceland by Eggert Ólafsson and Bjarni Pálsson Performed 1752–1757 by Order of His Danish Majesty*, revised English edition (Reykjavík: Örn og Örlygur, 1975). This account was the main source used by Uno von Troil in his letters from Iceland (see note 67 above).

75   Uno von Troil, *Letters on Iceland Containing Observations . . . Made During a Voyage Undertaken in the Year 1772 by Joseph Banks, Esq. F.R.S.* (London: 1780), p. 82.

76   Mekkin S. Perkins, 'Piracy in Iceland', *American-Scandinavian Review* 49:3 (1961), pp. 259–65.

77   von Troil, *Brev om Island*, p. 14.

78   Halldór Hermannsson, *Sir Joseph Banks and Iceland*, Islandica 18 (New York: Cornell University Library, 1928).

79   Björn Þorsteinsson, *Island*, p. 195.

80   Sigurður A. Magnússon, *Northern Sphinx*, p. 127.

81   Sir George Steuart Mackenzie, *Travels in the Island of Iceland during the Summer of the Year MDCCCX* (Edinburgh, 1811), p. 271.

82   Páll Eggert Ólason, *Jón Sigurðsson* (Reykjavík, 1929), vol. 1, pp. 30–2.

83   Ebenezer Henderson, *Iceland, or the Journal of a Residence in that Island during the Years 1814–1815*, 2 vols. (Edinburgh, 1818).

84   Paul Gaimard, *Voyage en Islande et au Groënland, exécuté pendant les années 1835 et 1836 sur la corvette* la Recherche, 8 vols. with Atlas (Paris, 1838–52); Lord Dufferin, *Letters from High Latitudes* (London, 1857).

85   In one of the Eddic poems, *Skírnismál*, it was Skírinir who brought Freyr's proposal of marriage to Gerður, beautiful daughter of a giant. He coaxed her and charmed her with magical spells so that she finally accepted.

86   Elfar Loftsson, *Island i Nato: Partierna och försvarsfrågan*, Göteborg Studies in Politics 9 (Göteborg: Författares bokmagasin, 1981), p. 27.

87   Páll Eggert Ólason, *Jón Sigurðsson*, pp. 357, 474.

88   Björn Þorsteinsson, *Island*, pp. 223, 268.

89   Hjörtur Pálsson, *Alaskaför Jóns Ólafssonar 1874* (Reykjavík: Menningarsjóður, 1975), pp. 12–25.

90   Heimir Þorleifsson, *Frá einveldi til lýðveldis: Islandssaga eftir 1830* (Reykjavík: Bókaverzlun Sigfúsar Eymundssonar, 1973), p. 52.

91   Ibid., pp. 63, 137; Björn Þorsteinsson, *Island*, p. 232.

92   Björn Þorsteinsson, *Island*, p. 236.

93   Bragi Guðmundsson and Gunnar Karlsson, *Uppruni nútímans: Íslandssaga frá öndverðri 19. öld til síðari hluta 20. aldar* (Reykjavík: Mál og menning, 1986), pp. 181–3; Björn Þorsteinsson, *Island*, pp. 242–3.

94   *Uppruni nútímans*, p. 183; Sigurður A. Magnússon, *Northern Sphinx*, p. 137; Björn Th. Björnsson, *Seld norðurljós* (Reykjavík: Mál og menning, 1982), pp. 62, 130.

95   The royal crown was removed from the coat of arms in 1944 when the republic was proclaimed. Every year on 1st December the students of the University still celebrate Independence Day, although it is no longer Iceland's national day. It is merely an old tradition.

96   This brief account of the historical development of the Icelandic coat of arms has been supplied by the Icelandic National Archivist, Ólafur Ásgeirsson.

97   These accounts are reproduced in *Uppruni nútímans*, p. 186. See also Halldór Guðmundsson, *Loksins, loksins* (Reykjavík: Mál og menning, 1987), pp. 128–9.

98   *Iceland 1986*, pp. 50–1.

99   Halvar G. F. Sundberg, *Folkrätt* (Uppsala: Norstedt, 1944), pp. 31–2.

100   Sigurður A. Magnússon, *Northern Sphinx*, pp. 139–40. As king of Sweden 1950–73, Gustaf VI Adolf shared an interest in archaeology with Dr Kristján Eldjárn, president of Iceland 1968–80.

101   Albert Engström, *Åt Häcklefjäll* (Stockholm: Bonnier, 1911).

102   Winston S. Churchill, *The Second World War*, vol. 3, *The Grand Alliance* (London: Cassel 1950), p. 120.

103 Þór Whitehead, *Íslandsævintýri Himmlers 1935–1937* (Reykjavík: Almenna bókafélagið, 1988). The same author continues the story of Iceland in World War II in his books *Ófriður í aðsigi* (1980) and *Stríð fyrir ströndum* (1985), from the same publisher.

104 *Uppruni nútímans*, p. 261.

105 Winston S. Churchill, *The Second World War*, Vol. 1, *The Gathering Storm*, revised ed. (London: Cassel, 1949), p. 540.

106 Ibid., p. 605.

107 *Uppruni nútímans*, p. 263.

108 Churchill, *The Gathering Storm*, p. 558.

109 Elfar Loftsson, *Island i Nato*, pp. 129–31; Björn Þorsteinsson, *Island*, pp. 257–9; Michael T. Corgan, 'Franklin D. Roosevelt and the American Occupation of Iceland', *Naval War College Review*, Volume XLV, Number 4 (Autumn 1992), Newport, RI (pp. 34–54).

110 See the section on 'Inflation: On the Way to Balance' in Chapter 6.

111 Elfar Loftsson, *Island i Nato*, p. 46.

112 *Uppruni nútímans*, pp. 276–8.

⊰⊱ Chapter 2 ⊰⊱

Eddas and Sagas

If you find a friend
you fully trust
and wish for his good-will,
exchange thoughts,
exchange gifts,
go often to his house.
*Hávamál 44 in W. H Auden's
translation*

Introduction

THE OLD ICELANDIC LITERATURE which has been preserved for
posterity—the Eddic and skaldic poems and the sagas—was originally
oral. It was handed down from generation to generation through learning by heart. It lived for centuries on the lips of the people.

The oldest works are the poems of the *Elder Edda*. These are written
in two main alliterative metres, known as *ljóðaháttur* ('song metre',
as in the epigraph to this chapter) and *fornyrðislag* ('old lore metre').
It must have been relatively easy to memorize the Eddic poems. Like
the Homeric poems, they contain mythological motifs and tales of
legendary heroes. The early migrations of the Germanic peoples provide a background to these legends. The poems were performed all
over Scandinavia and among other Germanic-speaking peoples in
Europe, often in chieftains' halls and kings' courts, but no doubt also
in lowlier settings, such as markets. The authors were anonymous.

Skaldic poets, on the other hand, are often known to us by name.[1] On ceremonious occasions the *skald* or poet—like the Icelander Egill Skalla-Grímsson (*c*.910–90)—declaimed praise poems to a king or earl. The skalds wove highly complex kennings into an intricate metrical structure of rules for rhythm, alliteration, and assonance. Their poems make frequent use of a figure known as a *kenning* or periphrasis. Battle, for example, can be called 'the song of weapons'; blood is 'the dew of slaughter'; gold is 'the dragon's bed'.

It was not until the twelfth and thirteenth centuries that these Eddic and skaldic poems were written down. This was done in Iceland, where the literature grew and received its distinctly Icelandic stamp.

The first Icelandic historians usually bore the epithet 'the learned'. One of them, Sæmundur Sigfússon (1056–1133) wrote in Latin, but none of his work survives. His contemporary Ari Þorgilsson (1067–1147) was something of a pioneer in that he wrote in the vernacular.

History and legend were also recorded in Denmark (*Gesta Danorum* of Saxo Grammaticus) and to some extent in Norway, but the writers in these two countries used Latin. While the rest of Scandinavia was witnessing the dawn of literature, Sweden was silent. In England, on the other hand, the Anglo-Saxons had begun to write their history in their native language several centuries earlier.

The Icelanders were virtually alone in Scandinavia in this literary achievement. As Sven B. F. Jansson says, a major part of Old Norse literature was not just written down in Iceland, it was *created* there; 'in both form and content it bears the stamp of brilliant Icelanders and therefore belongs to the history of Icelandic literature. It rightly occupies a prominent place in the history of world literature, of Germanic literature, and of Nordic literature.'[2]

The world thus owes a debt of gratitude to 60,000–70,000 Icelanders. Without them, only a paltry remnant of the Norse cultural heritage would have been preserved. It would have consisted largely of runic inscriptions.

How was this literary achievement possible?

One factor was the powerful Icelandic farmers, whose big farms (*höfuðból*) provided a setting where family pride, memories of the ancient heritage, and the narrative art were highly treasured. The constitution of the commonwealth, with its lack of a suffocating central government, left the field free for individualists.

Another important precondition was the isolated location in the North Atlantic, far from the wars and upheavals of continental Europe. This left the Icelanders free to create literature without disturbance. Here the settlers were safe, yet still in a position to benefit from enriching contacts with their kinsmen in Scandinavia and with the civilization of the British Isles. The Icelanders always looked forward to the spring, when they could set sail for distant destinations, to Greenland and North America in the west, to Constantinople and even to Palestine in the east.

Perhaps the most positive factor for the Icelandic literary achievement was the way in which the country was converted to Christianity. As we have seen, this was accomplished without friction. Whereas in continental Europe the coming of Christianity had often led to radical breaks with old customs and traditions, in Iceland the new was peacefully and harmoniously grafted on to the old. Icelanders retained a passionate interest in their past, in their own tales and language. This interest is still a distinctive characteristic of today's Icelanders.

Among the pagan Germanic peoples the art of writing had been technically restricted. Before their conversion to Christianity they could only carve runes. It is mostly the inscriptions on stone that have survived. They are most numerous in Sweden, where there are over two thousand. Runes were also commonly inscribed on organic material, such as wood, which has seldom been preserved. The inscriptions were made by 'scratching', as shown by the use of the word *rísta*. The fact that this verb is also used of stone inscriptions suggests that the normal way of writing runes was to scratch them, originally on a softer surface such as wood, leather, or soft metal. Another commonly used verb is *fá* 'to paint', which shows that the runes could have been coloured.

Christianity expanded the art of writing. It brought parchment and Latin letters. The Icelanders were quick to learn the alphabet. They learned to write in their native tongue and not, as was the rule elsewhere in Europe, in Latin. It was therefore natural for them to record their memories and express their thoughts in the vernacular. They felt intellectually free and inspired.

Iceland soon acquired a number of literate priests and laymen. They combined a growing store of knowledge—for example, in the Latin language and Greco-Roman culture—with the gift of composition and a living interest in their own country. Their choice of topics included everything from translations from Latin, such as saints' lives or the dialogues and homilies of Pope Gregory the Great, to Germanic mythology, heroic poems, and sagas about distinguished families, their travels, adventures, disputes, and bloody family feuds. The events in these poems and sagas took place not just in Iceland but also in other countries where the Vikings had roved and sailed.

All this was recorded by the Icelanders—travelled, inquiring, and often highly talented people—in an expressive language with short sentences, keen observations, and witty exchanges. This language bubbles forth in the Icelandic sagas, simple and crystal-clear as a mountain stream. It is conveyed in the fresh, unforced style of the oral narrator, with tension, charm, and sometimes with elements of humour.

Most languages have taken shape and changed in a number of phases. A good example is English, with its division into Old English (Anglo-Saxon), Middle English, and Modern English. Icelandic, on the other hand, has escaped such radical changes, just as it has largely escaped becoming split into different dialects. Despite Iceland's considerable size, its inhabitants have never had any difficulty in understanding each other. The pronunciation has changed, though normally in the same way in all parts of the country. Most of the vocabulary is preserved unchanged, as are the basic grammatical rules. This means that modern written Icelandic to all intents and purposes starts with the commonwealth era, when the Old Icelandic literature was written down.[3]

It is in the poems and sagas written in this Old Icelandic—scarcely different from Modern Icelandic—that we meet the men and women of yesteryear, their gods and heroes.

The Icelandic Manuscripts

The soul of the Nordic peoples is
concealed in Icelandic books.

Halldór Laxness, Íslandsklukkan

The medieval Icelandic manuscripts were written or copied by monks, priests, and literate laymen, using goose quills on parchment made from calfskin (vellum). Some of these books were brilliantly illustrated. Most of the manuscripts, however, both the originals and the many transcripts, have been lost down the ages. They were blackened by soot. They were stained by greasy fingers. They were read to pieces. They mouldered in damp dwellings or were destroyed out of ignorance. Many manuscripts disappeared forever in shipwrecks or burning libraries.

The ancient Icelandic manuscripts which have been preserved for posterity, mostly in Denmark and Sweden, often had remarkable vicissitudes. Many ended up in Sweden in the seventeenth century, in the days when she was a great power. The first examples arrived there by a fortunate quirk of fate, while others later came as a result of organized purchases. They were taken to Sweden by a series of Icelandic bibliophiles, who were welcomed with open arms, since they brought manuscripts of the *Edda*, the legendary sagas, and the Icelandic family sagas. But the Swedish antiquarians were not content just to collect and preserve Icelandic manuscripts. Rather than merely storing them in archives and libraries, they made them available to the Swedish reading public. Thanks to excellent cooperation between Icelanders and Swedes, many romantic sagas about ancestral heroes and kings were translated into Swedish. This type of legend—known as *fornaldarsaga* 'saga of ancient times'—is a mythical-heroic tale of fantastic events which usually took place in countries other than Iceland or Norway. These sagas were printed in rapid succession in the period 1664–97. After a lengthy pause between 1698 and 1718, coinciding with the reign of Charles XII and the Great Northern War, publication continued during the eighteenth century.

The most notable year in this connection was 1697, when Johan

Peringskiöld published Snorri Sturluson's *Heimskringla* in Stockholm. We have seen that this great work is mainly a history of the kings of Norway until 1177, but it is also of great interest to Swedes because it opens with *Ynglinga saga*, a partly mythical account of the Swedish Yngling dynasty, tracing their line from the gods.

The first in the series of learned Icelanders to come to Sweden was Jón Jónsson from the farm of Rúgstaðir. He had been expelled from the Latin School at Hólar in northern Iceland. As a Danish subject, Jón was captured by Swedes in 1658 when the ship on which he was sailing to Copenhagen was boarded by Swedes and taken to Gothenburg. Thanks to the Steward of the Realm, Per Brahe the Younger, Jón came to Uppsala University, where his work was highly valued by the College of Antiquities. He took the surname Rúgmann after his birthplace in Iceland.

Other famous Icelandic manuscript collectors who worked for Sweden in the latter half of the seventeenth century were Guðmundur Ólafsson (died 1695), who succeeded Rúgmann, and Jón Eggertsson. Guðmundur displayed the customary Icelandic diligence. He worked doggedly, for example, on an Icelandic dictionary—Lexicon island-

The title page of Snorri Sturluson's Heimskringla, *first published 1697 in Stockholm by the Swedish scholar Johann Peringskiöld. As we have seen in Chapter 1,* Heimskringla *takes its name from the first two words of this great work, 'Kringla heimsins', the orb of the world, orbis terrarum.*

icum—which was never completed. However, his somewhat bureaucratic superior, Johan Hadorph, complained that Guðmundur had a dangerous thirst for strong spirits.

Jón Eggertsson did outstanding work for Sweden in two ways. He sought out manuscripts in Iceland, and he made transcripts in Copenhagen, including Snorri's *Heimskringla*. Shortly before his death (1689) he was released from a Danish prison thanks to the Swedish envoy in Copenhagen. He was posthumously honoured in Sweden, where Icelanders and Swedes vied to sing his praises.[4]

The College of Antiquities considered offering a post to Árni Magnússon (1663–1730), the most famous manuscript collector of the time. The idea was never realized, however.[5] Instead the learned Icelander settled down as professor at the University of Copenhagen, where he created a celebrated collection of manuscripts, known as the Arnamagnæan Collection. A large number of transcripts and most of the printed books perished in the great fire of Copenhagen in 1728, the tragedy which provoked Árni's words: 'There are the books which are to be had nowhere in the world.'[6] Later research has shown, however, that Árni and his colleagues managed to rescue most of his irreplaceable Icelandic manuscripts. These he bequeathed, along with his books and his considerable fortune, to the University of Copenhagen. The manuscripts were to be preserved in a separate section. According to the will, which Árni and his Danish wife Mette signed the day before his death, they were to be used for research by 'native-born Icelandic students'.[7]

Remarkable work in the spirit of Árni was performed by the Icelander Grímur Thorkelin (1752–1829). He was highly esteemed in both London and Copenhagen. In London he was invited to take charge of the British Museum, but he turned down this distinguished post, preferring to continue his philological research in Copenhagen. There he published many Icelandic manuscripts, and in 1815 he issued the first printed edition of the Anglo-Saxon epic *Beowulf*. In the British Museum Grímur had transcribed the only surviving manuscript of the poem, which deals with the exploits of the eponymous hero in the wars between Germanic tribes in the Dark Ages. It is of interest not least for its literary quality.[8] The manuscript is dated to the end of the tenth century or slightly later.

The work on Icelandic manuscripts in Copenhagen first took organized form in 1772, when the foundation of the Arnamagnæan Commission initiated the publication of the old writings. Since then the work has continued according to carefully formulated plans and goals. A great incentive to this was the romantic movement at the start of the nineteenth century, with its interest in folk culture, national character, and the native language. The Danish poets Adam Oehlenschläger and N. F. S. Grundtvig and the philologists and antiquaries Rasmus Christian Rask and Carl Christian Rafn did splendid pioneering work. Most of the research and publishing, however, was done by Icelanders. This is natural. They have inherited the language of the manuscripts as their birthright. Their studies have covered a broad field, with topics such as history, legislation, the family sagas, the bishops' sagas, the chivalrous sagas, the Eddic poems, the *rímur*, and the lives of the saints.

The *ríma* (plural *rímur*), a specifically Icelandic poetic art, is reminiscent of the romantic medieval ballad. The *rímur* have end rhymes (hence the name) and were sung by a soloist to a rhythmic beat. In the old days, the *rímur*-poems were highly popular among the country people when they assembled during the long winter evenings. Some *rímur* have been described as 'poems composed by turning written sagas into verse'.[9]

The year 1956 saw the foundation of the Arnamagnæan Institute in Copenhagen. The first director was the Icelandic poet and philologist Jón Helgason. The coming of the institute had a historical connection with the desire of the newly established republic to bring the documents and manuscripts 'home to Iceland'. This demand met stubborn opposition. Finally, however, the parties agreed that Denmark would return manuscripts of particular concern to Iceland. The repatriation began one sunny spring day in 1971, when a Danish naval vessel dropped anchor in Reykjavík harbour. Its cargo was the most valuable Icelandic manuscripts. They were transported from the wharf, past cheering crowds and rows of children carrying Danish and Icelandic flags, to the University of Iceland. In the great hall of the university, the manuscripts were ceremoniously handed over—a momentous milestone in the history of the Nordic countries.

A manuscript institute had been founded in Reykjavík in 1962. The manuscripts which were acquired with that first precious shipment

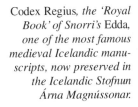

Codex Regius, *the 'Royal Book' of Snorri's* Edda, *one of the most famous medieval Icelandic manuscripts, now preserved in the Icelandic Stofnun Árna Magnússonar.*

were the *Codex Regius* of the *Elder Edda*, from the end of the thirteenth century, and *Flateyjarbók*, which contains sagas of the Norwegian kings. *Codex Regius* (The Royal Book) takes its name from the long period during which it was kept in the library of the Danish king, while *Flateyjarbók* once belonged to a farmer on the island of Flatey in Breiðafjörður. He gave it to Brynjólfur Sveinsson, Bishop of Skálholt, who sent it by royal request in 1659 to Frederik III of Denmark. Brynjólfur would have preferred to set up a press at Skálholt to print the book. His wish was not to be fulfilled until twenty-five years later, when the first manuscripts were printed in Iceland—at Skálholt in 1684; they included four short sagas (*þættir*) from the saga of Ólafur Tryggvason.

It took 113 calfskins to make *Flateyjarbók*, the thickest of all the Icelandic manuscripts. Written around 1387, it is also one of the most beautiful. The initial letters of the individual sagas are decorated with elegant paintings. Medieval Icelandic book illumination is otherwise largely confined to law-books and ecclesiastical manuscripts.

Another treasure restored to Iceland is *Skarðsbók*, written in a monastery in 1363. It is one of the most beautifully illustrated Icelandic manuscripts, and it is well preserved. It contains the text of the law-book *Jónsbók*.[10]

The return of the manuscripts was a magnanimous gesture on the part of the Danes, and it was highly appreciated by the Icelanders, especially since, as Jónas Kristjánsson says, 'We Icelanders are poor in remains from antiquity'.[11] For the Icelanders it was natural to call their new manuscript institute after the great collector, Stofnun Árna Magnússonar (Árnastofnun, The Arnamagnæan Institute). It is well worth a visit. A reproduction of Árni's portrait meets the visitor. The Danish gift has greatly increased the attraction of the institute for both philologists and historians. The Icelanders are immensely proud of their manuscripts. As Jónas says, they mean as much to them as historic buildings and royal palaces mean to other nations.

The Icelandic manuscripts which came to Sweden in the seventeenth century are still preserved in Uppsala University Library, which has a manuscript of Snorri's *Edda* from the early fourteenth century, and in the Royal Library in Stockholm, which preserves one of the oldest Icelandic manuscripts, a collection of sermons known as the Icelandic Homily Book. For historical reasons, these manuscripts are regarded as an integral part of the Swedish cultural heritage.

The question of where the Icelandic manuscripts should be preserved has several different aspects, concerning both research and historical tradition. Modern techniques of reproduction mean that researchers generally do not care so much where an original manuscript is preserved. For the Swedish state, however, with its trophies of war such as *Codex Argenteus*—the unique Silver Bible in the Gothic language which was brought to Sweden as a war trophy from Prague in 1648 and is now in Uppsala University Library—there is concern about the setting of a precedent. The British Library in London and the university libraries in Oxford and Edinburgh are in a similar situation. Some of the Icelandic manuscripts in the British Library were collected by the naturalist and patron of the sciences Sir Joseph Banks during his expedition to Iceland in 1772.

Icelanders with their passion for the past—as exemplified in Halldór Laxness's novel *Íslandsklukkan*—see the issue in a completely different light. They regard the Icelandic manuscripts as a part of their history and literature. They cannot avoid thinking of the symbolic value of an artefact. For them the act of chopping down an old, cracked bell at Þingvellir denoted the loss of Iceland's freedom.

Since Iceland was part of the kingdom of Denmark for so many centuries, it is understandable that the desire of the Icelanders to regain their manuscripts was eventually heeded in Copenhagen. The consideration of setting a precedent did not weigh as heavily as in other old European countries. Moreover, the matter rested on a different foundation: the Icelandic manuscripts were part of a joint Icelandic-Danish patrimony, which was ripe for division when the Republic of Iceland was founded in 1944. It was achieved as a result of negotiation and a decision by the Danish parliament. The return of Icelandic manuscripts was granted as a gift from Denmark. The Danish gesture deserves admiration. The Danes showed, in the words of an Iceland historian, 'a consideration which is rare in international relations'.[12]

The foundation of the Arnamagnæan Institutes in Copenhagen and Reykjavík has meant an enormous increase in research into Icelandic manuscripts and publication activities based on the manuscripts. Both the institutes are of an international character, visited by scholars from many parts of the world with an interest in the Icelandic literary heritage.

Snorri's *Edda*

Norse mythology—like that of the Greeks—grew step by step. In earliest times the Germanic peoples believed in invisible beings that lived in trees, cairns, and other objects, and in natural phenomena like the sun, the moon, and lightning. Alongside this primeval cult, the poems of the *Elder Edda* reveal how the creative poetic imagination produced systematized ideas of a universe with gods and goddesses, humans, giants, and dwarfs. We follow them in their dealings right from the creation of the world. We are involved in their destinies and adventures all the way until the great winter (*Fimbulvetur*) which precedes the destruction of the gods (*Ragnarök*) and the rebirth of the world.

A coherent presentation of Norse mythology is given by Snorri Sturluson in his *Edda*.[13] Many qualities make this one of the masterpieces of medieval literature.

From the section in Snorri's *Edda* on the deluding of Gylfi (*Gylfaginning*), together with the poems in the *Elder Edda*,[14] we obtain a clear picture of the polytheistic religion of the Germanic peoples. The expressive imagery of *Gylfaginning* gives us a rounded picture of the

Æsir, with all their faults and merits, their attributes and exploits. Snorri's *Edda* contains two other sections—introduced by Bragi, the husband of Iðunn and the god of poetry—on kennings and 102 different verse metres. Snorri's *Edda* was to have a lasting influence on later writers and poets.

According to the prologue, the gods originated in Troy in Asia, whence the name Æsir. From here Odin (Icelandic Óðinn) and his followers, who 'were looked on as gods rather than men', came through Germany and Jutland to Svíþjóð (the people of the Swedes—compare the Anglo-Saxon *Swêoþeod* and *Swêorice*—originally in the limited sense of the northern Swedes, but now the Icelandic word for the whole of Sweden). There Odin chose for himself a home which is now called Sigtuna. His son Yngvi became king of Svíþjóð, thus founding the pagan dynasty of the Ynglings.

Gylfaginning begins with King Gylfi of Svíþjóð, 'a wise man and skilled in magic', making his way to Ásgarður, the enclosure of the Æsir. He there appears in the likeness of a weary old traveller, Gangleri. He asks a number of questions about the gods, but they delude him, hence the title. They distort his vision by spells so that, when he enters Valhalla, he sees a hall so lofty that he can hardly see over it; it is roofed with golden shields, like a shingle roof.

Gangleri's questions are answered in turn by the three chieftains Hár (High One), Jafnhár (Just-as-high), and Þriði (Third). This device provides a natural framework for the myths that are recounted in *Gylfaginning*.

The chaos of Greek mythology has its counterpart in the open void of Norse myth—Ginnungagap—where mild, windless weather prevailed at the dawn of time. This void was filled to the north with a heavy mass of ice and hoar-frost from Niflheimur, the world of cold. But the southern part of Ginnungagap was brightened by the sparks and glowing embers flowing from Múspellsheimur, the world of light and fire.

This encounter of ice and fire engendered the world. Life appeared, in the form of the primeval giant Ymir and a cow named Auðhumla. She licked the salty blocks of ice, out of which there appeared a man called Búri. He had a son called Bor, who married the giant's daughter Bestla; together with her he had three sons, Odin, Vili, and Vé.

Bor's sons killed the giant Ymir and laid him in the middle of Ginnungagap. From his body they made the world. His blood became the oceans and lakes, his flesh the earth, his bones the mountains. His teeth and broken bones were used to make rocks and pebbles. They made the sky out of his skull. They set it over the earth, with a dwarf under each corner; their names were East, West, North, and South.

The gods used Ymir's eyebrows to build a fortress, called Miðgarður 'the middle court', which is our earth. Miðgarður was to be a stronghold against the giants. These are abetted by the malicious conspirator Loki, father of the terrible wolf Fenrir, the world serpent Miðgarðsormur, and the goddess Hel who rules the kingdom of the dead.

When the sons of Bor were walking along the sea-shore, they found two tree-trunks, from which they made humans. The sons of Bor gave them clothes and names; the first man was called Askur (Ash-tree) and the first woman Embla (?Elm). These are the progenitors of mankind. They were given Miðgarður to live in.

The battle between the Æsir and the giants, a never-ending strife between the forces of good and evil, is also symbolized in the myth of the ash Yggdrasill. This is the mightiest tree of all. Its branches spread all over the world and reach up over heaven. This world-tree is held in place by three roots. One of them extends over Niflheimur, the cold northern part of Ginnungagap. The serpent Níðhöggur endangers the world by gnawing at the root from below.

By another of the tree's roots lies the well of Mímir, a source of wisdom, where the All-father Odin once sacrificed an eye for a drink from the spring. On each of Odin's shoulders there sits a raven, one called Huginn (Thought), the other called Muninn (Memory). They fly off at dawn and tell him on their return of all they have seen and heard. Odin himself rides the eight-legged horse Sleipnir.

Under the third root of Yggdrasill lies the holy spring of Urður, where the gods hold their court of justice. Three maidens known as Norns live by this spring. Every day they take water from the well and sprinkle it over the ash to ensure that its branches do not wither. As long as the ash lives, the world will persist.

The Norns are the fates of Norse mythology. Their names are Urður, Verðandi, and Skuld (Past, Present, and Future). They carve runes and mete out destiny to the children of men. Apart from these Norns of godly stock there are other Norns, some belonging to the family of the elves, some belonging to the family of the dwarfs. 'The good Norns who come from good stock shape good lives, but those who meet with misfortune owe it to the evil Norns.'[15]

To get to Ásgarður, their fortress and place of assembly at the third root of the world-tree, the Æsir ride over the bridge Bifröst (the moving bridge), the rainbow that leads from earth to heaven. The bridge is guarded by Heimdallur. His horse is named Gulltoppur. He needs less sleep than a bird and can see a hundred leagues in every direction, whether it is night or day. He can also hear the grass grow. When he blows his Gjallarhorn to signal doomsday (Ragnarök), it is heard all over the world.

Snorri's description of the origin of the wind is another example of the fantasy that permeates *Gylfaginning*:[16]

> Then Gangleri asked: 'Where does the wind come from? It is so strong that it stirs up great seas and fans fire into flame, yet, strong as it is, it can never be seen, so marvellously is it made.'
> High One said: 'I can easily tell you that. At the northern end of the sky sits the giant called Hræsvelgur [Corpse-swallower]. He has the form of an eagle, and when he spreads his wings for flight a wind arises from under them, as it says here:

> > The one who squats at the end of the sky
> > is known as Engulfer-of-corpses
> > a giant in eagle form;
> > they say from his wings
> > comes the wind
> > of this world.'

Odin is the god of wisdom, runes, and poetry. His wife is Frigg, the chief of the goddesses who, like Freyr and Freyja, has power over fertility. Place-names like Odense in Denmark and Odensala in Sweden testify to the extent of Odin's cult; his Anglo-Saxon equivalent Woden still survives in the place-name Wednesbury. He is not only *Alfaðir*, father of all the gods, but also *Valfaðir*, the father of those slain in battle. With the help of his shield-maidens, the Valkyries, he takes the fallen heroes to Valhalla, a magnificent, golden-roofed fortress

*Odin depicted in a manu-
script, now preserved in the
Stofnun Árna Magnússonar.*

with 540 doors. There the dead are revived as Odin's champions, the Einherjar.

The Einherjar in Valhalla live a life befitting a warrior. Every day at dawn they go out to battle. When breakfast time comes, they ride back to the hall, unharmed and reconciled. Back in Valhalla, a feast awaits them; they sate themselves with pork from the boar Sæhrímnir, which is boiled every day and comes back to life every evening. They drink their fill of mead, which is served by the Valkyries.

Thor (Icelandic Þór) can be compared to Hercules for his sheer strength. His weapons are the hammer Mjölnir, a belt of strength, and a pair of iron gauntlets—he cannot do without these when he grips the shaft of his hammer. He is married to Sif. His power may be illustrated by the following tale.

It is chiefly Thor who protects the Æsir against giants and trolls. Once a giant, claiming to be a builder, offered to construct a mighty stronghold for the Æsir. He undertook to accomplish this in one winter, with the help of his stallion Svaðilfari. His reward was to be no less than Freyja, the fairest of the goddesses. The giant builder also wanted the sun and the moon. It was agreed that, if the fortress was not completed by the first day of summer, the giant would forfeit all payment. The agreement had been confirmed with many oaths, for the giant did not feel safe working among the Æsir without safe conduct if Thor should come home. At that time Thor was away in the east, fighting trolls.

The construction work proceeded quickly. When only three days remained and the gods saw that the giant was likely to fulfil his side of the bargain—only the gateway remained to be built—they began to fear that they would lose Freyja to Jötunheimur, the home of the giants and trolls. Nor did they wish to destroy the heavens by taking away the sun and the moon. To avoid having to fulfil the agreement, they consulted the ingenious Loki. He turned himself into a mare, who came running that evening out of the woods, whinnying to the giant's stallion. When Svaðilfari saw the mare he became frantic, broke his traces, and galloped after her. The builder, seeing that he would fail to perform his feat, flew into a rage. He thus revealed himself to be a mountain giant. The Æsir felt no obligation to keep any agreement with a giant. They called on Thor. Wielding his hammer, he made short work of the giant.

Not long afterwards, Loki gave birth to a foal. It was Sleipnir, Odin's eight-legged horse, 'and amongst gods and men that horse is the best'.[17]

It would take too much space here to dwell on Snorri's account of all the contests in which Thor was outwitted by Útgarða-Loki, a magician-giant from Jötunheimur. Thor may be strong, but Útgarða-Loki is all the more sly and cunning. Thor is repeatedly outfoxed, through delusions, ingenuity, and ruses. When Thor, for example, rashly undertakes to drain a horn in three draughts, the task is too great for him. He swallows such great gulps that he has to pause for breath, but no matter how hard he drinks, the level in the horn does not appear to sink.

The explanation was simple, although Thor failed to see it. The other end of the horn was in the sea. Thor had nevertheless managed to drink so much that the level of the ocean had dropped. Thor had caused the first ebb tide.

Thor is constantly involved in ferocious battles or hilarious contests with giants, or in search of his stolen hammer. He gets around on foot, wading through rivers, or in a wagon pulled by two goats with teeth-gnashing names, Tanngnjóstur and Tanngrisnir. Wherever he moves, thunder is heard; the word *thunder* comes from the name of Thor's Anglo-Saxon equivalent Þunor. People dread the unknown, the frightening things which can be seen or heard but not explained. For that reason, the cult of Thor was widespread. He had to be propitiated through sacrifice.

Thor's name survives in Thurs-day, as well as in many Scandinavian personal names (Icelandic Þór, Þóra, Þórir, Þorleifur, Þórólfur, Þorsteinn, etc.) and in place-names (Þórsmörk in Iceland, Tórshavn in the Faroes, Torshälla in Sweden, Torslunde in Denmark). His Anglo-Saxon counterpart is remembered in the English town of Thursley.

The sea-god *Njörður* lives at Nóatún. He belongs to the Vanir, a different race of gods from the Æsir. He has a son Freyr and a daughter Freyja. Njörður controls the path of the wind. He can still sea and fire. People call on him for seafaring and fishing. The fishing village of Njarðvíkur was named after Njörður.

Njörður's wife is called *Skaði*. She is the daughter of Þjassi, the giant who once abducted the goddess Iðunn and her apples of youth. Skaði wanted to live in the homestead which her father had owned in a mountainous land named Þrymheimur. But Njörður wanted to live near the sea. They came to an agreement that they should spend nine nights at Þrymheimur and nine nights at Nóatún. When they returned from Þrymheimur to Nóatún, however, Njörður complained. He was tired of the mountains and the howling of the wolves. He preferred the song of the swans. Then Skaði complained in the following words:[18]

> I could not sleep
> by the shore of the sea
> for the noise of the mew
> that awakened me,
> the bird that flew
> each dawn from the deep.

Skaði thereupon returned to the mountains. She settled in Þrymheimur, where she skis a great deal and shoots animals with her bow.

Even the gods can have their marital problems.

Freyr controls the rain and the sunshine. He owns the ship Skíðblaðnir.

As the god of fertility, he can be invoked for peace and plenty. His sister *Freyja* can be called on for help in love affairs. She drives a chariot pulled by cats. Freyja is also called Vanadís, the goddess of the Vanir.

Freyr once fell in love with the beautiful Gerður, a giant's daughter. He knows how unbearable it feels to have to wait for one's beloved:[19]

> One night is long,
> long is a second,
> how shall I three endure?
> shorter to me
> has a month often seemed
> than this half bridal-eve.

Odin's son *Týr* is something of a war-god. He is ever eager for battle, bold to the point of foolhardiness. One proof of his daring came when the gods enticed the wolf Fenrir to allow the fetter Gleipnir to be put on him. The wolf did not believe that they would release him afterwards, so he demanded as a pledge that Týr should put his hand in his mouth. Then, when the gods would not set Fenrir free, he bit off Týr's hand at the wrist, the place which the Icelanders called the wolf-joint (*úlfliður*).[20]

According to Snorri's *Edda*, the fetter Gleipnir was forged by some dwarfs to hold the wolf Fenrir, who had burst his stout iron shackles. Gleipnir was a remarkable fetter:[21]

> This was made from six things: the noise a cat makes when it moves, the beard of a woman, the roots of a mountain, the sinews of a bear, the breath of a fish, and the spittle of a bird. Now, although you may not have known this before, you can easily prove that you are not being told a falsehood, since you will have observed that a woman has no beard, a cat makes no noise when running, a mountain has no roots.

The bear's sinews were the only part of the fetter that exist in reality. Gleipnir was five-sixths the product of a different world.

Despite its strength, the fetter was as smooth and soft as a silk ribbon. The Æsir called the wolf and showed him the 'silken band' and asked him to break it. They said that he would almost certainly be able to snap it. The wolf answered. 'This ribbon looks to me as if I could gain no renown from breaking it—it is so slight a cord; but if it has been made by guile and cunning, slender though it looks, it is not going to come on my legs.' He went on: 'If you bind me so that I can't get free, then you will sneak away so that it will be a long time before I get any help from you. I don't want to have that ribbon put on me. But rather than be accused of cowardice by you, let one of you place his hand in my mouth as a pledge that this is done in good faith'. None of the gods was willing to risk a hand until Týr volunteered. When the wolf began to struggle against the fetter, it tightened; the more he struggled, the tighter it got. All the gods laughed except Týr. He lost his hand.

Ægir is the master of the sea and *Rán* its mistress. Their nine daughters—with names like Bylgja, Hrönn, Bára, and Kólga—are the waves (or billows—a word borrowed into English from Old Norse *bylgja*). In Snorri's *Edda* Ægir is described with imaginative synonyms like 'the brother of the wind and fire'. Once Ægir laid on a feast for the gods. They all turned up, except Thor who—as so often—was away in the east fighting giants. When the gods had taken their seats in Ægir's hall, he ordered gleaming gold to be carried in; it shone and lit up the hall like fire. Since then gold has been known by the kenning 'Ægir's fire'.

Loki, the instigator of all deceit, sometimes used his cunning and magic to solve problems for the gods. More often, however, he brought them into difficulty. He cut off Sif's wonderful golden hair. He stole Freyja's Brísingamen, the marvellous necklace made by the dwarfs. He helped Þjassi when, in the guise of an eagle, he abducted Iðunn and her apples of youth from Ásgarður; this loss soon made the gods grow old and grey. The theme of the alluring apples recurs in the Greek myth of the golden apples of the Hesperides, which were guarded by a dragon. The giant Atlas plucked the apples for Hercules, who relieved him for a while of the task of bearing the celestial globe on his shoulders.

The foulest deed perpetrated by Loki was when he tricked the strong but blind god *Höður* into slaying his brother *Baldur*.[22]

Baldur the Good, son of Odin and Frigg, was far above all evil in life. He and his wife *Nanna Nepsdóttir* lived in Breiðablik, a fortress with an extensive view, a place totally without impurity. They had a son *Forseti*, the god of justice. The Icelandic noun *forseti*, like English *president* and *chairman*, denotes the person in the prime seat, for example in a court of justice. Forseti reconciled all those who came to him with legal disputes.

Baldur the Good was the darling of the gods. He was the wisest, most eloquent, most merciful of them all, besides which he was wondrously fair. He radiated beauty. A variety of mayweed with white petals has been likened to Baldur's brow.[23]

Baldur had ominous dreams portending a violent early death. He told these dreams to the other gods, who resolved to protect him against all manner of danger. Frigg exacted an oath from all the things in the world, that they would not harm Baldur. The gods were no longer worried after this. Nor was Baldur. The gods amused themselves by throwing stones and spears at Baldur, knowing that they could not hurt him in the least.

But Loki did not like this. Appearing in the shape of an old woman, he asked Frigg whether she really had extracted an oath from everything in the world. Frigg revealed that she had made one exception: a little bush called the mistletoe, which grew west of Valhalla, was considered too young to swear an oath. Loki found the mistletoe. He went to the gods' assembly place. There he sought out Höður, who was standing at the edge of the circle of people, because he was blind. Loki persuaded Höður to do as all the other men were doing, to throw darts at Baldur. 'Show Baldur honour like other men. I will show you where he is standing; throw this twig at him.' Höður threw it, with Loki taking aim for him. Baldur fell dead to the ground.

Hermóður, son of Odin, offered to ride on Sleipnir to Hel, the goddess of the dead, to offer a ransom for the return of Baldur. After nine days of riding through dark, deep valleys, Hermóður came to the river Gjöll, which separates the realm of the dead from the world of the living. He rode over the gold-thatched bridge, past the guardian maidens, through the gates of Hel, and right up to the hall. There he saw Baldur sitting on the high-seat. He implored Hel to let Baldur ride back with him to the Æsir. Hel agreed to this on one condition. She wanted proof that Baldur was loved as much as people said. The condition was that everything in the world, both living and dead, should weep for him. And everything did, even the stones and the metals, 'just as you will have seen these things weeping when they come out of frost and into the heat'. Finally, the Æsir came to a giantess named Þökk, presumably Loki in a new disguise, who refused to weep Baldur out of Hel.

The Greeks have an equivalent to this story in the myth of Orpheus, who charmed all living creatures with the tones of his singing and his lyre, and even made the stones and trees follow him. When his beloved Eurydice died, he soothed the heart of Hades to let her return to the world of the living. The only condition was that Orpheus should not look back at Eurydice until they had reached the daylight. Yet as they neared the sunlight, Orpheus could not help looking round. He lost her forever.

Loki received his punishment. No one can escape his destiny. All must pay for their deeds.

Seeking safety from the enraged gods, Loki built himself a house with four doors, so that he could see out in all directions. When someone approached the house, he would turn into a salmon and conceal himself in a waterfall known as Fránangursfoss. The time of retribution was near. Loki's hiding-place was discovered by the far-sighted Odin as he sat in his high-seat Hliðskjálf and gazed out over the world.

When they reached the waterfall, the Æsir tried to catch Loki in a net. Loki, however, lay between two stones so that the net passed over him. The Æsir, noticing that there was something alive there, fastened weights to the net so that nothing could pass under it. But Loki escaped by jumping over the rope.

This time the gods saw where he had gone. They made a third attempt to catch him in the net. They split up into two groups, while Thor waded in mid-stream. When Loki once more made a bold leap over the rope, Thor caught him and clutched fast by squeezing him hard at the tail. That is why the salmon tapers towards the tail.

The gods exacted a terrible revenge. They fettered Loki in a cave, bound over the edges of three sharp stones, under the dripping venom of a poisonous snake. But *Sigyn*, Loki's wife, protects him by holding a bowl to catch the poison. When the bowl is full, she goes to empty it. In the meantime the venom drips on Loki's face, which makes him jerk so violently in his fetters that the whole earth shakes. That is the cause of earthquakes.

These extracts from the *Prose Edda* should give a fair taste of the world of Norse mythology as narrated by Snorri Sturluson.

These myths are not an isolated Norse invention. Comparisons with Celtic, Roman, Greek, and Indian mythology show they are part of an Indo-European cultural heritage. Our friend Jacques de Wærn, archivist and heraldist at the National Archives in Stockholm, has sent us an interesting comparative study on this topic. It is reproduced as an appendix to this book.

Völuspá

The biblical creation story told in the first chapter of the book of Genesis has its Norse counterpart in the introduction to *Völuspá* (The Sibyl's Prophecy), the first poem in the *Elder Edda*. Whereas the Bible tells us that the world was created by God, the ancient seeress in *Völuspá* describes the origin of the world in a completely different way.

Völuspá has been translated into English several times.[24] The life of the Æsir is described in the following verses:[25]

> At Iðavöllur met
> the mighty gods,
> shrines and temples
> they timbered high;
> forges they set,
> and they smithied ore,
> tongs they wrought,
> and tools they fashioned.
>
> In their dwellings at peace
> they played at tables,
> of gold no lack
> did the gods then know,—
> till thither came up
> giant-maids three,
> huge of might,
> out of Jötunheimur.

The busy building and handicrafts and the carefree board-games of the Æsir at their abode called Iðavöllur are disturbed, however, by evil, personified by the cunning, malicious Loki. The death of the pure-hearted Baldur—'the greatest misfortune ever to befall gods and men', as Snorri writes—was an omen of the final struggle of the gods against giants and monsters.

Ragnarök, the fate of the gods,[26] begins with a terrible winter, when heavy snow whirls from every direction. Three winters with piercing winds follow in succession, with no summer, no warming sun in between.

Brother slays brother in merciless battles all over the world. Wolves swallow the sun and the moon. The stars in heaven cease to shine. The earth quakes. Mountains collapse. All fetters burst, so that Loki is set free. The wolf Fenrir also breaks loose, with fire spouting from his eyes and nose. The world-serpent, Miðgarðsormur, spews his venom through air and water. The heavens are rent asunder. The bridge Bifröst breaks when the sons of Múspell ride over it, with the fiery giant Surtur at their head. In their train come Fenrir and the world-serpent, Loki and all the frost-giants.

Then the ash Yggdrasill trembles. Heimdallur the watchman blows his Gjallarhorn to summon the gods to the final battle on the plain of Vígríður. There the giants, the monsters, and the Æsir fall. The wolf Fenrir swallows Odin. His son Víðar avenges the All-father by killing the wolf. Then Surtur spouts fire all over the earth, thus consuming the world.

This destruction of the rulers and the rebirth of the world are described in two frequently cited verses:

> The sun turns black,
> earth sinks in the sea,
> the hot stars down
> from heaven are whirled;
> Fierce grows the steam
> and the life-feeding flame,
> till fire leaps high
> about heaven itself.

> Now do I see
> the earth anew
> rise all green
> from the waves again;
> the cataracts fall,

and the eagle flies
and fish he catches
beneath the cliffs.

The first verse conjures up a volcanic eruption. 'This vivid picture of creation and destruction was surely most likely to emerge in Iceland itself.'[27] The second verse is a vision of the dramatic Icelandic landscape at peace.

The imagery in *Völuspá* about the reborn world also has some bright tones. The Æsir meet once again to play at tables at Iðavöllur. Baldur is expected back in Valhalla. At the southern end of the heavens stands Gimli, the eternal home of the righteous, the fairest of all houses, with its roof of gold. In a hall known as Brimir there is plenty to drink for those who so wish. There is also a hall which glistens with red gold. It is called Sindri. According to some modern-day Icelanders, this hall was built by an artistic dwarf of the same name.

This closing scene of *Völuspá* has forever etched itself into the minds of many Icelanders. Five hundred impoverished Icelanders who emigrated to Canada at the end of the nineteenth century founded the small town of Gimli in Manitoba. It lies north of the city of Winnipeg, just west of the south tip of Lake Winnipeg. In Iceland one meets the name Gimli in the name of at least one house in central Reykjavík from the turn of the century.

Hávamál

The second poem in the *Elder Edda* is really a collection of poems. *Hávamál* (Sayings of the High One—Odin) takes its name from its ritual and mythological passages. They depict events in Odin's life, such as love affairs, magical spells, and runic carvings. We also learn how Odin acquired the precious mead of poetry from Gunnlöð, daughter of the giant Suttungur.

Scholars appear to be in agreement that *Hávamál* was originally composed in Norway. One clue is the reference in verse 50 to a pine tree (*þöll*) with its bark and needles.

Perhaps the most readable part of the poem is the introductory collection of proverbs and advice on manners. Many of them are reminiscent of the proverbial teachings in the Old Testament (Proverbs and Ecclesiastes).

The reader is given a picture of a society where one has to be on one's guard. Essential assets are 'a mind full of sense', an ability to distinguish friends from foes, and to drink mead in moderation. It is difficult to cope alone; one must have kinsmen and good friends. In other words, we see 'all possible sides of everyday life through the eyes of an experienced, broad-minded, and utilitarian pagan peasant.'[28]

The closing verse (no. 76) of the proverbial section has a higher outlook, however. We see life in the perspective of eternity, 'sub specie aeternitatis'. This verse praises the value of being held in esteem by future generations.

Qualities like friendship and hospitality, moderation and wisdom, kinship and honour are exalted throughout the poem. These ideals— combined with easily wounded pride, death-defying courage, and a belief in destiny—evidently guide the conduct of the heroes of the Icelandic sagas. Since they help to explain their actions, it may be interesting here to pause to consider some of the most famous stanzas (or half-stanzas) in *Hávamál*. They are taken from the translation by Henry Adams Bellows.

1   Within the gates
     ere a man shall go,
     (full warily let him watch,)
     full long look around him;
     for little he knows
     where a foe may lurk,
     and sit in the seats within.

10   A better burden
     no man may bear
     for wanderings wide than wisdom;
     it is better than wealth
     on unknown ways,
     and in grief a refuge it gives.

34   Crooked and far
     is the road to a foe,
     though his house on the highway be;
     but wide and straight
     is the way to a friend,
     though far away he fare.

43   To his friend a man
      a friend shall prove,
      to him and the friend of his friend;
      but never a man
      shall friendship make
      with one of his foeman's friends.

44   If a friend thou hast
      whom thou fully wilt trust
      and good from him wouldst get,
      thy thought with his mingle,
      and gifts shalt thou make,
      and fare to find him oft.

47   Young was I once
      and wandered alone,
      and nought of the road I knew;
      rich did I feel
      when a comrade I found,
      for man is man's delight.

50   On the hillside drear
      the fir-tree dies,
      all bootless its needles and bark;
      it is like a man
      whom no one loves,—
      why should his life be long?

63   tell one thy thoughts
      but beware of two,—
      all know what is known to three.

72   A son is better
      though late he be born
      and his father to death have fared;
      memory-stones
      seldom stand by the road
      save when kinsman honours his kin.

76   Cattle die,
      and kinsmen die,
      and so one dies one's self;
      but a noble name
      will never die
      if good renown one gets.

133   none so good is found
      that he faults has not,
      nor so wicked that nought he is worth.

138   profit thou hast if thou hearest,
      great thy gain if thou learnest.

For us children of a later age, the Norse myths may sometimes appear remote, preposterous, of no concern to us. Such a first impression does not stand up to close consideration. Like the *Iliad* and the *Odyssey*, the Eddic poems are replete with magnificent poetry, often with humorous elements, and a creative fantasy which raises the spirit above everyday concerns. They have also served as a source of inspiration to new literary and artistic expressions in the works of many Icelandic authors and artists.

The conceptual world of Norse mythology is far from dead. It still survives in Scandinavia and elsewhere, in deeply rooted customs, folktales, and legends. The gods and goddesses, giants and dwarfs still haunt the imagination. The modern languages give us daily reminders of the pagan cultural heritage of the Nordic people. Not just in Iceland but throughout Scandinavia, as well as in the British Isles, we find this heritage in personal names, place-names, titles of journals like *Fjölnir* and *Skírnir*, runic inscriptions, and archaeological finds. In Iceland today there are vessels with names like *Andvari, Baldur, Draupnir, Freyr, Frigg, Gulltoppur, Hrungnir, Huginn, Muninn, Óðinn, Sleipnir, Þór*, and *Ymir*.

The days of the week in English still bear the names of Germanic gods. Sunday and Monday are called after the sun and the moon. Tuesday takes its name from the Anglo-Saxon war-god Tiw (equivalent to Týr), Wednesday from Wôden (Óðinn), Thursday from Þunor (Þór), Friday from the goddess Frig (Frigg), while Saturday bears the name of the Roman god Saturn. Modern Icelandic, however, retains only the words for the sun and the moon in *sunnudagur* and *mánudagur*. The other days have been deprived of their pagan connotations: *týsdagur* has been replaced by *þriðjudagur* 'third day', *óðinsdagur* has become *miðvikudagur* 'mid-week day', *þórsdagur* is now *fimmtudagur* 'fifth day', and *frjádagur* has become firmly Christianized as *föstudagur* 'fast-day'. Saturday in Iceland is *laugardagur* 'bath-day'.

Pagan Germanic religion is thus a concrete part of our cultural heritage, untainted by the distasteful manner in which it was exploited by the Nazis. The Germanic gods and myths were best preserved in Scandinavia. For this the world is indebted to Iceland, and in particular to Snorri Sturluson and his *Edda*.

The Swedish prime minister Olof Palme, who visited Iceland in

December 1984 (little more than a year before his assassination), brought up this topic. During a lecture at the University of Iceland entitled 'The Nordic Countries and the World' he said that we must seek the source of Nordic culture in Iceland. He quoted the words of a Swedish historian: 'Never at high latitudes has so much of note been created by so few'.

When Palme broached the subject of a Nordic nuclear-free zone, he put his manuscript to one side and spoke plainly. He conjured up the probable consequences of a nuclear war: an atomic winter which could destroy all human life on earth. He did so by warning of a *Ragnarök* and by using Snorri's term *Fimbulvetur* to describe the terrible winter that would ensue.

The Icelandic Sagas

Authors have always written for a
minority, except of course when the
Icelandic sagas were read and
understood by the whole nation.

Doris Lessing in a television interview
in Reykjavík, June 1986

In three of the most famous Icelandic sagas—*Laxdœla saga, Njáls saga*, and *Egils saga Skalla-Grímssonar*—the interest is concentrated on the members of some closely related powerful families. The child of a leading character in one saga can appear as the leading character in another saga. The mutual relations of these powerful men, their travels and vicissitudes illustrate events over several generations, beginning with the emigration from Norway and the colonization of Iceland and continuing until a few decades into the eleventh century.

These three sagas, like another saga which we shall consider in this section, *Grettis saga*, are genuinely Icelandic in their themes and their outlook on life. About this there can be no doubt. But they were not written down by a people in isolation. The affirmation of courtly manners which is typical of medieval European chivalrous literature is also evident in *Laxdœla saga*, where the French loan-word *kurteisi* 'courtesy' is a term of high praise. The clash of pagan Norse and

Christian European virtues finds expression at several points in *Njáls saga*.

The events in *Egils saga* and *Laxdæla saga* are enacted chiefly in western Iceland, while *Njáls saga* is based in the south and *Grettis saga* in north-west Iceland.

Let us begin with *Laxdæla saga*.[29] One of its remarkable personages is Melkorka, daughter of the Irish king Mýrkjartan. At the age of fifteen she was carried off as a slave to Scandinavia. She was later brought to Iceland by the chieftain Höskuldur Dala-Kollsson, who bought her at a market held by the King of Norway. The seller told Höskuldur that the woman was a mute.

Since Melkorka was a proud princess and Höskuldur was already married, she spoke not a word to him for years. He had no reason to believe that she was not a mute. One sunny morning, however, when Höskuldur was out seeing to his farm, he heard the sound of voices coming from a stream at the foot of the sloping homefield. He recognized the speakers as Melkorka and their little son Ólafur. She was talking busily to the child.

Ólafur grew up to achieve great fame and power. His love of finery earned him the epithet *pái* 'peacock'. He married Þorgerður Egilsdóttir from Borg in Borgarfjörður. She was the daughter of the Viking and poet Egill Skalla-Grímsson, the leading character in the saga that bears his name.

Ólafur the Peacock and Þorgerður had several children, including Kjartan Ólafsson, one of the three main characters in *Laxdæla saga*. Women play a prominent role in this romantic saga. The central part of the saga develops into an eternal triangle involving Kjartan, his foster-brother Bolli Þorleiksson, and Guðrún Ósvífursdóttir, a proud and passionate woman. Before she married for the first time, she had four dreams which were interpreted as portending that she would marry four times.

The drama begins with Kjartan and Guðrún falling in love. Bolli was also attracted to her. When Kjartan and Bolli agreed to sail to Norway, Guðrún wanted to join them. 'That's out of the question,' said Kjartan. 'So wait for me instead for three years.'

During their stay in Norway with King Ólafur Tryggvason, both Kjartan and Bolli were baptized. The king at this time was trying to force the entire Icelandic people to convert to Christianity, with the aid of his court priest Þangbrandur. When the three years had passed, Bolli returned to Iceland, but four Icelanders, including Kjartan, were held as hostage by the king. Kjartan was well treated by the king and his sister Ingibjörg, 'the loveliest woman in all Norway'.

Back in Iceland, Bolli often visited Guðrún. She asked him if there was anything besides the king's friendship which was keeping Kjartan in Norway. Bolli replied that Kjartan spent a lot of time with Ingibjörg. At the same time, Bolli asked Guðrún not to wait any longer for Kjartan but to marry him. She reluctantly agreed, but only after some time and much persuasion.

Kjartan returned to Iceland hoping to marry Guðrún, but when he heard of her marriage to Bolli he chose another woman named Hrefna. On hearing of this, Guðrún—who was still deeply in love with Kjartan—fell into despair. She incited Bolli to kill Kjartan, but Bolli immediately regretted the deed.

After the killing, Bolli rode home to Guðrún, who came out to meet him. She asked him how late in the day it was. Bolli answered that it was around noon:[30]

> Then Guðrún said, 'Morning tasks are often mixed: I have spun yarn for twelve ells of cloth and you have killed Kjartan.'
> Bolli replied, 'This luckless deed will live long enough in my mind without you reminding me of it.'
> 'I do not think it luckless,' said Guðrún. '. . . what I like best is that Hrefna will not go laughing to bed tonight.'
> Then Bolli said, in sudden fury, 'I doubt if she will turn any paler at the news than you, and I suspect you would have been less shocked if I had been left lying on the field of battle and Kjartan had lived to tell the tale.'

Guðrún married—as fate had determined—no less than four times. She spent her old age in great sorrow. She became the first nun in Iceland.

Once Guðrún received a much longed-for visit from her son Bolli. They sat together for a long time, speaking of many things. He asked, 'Will you tell me something, mother, that I am very curious to know? Which man did you love the most?' Guðrún gives a brief characterization of each husband, but without answering the question. Bolli repeats it. 'You have not told me yet which man you loved the most.

There's no need to conceal it any longer now.' Then Guðrún answers: 'I was worst to the one I loved the most.'

We have now seen the fate of the son and grandson of Höskuldur Dala-Kollsson by his concubine Melkorka. Höskuldur also had children by his wife Jórunn; one of these was a daughter, Hallgerður. In *Laxdœla saga* she is only mentioned in passing, but she plays one of the main roles in *Njáls saga*. Hallgerður had long, thick hair. She was handsome and tall, as her nickname *langbrók* (Long-Breeches) suggests, and she was beautiful. But she was also quick to take offence and vengeful, treacherous and inclined to steal. When her uncle Hrútur once saw her playing as a child, he immediately discerned the different sides of her character. 'The child is beautiful enough, and many will suffer for her beauty; but I cannot image how thief's eyes have come into our kin.'[31]

Hallgerður marries the chivalrous Gunnar of Hlíðarendi, close friend of the wise Njáll. Gunnar falls for her beauty when he meets her at the assembly at Þingvellir. Later, however, he repeatedly has reason to regret his choice of wife. Once he slaps her on the cheek when he discovers that she has stolen food.

It is largely because of her intrigues that Gunnar gets involved in blood-feuds with many killings. For this he and his brother Kolskeggur are condemned by the Althing to exile for three years. When it comes to the point, however, Gunnar cannot bring himself to leave his home:[32]

> When he was ready to leave, he embraced them all one by one. The whole household came out to see him off. With a thrust of his halberd he vaulted into the saddle, and rode away with Kolskeggur.
> They rode down towards Markar River. Just then Gunnar's horse stumbled, and he had to leap from the saddle. He happened to glance up towards his home and the slopes of Hlíðarendi.
> 'How lovely the slopes are,' he said, 'more lovely than they have ever seemed to me before, golden cornfields and new-mown hay. I am going back home, and I will not go away.'

Because he defies the judgement of the court in this way, Gunnar is outlawed. This means that anyone is free to kill him with impunity.

One day, just before dawn, when Gunnar is the only man at Hlíðarendi, together with Hallgerður and his mother Rannveig, a large band of men mount a surprise attack. Gunnar defends himself with his bow and arrows, but one of the assailants cuts the string of his bow. In this predicament, Gunnar turns to Hallgerður:[33]

> 'Let me have two locks of your hair, and help my mother plait them into a bow-string for me.'
> 'Does anything depend on it?' asked Hallgerður.
> 'My life depends on it,' replied Gunnar, 'for they will never overcome me as long as I can use my bow.'
> 'In that case,' said Hallgerður, 'I shall now remind you of the slap you once gave me. I do not care in the least whether you hold out a long time or not.'
> 'To each his own way of earning fame,' said Gunnar. 'You shall not be asked again.'
> Rannveig said, 'You are an evil woman, and your shame will long be remembered.'

This frequently cited exchange reveals not only Hallgerður's bitterness and vindictiveness but also Gunnar's self-control in the face of death, which finds expression in his sarcastic reply to Hallgerður. Both he and his mother have a strong sense of the value of a good reputation after one's death.

Similar fateful scenes are enacted in *Egils saga Skalla-Grímsson*, which may be the work of Snorri Sturluson (see Chapter 1). This saga begins by telling of Egill's forefathers in Norway. We then follow Egill himself on his many Viking forays to east and west alike, before he settles down in Iceland as a very wealthy man. He lives first at a farm called Borg in the west, but spends the last years of his life with his son-in-law at Mosfell close to Reykjavík.

One recurrent theme in the saga is the conflict in Norway between defiant chieftains and petty kings on the one hand, and the growing central power of the crown on the other. The latter is represented by Haraldur hárfagri and his descendants. Haraldur swears neither to cut nor comb his hair until he is sole king of Norway. One of the chieftains who suffers from Haraldur's resolute enforcement of his authority is Egill's grandfather, Kveld-Úlfur (Evening-Wolf). He got his name because he was tired and irritable in the evenings. Many people believed that he had supernatural powers.

When King Haraldur attacks and kills Kveld-Úlfur's son Þórólfur, a terrible revenge is taken by Kveld-Úlfur and Grímur, his other son. Grímur is a head taller than other men, and he grows bald at an early age, which earns him the name Skalla-Grímur. In a battle where the ageing Kveld-Úlfur goes berserk, he and Skalla-Grímur slay two of Haraldur's cousins and more than fifty of their men. The battle takes place on a ship which previously belonged to Þórólfur. They seize the ship and its entire cargo as booty and sail off to sea.

They had no choice. With the king as an enemy they could hardly have stayed in Norway. They sailed for Iceland with their women and children. Kveld-Úlfur died on the voyage. Skalla-Grímur landed by a fiord in the west, in an area rich in bogs, extensive forests, salmon rivers, places for hunting seal and fishing, for retrieving stranded whales and driftwood along the coast. He built the farm of Borg a little way in from the coast. He called the fiord Borgarfjörður. He drove his cattle to a headland where there were many swans, hence the name Álftanes. He had a son named Egill.

The struggle with the Norwegian king continued in the next generation. When Egill Skalla-Grímsson sailed to Norway as a young man, he soon found himself in conflict with Haraldur's son, Eiríkur blóðöx (Eric Bloodaxe), and his queen Gunnhildur. This lady is described as a skilled magician. During a feast when a very thirsty Egill downs one horn of ale after another, she tries to kill him by poisoning his beer. Egill throws the horn away and kills the host. New disputes end with Egill killing one of the king's sons. Egill has to escape. Before he does so, however, he raises a pole of insult (*níðstöng*), on which he carves runes with spells directed against Eiríkur and Gunnhildur: may the guardian spirits (*landvættir*) drive them out of the country.

The spell worked. Eiríkur fled from Norway to England, where he made himself king of the fortified town of Jórvík (York) and came into conflict with the Christian king Aðalsteinn (Ethelstan) of England. Or, as Egill later put it in his poem to his best friend Arinbjörn:[34]

> The cross-grained King
> Kept house at York,
> Where the barren beaches
> Are beaten by rain,
> The sodden coastline
> Soaked and stormy;
> There in helmet of horror
> Sat the heroic one.

Little suspecting any malice, Egill is shipwrecked on this sodden coast. Egill curses his bad luck; he does not know that it is the magic of Queen Gunnhildur that brings him to York. He soon stands face to face before the king and queen. They condemn him to die the following morning. But he saves his life by a virtual miracle. During the night before his execution, he composes a poem of praise to the king. It is rightly named his head-ransom (*Höfuðlausn*).

On an earlier occasion, we read that King Aðalsteinn the Victorious defeats an invading Scottish army with the aid of Egill at the head of a large muster of men. As a reward for this the king gives him two chests full of silver. The pious king becomes a close friend. Egill allows himself to be 'prime-signed', a preliminary form of baptism whereby he is blessed with the sign of the cross but still remains a pagan deep down. Egill is happiest when fighting duels with spear and sword, or setting out in the spring to go raiding, or drinking ale and composing poems in the company of true friends.

Wherever he went, Egill always took the chests of silver from King Aðalsteinn. He would not lose them for the world. As an old man he grew stiff, hard of hearing, and blind. One evening he rode away from home with the chests, accompanied by two slaves. The following morning, the people at Mosfell saw Egill wandering around on a hill, without the slaves and without the chests. He said that he had killed the slaves and hidden the treasure.

To this day, no one knows where Egill buried the silver.

In the account of a feast in the hall of King Aðalsteinn, the saga paints a full-size portrait of Egill after he has sat down in the high-seat opposite the king. At that feast in his honour, Egill was deeply distressed about his dear brother Þórólfur, who had just been killed in the victorious battle against the Scots on Vínheiði ('Vin Moor') by Vínskógar ('Vin Forest') in Norðimbraland (present-day Northumberland).[35]

> There Egill sat, his shield at his feet and his helmet on his head. He had his sword across his knees and kept pulling it part of the way out of the scabbard, then thrusting it back. He sat bolt upright but his head was bent low.
> Egill was a man who caught the eye. He had a wide forehead, bushy eyebrows and a nose, not long, but impressively large. A great broad beard grew on a chin as massive as his jaws; his neck was stout and his

shoulders heavy, far heavier than those of other men. When he grew angry there was a hard, cruel look on his face. He was far above normal height but well-proportioned and though he once had a head of thick wolf-grey hair, he had grown bald early in life.

There he sat, just as we describe him, with one eyebrow sunk down right to the cheek and the other lifting up to the roots of the hair. His eyes were black and his eyebrows joined in the middle.

Egill, however, quickly changed the expression of his face, where the movements of his eyebrows mirrored his feelings. When King Aðalsteinn handed him a fine big bracelet, Egill put it on his arm and his eyebrows went back to normal. Egill's mood grew more cheerful when the king gave him the two chests of silver, and he composed this verse:

> In bitterness my brows
> Beetled over my eyes;
> Now my forehead had found one
> To smooth its furrows:
> The King has conquered
> My louring cliff-face,
> The granter of gifts,
> The gold-flinger.

Egill is depicted with something of a dual nature. On the one hand he is shown as a coarse, greedy, cruel Viking. On the other hand, he has redeeming features such as courage, loyalty to friends, and the ability to express true human emotion in his soulful poetry.

This side of his complex nature is revealed in his masterly lament *Sonatorrek* (The Great Loss of My Sons). The background to its composition was that Egill, in despair over the death of his sons Böðvar and Gunnar, went to bed and refused to eat or drink. He obviously intended to take his own life in this way. His daughter Þorgerður managed to trick him into drinking milk and composing a poem:[36]

> My own choice, father, would be for us to keep going a little longer. Then you can compose a dirge for Böðvar, and I'll carve the poem in runes on a log. After that we can die if we want to. I think it will be a long time before your son Þorsteinn makes a poem in memory of Böðvar. Nor will it do if Böðvar isn't honoured with a funeral feast.

As he worked on the dirge, Egill regained his strength. It developed into one of the most moving poems of ancient times.

When Egill died, his kinsmen, following heathen custom, set him in a burial mound with his weapons and clothes. After the adoption of Christianity his bones were moved into a church. When the church was demolished, bones of an unusual size were discovered under the altar. The priest, wanting to test how thick the skull was, struck it as hard as he could with an axe. It neither broke nor dented. The bones could only have belonged to Egill Skalla-Grímsson.

Another famous Icelandic saga is *Grettis saga Ásmundarsonar*. The hero is Grettir, a mighty champion and poet, a loner and a powerful swimmer. In his twenty years as an outlaw he has many adventures. Grettir was famous for his violent temperament, his sudden rage, his physical strength, and his fear of darkness. As soon as it got dark, he imagined he saw ghosts and malicious trolls. He grew up at the family farm of Bjarg near Miðfjörður in north-west Iceland, but he travelled all round the island, as well as to Scandinavia. The saga relates how Grettir and his ancestors travelled to Norway and all over Iceland. At the age of fourteen Grettir was exiled for three years on account of manslaughter. Later on he was outlawed. As a hunted outlaw, he sought refuge near the end of his life on Drangey, a little island in Skagafjörður, one of the deep fiords on the north coast. From this island he swam up the fiord one afternoon in the ice-cold waters of the North Atlantic. The tide was with him. The weather was perfectly calm. He took powerful strokes and came ashore at Reykjanes, when the sun had set.

Grettir's many misfortunes were mostly a consequence of his life-and-death duel with Glámur, a ghost, or rather a living corpse (*draugur*). Glámur was a Swede who had been killed by a supernatural being as he sat watching sheep for the farmer Þórhallur of Þórhalls-staðir in Forsæludalur. Glámur had never been given a burial in consecrated earth. Soon afterwards, he started haunting people by day and by night. He would sit astride houses at night and kill both people and animals in the valley. During the summer, when the sun was at its highest, he would disappear. But when the days grew shorter and autumn darkness spread over the district, Glámur returned to torment all living creatures in the valley.

When Grettir heard of the hauntings, he rode over to Þórhallsstaðir and offered to stay there with the farmer. Þórhallur was grateful, since no one else dared to visit him any longer. During the third night at the farm, a night with clear moonlight and drifting clouds, Grettir managed to defeat the ghost after a wild wrestling match. Just as Glámur fell to the ground, the sky drifted away from the moon. He gave Grettir a sharp look. It made him turn pale. He was so overwhelmed by everything—fatigue after the fight and the sight of Glámur's fixed stare—that he could not draw his sword but was lying almost half-dead on the ground. Glámur pronounced a curse on Grettir. It ended with some words which Grettir would never forget:[37]

> Up until now your deeds have brought you fame, but from now on outlawry and slaughter will come your way, and most of your acts will bring you ill luck and misfortune. You will be made an outlaw and always forced to live by yourself in the wilderness. I also lay this curse on you: you will always see before you these eyes of mine, and they will make your solitude unbearable, and this shall drag you to your death.

At the same instant as Glámur had pronounced his curse, Grettir was released from his powerlessness. He drew his sword and chopped off Glámur's head.

Old Icelandic literature has always been a priceless part of the cultural heritage of the Icelanders. The old poems and sagas have captivated readers for centuries, spellbinding them, seizing their imagination and giving them the spiritual strength with which to survive times of material destitution and adverse circumstances.

The Icelanders are a small nation, but they have always shown themselves to be interested in reading, stoically conscious of their history—not least during the many centuries of foreign rule, when they suffered ceaseless repression and poverty, famine, natural disasters, and epidemics. Indomitable Icelanders of this type are brought to life by Halldór Laxness in his novel *Independent People*.[38]

Icelanders in general retain their great interest in the sagas today. They speak, write, and make films about events in the sagas. It sometimes even appears as if many Icelanders—whether they be farmers, craftsmen, fishermen, or academics—feel that they are closely related to the figures in the sagas. It can happen that an Icelander changes course in the middle of a sentence when he is reminded of a passage from a saga. Icelandic newspapers from time to time publish absorbing articles about the sagas, their heroes, and the motives that may have dictated their actions. In 1936 W. H. Auden was impressed to hear a kitchen-maid in the country 'give an excellent criticism of a medieval saga'.[39]

The sagas continue to inspire new works of art. Halldór Laxness's novel *Gerpla* is based on *Fóstbrœðra saga*,[40] and Ágúst Guðmunds- son's film *The Outlaw* (1981) is based on *Gísla saga Súrssonar*.[41] The film director Hrafn Gunnlaugsson was generally inspired by the mo- tifs, the atmosphere, and the milieu of the Icelandic sagas when he wrote the screenplay for his award-winning *When the Raven Flies* (1984). This film shows how a young Irishman comes to Iceland to take revenge on the Icelandic Vikings who once, while plundering in Ireland, cruelly killed his parents before the young boy's eyes and abducted his sister.

Hrafn also attracted international attention for his film *In the Shadow of the Raven* (1988). The leitmotif is borrowed from the courtly romance of Tristan and Isolde, of which the medieval Icelan- ders had their own version in *Tristrams saga*.[42] Tristan and Isolde drink a love potion made of many kinds of flowers and herbs. When they have drained it, they are united in such a passionate love that nothing can stand between them, even though they come from two hostile families. Hrafn's film, like Richard Wagner's musical drama, is a tale of love, jealousy, hate, revenge, and forgiveness. The violent action and swift rhythm of the film hold the viewer in an iron grip. It was filmed in the shimmering light and the virtually treeless landscape of Iceland, with a stranded whale, black ravens, geysers, a lagoon with icebergs and roaring torrents. Thanks to this natural backdrop, the drama has a specifically Icelandic frame, which gives it intensity and the correct atmosphere.

The Christianization of Norway and Iceland serves as the fateful background to Hrafn's subsequent film, *The White Viking* (1991).

For many reasons—perhaps primarily their realistic style, their inherent drama, and the pithy depiction of people and settings—the Icelandic sagas have served as a model for many classic writers throughout Scandinavia. Examples include Adam Oehlenschläger, August Strindberg, Selma Lagerlöf, and Henrik Ibsen.[43]

Outside Scandinavia as well, the sagas have exerted an influence on writers. One such is Sir Walter Scott. Many of his novels are based on historical tales which he had heard from his grandfather. It has been pointed out that there are striking similarities between some of these novels and the Icelandic sagas. Since it is known that Scott had read some Icelandic sagas—such as *Eyrbyggja saga* with its romantic colouring and its dramatic recreation of historical events[44]—it can reasonably be assumed that they influenced his writing. He was also interested in Norse folk belief, the world peopled by supernatural beings such as dwarfs, elves, and ghosts.[45] Following Scott, other Scottish writers, such as Robert Louis Stevenson and R. M. Ballantyne, were also influenced by the Icelandic sagas.

Scholars of literature have speculated about the extent to which the Icelandic saga may have influenced, directly or indirectly, the hard-boiled, realistic narrative technique of Ernest Hemingway. No direct link is known between them. Yet Hemingway's style and that of the Icelandic saga undeniably show similar features. But the similarity is limited. If one looks more closely below the surface—at milieux, values, and ideals—one sees no close affinity. On the contrary. The heroes of the Icelandic sagas and the characters in Hemingway's novels belong to completely different epochs. These men and women live in radically different worlds.[46]

The characters in the sagas—such as the champion swimmer Grettir—are still very much alive for today's Icelanders. In the summer, some of them emulate Grettir's feat of swimming from Drangey to the mainland.

A feat of swimming of a much more serious kind was performed a few years ago. In March 1984, when the little fishing-boat *Hellisey VE*, with her crew of four, suddenly overturned at midnight one night on the high seas and started to sink, the four men began to say the Lord's Prayer. Two of them disappeared into the deep at once, and ten minutes later the 24-year-old captain also drowned.

The sole survivor was the 20-year-old seaman Guðlaugur Friðþórsson. In ice-cold water (5°C) he swam against the tide for five or six hours towards the island of Heimaey. He took his bearings from the lighthouse there and the stars of the cloudless night sky. As he neared the underwater rocks by the coast, he saw beyond them a sheer precipice. He knew that if he swam in that direction, he would probably be crushed against the cliff. Instead he swam out again. Further away he saw a more suitable landing place, where he pulled himself on to the shore. After two hours of walking barefoot over pathless terrain with sharp lava rocks, he stumbled on bloody feet into a house in the town of Vestmannaeyjar.

When doctors in Iceland and the USA later examined Guðlaugur, they said that he had saved his life through an incredible combination of physical and mental strength. This exploit has been immortalized in the documentary film *Reginsund* (The Enormous Swim) by Páll Steingrímsson, himself from Vestmannaeyjar. In the film Guðlaugur says: 'While I was swimming I thought a lot about God. I never doubted that I would manage it.'

Notes to Chapter 2

1   Lee M. Hollander, *The Skalds: A Selection of Their Poems, with Introduction and Notes* (Ann Arbor: University of Michigan Press, 1968), p. 13.

2   Sven B. F. Jansson, 'Forntidens litteratur', in *Ny illustrerad svensk litteraturhistoria*, 2nd ed. (Stockholm: Natur och Kultur, 1967), vol. 1, p. 3.

3   See 'The Icelanders and their Language' in Chapter 6.

4   Gun Nilsson, 'Den isländska litteraturen i stormaktstidens Sverige', *Scripta Islandica* 5 (1954), pp. 19–41.

5   Ibid., p. 29.

6   Hans Bekker-Nielsen and Ole Widding, *Arne Magnusson: The Manuscript Collector*, trans. Robert W. Mattila (Odense: Odense University Press, 1972), p. 48. In Halldór Laxness's *Íslandsklukkan* the same words are put into the mouth of Arnas Arnæus, the learned man of the world, for whom Árni Magnússon was the prototype; see 'Trade Monopoly and Natural Disasters' in Chapter 1.

7   Bekker-Nielsen and Widding, *Arne Magnusson*, p. 55.

8   See Kevin S. Kiernan, *The Thorkelin Transcripts of Beowulf*, Anglistica 25 (Copenhagen: Rosenkilde and Bagger, 1986). Of the many editions see, e.g. F. Klaeber, *Beowulf and the Fight at Finnsburg*, 3rd ed. (Boston: Heath, 1950). An easily available verse translation of *Beowulf* is that by Michael Alexander (Harmondsworth: Penguin, 1973).

9   Jónas Kristjánsson, 'The Literary Heritage: Eddas and Sagas', in *Icelandic Sagas, Eddas, and Art: Treasures Illustrating the Greatest Mediaeval Literary*

Heritage of Northern Europe (New York: The Pierpont Morgan Library, 1982), p. 10.

10 Jónas Kristjánsson, 'Heimkoma handritanna', *Árbók Háskóla Íslands* 1981, pp. 39–42 and 49–54.

11 Ibid., p. 57.

12 Björn Þorsteinsson, *Island*, Politikens Danmarkshistorie (Copenhagen: Politiken, 1985), p. 290.

13 The following account is based on *The Prose Edda of Snorri Sturluson: Tales from Norse Mythology*, trans. Jean I. Young (Berkeley: University of California Press, 1973). In our quotations from this and other English translations of Old Icelandic works, proper names have been changed into Modern Icelandic in accordance with the principles stated in the Introduction.

14 Sigurður Nordal points out in his introduction (p. 8) to the translation mentioned in the previous note that the title *Edda*, which may mean 'Poetics', originally refers only to Snorri's prose work. The application of the title to the mythological and heroic poems of the so-called *Elder Edda* or *Poetic Edda* is 'a seventeenth-century misunderstanding'.

15 *The Prose Edda*, p. 44.

16 Ibid., pp. 47–8.

17 Ibid., pp. 66–8.

18 Ibid., p. 52.

19 Ibid., p. 62.

20 In Modern Icelandic the word *úlfliður* has been replaced with *úlnliður* as the term for the wrist. This change is the work of learned men, who have shown the form with *úlf-* 'wolf' to be folk etymology, and have introduced the form with *úln-* to show the original relationship with *öln* 'forearm' (Latin *ulna*, English *ell*).

21 *The Prose Edda*, p. 57.

22 Ibid., pp. 80–4.

23 Stinking mayweed (*Anthemis cotula*) is known as Balder's Brae in Northumberland; see Geoffrey Grigson, *The Englishman's Flora* (St Alban's: Paladin, 1975), p. 401.

24 There is still no 'definitive' translation of the *Elder Edda*. Perhaps the best version on philological grounds is that by Henry Adams Bellows, *The Poetic Edda*, Scandinavian Classics 21 and 22, 2 vols. in 1 (New York: American-Scandinavian Foundation, 1923). There are two easily available translations with little or no scholarly apparatus: Patricia Terry, *Poems of the Vikings: The Elder Edda* (Indianapolis: Bobbs-Merrill, 1969); W. H. Auden and Paul B. Taylor, *Norse Poems* (London: Athlone Press, 1981).

25 Bellows, *The Poetic Edda*, pp. 5, 24. Besides modernizing the spelling of Icelandic names, we have taken the liberty to arrange Eddic stanzas in six or eight short lines, following the principle of modern editions of the *Elder Edda*.

26 *Ragnarök* literally means 'the fate of the rulers'. The expression 'Twilight of the Gods' (German *Götterdämmerung*) is a translation of Old Icelandic *ragna-*

røkr, which is used by Snorri as a synonym for *ragnarök*. See John Stanley Martin, *Ragnarök: An Investigation into Old Norse Concepts of the Fate of the Gods*, Melbourne Monographs in Germanic Studies 3 (Assen: Van Gorcum, 1972), pp. 3–5.

27   R. Ellis Davidson, *Gods and Myths of Northern Europe* (Harmondsworth: Penguin, 1964), p. 209.

28   Björn Collinder, p. 24 of his introduction to the Swedish translation, *Den poetiska Eddan* (Stockholm: Forum, 1972).

29   *Laxdæla Saga*, trans. Magnus Magnusson and Hermann Pálsson (Harmondsworth: Penguin, 1969).

30   Ibid., ch. 49.

31   *Njal's Saga*, trans. Magnus Magnusson and Hermann Pálsson (Harmondsworth: Penguin, 1960), ch. 1.

32   Ibid., ch. 75.

33   Ibid., ch. 77.

34   *Egil's Saga,* trans. Hermann Pálsson and Paul Edwards (Harmondsworth: Penguin, 1976), ch. 78.

35   Ibid., ch. 55.

36   Ibid., ch. 78.

37   *Grettir's Saga*, trans. Denton Fox and Hermann Pálsson (Toronto: University of Toronto Press, 1974), ch. 35.

38   Halldór Laxness, *Independent People: An Epic*, trans. J. A. Thompson (New York: Knopf, 1946). See the section on Halldór Laxness in Chapter 4.

39   H. Auden and Louis MacNeice, *Letters from Iceland* (London: Faber, 1937), p. 213.

40   *Gerpla* has been translated into English by Katherine John as *The Happy Warriors* (London: Methuen, 1958). *Fóstbrœðra saga* has been translated by Lee M. Hollander in *The Sagas of Kormák and the Sworn Brothers* (Princeton: Princeton University Press, 1949).

41   *The Saga of Gisli*, trans. George Johnston (London: Dent, 1963).

42   *The Saga of Tristram and Ísönd*, trans. Paul Schach (Lincoln: University of Nebraska Press, 1973).

43   Peter Hallberg, *The Icelandic Saga*, trans. Paul Schach (Lincoln: University of Nebraska Press, 1962), p. 149.

44   *Eyrbyggja Saga*, trans. Hermann Pálsson and Paul Edwards (Harmondsworth: Penguin, 1989), pp. 1–2.

45   Kirsten Wolf and Julian Meldon D'Arcy, 'Walter Scott og Eyrbyggja', *Skírnir* 162 (1988), pp. 257–8, 267–8.

46   Hallberg, *The Icelandic Saga*, pp. 78–80. Cf. Sigurður A. Magnússon, *Northern Sphinx: Iceland and the Icelanders from the Settlement to the Present* (London: Hurst, 1977), p. 75.

❧ Chapter 3 ❧

Folk Belief and Folktales

Distance makes the mountains blue
and the men great.

Jóhann Sigurjónsson in his play
Eyvindur of the Mountains

Introduction

THE COLLECTING AND RECORDING of legends and folktales began in
an organized way as a result of stimulus from the romantic movement
in Germany in the early nineteenth century. This in turn was a reaction
to the Enlightenment, with its boundless faith in reason, its scepticism
towards religion, and its alleged lack of a sense of history. The romantic philosophers and authors, composers and painters longed instead
to escape from the grey reality of everyday life. They wanted free
scope for imagination and emotion. The political dimension of the
romantic movement—patriotism and an aspiration for freedom from
oppression—was a consequence of the foreign rule of Napoleon.

The German romantics thus turned to popular and national culture,
to their native language, to their own folk belief, tales, and legends.
The Middle Ages, which had previously been disparaged, became the
focus of attention. In cultural centres such as Dresden, Heidelberg, and
Vienna, interested connoisseurs assembled for reading evenings. They
also applauded musical soirées, where the programme could include
the *Lieder* of Franz Schubert and the romances of Robert Schumann—

sometimes rendered by his wife Clara, a brilliant concert pianist. It is against this cultural background that we must see the origin of the fairy tales published in 1812–14 by the brothers Jakob and Wilhelm Grimm, and the growing interest in folklore.

The influence of the German romantics spread rapidly, like ripples on a pond, to England (Coleridge), France (Madame de Staël), and Scandinavia.

Iceland had its own Heinrich Heine in the romantically coloured Jónas Hallgrímsson (1807–45), who wrote lyrical nature poems. This Icelandic national poet had many strings on his bow. He was a scientist who had studied the Icelandic landscape. His enraptured poems in the journal *Fjölnir*—with motifs such as rambling in the mountains around Þingvellir, and the immortal characters in the Icelandic sagas—roused the slumbering national feeling of his compatriots. Along with the rest of Fjölnir's men, he thus laid the foundation for Jón Sigurðsson's struggle for independence. He saw the cultural value of the distinctive national character of the Icelanders, as revealed in sagas and legends. He took up the torch from the great men of the commonwealth, and he passed the message on in his poems.

It may be mentioned in passing that Jónas Hallgrímsson is still widely read: generation after generation of Icelanders continue to read his poems. They are frequently recited and quoted. A collected and revised edition of his works was published in 1989.[1]

In the mid-nineteenth century, Jón Árnason, librarian at the then Diocesan Library in Reykjavík (now the National Library), published his *Íslenzkar þjóðsögur og æfintýri* (2 vols., 1862–64). Produced in collaboration with German scholars, it is dedicated to Jakob Grimm. It was a magnificent cultural achievement. The Icelanders had already written down their classical sagas; now their folktales were also saved from oblivion. The rescue may have come at the last minute. The national hero Jón Sigurðsson had sounded an eloquent warning of this danger in an article in 1860:[2]

> We attach a low value to the folktales that surround us. Wherever we turn, they shoot up around us like little flowers. They grow with us in our youth. They live under the tongues of our mothers and foster-mothers. They could grow into beautiful oaks and flower-gods. But they

disappear before that, because we throw them away like withered autumn hawkbits.

Through Jón Árnason's work and comparable collections,[3] we still have access to countless folktales and legends,[4] stories with elements of superstition and details of remarkable customs of hoary antiquity. Sometimes they go back to hazy memories of pagan times, sometimes to the dawn of history, when people still clearly perceived both Jesus Christ and the Devil as concrete figures.

Our newly Christianized forefathers also believed in a world inhabited by 'the other people', creatures belonging to the hidden people (*huldufólk*). They lived underground and inside mountains, cairns, and mounds. They were invisible to most ordinary mortals. They were similar to us in many ways, and like us they could also be good or evil. In fact, they reflected the entire gamut of human qualities, feelings, and passions. Like the brownie, a friendly fairy woman (*huldukona*) could bring fortune and prosperity to a farm. Wights (*vættir*) protected a place or a country, as long as nobody worried or enraged them.

Some Well-known Folktales and Legends

The phantasmagoria of popular belief also included hostile terrors such as elves who lived in boulders and burial mounds, and ugly trolls from distant mountains. In Icelandic folk belief these trolls are usually depicted as lascivious giantesses. According to the tale of 'Trunt, Trunt, and the Trolls in the Fells', a man out picking Iceland lichen (for its edible fronds) is captured and carried off by one such troll woman. After three years, he appears before his friends, now in the form of a horrible troll. He no longer believes in God, but in 'trunt, trunt, and the trolls in the fells'.[5]

This tale reflects the powerlessness of a poor little human against dreadful giants. It reminds us of other tiny literary figures, such as Thumbelina, Hans Christian Andersen's delicate poetic creation. In a similar way, Jonathan Swift in his ironic social satire *Gulliver's Travels* lets the shipwrecked Gulliver meet the Lilliputians. For him they are microscopically small, but they still manage to tie him down while he sleeps. This takes place on his first voyage. On the next one,

Gulliver finds himself in the reverse situation, as a terrified midget among the giants of Brobdingnag, 'these enormous barbarians'. One of the giants holds him carefully like an insect between his finger and thumb. Another shuts him in a little box for safe keeping.[6]

These distorted pictures of reality all have the same moral. Man's encounter with the rest of the world would do better for some tolerance, consideration, and mutual respect.

In the Icelandic sagas—as in some of Edgar Allan Poe's classic short stories—we meet ghosts, restless spirits who return to torment the living in various ways. Ghosts occur frequently in Icelandic folktales. A ghost may not mention the name of God, nor any person's name containing the name of God (Icelandic *Guð*, a common element in names of both men and women, like the Greek *Theo* in Theodore, Theodora, and Theophilus). The ghost in the tale of 'The Deacon of Myrká' therefore calls his beloved Guðrún by the name 'Garún'.[7]

In Icelandic folk belief one should beware of meeting ghosts, who can appear in the form of *draugar* (living corpses), or as *fylgjur* (accompanying spirits). If sent to hurt or kill a person, they are known as *sendingar*. These 'emissaries' are conjured up by magic and sent to wreak vengeance; they are usually ghosts who have been raised from the dead and forced to do the will of the person who conjured them up. They are always sent to cause harm to an enemy.

As regards *fylgjur*, the inherited popular conceptions have varied. In ancient times, up until the eighteenth century, a *fylgja* was considered benevolent, an accompanying spirit guaranteeing protection. It could appear in the form of a woman or an animal. It often reflected some aspect of a person's character. A cunning person, for example, could be accompanied by a fox. In the eighteenth century, however, people began to fear the *fylgja*. It was said to be a sort of ghost, persecuting a family with disease and misfortune over many generations. People believed that frustrated love could conjure up a *fylgja*.

In popular belief there were also black magicians with the power to revive the dead. One famous example of a person with this dangerous faculty was Doctor Johann Faust of the University of Heidelberg, who lived in the sixteenth century. In Iceland we have Loftur Þorsteinsson, a gifted student at the Latin School at Hólar in northern Iceland, who lived in the eighteenth century.[8] Transformed and given new depth by the creative imagination, the former appears in the literary master-pieces by Marlowe and Goethe, and the latter in the play *Loftur the Magician* by the poet and playwright Jóhann Sigurjónsson (1880–1919). This is based on the motif of an Icelandic folktale, as is the same writer's *Eyvindur of the Mountains*, a play about an outlaw in the eighteenth century, which has been performed on several stages in Europe.[9]

Iceland is an extensive, sparsely populated island. In its variegated landscape—with white glaciers and slumbering volcanoes, raging waterfalls and black or grey-green fields of lava, with flowering mead-ows and snow-capped mountains—there is plenty of room for the supernatural beings of popular belief. In bygone days, storytellers could bring them to life with such intensity that the listeners felt they could see them and started to dream about them. These fairies and elves, these giants and ghosts stood out so clearly in their imagination that it must have appeared beyond all doubt that they really existed. The listeners were at once captivated and terrified by the stories of these beings from the other world.

As the father of the house read stories aloud by the flickering flames of the hearth, or by the light of a reeking whale-oil lamp, the darkness was compact outside the window of dried animal cauls or hides. It was important to stay indoors all night, to keep out of reach of trolls, until they were put to flight by the ringing of a bell or the slanting rays of the rising sun.

The belief in magic and devil-worship was reflected in hysterical notions about witches. It was said that they flew on magic staffs to give themselves in vile orgies to the prince of darkness. Blind, irra-tional hatred of supposed witches—often old women living on their own—degenerated in the sixteenth and seventeenth centuries into barbaric witch trials, which sent many unfortunate women to die at the stake throughout Europe.

There were also witch trials in Iceland in the seventeenth century, although on a relatively small scale. About twenty men men were condemned and executed for witchcraft, but only one woman. In bygone Iceland there was a principle that violence against women could never be accepted.

Superstition and magic also gave rise to customs which have survived to our times, although we may be unaware of their mythical origin. Bonfires, maypoles, and the like are all relics of pre-Christian belief.

The Norsemen who colonized Iceland knew nothing of the *land-vættir*, the guardian spirits of the country. They did not know how to behave so as not to upset these spirits. They had to be shown respect. The pagan law of Iceland (*Úlfljótslög*) began with a statute based on this belief. Before land was sighted, a sailor with a dragon's head at his prow had to take it down; the sight of the gaping jaws of the dragon could frighten the guardian spirits of the country.[10]

Once, towards the end of the tenth century, the guardian spirits protected Iceland from an attack by the Danish king Haraldur blátönn (Harald Bluetooth). Snorri Sturluson tells the story in his *Ólafs saga Tryggvasonar*, which is part of *Heimskringla*, his history of the kings of Norway.[11] According to the saga, Haraldur proposed to sail with his army to Iceland to exact vengeance for the mockery which all the Icelanders had shown towards him. There was a law in Iceland that everyone was to compose a lampoon about King Haraldur and his bailiff Birgir. The reason for the lampoon was that an Icelandic vessel had stranded in Denmark, where the Danes declared it a wreck and seized all the property.

To prepare for this expedition, Haraldur asked a warlock to swim to Iceland in the shape of a whale and reconnoitre the country. This proved to be a difficult undertaking for the warlock. No matter what coast he tried to land at, he was prevented by the guardian creatures, in the shape of a dragon, a bird of prey, a bull, and a giant.

It was consequently natural for the Icelanders to choose these guard-ian creatures as the heraldic figures which support the crowned shield in the national coat of arms. This was introduced in 1918, at the same time as Iceland received her own national and merchant flags. When the republic was proclaimed in 1944, the royal crown was removed from the arms, but the *landvættir* remain. They are also depicted on Icelandic coins, stamps, and on the façade of the Althing.

The leading character in many legends is the Icelandic historian Sæmundur Sigfússon (1056–1133), who studied in France in the elev-enth century, presumably at a monastic school—folk belief identifies it with the Black School, an institution run by the Devil in northern

Anyone who visits the University of Iceland today will see a concrete reminder of the legend of 'Sæmundur and the Seal'. The view in front of the main building is dominated by an eye-catching sculpture by Ásmundur Sveinsson (1893–1982). It shows Sæmundur astride a seal, with his psalter in hand.

France. It is understandable that Sæmundur is the subject of so many tales. He was not just a learned historian, a priest, and the owner of a large ancestral estate at Oddi in southern Iceland. This Icelandic Faust was also evidently shrewder than Old Nick himself. Sæmundur was able to outwit him, as we shall now see in the legend of 'Sæmundur and the Shadow'.[12]

> In the Black School there was a rule that all students should attend for three years. Those who finished their studies in the same year all had to leave the school on the same day and at the same hour. The Devil would then take the last one to come out through the door. The students therefore drew lots to decide who would be the last to leave.
>
> Once there were three Icelanders at the school: Sæmundur, Kálfur, and Hálfdan. They were all due to leave together after three years of study. To the delight of his comrades, Sæmundur offered to leave last. As he stood in the doorway, the sun shone in on him and reflected his shadow on the wall. As the Devil was about to seize him, he said, 'I am not the last. Don't you see the one behind me?'
>
> The Devil snatched at the shadow, taking it to be a person, while Sæmundur narrowly escaped through the door. From that day forth, Sæmundur never had a shadow, since the Devil had kept it.

According to another tale, it was on the back of a seal that Sæmund-

ur returned to Iceland, where he settled at Oddi as a priest.[13] The legend
of 'Sæmundur and the Seal' has been retold in the following words:[14]

> As Sæmundur, Kálfur, and Hálfdan were returning from the Black
> School, they heard that the living of Oddi was vacant. So they all hurried
> to the king, and each asked it for himself. The king, well knowing with
> whom he had to deal, promised it to him who should be the first to reach
> the place. Upon this Sæmundur immediately called the devil to him and
> said, 'Swim with me on your back, to Iceland; and if you can bring me
> to shore without wetting the skirt of my coat, you shall have me for your
> own.' The devil agreed to this, so he changed himself into a seal and
> swam off with Sæmundur on his back. On the way Sæmundur amused
> himself by reading the book of the Psalms of David. Before very long
> they came close to the coast of Iceland. When he saw this he closed the
> book and smote the seal with it upon the head, so that it sank, and
> Sæmundur swam to land. And as, when Sæmundur got to shore, the
> skirts of his coat were wet, the devil lost the bargain, but Sæmundur got
> the living.

The legend of 'Sæmundur and the Witch in Saxony' is about one of
the learned man's erotic escapades. He had adventures like these both
as a student and later on as an established priest. Sæmundur had
promised to marry a Saxon woman with magical powers, but he failed
to keep his word. Many years later, she determined to avenge herself
by sending him a gilded chest with the instructions that only he was
allowed to open it. When a messenger came with the chest, Sæmundur
was in church. He was not in the least surprised, since he himself was
well versed in the black art, and suspected what the chest might
contain. He welcomed the messenger and asked him to put the chest
on the altar. It lay there that night. The next day, Sæmundur rode with
the chest up to the top of Mount Hekla, where he threw it down into
a crevice. Hekla then began to spout fire for the first time.

There is a similar ending to the tale of 'Katla or Katla's Chasm', but
it begins differently:[15]

> Once upon a time there was a monastery with a church at Þykkvabæjar-
> klaustur. It is said that its bell was so loud that it could be heard ringing
> far out on the sandy plain—particularly important in this age of magic
> and witchcraft. The abbot had a housekeeper whose name was Katla.
> She was experienced in the black art. She owned a pair of magic trousers
> which gave the wearer the ability to run without getting tired. Many
> people, even the abbot, were afraid of her because of her magic. At the
> same place there was a shepherd whose name was Barði. He often had

to endure sharp reproaches from Katla if there were any sheep missing when he drove them into the fold.

Once in the autumn the abbot and his housekeeper went off to a feast. Before they came home, Barði was to round up the sheep, but he could not find them all. He thought of solving the problem by putting on Katla's trousers. With their help he was able to run and round up the herd. When Katla came home she understood that Barði had borrowed her trousers. She carried him away in secret and suffocated him in a barrel of curds, where she let the body lie.

No one knew what had become of Barði. Towards the end of winter, when the curds in the barrel were running low, people could hear these words being spoken to Katla: 'Barði will soon show himself.' When she realized that her evil deed would be discovered, and that it would cost her dear, she pulled on her trousers. Running out of the monastery, she headed north-west to the glacier. Up on the glacier she threw herself down into a chasm. At least, that is what people believed, since they never saw her again. Soon afterwards, a glacial outburst began, running down towards the monastery. It was believed that it had been caused by her black magic. Ever since then, the chasm has been called Katla's Chasm.

Like Sæmundur the Wise, Einar the priest was experienced in the black art. So was his son Þórarinn, who was known as a wizard. This is the subject of the tale 'Einar Attracts a Whale by Magic'.[16]

Once there was such a famine in the district that Einar was forced to use magic to entice a whale. . . . When the priest came to a place where whales were often stranded, he dug himself down in the sand. Meanwhile he told his son Þórarinn to keep a close watch on the sea. The weather was clear. Down in his trench, the priest said charms, while Þórarinn observed the changing weather. Finally, he told his father that it was getting dark over the sea. The priest said that they could now expect something to happen. He continued to recite his spells louder than ever. At once a huge bank of clouds drifted over the sea, and a strong north wind drove high waves towards the shore. An enormous whale was thrown up on to the beach. The priest then crawled out of his hiding place in the sand. He ordered the men to cut up the whale, carry it back to his house, and boil it. No one was to eat any of the whale before this was done.

The priest let a pauper eat the first bit, but he fell down dead. Then the priest ate some of it himself, but he took no harm. He then told them all that it was safe to eat. Neither he nor any other man took any harm. It is said that he saved the entire parish by means of this whale, for which he took no payment.

It was only the pauper who had to pay with his life, and possibly his soul.

Let us round off with a well-loved tale, 'My Jón's Soul'.[17] It has been congenially visualized in a series of drawings by the Icelandic painter Muggur, who is presented in the next Chapter.

> There were once an old cottager and his wife, who lived together. The old man was rather quarrelsome and disagreeable, and, what's more, he was lazy and useless about the house; his old woman was not at all pleased about it, and she would often grumble at him and say the only thing he was any good at was squandering what she had scraped together—for she herself was constantly at work and tried by hook or by crook to earn what they needed, and was always good at getting her own way with anybody she had to deal with. But even if they did not agree about some things, the old woman loved her husband dearly and never let him go short.
>
> Now things went on the same way for a long time, but one day the old man fell sick, and it was obvious that he was in a bad way. The old woman was sitting up with him, and when he grew weaker, it occurred to her that he could hardly be very well prepared for death, and that this meant there was some doubt as to whether he would be allowed to enter Heaven. So she thinks to herself that the best plan will be for her to try and put her husband's soul on the right road herself. Then she took a small bag and held it over her husband's nose and mouth, so that when the breath of life leaves him it passes into this bag, and she ties it up at once.
>
> Then off she goes towards Heaven, carrying the bag in her apron, comes to the borders of the Kingdom of Heaven, and knocks on the door.
>
> Out comes Saint Peter, and asks what her business may be.

The tale 'My Jón's soul' has been visualized in a series of seven drawings by Muggur. Here we see the last three scenes in the series. — To the left: The old woman debated in vain with the Blessed Virgin Mary. — In the middle: She flung the bag with the soul of her Jón far into the halls of heaven. — To the right: She returned home, pleased and with a happy smile on her face.

'A very good morning to you, sir,' says the old woman. 'I've come here with the soul of that Jón of mine—you'll have heard of him, most likely—and now I'm wanting to ask you to let him in.'

'Yes, yes, yes,' says Peter, 'but unfortunately I can't. I have indeed heard of that Jón of yours, but I never heard anything good of him yet.'

Then the old woman said: 'Well, really, Saint Peter, I'd never have believed it, that you could be so hard-hearted! You must be forgetting what happened to you in the old days, when you denied your Master.'

At that, Peter went back in and shut the door, and the old woman remained outside, sighing bitterly. But when a little time has passed, she knocks on the door again, and out comes Saint Paul. She greets him and asks him his name, and he tells her who he is. Then she pleads with him for the soul of her Jón—but he said he didn't want to hear another word from her about that, and said that her Jón deserved no mercy.

Then the old woman got angry, and said: 'It's all very well for you, Paul! I suppose you deserved mercy in the old days, when you were persecuting God and men! I reckon I'd better stop asking any favours from you.'

So now Paul shuts the door as fast as he can. But when the old woman knocks for the third time, out comes the Blessed Virgin Mary.

'Hail, most blessed Lady,' says the old woman. 'I do hope you'll allow that Jón of mine in, even though that Peter and Paul won't allow it.'

'It's a great pity, my dear,' says Mary, 'but I daren't, because he really was such a brute, that Jón of yours.'

'Well, I can't blame you for that,' says the old woman. 'But all the same, I did think you would know that other people can have their little weaknesses as well as you—or have you forgotten by now that you once had a baby, and no father for it?'

Mary would hear no more, but shut the door as fast as she could.

For the fourth time, the old woman knocks on the door. Then out comes Christ himself, and asks what she's doing there.

Then she spoke very humbly: 'I wanted to beg you, my dear Saviour, to let this poor wretch's soul warm itself near the door.'

'It's that Jón,' answered Christ. 'No, woman; he had no faith in Me.'

Just as He said this He was about to shut the door, but the old woman was not slow, far from it—she flung the bag with the soul in it right past him, so that it hurtled far into the halls of Heaven, but then the door was slammed and bolted.

Then a great weight was lifted from the old woman's heart when Jón got into the Kingdom of Heaven in spite of everything, and she went home happy; and we know nothing more about her, nor about what became of Jón's soul after that.

Surviving Belief in the Supernatural

We can understand the origin of folk belief and legends if we take an imaginative leap into the past.

We have already delineated the conceptual world of the medieval Norsemen. It combined ideas of pagan origin with clerical teachings about life as a duel between God and the Devil. The church was the centre of every community, but 'the other people' were ever-present as well.

When people saw the bewitching dance of the mists over the wet meadows, they imagined that they could see enticing elves and friendly fairies and brownies. But there were also hidden creatures who instilled fear: giants and trolls, dark elves and dead people returning to haunt the living. Our forefathers lived in poorly lit homes, surrounded by a menacing darkness. They were afraid of malicious beings in the wilderness; they feared ghosts in moonlit cemeteries with mossy gravestones.

Theirs was a completely different environment from our own. We live in a world of electric light, technology, and computers. We are surrounded by aeroplanes, express trains and underground trains, buses and cars, neon signs and loudspeakers. We live in homes where television, video, and radio compete with the telephone and the record-player for our attention.

Because of these technological changes, 'neo-religious fashions'[18]—like theosophy, spiritualism, religious sects—and modern school education, it is understandable that old superstitions are tending to wane or disappear. They are rapidly being put to flight, like the morning dew in the warming rays of dawn, or as the bold rainbow over the heavens disappears just after the sun has fully burst forth through the rain.

In this respect Iceland is probably similar to most other countries. It nevertheless seems as if superstition in various forms and the belief in ghosts still has a remarkably strong grasp on the minds of the Icelandic people. Recently published surveys, as we shall see later, show that about half of the population still believe in the existence of some sort of 'hidden people'.

This is explained not least by the dramatic quality of the Icelandic landscape with its ever-changing colours. In this land of ice and fire, framed by glaciers and slumbering volcanoes, there is plenty of room for all the creatures of folk belief. We may sense their presence as our gaze gets lost in the direction of sulphurous geysers and steaming hot springs, or we may be captivated by the play of light over the endless heaths, or by the swirl of the mists over plains of lava, coal-black with their gravel and boulders.

We may mention some examples of these survivals of superstition in Iceland.

According to popular belief, humans should avoid certain places which are frequented by elves. Some Icelandic guides advise tourists not to climb certain cairns; instead they should add a stone to the pile. Above all, no one should build on these enchanted spots (*álagablettir*), whether they are cairns, mounds, giant rocks, or meadows belonging to the hidden people. It is likely that notions of this kind are based on a combination of superstition and practical experience over many centuries. These enchanted spots have occasionally been the scene of avalanches, landslides, and similar disasters.

Early in the twentieth century, the Swedish writer and artist Albert Engström, when visiting a clergyman in northern Iceland, saw one such enchanted spot. He faithfully records the clergyman's telling statement about associated ideas in Icelandic folk belief:[19]

Suddenly I observed that I was walking in unusually long grass.
'Why has this not been mown?'
He was slow to answer.
'Well, this is an *álagablettur*. There are meadows which have belonged to the hidden people from time immemorial, and no one is allowed to mow them. Not that I believe in the like, but you can't eradicate that belief in the people here. I would prefer to tend the rectory land properly and use it to the full, but it would cause such bad blood in the district that I would make myself impossible. If anyone mows these *álagablettir*, there is always a misfortune at once: a horse dies, a sheep dies, or something even worse happens. The hidden people are like us, they keep house like us, they eat as we do, and they have livestock. People put out food for their children, milk and so on. And one has to organize one's life in part so as not to disturb them. I don't fish in the river, for example, when the hidden people leave special signs to show that it is their turn to fish.'

On one occasion, rationally minded American military personnel, not believing in supernatural phenomena, ignored the warnings of the local populace and started building in one such dangerous spot. The project was a complete failure.

The Icelanders still show great respect for enchanted spots. In Kópavogur, the neighbouring town of Reykjavík, there were plans in 1987—according to a highly publicized television report—to widen a narrow part of a road known as Álfshólsvegur, literally 'Elf-Hill Road'. The narrow section was occasioned by a huge rock sticking out into the road. The road builders tried to remove the rock by boring through it with a pneumatic drill. The drill bit inexplicably broke. The roads department therefore decided not to disturb the elves who lived there. The rock was allowed to stand where it was. It is still there today.

There sometimes appears to be magic power in words, particularly in Iceland. An Icelandic pacifist once thought that she could prevent one of NATO's naval manoeuvres which was planned to take place near her home by a western fiord. Her approach was traditional in style: she declaimed an abusive poem. The manoeuvre was indeed cancelled, because of unexpected bad weather. Storms blew in over the fiords. Actually, there are few places in the world where the winds can blow so violently and so suddenly as in Iceland.

This picture of surviving superstition in Iceland would not be complete without an account of the hauntings that have taken place at Höfði.[20]

Höfði, a name which means 'headland', is a wooden house in Jugend style built in 1909 on an expansive site in Reykjavík, near the open sea. It was prefabricated by a factory in Norway, which gave the entrance hall the typically Norwegian 'dragon style'. Having been shipped to Iceland, it was assembled by Icelandic craftsmen to become the residence of the French consul Brillouin. He soon came into conflict with the authorities, since he had built the house without waiting for planning permission. This controversy was settled in Brillouin's favour. Iceland chose to turn a blind eye to the matter—'out of consideration for the ties of friendship with France'. Besides, people thought the house was beautiful. Yet Monsieur Brillouin did not stay long in Höfði, allegedly because his new house was haunted.

For the first fifty years of its existence, Höfði had nearly ten different owners who succeeded each other in rapid succession. One of them was the lawyer and poet Einar Benediktsson (1864–1940). During his period as an official in northern Iceland he had once questioned a young girl named Sólborg Jónsdóttir. She was suspected of incest, having given birth to a child allegedly by her own brother. This case, known as the Svalbarð Case,[21] had been judged by the young Einar Benediktsson in his capacity of county sheriff. Immediately afterwards, when he was playing cards with a clergyman and a few other people in the living-room of the big farm and rectory of Svalbarð by Þistilfjörður, the girl was heard to scream. In her despair over the verdict—the child was to be taken from her—she had locked herself in a room and taken her own life by swallowing poison.

The thought of Sólborg's tragic suicide was to haunt Einar for the rest of his life. He was a highly sensitive person. Perhaps he had a guilty conscience. At all events, he often had hallucinations where he thought he could hear or see the girl. A little later, Einar was being rowed over a river. The ferryman must have seen Sólborg's ghost, since he asked Einar: 'Aren't you going to pay for the girl too?'

Several years after the Svalbarð Case, Einar Benediktsson bought Höfði. But he was afraid of the dark. He was also tormented from time to time by the sight of the girl's ghost.

Between 1938 and 1951 Höfði was occupied by diplomats. It was last the residence of the Head of the British Mission, John Greenway, a bachelor who was afraid of ghosts. Höfði had its obvious qualities as an official residence. Mr Greenway, however, could not sleep peacefully at night, because of the clamour of ghosts. He could not bear it. He sent one dispatch after the other to the Foreign Office, asking for a new residence instead of Höfði. The Foreign Office finally acceded.

Since 1958, the house has been owned by the city of Reykjavík and used for special occasions. The historical building is ideal for the purpose. It is a delightful house, with a breathtaking view of sky and sea.

About a decade ago, the harmony at Höfði was disturbed by new hauntings. The glasses on the trays, for example, were known to jump. The neatly folded linen napkins fell to the floor, as did the great painting in the dining room, even though the nail sat fast in the wall. Door handles came loose. When the guests had gone home in the evening, all the lights would suddenly go out. The staff felt that something was moving in the house.

Then a Danish-born woman, Ása Skarphéðinsdóttir, had the idea of speaking to the ghost. She reproved it in firm but friendly terms. According to her own account, the ghost disappeared after this conversation. Since then, no hauntings have been reported from Höfði.

Ása Skarphéðinsdóttir's action may sound like a fantastic invention. It has been confirmed, however, by the janitor of Höfði, who was present on the occasion. He emphasizes that Ása Skarphéðinsdóttir is calm, balanced, and of sound judgement. In his view, the events may have a natural explanation, but he is personally convinced that Ása firmly believed that they were caused by a ghost.

In October 1986 Höfði achieved world fame. After just ten days of hectic preparations, it was used for the summit meeting of the super-power leaders Ronald Reagan and Mikhail S. Gorbachev. The meeting was followed by about three thousand foreign journalists who invaded Iceland.

This historic meeting suddenly brought the Icelandic people into the limelight. Iceland and Reykjavík found their place on the world map, in a wholly positive way. This has manifested itself in a growth in tourism since the summit meeting. Moreover, 'the Reykjavík spirit' became synonymous all over the world with hopes of peace and détente between nations.

Icelandic Superstition as a Subject of Scientific Study

In 1974 the University of Iceland conducted a nationwide survey of the Icelanders and the extent of their religiosity, Bible-reading, and participation in spiritualistic meetings, and their attitudes to paranormal phenomena of various kinds: telepathy, clairvoyance, psychic dreams, and superstition. In the latter area the questions dealt with the hidden people, accompanying spirits, and enchanted spots.

The study covered 1,132 people aged 30–60, selected at random from the population registers. The questions were answered by 902 people. The study was thus representative of the entire Icelandic population, which was then about 220,000.[22]

The questions concerning superstition obtained the following responses, expressed as percentages:

The existence of hidden people (*huldufólk*)

impossible	10
improbable	18
possible	33
probable	15
certain	7
don't know	17

The existence of accompanying spirits (*fylgjur*)

impossible	5
improbable	12
possible	35
probable	21
certain	16
don't know	11

The existence of enchanted spots (*álagablettir*)

impossible	5
improbable	14
possible	35
probable	22
certain	11
don't know	13

The proportion of Icelanders who said that they believed in accompanying spirits or regarded their existence as possible was thus 72 per cent. For enchanted spots the corresponding figure was 68 per cent and for the hidden people 55 per cent.

Notes to Chapter 3

1   *Ritverk Jónasar Hallgrímssonar*, 4 vols. (Reykjavík: Svart á hvítu, 1989).

2   The quotation is taken from Jón Árnason, *Íslenskar þjóðsögur og ævintýri*, reissue in 6 vols. (Reykjavík: Þjóðsaga, 1961).

3   Our account is based mainly on Jón Árnason's collection, together with Einar Ólafur Sveinsson's *Íslenzkar þjóðsögur og ævintýri með myndum eftir íslenzka listamenn* (Reykjavík: Leiftur, 1944). A representative sample has been translated into English by Jacqueline Simpson, *Icelandic Folktales and Legends* (London: Batsford, 1972); see also her *Legends of Icelandic Magicians* (Cambridge: Brewer, 1975). Alan Boucher has translated three volumes of folktales, published in Reykjavík in 1977 by the Iceland Review Library: *Ghosts, Witchcraft and the Other World*; *Elves, Trolls and Elemental Beings*; and *Adventures, Outlaws and Past Events*.

4   Folklorists often apply a rough classification of tales into legends (Icelandic *þjóðsagnir*), which are told as true stories, and other kinds of folktales which are told as entertaining fantasies, such as fairy tales (Icelandic *ævintýri*, German *Märchen*) and jocular tales. See Simpson, *Icelandic Folktales and Legends*, p. 3.

5   Simpson, *Icelandic Folktales and Legends*, pp. 78–9.

6   Jonathan Swift, *Gulliver's Travels* (1726). When this Irish writer (1667–1745) wrote *Gulliver's Travels* he was 58 years old. He was disillusioned with life and had grown into an embittered misanthrope, but he had polished his style to perfection. *Gulliver's Travels* thus became a witty, entertaining satire on humanity and its weaknesses, and especially on English society after 1720. The Emperor of Lilliput represents King George I, while the treasurer Flimnap stands for the prime minister, Robert Walpole.

7   Simpson, *Icelandic Folktales and Legends*, pp. 132–6.

8   See the tale of 'Loft the Enchanter' in Boucher, *Ghosts, Witchcraft and the Other World*, pp. 23–8. Jóhann Sigurjónsson's play *Galdra-Loftur* has been translated as *The Wish* by Einar Haugen in his *Fire and Ice: Three Icelandic Plays* (Madison: University of Wisconsin Press, 1967).

9   Jóhann Sigurjónsson, *Eyvindur of the Mountains*, trans. Francis P. Magoun (Reykjavík: Helgafell, 1961). The folktale of 'Eyvind of the Fells' is retold in Boucher, *Adventures, Outlaws and Past Events*, pp. 45–56. See also Chapter 4, 'Icelandic Literature in the Twentieth Century: A Survey'.

10   Jón Jóhannesson, *A History of the Old Icelandic Commonwealth: Íslendinga*

Saga, trans. Haraldur Bessason (Winnipeg: University of Manitoba Press, 1974), p. 94.

11   Snorri Sturluson, *Heimskringla: History of the Kings of Norway*, trans. Lee M. Hollander (Austin: University of Texas Press, 1964), pp. 173–4 (*Ólafs saga Tryggvasonar*, ch. 33).

12   This legend, along with other stories about Sæmundur, can be read in Boucher, *Ghosts, Witchcraft and the Other World*, pp. 13–20.

13   A statue outside the main entrance to the University of Iceland depicts Sæmundur astride a seal, with his psalter in his hand. See the section on the sculptor Ásmundur Sveinsson in Chapter 4.

14   *Icelandic Legends*, trans. George E. J. Powell and Eiríkur Magnússon (London, 1864), pp. 230–1.

15   A version of this can be found in Powell and Magnússon, *Icelandic Legends*, pp. 134–5.

16   Jón Árnason, *Íslenskar þjóðsögur og ævintýri*, vol. 1, p. 513.

17   Simpson, *Icelandic Folktales and Legends*, pp. 196–9. Lars Svensson, in 'Om sagan om Jóns själ', *Gardar* 9 (1978), pp. 17–22, points out how this folktale inspired the poet Davíð Stefánsson to write the play *Gullna hliðið* (translated as *The Golden Gate* by G. M. Gathorne Hardy in *Fire and Ice*, ed. Einar Haugen). This popular play was first performed in 1941 by the Reykjavík Dramatic Society and revived in 1976–77 by the Icelandic National Theatre, produced by Sveinn Einarsson.

18   Sigurbjörn Einarsson, 'Islands tusen år', in *Våra nordiska syskonkyrkor* (Stockholm: Proprius, 1985), p. 89.

19   Albert Engström, *Åt Häcklefjäll* (Stockholm: Bonnier, 1913), part 2, p. 22.

20   On Höfði see *Húsverndun* (Reykjavík: Torfusamtökin, 1986), pp. 40–1, and Leifur Blumenstein, *Byggingarsaga Höfða* (1985). Cf. Sir Andrew Gilchrist, *Cod Wars and How to Lose Them* (Edinburgh: Q Press, 1978). See also Björn Th. Björnsson, *Seld norðurljós* (Reykjavík: Mál og menning, 1982), pp. 19–20.

21   This case forms the basis for a novel by Thor Vilhjálmsson, *Grámosinn glóir* (The Grey Moss Glistens, 1986). See Chapter 4, 'Icelandic Literature in the Twentieth Century: A Survey'.

22   For an evaluation of the 1974 study and comparable studies in Britain, Sweden, the USA, and elsewhere, see Erlendur Haraldsson, 'Representative National Surveys of Psychic Phenomena' in *Journal of the Society for Psychical Research* 53:801 (1985). Erlendur claims that these studies suggest that the belief in telepathy and psychic dreams is more widespread than was previously assumed.

⁂ Chapter 4 ⁂

The Cultural Heritage as a Source of Inspiration

Forgive us for being a people of
history and not being able to forget
anything.
Halldór Laxness, Íslandsklukkan

Introduction

FROM THE FALL OF THE ICELANDIC commonwealth in 1262, the country was for centuries an isolated colony, far away in the North Atlantic. For superstitious Europeans on the continent, Iceland gave the impression of being an exotic island of magic, with sulphur-spouting volcanoes. The struggle for independence and the coming of new communications helped to break the isolation. Iceland was opened to the surrounding world and a wave of international influences. In the twentieth century these have poured in over the Icelandic people at an increasing speed. The influence on Icelandic society and culture has been significant. This deserves to be mentioned, because it is an essential feature of modern Icelandic life.

Nevertheless, the following survey will concentrate on some of the many Icelanders for whom the native cultural heritage is and will remain their permanent foundation. It has been said that every other Icelander is a poet or a painter. Most of them have a profound national feeling. They include, first and foremost, a large number of poets, authors, and dramatists, all the way from Snorri Sturluson (1179–1241), the poet-priest Hallgrímur Pétursson (1614–74), and the poet Jónas Hallgrímsson (1807–45), one of the first standard-bearers in the struggle for independence. The tradition was continued by men whom we have already met on these pages, like Matthías Jochumsson (1835–1920), Einar Benediktsson (1864–1940), Jóhann Sigurjónsson (1880–1919), and Hannes Hafstein (1861–1922). Equally unforgettable are the prose writer Gunnar Gunnarsson (1889–1975), the playwright Guðmundur Kamban (1888–1945), and the novelist Halldór Laxness (born 1902).

It is unlikely that anyone was better than the poet Steinn Steinarr (1908–58) at interpreting the brooding despair of youth and the social criticism fostered by the crisis of the 1930s. He was unemployed and could not afford to go to school.

From later decades we may mention, for instance, the poets Einar Bragi, Steinunn Sigurðardóttir, and Þórarinn Eldjárn. A particularly strong love of Iceland is shown by Jón Helgason, Snorri Hjartarson, Hannes Sigfússon, Jón úr Vör, Jón Óskar, Hannes Pétursson, and Matthías Johannessen. Since 1959, Matthías has been one of the editors of the largest newspaper in Iceland, *Morgunblaðið*. Prominent dramatists include Jökull Jakobsson, Kjartan Ragnarsson, Guðmundur Steinsson, Birgir Sigurðsson, Svava Jakobsdóttir, and Jónas Árnason. It is difficult to know where to end the list; it could easily be prolonged, since Iceland has so many gifted writers and artists. It is perhaps best to conclude the enumeration with Thor Vilhjálmsson, who in 1988 won the Nordic Council's Prize for Literature for his novel *Grámosinn glóir* (The Grey Moss Glistens).[1]

Naturally, pride of place goes to Halldór Laxness, winner of the Nobel Prize for Literature in 1955. The matter of most of his novels comes from Icelandic history or from Icelandic folk belief.

Motifs from popular beliefs and folktales have also inspired many prominent visual artists. Along with the sculptors Einar Jónsson and Ásmundur Sveinsson we may mention at least four of Iceland's most famous painters, Ásgrímur Jónsson, Guðmundur Thorsteinsson 'Muggur', Jóhannes Kjarval, and Gunnlaugur Scheving. This circle of

Carta Marina was published in Venice in 1539 by the Swedish cartographer Olaus Magnus as a map and a description of the Nordic countries, including Iceland. As such, it is far from being accurate. As a counterpart, the sailing vessels, the gigantic whales and sulphur-spouting volcanoes, depicted in Carta Marina, appeal to our imagination. We also see before us Hekla with its dazzling snowfield and almost feel the smell from the 'eternal sulphur fire'. Carta Marina no doubt received many readers. In folk belief the volcano Hekla was said to be the 'door to the fires of Hell'.

creative artists also includes composers like Jón Leifs and Jón Ásgeirsson, Atli Heimir Sveinsson, and Þorkell Sigurbjörnsson.

Most Icelandic artists have also been captivated by the unique landscape of the island, by visions of fishing and the ocean, the daily struggle for food. This is a characteristic feature of many Icelandic artists—wherever they may be. Examples are Jóhannes Geir (born 1927), with his paintings of ships and horses in motion, and the naive painter Ísleifur Konráðsson (1889–1972). Ísleifur, an unschooled worker from one of the western fiords, did not make his début until the age of 72. With his dreamy, lyrical works, the graphic artist and painter Jón Reykdal (born 1945) helps us to see the links between man and the Icelandic landscape. Other admired painters are Þórarinn B. Þorláksson (1867–1924), Jón Stefánsson (1881–1963), Kristín Jónsdóttir (1888–1958), and Júlíana Sveinsdóttir (1889–1960). Talented representatives of the modern pictorial idiom are Þorvaldur Skúlason (1906–84), Svavar Guðnason (1909–88), and Karl Kvaran (1924–89).

The painters Louisa Matthíasdóttir (born 1917) and Nína Tryggvadóttir (1913–68) show their fascination with their native Iceland, and so also in his special way does Erró (born 1932). This is despite the fact that they have long been settled abroad, the first two painters in the USA, Erró in France. Although they have ended up in other climates, in alien environments, they have not forgotten their roots. Nína is now dead, but she accomplished a great deal during her life, including oil paintings and stained glass with motifs from history and the sagas, and the light-reflecting mosaics on the chancel wall of Skálholt Cathedral, where a picture of Christ presents itself to the congregation.

Louisa and Erró come to Iceland occasionally to paint and exhibit their works. Icelandic landscapes are especially typical of Louisa's paintings. She is known for her stylized horses and sheep, which contrast sharply against sun-drenched grassy slopes on a background colouring of bright-hued mountains, ultramarine fiords, and distant blue skies. One cannot fail to be struck by the way this country's poets and authors, visual artists and composers have been bewitched by such national sources of inspiration as the Icelandic sagas, folksongs, and Eddas, historical events and bygone leaders.

In 1989 Erró (alias Guðmundur Guðmundsson) donated about two thousand of his works to the town of Reykjavík. They include oil paintings, water-colours, lithographs, drawings, collages, sketches, and diaries. They range over his entire career, right from the days when, as a boy, he was given some tubes of paint and scraps of canvas by Jóhannes Kjarval. This was a welcome gift, which inspired in him the dream of becoming an artist. Erró has been described as a 'pop artist' and people have spoken of a special 'Erró style'. He himself dislikes hackneyed phrases and labels. He experiments, ever searching, never getting stuck in any one artistic vein. For him a painting is 'a sort of journey through form, space, and style'.

Erró is undoubtedly the best-known modern Icelandic visual artist. Art museums and wealthy collectors all over the world compete to acquire works by this master. Yet Erró prefers to donate them to Iceland. The idea is that they will decorate the walls of the stone houses at Korpúlfsstaðir, a large farm north of Reykjavík built in the jubilee year of 1930, but ultimately going back to the Middle Ages. Reykjavík will thus gain yet another artistic citadel. It already has the National Art Gallery and the Trade Union Gallery, as well as museums with the works of Einar Jónsson, Ásmundur Sveinsson, and Sigurjón Ólafsson (all sculptors), and Ásgrímur Jónsson and Jóhannes Kjarval (painters).

In this connection we may also mention artists such as Einar Hákonarson (born 1945), a skilled exponent of many art forms, the graphic artist Ragnheiður Jónsdóttir (born 1933), Ásgerður Búadóttir (born 1920), who weaves in wool and is known for her tapestries with applied horsehair, the stained-glass artist Leifur Breiðfjörð (born 1945), the goldsmith Jens Guðjónsson (born 1920), and the visual artist Sigrún Guðjónsdóttir ('Rúna', born 1926), who expresses herself in ceramics, design, and painting. Rúna and her husband, the sculptor Gestur Þorgrímsson, have decorated a whole wall in the new dining-room of the Nordic Cultural Centre at Hässelby Castle outside Stockholm in Sweden.

Thanks to all these imaginative Icelanders, we have clearly delineated pictures of what is genuinely Icelandic. We shall not forget them. Thanks to them, it is also easier to understand Icelanders today.

The principles by which a selection is made can always be debated. Some subjectivity is inevitable. Our small selection could easily have been increased, but it would have made the book cumbersome to handle and dry as dust. The purpose of this book is to communicate some insights about Iceland yesterday and today. It is not intended to serve as an encyclopaedia.

On this matter it is worth listening to what Albert Engström has to say. In his account of his visit to the island he points out that Iceland had been described by only three other Swedes before him:[2]

> My predecessors have also freed me from the otherwise inescapable duty of providing a revision course in Icelandic history and geology. Consult a good encyclopaedia! The truly curious person can buy Herrman's book, the Teutonic thoroughness of which will satisfy even the greatest thirst for knowledge.

What the small population of Iceland has achieved—especially in the field of culture—deserves admiration. We all know that there is a continuous literary tradition in Iceland from Snorri's *Edda* and the family sagas. More books per inhabitant are published in Iceland than anywhere else in the world. It is not unusual to see more than 500 new titles in the bookshops before Christmas each year, including Icelandic novels and biographies, translations of foreign literature, and magnificently illustrated works.

Authors

Icelandic Literature in the Twentieth Century: A Survey

Our country will not fight with the force of arms,
But with the Vikings of the spirit, for position and honour.
Einar Benediktsson, 'Varangians'

Icelandic literature in the nineteenth century bore the stamp of the independence struggle and the German romanticism which came to Iceland via Denmark. It was a song of praise to nature, to the excellence of Iceland and its former glory, when the heroes of the sagas rode around the country.

Realism began to make an impact on Icelandic literature in 1882, when four Icelandic students in Copenhagen, influenced by the theories of the Danish critic Georg Brandes, started issuing the journal *Verðandi*. Three of them are ranked among the most important authors of the period. Gestur Pálsson (1852–1891) was a major pioneer of the Icelandic short story. Despite his brief life and the limited scope of his production, his stories are always certain to find a place in any selection of Icelandic short stories. Einar H. Kvaran (1859–1938) was a good novelist who also wrote plays, short stories, and poems. He was one of the most influential Icelandic authors at the turn of the century, but he was gradually left in the shadow by younger writers. At an early age Einar made the acquaintance of spiritism, in which he was later deeply involved. The poet Hannes Hafstein (1861–1922) was only twenty-one when he published his first poems in *Verðandi*. He introduced a new, fresh tone of masculinity and hedonism in his poetry. Some of his youthful lyrics live on in the minds of the people, and they are still sung today. Hannes was a celebrated, elegant man, who was engaged in politics from an early age. He reached the pinnacle of esteem when he became the first Minister for Iceland after the country was granted limited home rule in 1904.

Other poets of the *Verðandi* generation were all influenced more or less by realism. The poet Stephan G. Stephansson (1853–1927) emigrated to Canada at the age of twenty. There he became a farmer, breaking ground in three different places. Despite hard labour from dawn to dusk, he composed poems during sleepless nights, producing a larger quantity—and of a higher quality—than most other Icelandic poets before or since. He was a spokesman for the unfortunates of society, a radical and an ardent pacifist.

Þorsteinn Erlingsson (1858–1914), who studied law at Copenhagen University in his youth, was one of the first Icelanders to become a committed socialist and atheist. He wrote satirical political poetry, but at the same time he composed sensitive love poems and nature poems.

Einar Benediktsson (1864–1940) published several collections of poems. He translated Ibsen's *Peer Gynt* into Icelandic, boasting that he had translated it into the original language. We have already met him in Chapter 1 as the man who advocated an Icelandic flag with a white cross on a blue background. He was a widely travelled adventurer, with a flash of humour in his eye. It is said that he once sold the Northern Lights, Aurora Borealis, to an American businessman. On the subject of this rumour, Einar himself once told a relative, according to a monograph on him written by the art historian Björn Th. Björnsson, 'That is a damned lie. You know yourself, cousin, that it is a gross lie. They will be saying that I would sell the next earthquake.' And he roared with laughter.[3] Einar was a high-minded poet, with a loyal band of admirers who considered him to be the poets' poet, and who were proud to be able to recite his poems from memory.

Like his fellow poet Stephan G., Guðmundur Friðjónsson (1869–1944) was a farmer all his life. He had almost as many children as Bach. He was nevertheless able to produce ten collections of short stories, five volumes of poetry, and a few books of essays. Some people thought that he was conservative. The truth was that he held fast to ancient virtues and admired those who stoutly defied hardship and were true to their patrimony, instead of fleeing their responsibilities and rushing off to America in the hope of easily gotten gain.

Finally, we may mention Jón Trausti (1873–1918), a self-taught man of the people who studied printing but wrote several novels in his spare time. He began by writing in a spirit of realism, but then turned to historical novels.

In their hearts of hearts, all the writers of this period were farmers, and Iceland was an agrarian society. Shortly after the turn of the century, however, there were radical changes, which went hand in hand with the progress of the independence movement. The Icelanders acquired a degree of self-government and began themselves to take over the transport of merchandise to and from the country. Whereas the only work had previously been on the farms, people could now find employment in the fishing stations and towns that were growing up on the coast. Everything began to open up, pointing the way forward to progress.

In the first decades of the century, some young Icelanders left the country and began to write in foreign languages. Jóhann Sigurjónsson (1880–1919) was the first. He went to Denmark at the age of nineteen to commence the study of veterinary medicine. When he still had a year of the course left he gave it up and began to write in Danish. He specialized in drama and wrote many plays, the best of which described Icelandic folk life. The play *Fjalla-Eyvindur* (*Eyvindur of the Mountains*) from 1911 attracted so much attention that it was filmed in Sweden; Victor Sjöström's film from 1918, *The Outlaw and His Wife,* is still reckoned among the classics of the silent cinema.[4] Jóhann also wrote fine poems, in both Danish and Icelandic, including one in free verse, foreshadowing modernism.

Gunnar Gunnarsson (1889–1975) was a farmer's son from eastern Iceland. At the age of eighteen he went to Denmark, and four years later he published his first book in Danish, *Digte* (Poems, 1911). He achieved success with his novels about Icelandic life and history. Among his novels we may mention four which have been translated into English, *Guest the One-Eyed, Seven Days' Darkness, The Sworn Brothers,* and *The Black Cliffs.*[5] His great autobiographical cycle *Kirken paa Bjerget* (The Church on the Mountain) contains fresh, tender, and captivating reminiscences of his childhood; they can be read in English in *Ships in the Sky* and *The Night and the Dream.*[6] Gunnar wrote in Danish. After thirty-two years abroad, however, he returned to Iceland in 1939; he settled in his native district on the east coast and began to write in Icelandic. Halldór Laxness translated *Kirken paa Bjerget* into Icelandic, and Gunnar Gunnarsson himself introduced Halldór Laxness in Denmark through his translation of *Salka Valka*. The television opera *Vikivaki*, by the composer Atli Heimir Sveinsson and with a libretto by the author Thor Vilhjálmsson, is based on the highly imaginative novel of the same name by Gunnar. Thus is the message passed on from one generation to the next.

Guðmundur Kamban (1888–1945) was the third Icelandic author who wrote in Danish. He was an ambitious playwright and novelist, who absorbed the new currents in philosophy and science. His play *Hadda Padda* (1914)[7] was made into a silent film. Guðmundur himself took a keen interest in film production.

Kristmann Guðmundsson (1901–83) moved to Norway in 1924 and two years later published his first collection of stories in Norwegian, *Islandsk kjærlighet* (Icelandic Love). In the following thirteen years he wrote novels in Norwegian which attained great popularity and were translated into many languages. In 1939 he returned to Iceland, where he wrote a large number of novels in his native language.

Nonni (1857–1944) may be included in this list of roving Icelandic writers, although he followed a highly unusual career. When he was twelve years old he came into the care of a French Catholic count who financed his studies. Jón Sveinsson, as his real name was, became a Jesuit, studied theology and philosophy in the Netherlands and England, and was ordained. As long as his health permitted, he also taught at a Latin School in Copenhagen. When he gave up teaching at the age of fifty-five, he began to write children's books in German, freely based on his childhood memories from Iceland. They became extremely popular and have probably been translated into more languages than the books of any other Icelandic writer. The best known are *Nonni* (1913), *Nonni und Manni* (1915),[8] and *Auf Skipalón* (1928).

The foundation in 1911 of the University of Iceland started a cultural revival that was particularly valuable for the development of the Icelandic language, the maturity of literature, and research into the history of the country. In 1918 Iceland became a sovereign kingdom in personal union with Denmark, which the Icelanders were able to end unilaterally after a period of twenty-five years. It was generally known that they wanted to establish an independent republic after the agreement expired. All this helped to free the people from old burdens and increase the courage and optimism of the nation.

It was no coincidence that the years 1918 and 1919 saw the publication of four books, each in its own way marking a turning-point: *Söngvar förumannsins* (The Beggar's Songs) by Stefán frá Hvítadal, *Svartar fjaðrir* (Black Feathers) by Davíð Stefánsson frá Fagraskógi, *Fornar ástir* (Ancient Loves) by Sigurður Nordal, and *Barn náttúrunnar* (Child of Nature) written by a precocious genius, the farmer's son Halldór Laxness (born 1902). Stefán frá Hvítadal (1887–1933) introduced a new tone into Icelandic poetry, which corresponded to the demands of a new age for a free lifestyle and more open attitudes, especially towards love. Young people welcomed his poems, but older moralists were appalled by his laxity. Stefán contracted tuberculosis at an early age, lost one leg, and never enjoyed full health afterwards. Poverty and a large family of children on a meagre farm in the remote countryside clipped his poetic wings and led to a death in middle age. Davíð Stefánsson frá Fagraskógi (1895–1964) had also been ill during his childhood. He did not take his school-leaving certificate until the age of twenty-four. In the same spring he published his first collection of poems, which met with instant acclaim. No other Icelandic poet has been able to sing his way so easily into the hearts of the people as Davíð. He struck much the same chords as Stefán frá Hvítadal, praising love and wine, attacking narrow-mindedness, hypocrisy, and pretence. He was a true freedom-lover and a spiritual leader with a profound sympathy for those who were worst off. He produced many collections of poems. He was also acclaimed for his play *Gullna hliðið* (*The Golden Gate*), which is based on the tale of 'My Jón's Soul'.[9] Sigurður Nordal (1886–1974) is without doubt best known for his long service as professor of Icelandic literature at the University of Iceland and for his expertise in Icelandic culture, past and present. *Fornar ástir* (Ancient Loves) is a remarkable work of Icelandic literature in that the prose poems in that collection foreshadowed the upheaval in poetic form which was later to revolutionize Icelandic poetry, although Sigurður at that time was an opponent of modernism.

Four of the poets who made their début in the 1920s were to be significant figures in Icelandic literature for the rest of their lives. Guðmundur G. Hagalín (1898–1985) published his first book *Blind-*

sker (Sunken Rocks) in 1921; it contained stories, adventures, and poems. With *Virkir dagar* (Workdays, 1936–8), a series of books based on interviews with a wise, tough shark skipper, Guðmundur showed himself to be a good exponent of a genre which has sadly degenerated in recent years. One of his best-known works is *Kristrún í Hamravík* (1933).

Þórbergur Þórðarson (1889–1974) published a small volume of lyrics in 1922 under the title *Hvítir hrafnar* (White Ravens), which differed from almost all previous Icelandic poetry. But it was not until his *Bréf til Láru* (Letters to Lára, 1924), that he confirmed his position as one of the most eminent Icelandic writers. In this book, written as a series of letters, he criticized society, praising the social democratic ideology and attacking agrarian culture and the clergy. Þórbergur is distinctive in that the basic themes in his central works are autobiographical. They are *Íslenzkur aðall* (Icelandic Nobility), *Ofvitinn* I–II (The Genius), and *Í Suðursveit* (In the South Country), issued between 1938 and 1975. Other well-known works are the six-volume *Ævisaga Árna prófasts Þórarinssonar* (The Life-Story of Dean Árni Þórarinsson) and the two-volume *Sálmurinn um blómið* (The Hymn of the Flower). Þórbergur was a skilled Esperantist, writing a great deal in that international language, including courses in Esperanto. In his early years he was also an energetic collector of proverbs and folklore.

Tómas Guðmundsson (1901–83) made his début as a poet in 1925 with the book *Við sundin blá* (By the Blue Sound), but he failed to attract much attention. His breakthrough did not come until 1933, with a collection of poems entitled *Fagra veröld* (Beautiful World). Although Tómas was born and grew up in the countryside, it was obvious that the young capital had acquired its first poet. He wrote cheerful, humorous poems about his town, which was depicted as charming, in contrast to the fearful picture which the farmers had always had of Reykjavík.

Jóhannes úr Kötlum (1899–1972) published his first collection of poems, *Bí bí og blaka*, in 1926, and remained until his death one of the most productive of Icelandic poets. He started his career as a traditional idealistic poet in the spirit of the people, but he sympathized with Communist internationalism during the depression and subsequently never changed his stance, regardless of what happened.

When he was around fifty, he turned his back on the traditional forms of poetry and succeeded in renewing his style so thoroughly that from this point on he was virtually on a footing with the youngest innovators in Icelandic poetry. His first collection of free verse was *Sjödægra* (Seven Days, 1955). Jóhannes also wrote a large number of children's verses, which almost all Icelandic children imbibe along with their mothers' milk.

The 1930s was a decade of bitter class conflict as a result of the great depression, when the common people lived a life of hardship. As one might expect, the poets took the side of the underdogs in their struggle against those with power and money, and this made its mark on the literature of the day. It was during this decade that Halldór Laxness, who is treated separately in the next section, published *Salka Valka*, *Independent People*, and *World Light*. A large number of new authors made their appearance, but here we shall confine ourselves to three poets and three prose writers who were to set their stamp on Icelandic literature in the following decades.

Steinn Steinarr (1908–58) made his début in 1934 with a collection of poems called *Rauður loginn brann* (The Red Flame Burned). The title was symbolic of the times. Steinn can be ranked without hesitation among the foremost Icelandic poets of this century. His first book already contains poems in free form, showing that Steinn was always open to innovation, although he never wholly abandoned traditional metrical forms. His last collection, *Tíminn og vatnið* (Time and the Water, 1948), is ostensibly traditional but has an inner form which is so modern that Steinn is often considered a precursor of the revolutionaries of poetic form. He himself felt a spiritual affinity with them, defending the new poetry when it provoked serious controversy in the early 1950s. 'The traditional form of poetry is finally dead,' he proclaimed then, and this slogan has often been quoted since.

Time and the Water

Time is like the water,
and the water is cold and deep
like my own consciousness.

And time is like a picture,
which is painted of water,

half of it by me.

And time and the water
flow trackless to extinction
into my own consciousness.

Steinn Steinarr
Translated by Marshall Brement[10]

Guðmundur Böðvarsson (1904–74) is one of the unschooled Icelandic farmers who has achieved a place among the country's leading
poets. His first book, *Kyssti mig sól* (A Sun Kissed Me, 1936), instantly aroused the interest and admiration of poetry-lovers. In his
poems he showed a facility to declare his humanistic view of life
without doing so at the expense of art.

Jón úr Vör (born 1917) made a quiet début in 1937 with his collection *Ég ber að dyrum* (I Knock on the Door). He was received with
the sort of cordial politeness that usually greets inexperienced newcomers. The reaction in 1946 was rather different, however, when he
published his most remarkable collection of poems, *Þorpið* (The Fishing Village). Although this was a fairly traditional description of life
in an Icelandic fishing station, all the poems were unrhymed, which
meant a revolution in form. He was castigated for this radical innovation, and many people have still not forgiven him.

Late Winter Months

And do you remember the long,
   milkless midwinter days,
  the near rotten fish,
  little cod, watered in a bucket,
  a wellhouse
    and the simple song of the water's flow,
  boats indoors
    some covered with canvas,
  sheep on a beach,
    and cold feet,
  and the evenings long as eternity itself,
one waited impatiently then
for good weather
and fresh fish.

And do you remember

one evening near dusk.
You stood on a beach with your fostermother.
You looked with fear at frozen oarlocks,
out at the fjord,
toward the sky—
you were expecting a small boat behind the headland,
and it did not come.
And the dusk became thick darkness and stormsounds,
silence
and tears on a pillow,
and you fell asleep alone in a bed that was too large.

And do you remember
    your happiness in the middle of the night,
    when you awakened and on your head
    was a workhardened palm
        and the back of a soft, warm hand
        was stroking your cheeks.

Your fosterfather was there
—and kissed you when you laid your hands on his neck.
And his sea-wet moustache was still cold.

And next morning there were blue catfish
    on the ice-covered doorstep,
        and the sun glistened on silver haddockscales—
    and on happiness in a poor man's house.

Jón úr Vör
Translated by Marshall Brement

Ólafur Jóhann Sigurðsson (1918–88) started his career at the age of sixteen, with a children's book entitled *Við Álftavatn* (At Álftavatn, 1934). He later became one of the most productive writers of novels and short stories in Iceland. His most famous works include the novel of contemporary life *Litbrigði jarðarinnar* (Shades of the Soil, 1947) and a trilogy about the journalist Páll Jónsson, on which he worked for twenty-five years. Of his collections of short stories we may mention *Speglar og fiðrildi* (Mirrors and Butterflies, 1947). Ólafur was best known for his prose works, but it was a collection of poems that won him the Nordic Prize for Literature in 1976.

Guðmundur Daníelsson (1910–90) made his début in 1935 with the novel *Bræðurnir í Grashaga* (The Brothers in Grashagi). He was later to publish many works, mostly novels, but also short stories, plays, and poems. His novels include *Hrafnhetta* (Raven's Hood, 1958) and *Sonur minn Sinfjötli* (My Son Sinfjötli, 1961). We may also mention two collections of short stories, *Vængjaðir hestar* (Winged Horses, 1955) and *Drengur á fjalli* (The Boy on the Mountain, 1964).

Stefán Jónsson (1905–66) made his début in 1936 with a collection of stories entitled *Konan á klettinum* (The Woman on the Cliff), after which he published several acclaimed collections of stories and novels for adults. He is best known, however, as one of the leading children's writers of his day. All his stories for children were reissued after his death in a fifteen-volume collection. He also wrote some songbooks and plays. Stefán's example and his enormous popularity as a writer for children furthered Icelandic children's literature. He has inspired others to write for children with the same care as is devoted to adult literature. His worthiest successor in this respect is Guðrún Helgadóttir (born 1935), whose first book about the twins *Jón Oddur og Jón Bjarni* (1974) had a mirthful tone which was loved by all children. She has since consolidated her popularity with books like *Undan illgresinu* (Under the Weeds, 1990), for which she won the Nordic Prize for Children's Books in 1992.

The proclamation of the republic from the law-rock at Þingvellir on 17 June 1944 overshadowed all other events in Iceland in the 1940s. It also influenced literature. In the same year, Snorri Hjartarson (1906–86) published his first collection of poems, called simply *Kvæði* (Poems). Then aged thirty-eight, he was no newcomer to art; he had attended art schools in Copenhagen and Oslo, and he had written a novel in Norwegian, *Højt flyver ravnen* (High Flies the Raven, 1934). His *Kvæði* is an incessant declaration of love for the country, the people, and the language. The same is true of his later work. He wrote nature poems following the aesthetics of traditional poetry. He was awarded the Nordic Prize for Literature in 1981 for his collection *Hauströkkið yfir mér* (Autumn Darkness over Me).

The years during and after the Second World War saw the greatest revolution in Icelandic literature since the age of the sagas. It took place among young poets who realized the great changes undergone by the Icelandic nation in modern times. They were scornfully termed 'atom poets' after a failed figure in Halldór Laxness's novel *Atóm-stöðin* (*The Atom Station*). The epithet was considered appropriate for the new poets, who departed from the traditional Icelandic alliteration and rhyme. Their style was neither rural romanticism nor realism; instead their poems were about life by the sea or life in the wide world. The entire world-view of the new poets had changed. They learned of the new trends represented by foreign poets, such as T. S. Eliot and the French surrealists. Yet the first books of the atom poets were not published until around 1950. They had not forgotten their literary heritage—although they were initially accused of this—but they did revolutionize the current view of the matter of poetry. Some, but not all of them, wrote works which were increasingly impenetrable.

Dymbilvaka (Holy Week), a collection of poems issued in 1949 by Hannes Sigfússon (born 1922), was the first book in this new spirit. Besides publishing five subsequent volumes of poetry, a novel, and two books of memoirs, Hannes translated a great deal of poetry from the other Scandinavian languages. He lived in Norway for twenty-five years, but he has recently moved home to Iceland.

Angel
(To Guðný)

No one grows old
who travels at the speed of light
said Einstein

And I saw no change in you
when we met again
after fifty years

I short of breath
grey with earthly age
you radiant
with the glory of heaven

What gentle god
cloaked you in eternity
for that fleeting moment
(that is a mortal life)

to deliver to me

like a promise
—before I left?

Hannes Sigfússon
Translated by Bernard Scudder

Einar Bragi (born 1921) made his literary début in 1950 with a collection of poems called *Eitt kvöld í júní* (An Evening in June). He has published seven volumes of his own poems and five collections of foreign poetry, including poems of the Norwegian Knut Ödegård and Gunnar Björling, a Swedish-speaking Finn, a collection of Lappish poetry, and a presentation of contemporary Greenlandic poetry. In 1992 he issued two thick volumes of his translations of twenty major plays of August Strindberg.

The Snare

Slowly

the snare tightens
around the narrow neck

and the moor bird
lifts up its voice
in anguish

then the world's bustle
is silenced for a while

men listen
in wonder to the song
and contrive new

snares.

Einar Bragi
Translated by Patricia Aylett[11]

Stefán Hörður Grímsson (born 1920) published *Svartálfadans* (Dance of the Black Elves) in 1951. He had previously written a collection of poems in traditional style in 1946. Stefán Hörður attracted attention once again in 1990, when he was awarded the newly instituted Icelandic Literary Prize; he won it for the collection *Yfir heiðan morgun* (Over a Clear Morning).

Winter Day

From the land's frigid face
the extinct eyes of lakes stare
at a grey February sky.

Of the wanderings of the restless winds
across the spacious vault
no news has been brought.

Mingled with colourless rime mist
the stillness has stiffened
on the breasts of white wastes.

Under the hollow shell of silence
solitary bass tones keep reaching out
when the ice heart beats.

On their spindly legs
men cross the snowfields
with mountains on their shoulders.

Stefán Hörður Grímsson
translated by Sigurður A. Magnússon[12]

Sigfús Daðason (born 1928) released his first book in 1951, *Ljóð 1947–1951* (Poems 1947–1951). He studied literature and philosophy at the Sorbonne in Paris. On his return to Iceland he became manager of the culturally radical publishing house Mál og Menning. He is at present a lecturer at the University of Iceland.

Jón Óskar (born 1921) published a volume of poems entitled *Skrifað í vindinn* (Written into the Wind) in 1953. A year before, however, he had made his literary début with a collection of short stories, *Mitt andlit og þitt* (My Face and Yours). He has since produced five collections of poems and two thick volumes of French poetry in translation. He has also written an autobiographical novel and published six volumes of memoirs.

These were the true atom poets. It was Einar Bragi who, on his return from Sweden in 1953, started the struggle for the recognition of the new poetry by issuing the periodical *Birtingur*. Others later published a journal under the same name (1955–68), defending not only the new poetry but also modernist currents in art as a whole. *Birtingur* had the following editors: Einar Bragi, the artist Hörður Ágústsson, Jón Óskar, and Thor Vilhjálmsson. What distinguished these atom poets from earlier poets was not just the change of form—the books mentioned above mixed alliteration and unrhymed verse—but also the new subjects and new attitudes to the matter. The poets had a more international orientation, although some of them wrote specifically about Iceland. Yet it was not the patriotic dream of agrarian Iceland that was reflected, but present-day society with cars, jazz, and foreign occupying forces.

Turning to Icelandic prose, we see that Thor Vilhjálmsson (born in Edinburgh in 1925) has a position similar to that of the atom poets in the field of poetry. He is a distinctive prose writer, regarded by many as the greatest innovator of the art since the end of the Second World War. He showed his modernist bent in *Maðurinn er alltaf einn* (Man is Always Alone, 1950), a collection of short prose pieces and poems. His first novel, *Fljótt, fljótt, sagði fuglinn* (Quick, Quick, Said the Bird), appeared in 1968. He has published over twenty books of different kinds. His novel *Grámosinn glóir* (The Grey Moss Glistens, 1986) won him the Nordic Council's Prize for Literature in 1988,[13] and in 1992 he received yet another prize for his literary achievements, this time from the Swedish Academy.

The impact of the atom poets was greater than expected. The second generation of poets showing their influence soon emerged. One of them was Jóhann Hjálmarsson (born 1939), whose collection in the spirit of the atom poets, *Aungull í tímann* (A Hook in Time), appeared in 1956. Two years later, Matthías Johannessen (born 1930) published *Borgin hló* (The Town Laughed), a collection of free poems about his home town, Reykjavík. In the years that have passed since then, Matthías has published a large number of books of widely varying kinds, including poetry, plays, short stories, essays, and interviews, mostly with authors and artists. For almost forty years he has worked for the largest daily newspaper in Iceland, *Morgunblaðið*, first as a journalist covering the arts, then as one of the two editors-in-chief.

The Land

I
The sun drifts
along the horizon
until it rushes full sail
out into the distant ocean,
coming next morning
with a new cargo
of lava, mountain and sea.

II
Our words
congealed lava
of thought
which at one time were fire,
mossgrown words.
And we are
burnt-out craters.

III
The land follows us
in a white gown,
but the craters are raised
fists
against heaven.

IV
We slept
under a clear sky
and awakened
into an unearthly
silence,
we saw the deserts come
to us
dressed in a quiet beige
morning:

An old sky descends to earth
in a transparent gown
and walks with the rays of the sun
across the lava

Matthías Johannessen
Translated by Marshall Brement

Vilborg Dagbjartsdóttir (born 1930) also followed in the footsteps of the atom poets with *Laufin á trjánum* (The Leaves on the Trees), which appeared in 1960. Since then Vilborg has been praised repeatedly for her poems on daily life, problems in Icelandic society, and women's fight for equal rights. Furthermore, she has been successful as a writer and translator of books for children.

Among the poets who emerged in the 1950s, a special position is occupied by Hannes Pétursson and Þorsteinn frá Hamri. Hannes Pétursson (born 1931) made his début with *Kvæðabók* (Book of Poems) in 1955, which was warmly received by lovers of conventional poetry, since he followed the traditional stylistic paths. Hannes has since then been an influential writer, publishing many collections of poems, short stories, scholarly works, folklore, and travel books. Þorsteinn frá Hamri (born 1938) aroused immediate interest in 1958 with his first book of poems, *Í svörtum kufli* (In a Black Cloak). In this and in later works he is both modern and traditional. Þorsteinn has written novels and popular tales, as well as ten collections of poems. He has also translated a large number of books.

Indriði G. Þorsteinsson (born 1926) made his début at the age of twenty-five with the short-story collection *Sæluvika* (Happy Week, 1951), since when he has written many novels. The best-known of them is *Sjötíu og níu af stöðinni* (Number 79 from the Station, 1955), a frequently reissued book which has also been filmed, as has his *Land og synir* (Land and Sons, 1963).

The short-story writer Geir Kristjánsson (1923–91) published a collection called *Stofnunin* (The Institute) in 1956. It won acclaim for its originality. He also wrote some unusual plays for the radio, but he is best known for his translations from Russian (Mayakovsky, Pasternak, Yevtushenko, Pushkin, Chekhov).

With Steinar Sigurjónsson (1928–92) the novel was given an innovative style, when his *Ástarsaga* (Love Story) appeared in 1958. His works describe harsh reality in a picaresque way.

At the youthful age of seventeen, Jökull Jakobsson (1933–78) published his novel *Tæmdur bikar* (Drained Cup), which he followed with some other novels. He is best known, however, for his many fine plays. Despite his early death, Jökull was able to revive Icelandic drama out of the period of decline that set in after the demise of Jóhann Sigurjónsson and Guðmundur Kamban. In Jökull's footsteps there have come playwrights such as Oddur Björnsson (born 1932), Jónas Árnason (born 1923), Guðmundur Steinsson (born 1925), Birgir Sigurðsson (born 1937), and Ólafur Haukur Símonarson (born 1947), all of whom have written plays for stage and radio, with excellent results.

The last literary début of the 1950s which we shall mention is that of Sigurður A. Magnússon (born 1928). He has worked in all genres of literature: novels, short stories, plays, poems, travel books, and essays. He has also been a respected critic of literature and drama, and a familiar voice in contemporary cultural debate. The work which is most likely to ensure his immortality is his cycle of autobiographical novels. The first volume in particular, *Undir kalstjörnu* (Under a Frosty Star, 1979), was highly praised.

Jakobína Sigurðardóttir (born 1918) was the oldest of the new writers to appear in the 1960s. A farmer's wife in northern Iceland for over forty years, she still found time to write many works of prose and poetry. She is best known for her novels—such as *Dægurvísa* (Popular Song, 1965)—and her collections of stories, for example, *Sjö vindur gráar* (Seven Grey Balls of Yarn, 1970).

Guðbergur Bergsson (born 1932) was twenty-nine when he made his début in 1961, with a novel in one hand, *Músin sem læðist* (The Sneaking Mouse), and a book of poems in the other, *Endurtekin orð* (Repeated Words). This says a great deal about the author. In the subsequent thirty years he has produced many books, both works of his own and translations. He trod new paths with his influential novel from 1966, *Tómas Jónsson metsölubók* (Tómas Jónsson Best-seller), and he has cultivated his style in later works. Guðbergur has translated many works by Spanish writers and South American poets. After Thor Vilhjálmsson, he is reckoned as the most productive innovator in Icelandic prose in the second half of this century.

The first published work of Svava Jakobsdóttir (born 1930) was a collection of short stories, *12 konur* (Twelve Women, 1965). They attracted attention because of the author's absurd symbolism, a style to which she has since remained faithful. Her first novel, *Leigjandinn* (The Lodger, 1969) is a symbolic description of an independent Iceland housing an American army. Her latest novel to date is *Gunnlaðar saga* (Gunnlöð's Saga, 1987), a profound novel with symbolism borrowed from the medieval literature of Iceland. Svava has also written plays.

The 1970s and 1980s saw the coming of a number of authors who have already produced many excellent works, although they may not have reached their literary peak yet. Steinunn Sigurðardóttir (born 1950) made her début at the age of nineteen with a collection of poems called *Sífelldur* (Ceaseless), since when she has published about ten books: novels, short stories, poems, and plays. Her novel *Tímaþjófurinn* (The Thief of Time, 1986) aroused considerable interest.

Pétur Gunnarsson (born 1947) published his first book of poems, *Splunkunýr dagur* (Brand-New Day), in 1973. Since then he has concentrated on the novel. He has been lauded for a number of humorous novels which capture life in Reykjavík in the author's childhood and youth. The first, *Punktur punktur komma strik* (Period, Period, Comma, Dash), appeared in 1976. Pétur is a graduate in philosophy from a French university.

Ingibjörg Haraldsdóttir (born 1942) graduated as a film director in Moscow and lived for several years in Cuba. She is a poet who published her first volume in 1974, *Þangað vil ég fljúga* (I Want to Fly There). In recent years she has presented good translations from Russian, working in particular with the novels of Dostoyevsky (*Crime and Punishment, The Idiot, The Brothers Karamazov*).

Þórarinn Eldjárn (born 1949) studied literature and philosophy in Sweden. His first book, *Kvæði* (Poems, 1974), went through four editions in five years, which is highly unusual for Icelandic books in general and probably unique in the case of an author's first collection of poems. He has since written many poems, novels, short stories, and plays, besides translating a number of books, especially from Swedish.

Sigurður Pálsson (born 1948) has studied drama and film production at a French university. He made his début in 1975 with a book of poems called *Ljóð vega salt* (See-Saw Poems), since when he has published some collections which have given him a place among the leading Icelandic poets of his generation. He has also written plays, besides directing, translating, and producing films.

Iceland's Only Kings

The birds point out our path long overgrown
lost beneath the turf and the tight wind
bends blades of grass that grow over ruins
of long-lost farms and overgrown paths

But the birds point out our path over grown turf
and ruins of farms where kings once sat
and wrote; kings of the poem and saga
in little farms with vastness in their heads

In their bright flight the birds display to us
the path that lies ever upwards and ahead
the path untouched by time and ruins and turf
the path through lines that kings laid down on skin

Lost are the farms and lost the windswept paths
But the path of the poem and saga still open and free

Sigurður Pálsson
Translated by Bernard Scudder

Einar Kárason (born 1955) is best known for his trilogy about the life of the poor in the tenements of Reykjavik: *Þar sem djöflaeyjan rís* (Where the Devil-Island Rises, 1983), *Gulleyjan* (The Golden Island, 1985), and *Fyrirheitna landið* (The Promised Land, 1989). He has also written collections of short stories and poems and chaired the Icelandic Authors' Union (Rithöfundasamband Íslands).

Einar Már Guðmundsson (born 1954) began his career with a collection of poems, *Er nokkur í Kórónafötum hér inni?* (Is Anyone Here Wearing Króna Clothes?, 1980). He later turned to novel-writing, with tales in the style of childhood memoirs, like those of Pétur Gunnarsson. They include *Riddarar hringstigans* (Riders of the Spiral Staircase, 1982) and *Vængjasláttur í þakrennu* (Wing-Beats in a Gutter, 1983).

Vigdís Grímsdóttir (born 1953) published her first book, *Tíu myndir úr lífi þínu* (Ten Pictures from Your Life) in 1983, but did not attract any great interest until her novel *Kaldaljós* (Cold Light) appeared in 1987. With her novel *Ég heiti Ísbjörg, ég er ljón* (My Name is Ísbjörg,

I Am a Lion, 1989) she reinforced her reputation. The novel was dramatized and played to full houses at the National Theatre in 1992.

Gyrðir Elíasson (born 1961) provoked immediate interest with his first collection of poems, *Svarthvít axlabönd* (Black and White Braces, 1983). Since then, Gyrðir has published about ten books, both poetry and prose, and he is considered one of the foremost Icelandic poets to have emerged in the last decade. He was the first to receive the Þórbergur Þórðarson prize for style in 1989.

Of the Last Descendant of Icarus

flap flap flap
somewhere
from above I chase
the sound up
the stairs in two/three steps
in the attic a man with a stick turns
his back to me and
walks out to the dormer
I creep un-
seen down
again but recall when I hear the cuckoo
clock strike those classic 12
strokes that on
the old work-
bench in
the attic
I saw
something
resembling half-
built wings.

Gyrðir Elíasson
Translated by Bernard Scudder

Guðmundur Andri Thorsson (born 1957) has only written two novels as yet—*Mín káta angist* (My Merry Anxiety, 1988) and *Íslenski draumurinn* (The Icelandic Dream, 1991)—but they are enough to arouse great hope for his future work. Hrafnhildur Hagalín (born 1965) enjoyed overnight success with her first play, *Ég er meistarinn* (I Am the Master). It played to full houses at the Reykjavík Civic Theatre in the 1990–1 season, and it won the young writer the Nordic Prize for Drama in 1992.

It remains for us to consider one of the most remarkable of modern Icelandic writers, Fríða Á. Sigurðardóttir (born 1940). In 1992 she was awarded the Nordic Prize for Literature for her novel *Meðan nóttin líður* (While Night Passes). The story is told by Nína, a successful, divorced, liberated career woman. One day she is sitting alone by her mother's deathbed. During her three-day vigil, she sees vivid pictures in her mind of six generations of women who have lived before her. Nína senses the huge gap between the secure society of yesterday's farmers and fishermen and today's torn existence. Her mother was born in a turf-roofed house in a sparsely populated area near the majestic Hornstrandir at the north-western tip of Iceland. It was a barren district, but it was harmonious and faithful to tradition. It was later depopulated and transformed into wilderness. In material terms, Nína has a good life in Reykjavík, but she feels rootless, foreign, lost. She looks back in her search for meaningful values which can serve for modern life. This cavalcade of memories is thus filled with soul-searching flashbacks; find your roots and liberate yourself.

In 1980 Fríða took her master's degree with a dissertation on the plays of Jökull Jakobsson. She then went on to translate and to write literature of her own. The prize-winning *Meðan nóttin líður* is her fifth book. She says that she has been influenced by Doris Lessing (whom she has translated), but her primary inspiration comes from the Icelandic family sagas, Halldór Laxness, and in recent years especially from Svava Jakobsdóttir. With her deep analysis of women's liberation in Iceland, Fríða convincingly shows that she is following in the great Icelandic narrative tradition. The reader cannot fail to be charmed.

Halldór Laxness

There is no sight more splendid than
Iceland rising from the sea.
Halldór Laxness, Íslandsklukkan

Icelandic farming society and the small fishing stations around the turn of the century and the First World War have been described with incredible vitality, accuracy, and colour by Halldór Laxness (born in Reykjavík in 1902). He won the Nobel Prize for Literature in 1955, 'for his vivid epic power, which has renewed the great narrative art of Iceland'. There is no room here to paint a detailed picture of him, although it would be tempting.[14] He is the student with a hunger for life and a thirst for knowledge who embraced Catholicism in the 1920s. He is the Catholic who became a socialist. He is the socialist who turned out to be at bottom a pragmatist, a humanist with a broad frame of reference and a marked sense of humour.

Halldór Guðjónsson took the surname Laxness after the farm where he grew up. When he converted to Catholicism he took the middle name Kiljan after an Irish saint, a martyr who worked as a missionary on the continent in the seventh century.

The following anecdote testifies to Halldór Laxness's quick wit and joking spirit, along with his ability for self-control in unexpected situations. The ever well-dressed author is driving homewards in his splendid Cadillac. As every Icelander knows, he lives in a beautiful white house called Gljúfrasteinn in Mosfellsdalur, which adorns the crest of a hill on the road from Reykjavík to Þingvellir. The sun is shining over the district. Everything is peaceful. In the middle of this narrow, winding dirt road, he suddenly meets a little Volkswagen. It is being driven at top speed down the middle of the road by a young driver. To avoid a crash, Halldór is forced to swerve into a ditch. Luckily, he is unhurt. He gets out of his Cadillac and brushes off the dust. He then turns to the youthful driver and asks with a charming smile, 'Is there anything else I can do for you, young man?'

In the 1930s and during the war years, Halldór Laxness wrote a series of fascinating novels about Iceland. He has also published collections of short stories and essays, plays, travel books, and auto-biographical works. One of the latter is his diary of the years 1922–3, which he spent at the Benedictine monastery of Saint Maurice de Clervaux in Luxemburg. This diary was lost for many years, but it was found in the National Library in Reykjavík in 1987 and published the same year under the title *Dagar hjá múnkum* (Days with Monks).

Halldór rediscovered Iceland, as it were, after many travels abroad as a young man. He had spells, for example, in Denmark, Sweden, and in the Luxemburg monastery where he learned Latin. In the USA he made the acquaintance of the social satirist Upton Sinclair (who wrote the novel *The Jungle* as an exposé of the meat-packing industry in Chicago), and he became a convinced socialist. He also spent time in Sicily and the Soviet Union.

For Halldór, getting to know the rest of the world was a way to see his beloved Iceland with new eyes. His works may communicate insight of a general, timeless validity, but they are also a concrete reflection of the people of Iceland, the struggling men and women, often from the bottom of the social scale, with their everyday toil, their harsh destinies and their bold dreams, and their thirst for education. It is hard to forget such courageous, proud, indomitable women as Salka Valka in her fishing station, Ugla the maid in *The Atom Station*, and Diljá, the symbol of passionate love and of life itself in *Vefarinn mikli frá Kasmír* (The Great Weaver from Kashmir, 1927). Laxness's portrayal of women in *Salka Valka* is revolutionary. The heroine does not want to be a pleasing female in the traditional role. She prefers to act like a man. Refusing to be a subdued woman, she wears trousers and buys a little fishing-boat.

In the 1930s and 1940s Halldór Laxness went on to write the novels *Sjálfstætt fólk* (*Independent People*), the tetralogy about Ólafur Kárason, *Heimsljós* (*World Light*), the trilogy *Íslandsklukkan* (Iceland's Bell), and *Atomstöðin* (*The Atom Station*).[15] *Íslandsklukkan* has been dramatized and staged by the Icelandic National Theatre. *The Atom Station* has been filmed by the Icelander Þorsteinn Jónsson, and it was turned into a musical by Hans Alfredson and performed by the Royal Dramatic Theatre in Stockholm in 1987. The subject matter of this work is still highly sensitive, since it concerns Iceland's independence.

Independent People describes the period 1900–21 in the history of Iceland. It is about Guðbjartur Jónsson (Bjartur í Sumarhúsum), a poor farm-hand working for a prosperous farmer. After eighteen years of toil he realizes his dream of becoming his own master. He procures a few sheep and buys a deserted croft just below the high heath, to which he gives the name Summerhouses. But his life is not an easy one. He and his family live in wretched circumstances. He loses two wives and four of his seven children—but not his favourite daughter Ásta Sóllilja, 'the flower of his life'. He has everything against him. But he does not give up, refusing to be beaten by the big farmer, by crop

Halldór Laxness, who was awarded the Nobel Prize for Literature in 1955, and his wife Auður. The picture was taken on a sunny spring day of 1990. It portrays Halldór and Auður in the library of Gljúfrasteinn, their home since 1945.

failure, or by repeated setbacks. He is finally forced to sell Summer-houses by auction. Not even then does he give up. He stubbornly continues his struggle to remain independent. He moves to another deserted farm, this time up on the heath itself. He is not entirely on his own—he still has his Ásta Sóllilja. She symbolizes for him all ethereal and butterfly-like beauty, everything that he cannot grasp himself. Bjartur and Ásta Sóllilja are living characters to the Icelanders. Florists in Iceland now sell a flower named after Ásta.

Bjartur fails in his struggle for economic independence. Was the struggle illusory? 'Sovereignty, independence are no more than words as long as the people live in poverty, suffering, and insecurity and cannot live a life befitting the inhabitants of this rich earth.'[16] Laxness's critique is broad in its temporal and geographical scope. It is not merely directed against Icelandic society in a time of change. Laxness the genius and the brilliant stylist has the ability to analyse problems in a way that is both poignant and universal in its validity.

In view of the political implications of this novel, it is hardly surprising that Halldór Laxness takes a critical view of Knut Hamsun's novel *The Growth of the Soil* (1917, for which the great Norwegian writer won the Nobel Prize in 1920), with its lyrical glorification of a bygone culture, the freehold farmer and his diligent toil. One cannot deny the brilliance of Hamsun's style, but this is not enough for Halldór Laxness. Like his contemporary Þórbergur Þórðarson—both of them began by shocking their fellow countrymen—Laxness wrote relentlessly ironic analyses of the one-sided lyrical romanticism of previous authors. What happened to the individual in the midst of all this nature-worship, this flight from reality? How could man survive?

The contrast between the two views of nature is brought out by Laxness in *Independent People*. We see how Bjartur resents the condescending attitude of the well-to-do members of the Young Icelanders' Association who go rambling in the barren mountainous wastes of Iceland, singing patriotic songs.

Knut Hamsun may be a controversial figure, but he is still justifiably read and admired, especially in Scandinavia. Like Isak Sellanrå, the leading character in *The Growth of the Soil*, Bjartur is a pronounced individualist. Like Isak, he is also sometimes at one with nature, with the flowering meadows and grassy slopes, the mossy heaths and sterile rocks in the shadow of the mountains. Here, in this mostly treeless landscape with its cairns and coal-black ravens, its babbling streams and roaring torrents, he meets the elves and fairies, the ghosts and trolls and other beings from the folktales, creatures who cannot be seen by the ordinary eye.

This rough, grassy landscape with its scattered white sheep looking from a distance like fluffs of cotton wool on the slopes, with its trout-lakes glittering in the sun, precipices rising steeply into the thin, crystal-clear air, where a keen-sighted eagle or falcon practises gliding in the air currents under an azure vault—of course such a landscape has its magical power, its inherent beauty. But a poor crofter, breaking his back to make sure that he and his family will survive, must take a different view. A famished child, crouching in front of an empty bowl, cannot be fed on beauty. It is not enough to say that everything is so beautiful.

Halldór Laxness was a highly deserving recipient of the Nobel Prize for Literature, and the newsreels of the prize-giving ceremony in Stockholm put Iceland on the world map. The Swedish Academy in the mid-1950s hesitated about how to award the prize. Malicious tongues said that their choice was between an imperialist, an alcoholic, and a communist, and indeed, the prize was awarded in turn to Winston Churchill in 1953, Ernest Hemingway in 1954, and Halldór Kiljan Laxness in 1955.

The works of Halldór Laxness are read throughout the world; they constantly reappear in new issues. He is the world's oldest living Nobel laureate in literature.

For Icelanders, Halldór Laxness is something of a national hero, as was graphically demonstrated at the celebrations to mark his ninetieth birthday in 1992. The highlight of this homage, which was covered by all the national media, was a torchlit procession to the author's home at Gljúfrasteinn.

The Dramatic Arts

Between 1897 and 1989, plays were performed by the Reykjavík Theatre Company at Iðnó, an old red timber building by the lake Tjörnin. Plays had of course been staged before this: the first theatrical performances and the first native plays came a century earlier, at the end of the eighteenth century. But it was at Iðnó that the Icelandic theatre—in the sense of conscious artistic creation—was born. If one defines theatre as full professional conditions for the exponents of the dramatic arts, then this did not come until 1950, when the National Theatre opened its doors. From 1964 the Reykjavík Theatre Company was also able to maintain a permanently employed ensemble and staff. These two theatres have since then had audiences which outnumber each year the population of Reykjavík and the neighbouring towns. This enormous interest in drama is one of the first features which strikes anyone who makes an acquaintance with the Icelandic theatre. In the high season one can often choose from among 15–20 different shows during the same week, performed by these and other theatres. They also include the Icelandic Opera (a private enterprise; the National Theatre also stages operas), the Icelandic Ballet (a state company which has grown under the aegis of the National Theatre), and the free professional groups that have emerged in the last few decades.

Theatrical activity is highly diversified. One of these independent groups, for example, specializes in puppet theatre.

Outside Reykjavík there is also a professional ensemble in the main town in the north, Akureyri, as well as some fifty or sixty amateur dramatic groups throughout the country. These amateurs deserve special mention. Year after year they have periods when they give up five or six evenings a week for rehearsals, performances, or tours to drama-hungry audiences in sparsely populated districts. Many plays are staged for children. About half of the repertoire consists of Icelandic plays. This applies not only to the amateurs, since Iceland consciously emphasizes native drama. The course was set by the Reykjavík Theatre Company in the 1960s and was soon followed by the National Theatre and other theatres. As a result, the greatest box-office successes in the past fifteen years have been written by contemporary Iceland playwrights, such as Jökull Jakobsson, Jónas Árnason, Guðmundur Steinsson, Birgir Sigurðsson, Kjartan Ragnarsson, to name but a few. Some of these plays have been successful in other countries: Guðmundur Steinsson's works have been staged in the Nordic countries, Germany, France, Poland, and Japan. Icelandic companies have also travelled abroad to give guest performances of native plays. The National Theatre ensemble, for example, played the group work *Inuk*, under the direction of Brynja Benediktsdóttir, at major drama festivals in twenty-two countries. The National Theatre also toured Europe with Guðmundur Steinsson's play *Stundarfriður* (A Brief Respite), produced by Stefán Baldursson, and Sveinn Einarsson's staging of Atli Heimir Sveinsson's opera *Silkitromman* (The Silken Drum) was performed at the great Bolívar Bicentennial in Caracas.

It is clear that theatre is deeply rooted among the Icelandic people. The pioneers in the eighteenth century were pupils at the Latin School at the bishopric of Skálholt. An annual coronation ceremony was enacted here, similar to the medieval feast of fools: one pupil was crowned king, while another was consecrated as bishop and preached a mock sermon. Later there came comic plays or scenes. When the school was moved to Reykjavík in 1846, comedies by Molière and Holberg were staged, as well as new plays by Icelandic writers.

A remarkable event in the history of Icelandic theatre was the première in 1864 of Matthías Jochumsson's *Skugga-Sveinn*, still regarded as the number one national play. It was first performed under the title *Útilegumennirnir* (The Outlaws). It is based on the many popular folktales about outlaws living in the desolate wastes of Iceland. The inspiration came from Sigurður Guðmundsson. His pupils, Matthías Jochumsson and Indriði Einarsson, took their motifs from Icelandic history, from the Eddic poems and the family sagas, from legends and ballads, while their forms were partly influenced by Shakespeare. The same can be said of Jóhann Sigurjónsson (1880–1919) and Guðmundur Kamban (1888–1945), although the latter also wrote plays about contemporary problems, after the breakthrough of realism around the turn of the century. Each of these currents contributed in its own way to the struggle for independence.

The Reykjavík Theatre Company was founded by amateur actors and craftsmen with an interest in drama, such as printers and carpenters. To quote Sveinn Einarsson, a well-known producer, writer, and historian of the stage, who has also been director of Iðnó and then of the National Theatre, the first year's work at Iðnó rewarded 'the fumbling efforts of various amateur groups to establish permanent theatrical activity in a nascent urban culture'.[17] The old Iðnó was congenial with charm and atmosphere. But it was far too small for the Reykjavík audiences. It was obvious that more space was needed.

The first answer was the National Theatre. With its 660 seats, and soon afterwards a second stage, many people around 1950 thought that the new theatre ought to be sufficient. The range of shows tripled overnight, but the theatres continued to be packed. Fortunately, it was decided to continue at the old Iðnó Theatre. The coming of the National Theatre naturally opened new doors; more vigorous contacts with the outside world were established.

The second answer came in October 1989, when the new Reykjavík Civic Theatre was ceremoniously opened and the Iðnó ensemble paraded on to the stage. The new theatre stands in Listabraut (Art Road), near the Kringlan shopping mall, which grew up in the 1980s in a newly built part of Reykjavík. Many ardent enthusiasts worked to accomplish this huge building project, which was brought to a successful close by the then mayor of Reykjavík, Davíð Oddsson. In his younger years he was a playwright and secretary of Iðnó, when Sveinn Einarsson was director of that theatre. The plans were already made in those days. When Sveinn Einarsson moved to the National Theatre, Vigdís Finnbogadóttir took over Iðnó and continued the fight for the cause, together with the artistes and staff of the theatre.

The Civic Theatre has already attracted interest abroad for its architecture. It was designed in close conjunction with people active in the theatre (one of the architects is also a leading actor, Þorsteinn Gunnarsson). There are two stages; the big theatre seats 570 people, while the little one seats 200. The repertoire during the first year consisted entirely of new works by Icelandic playwrights, including a dramatization by Kjartan Ragnarsson of the first two books in Halldór Laxness's tetralogy *World Light*.

Iceland has a flourishing artistic life. In winter it is not unusual for there to be 40–50 concerts per month in Reykjavík, and several new exhibitions of visual art are opened every week. In the last ten years, film production has developed considerably. Some of these films have achieved international success.[18] Another feature of artistic life in Iceland is the great interest in choir-singing.

Chess

The Icelanders have a passionate interest not only in theatre and cinema, but also in dramatic performances of a different kind—chess tournaments. All Icelandic Grand Masters in chess belong to the world élite. The first of them, Friðrík Ólafsson (born 1935), acquired the title in 1958. After Friðrík, five more Icelanders have received this title. It is not surprising, then, that Grand Masters in chess are eager to play in Reykjavík. In 1972, the Icelandic Chess Association hosted the exciting duel for the world championship between Boris Spassky and Bobby Fischer.

The American Willard Fiske (died 1904), a chess enthusiast, a patron of the arts and learning, and a great friend of Iceland, has left us a lively account of the Icelanders' passion for chess. In his book on the topic,[19] he cites as evidence a folktale from Grímsey. On this isolated island on the Arctic Circle, there was once a fourteen-year-old boy who had never left the island. His behaviour was therefore unrefined, but he did know one thing: how to play chess. His first trip to the mainland took him along with his father to the bishop's residence at Hólar in northern Iceland. When the bishop was passing, everyone took off his hat except the boy. On being reproached for this, the boy asked, 'Who then was that man?' One of the bystanders said, 'The bishop, you fool, the biggest priest in Iceland.' 'Oh, the bishop, does he play chess well? . . . But of course he does, for our parson is the second-best player in Grímsey,' said the boy in his way of thinking. This remark was reported to the bishop, who sent for the boy and asked him, 'What was it that you asked in the court?' The lad from Grímsey replied, 'I only asked one of your people if you played a good game of chess; for if you do, I should like to try one with you.' The bishop, who was also a skilled chess player, and exceedingly proud of his superiority, had to see his pride shattered as the boy quickly beat him in three straight games. When the defeated bishop asked the boy where he had learned how to play, the answer was: 'From my father and his people in Grímsey, for in the winter we play from early in the morning till late at night.' 'I should rather say,' exclaimed the humiliated bishop, 'that you learned it from the devil, and that you have been neglecting your prayers.' 'Why, if that be the case, I should be quite able to beat the fellow you mention, since I can beat the parson, and the parson, who is very good and pious, can beat anybody else.' This disarming reply from the gifted boy impressed the bishop, who admitted him to the cathedral school at Hólar, with excellent results. The boy later became a good and pious priest, well able to withstand the assaults of any adversary—even the devil.

Willard Fiske was just as impressed as the bishop. He gave the inhabitants of Grímsey a large number of chess boards and pieces. It was Fiske who founded the famous Icelandic Collection at Cornell University Library, to which he bequeathed his many books about Iceland.

According to Fiske and other authorities, the game of chess ultimately originated in India, where a game known as *cáturanga* was played. The name, meaning 'quadripartite', comes from Indian military strategy; when Alexander the Great was campaigning in India, he had to deal with Indian armies composed of four types of troops: infantry, cavalry, chariots, and elephants. In modern chess these have become pawns, knights, bishops, and rooks.

Much evidence points to close contacts between Icelanders and Englishmen at the time when chess was brought to Iceland. The Icelandic names of the chess pieces, for example—*kóngur, drottning, biskup, riddari, hrókur, peð*—are closer to the forms in English—*king, queen, bishop, knight, rook, pawn*—than to their German counterparts—*König, Dame, Läufer, Springer, Turm, Bauer.*[20]

Sculptors

Bertel Thorvaldsen

The most famous of all Icelandic sculptors is the 'Dane' Bertel Thorvaldsen (1770–1844). He was the son of an Icelander, and he spent almost all his artistic life in Rome, although—like the Norwegian-Danish writer Ludvig Holberg—he had grown up and received his education in Copenhagen. He can perhaps be best described as half-Icelandic, half-Danish.

Reference works, especially older editions, often contain misleading or incomplete data about Thorvaldsen's correct Christian name (Albert) and date of birth (1770), and about the fact that he inherited a rich artistic talent on his Icelandic father's side.[21]

Albert Thorvaldsen's grandfather, Þorvaldur Gottskálksson, pastor of Miklibær í Blönduhlíð at Skagafjörður in northern Iceland, built his own church. He decorated it tastefully with wood-carvings and oil paintings. In 1757, at great personal sacrifice, he sent all his three children—Ari, Gottskálk, and Ólöf—on the same ship to Copenhagen to receive an education. Ari became a goldsmith and Gottskálk a stonemason and wood-carver. Albert's grandmother, Guðrún, also came from a well-known Icelandic family where art and dexterity were highly valued.

Albert's father, Gottskálk Þorvaldsson, carved figureheads for ships. Most of them probably disappeared along with the ships, but one example of his work can be seen today: In Eckernförde by the Kiel Bight, the townspeople have set up a bronze cast of his figurehead *Gefjun* in a park. In the Eddic poem *Lokasenna* (Loki's Wrangling), Odin says that the goddess Gefjun knew the destinies of men as well as he did himself. The figurehead shows four heads rising out of the crest of a wave with Gefjun holding the reins. This unusual motif is taken from Snorri Sturluson's *Gylfaginning*. King Gylfi of Sweden had promised Gefjun as much land as she could plough in a day and a night. She then yoked four oxen to a plough, but they were no ordinary oxen: they were her sons by a giant from Jötunheimur. They ploughed so deep that they loosened a large piece of land which Gefjun set in the sea. This was the origin of Sjælland (Zealand) in Denmark, while the hole that was left became Mälaren, the lake on which Stockholm is situated. Snorri quotes a verse by Bragi the Old:[22]

> Gefjun dragged with laughter
> from Gylfi liberal prince
> what made Denmark larger,
> so that beasts of draught
> the oxen reeked with sweat;
> four heads they had, eight eyes to boot
> who went before broad island-pasture
> ripped away as loot.

There are no records in any Danish or Icelandic parish register of where and when Albert Thorvaldsen was born. There appears to be an acceptable explanation for this omission. Early in 1770, Gottskálk had married a Danish-born woman, Karen, who was expecting a child. They lived in Copenhagen. According to a persistent story from Skagafjörður, which is corroborated by other evidence, they visited Iceland that summer. Gottskálk wanted to meet his relatives again and show Karen his birthplace. The journey back to Denmark was repeatedly postponed because of bad weather. Just after they finally left Skagafjörður, their only son, Albert, was born on board the ship. Albert himself claimed that he was born on 19 November 1770.

Albert was an unusual Christian name in Denmark in the eighteenth century. In contrast, it does occur in the 1703 census of Iceland, which was conducted by the manuscript collector Árni Magnússon and the lawman Páll Vídalín.[23]

In his later years, Thorvaldsen signed official documents using the name Albert. The Icelanders always called him by this name. A treasure in Reykjavík Cathedral is a marble baptismal font with biblical motifs, sculpted in Rome by Thorvaldsen and donated to Iceland in

1838. The font bears his Latinized name, ALBERTVS THORVALD-
SEN. It is 'Albert' who is addressed in a poem of thanks for the gift
by Jónas Hallgrímsson:

> Albert Thorvaldsen
> gave it to his native land;
> how can the native land
> give thanks to Albert?

Bertel is probably a pet form of Albert. In any case, his surname
Thorvaldsen is clearly a Danicized form of the patronymic Þorvaldsson.

The finest collection of Thorvaldsen's austerely classical sculptures
can be seen in the Thorvaldsen Museum in Copenhagen, but he received commissions from all over Europe. A famous example is *The
Lion of Lucerne*, a monument to the Swiss who died during the French
Revolution.

Albert Thorvaldsen was proud of his Icelandic origin, but he did not
boast of it; he was averse to all forms of snobbery, vanity, and arro-
gance. After his triumphal return from Rome to Denmark in 1838, he
was hailed in the manner of a national hero or a saint. His own attitude
is illustrated in the following contemporary anecdote:

Thorvaldsen, about to be honoured by a visit from some Icelandic
representatives of the Nordic Archaeological Association, was struggling to pull on a pair of boots. They were too small for him. When
the visitors paraded into the room, an Icelandic professor stepped
forward with the association's mark of distinction and a genealogical
table. The table showed, according to the professor's pompous speech,
that Thorvaldsen was directly descended from the Norwegian king
Magnús Barefoot (died 1103). At that Thorvaldsen threw the boots to
one side and sighed, 'Well, well. Now I see why the boots don't fit.
Going barefoot runs in the family.'[24]

Einar Jónsson

The sculptor Einar Jónsson (1874–1954) was the subject of a doctoral
thesis by Ólafur Kvaran, who produced a portrait of the man himself
and the development of form and symbolism in his work.[25] The study,
which covers the period 1900–20, provides new, thought-provoking

approaches to the topic, showing, for example, how Einar Jónsson was influenced by theosophy and the mystical ideas of Emanuel Swedenborg.

Einar Jónsson's origin (a farm in southern Iceland) and his higher education (at the Danish Academy of Fine Arts, 1896–9) were typical of ambitious young Icelanders of the day. He developed further during long stays in foreign countries: in the art metropolises of Europe and in Philadelphia. It was in the USA in 1917–18 that he was commissioned to produce a statue of Þorfinnur karlsefni, the Icelander who is regarded as the first colonist in America. Þorfinnur's weapons reveal his Icelandic links. His scabbard bears Iceland's four guardian creatures in relief—the dragon, the bird of prey, the bull, and the giant—who thwarted the ambitions of the Danish king, Haraldur blátönn.[26]

Before Einar Jónsson's début as a sculptor, there was only one outdoor statue in Reykjavík. It was a work by Thorvaldsen, donated by the city of Copenhagen in 1874, when Iceland was celebrating the millenary of the settlement. Einar Jónsson remedied this deficiency. He created a number of bronze sculptures which now stand, covered by a green patina, in central Reykjavík. They depict prominent figures from Icelandic history, such as the first settler, Ingólfur Arnarson, the poets Jónas Hallgrímsson and Hannes Hafstein, King Christian IX, and the national hero Jón Sigurðsson. The latter statue, which stands outside the Althing, emphasizes Jón Sigurðsson's role as an orator and a pioneer. We may also mention the figure of Christ in Hallgrímskirkja, and the statue *Released from the Spell*, Einar Jónsson's interpretation of the legend of Saint George, the dragon, and the princess. He also planned a monument to Snorri Sturluson, but it never got beyond a sketch.

Many of Einar Jónsson's works around the turn of the century are characterized by his romantic temperament and religious brooding. He favoured motifs from Nordic mythology (Ymir and Auðhumla) and folk legends. The best known of these works is the statue of *The Outlaw*, which stands by the old cemetery in Reykjavík. It is based on the tale of an outlaw who had fled to the wilderness with his young wife. On her deathbed she asked him to bury her in consecrated ground. The statue depicts the outlaw carrying his wife's body tied to his back, with a child on his arm. He is followed by a dog on his night walk to the cemetery. The work shows influences of Auguste Rodin and the Norwegian sculptors Stephan Sinding and Gustav Vigeland. It also shows how Einar's soul was torn between realism and dreamy romanticism.

Allegorical symbolism is also seen in *The Guardian*, a ghost who watches over his graveyard to ensure that other dead people receive a burial. Another work with a similar motif is *Dawn*. It is based on the legend of the lone girl and the troll at the window, who is turned into stone by the oblique rays of the rising sun.[27] The morning sun has the same effect on night-trolls as the sight of Medusa's head in Greek mythology. According to Einar's own interpretation of the motif, the troll symbolizes narrow-minded hostility to culture, while the girl represents the Icelandic people, freeing themselves from the shackles of witchcraft with the aid of the morning sun. It stands for a new age with new ideas.[28]

As a young man, Einar Jónsson was a revolutionary, questioning all authority. He gradually lost the Christian belief of his childhood, finally ending up in a religious crisis. He found a way out of the labyrinth. One of the clues he followed was theosophy and the doctrine of correspondences elaborated by the visionary Emanuel Swedenborg.[29] Einar Jónsson thus gained peace of mind, while also being inspired to create allegorical motifs.

On his return to Iceland in 1920, the young firebrand became something of a mystic and philosopher. Modernistically inclined Icelanders have claimed that he also became a loner, who cut himself from the outside world and new ideas. Critics says that he isolated himself within the walls surrounding his studio and its park. Since 1923 it has been a state-owned museum. It has been described with some irony as 'very much a temple devoted to his own art and a centre for meditation on its spiritual truths'.[30]

Ólafur Kvaran's study suggests that such criticism is exaggerated. It can hardly be ruled out that posterity's verdict on Einar Jónsson's art will ultimately be more qualified and favourable.

Ásmundur Sveinsson

Anyone who visits the University of Iceland today will see a concrete reminder of the legend of 'Sæmundur and the Seal'. The view in front of the main building is dominated by an eye-catching sculpture by Ásmundur Sveinsson (1893–1982). It shows Sæmundur astride a seal, with his psalter in his hand. We have met this popular tale in Chapter 3.

This is one of Ásmundur's many masterpieces. The visitor will not soon forget it. One is tempted to return to it time and again—to be impressed by the perfection of form, to have the imagination fired by the choice of motif. In short, this sculpture, which preserves the memory of one of the first Icelanders to receive a university education, could scarcely have been placed in a better location.

Ásmundur Sveinsson has also been the subject of a doctoral thesis which appeared at the University of Aix-en-Provence in 1986.[31] The author, Gunnar B. Kvaran, tells how Ásmundur was born on the isolated farm of Kolsstaðir in western Iceland. He learned reading, writing, arithmetic, and the catechism at a primary school where the main emphasis was on the study of Icelandic sagas, legends, and the superstition which in Ásmundur's childhood still nourished the imagination of the people, at least in the countryside. Paintings and sculptures were totally unknown in his childhood home. The evenings—especially in the winter—were devoted to reading, whether in a group or individually.

Ásmundur was privileged to grow up in love and harmony with nature. His first profound visual impression was the beauty of a typically Icelandic treeless landscape with its shimmering light and its views of sloping meadows, lava fields, mountains, waterfalls, and the sea. The conceptual world of his youth was filled with images rooted in nature: the changes of the seasons, the hazy blue of the sea and the skies. This was to be a strong expressive force in his later creations.

He came as an adult, accompanied by a local priest, to Reykjavík, where he learned wood-carving, modelling, and drawing. After tentative studies in Reykjavík (1915–19) and a winter in Copenhagen, where he was not happy, he took his first real steps in sculpture at the Royal Academy of Fine Arts in Stockholm (1920–6). Here he became a devoted pupil of Carl Milles, that master of movement. He was influenced by the archaic Greek style of Milles and Aristide Maillol. The teacher and the pupil evidently had an intellectually fruitful exchange of ideas, which no doubt helped to develop the personal elements in the young Icelander's future sculptures.

It was under the influence of early Greek art that Ásmundur in 1922 made the first design (in plaster) of *Sæmundur on the Seal*. In 1927 he donated a new, slightly different version of the same motif (also in plaster) to the city of Paris when it was celebrating its bimillenary. In both variants the movement and the inherent tension are depicted expressively, as Sæmundur whacks the seal on the head with the psalter. Ásmundur gave the seal ears, indicating that it was no ordinary seal, but a chimera.

Ásmundur's sojourn in Paris (1926–9) was well used for continued studies in art and new contacts. In Paris and other centres of art, cubists and surrealists were now successfully storming the museums and salons. Ásmundur was influenced by representatives of cubism and abstract art, such as Henri Laurens, Pablo Picasso, and Henry Moore.

One of Ásmundur's Icelandic admirers once said to him, 'There are those who say that you are like Henry Moore. What do you think yourself, Ásmundur?' His reply was at once humble and disarming: 'If some people think so, then I can only be proud of it.'

It is true that Henry Moore and Ásmundur Sveinsson have a great deal in common in their works: they both forge links with bygone ages, they both give form to their perceptions of the landscape. At the same time, it is probably wise to remember the old saying that comparisons are odious.

In Iceland there are some connoisseurs who feel that Ásmundur Sveinsson, although his international reputation is not as great as Henry Moore's, will in the long run be regarded as being at least as remarkable an artist. Ásmundur is perhaps more versatile and more imaginative. He has a uniquely rich breadth. He is also the great seeker, always on the lookout for new horizons. His sculptures burst with incredible energy and powerful emotions, while retaining an unusual suppleness and grace. Ásmundur developed throughout his life, and development blossomed for him. Like Carl Milles, he was a great innovator in one field after another.

In the middle of the 1930s Ásmundur created such famous sculptures in abstract style as *The Water Carrier*, *The Washerwomen*, and *Mother Earth*. He returned to *Egils saga* for inspiration for his works named *Head Ransom* and *Lament* (after *The Great Loss of My Sons*)— the background to these poems is sketched in Chapter 2. Female figures, biblical and mythological motifs, and the music of the seas were recurrent elements in his work. Towards the end of his life, he took a particularly keen interest in modern technology. This found expression in sculptures such as *Through the Sound Barrier*, *Electricity*, *The Face of the Sun*, and *The Spark of Life*.

Ásmundur's work was initially greeted with scepticism and suspicion in Iceland. His life was sometimes difficult, with little money to spend on housing or materials. His problems were exacerbated by his preference for creating large-scale sculptures for outdoor display.

Many of Ásmundur's works are now assembled in a domed building in Reykjavík; the unusual architecture of Ásmundarsafn is the artist's own design. It is said that, when the house was being built, Ásmundur himself undertook the heaviest jobs, including casting the concrete. Other works by this great sculptor adorn outdoor locations in Reykjavík and the neighbouring towns.

One of these works is, as we have seen, the final version of *Sæmundur on the Seal*. The sculpture was erected in 1970. In 1975 it was cast in bronze, on the initiative of the Student Union with the collaboration of the poet and newspaper editor Matthías Johannessen.

Ásmundur is one in a line of prominent Icelandic sculptors. Others include Sigurjón Ólafsson (1908–82) and Gerður Helgadóttir (1928–75). Gerður, who studied with Ossip Zadkine in Paris, is also known for her reliefs and stained glass; the latter can be admired at Skálholt Cathedral. Talented representatives of modernism are the sculptors Jón Gunnar Árnason (1931–89), whose artistic quest led him to original forms of expression, and Jóhann Eyfells (born 1923). Jóhann has been active as a professor of art in Florida, but his works are clearly influenced by the Icelandic lava landscape. The enormous power inherent in his sculptures reminds us of the uncontrollable, fiery flow of lava.

Painters

Nature does not only have its right in
art. It is also a life-giving force, in
exactly the same way as abstract
beauty is an indispensable condition
for art.

Gunnlaugur Scheving

Ásgrímur Jónsson

Like his contemporary, Einar Jónsson, the landscape painter Ásgrímur
Jónsson (1876–1958) is an outstanding artist whose work bears the
palpable influence of Icelandic folk belief and legend. Ásgrímur himself has explained this in his autobiography, referring to some childhood impressions:[32]

> A description of my early impressions from the mountains would be
> incomplete if I only dwelled on their beauty, the play of colour, the
> dignity. In the minds of us children, the mountains were the home of a
> marvellous people, who tickled our imagination no less than elves and
> fairies. These elusive people, who alone knew the breadth of all secrets,
> were the outlaws. I am convinced that there were few young people who
> did not believe in their existence. I think we even imagined we saw them
> retreating to the mountains and the glaciers when the shadows length-
> ened in the evenings.

Ásgrímur's profound knowledge of folklore was undoubtedly due in
part to the evening vigils in his childhood home, when the long winter
evenings were spent doing needlework, knitting, and other handicrafts
while listening to the sagas and tales that were read aloud by the light
of the oil-lamp.

Like a number of other Icelandic artists, Ásgrímur grew up in a poor
home. He was the oldest of a family of five children on a small farm
in the south. Even as a child he showed his inclination for sculpting
with whatever was available (clay, moss, bits of wood) and for drawing. He once drew a picture of the volcano Hekla with the aid of a
chalk and the pigment from the 'blue bag' that was used for washing
whites.

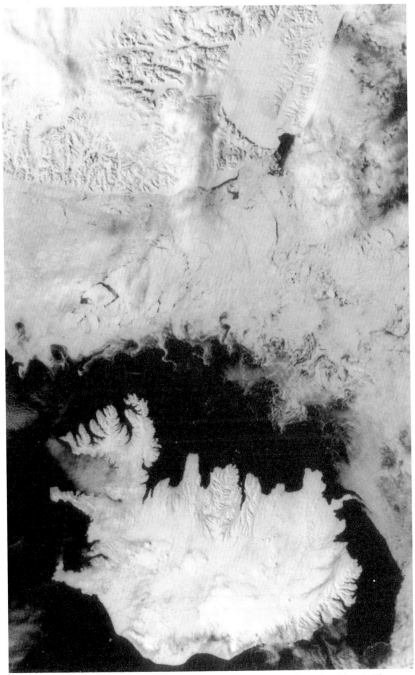

24 *A satellite photo showing Iceland and a part of eastern Greenland (top). The photo was taken on 17th March 1979.*

25 *The results of soil conservation can clearly be seen on this picture from eastern Iceland. The mountain Snæfell in the background. See pp. 265-71.*

26 *Volunteers for soil conservation.*

27 *Alone in the wilderness.*

28 *Hopeful growth for the future.*

29 *Icelandic fishermen toiling for their daily bread. One of Gunnlaugur Scheving's marine paintings, painted between 1960 and 1970. See pp. 192-5.*

30 The Night-Troll in the Window, *painting by Ásgrímur Jónsson (1905). See p. 188.*

31 Ruins of an old turf-house *as depicted in a retrospective dream by the artist, Jóhannes Kjarval. Oil painting from around 1950. See pp. 190-91.*

Hedder du Trold saae den lille Prinsesse

32 Is Your Name Troll? *Drawing by Muggur (1924). See p. 190.*

33 Earth of Fire *by textile artist Ásgerður Búadóttir (1991), made for the Industrial Loan Fund (Iðnlánasjóður) in Reykjavík. See p. 147.*

34 On the hidden coast, *painting by Jóhannes Kjarval (1935).*

35 *The altarpiece in the church of Skálholt, mosaic by Nína Tryggvadóttir (1964-65). See p. 146.*

36 *An embroidery by Rakel Sigurðardóttir-Rosenblad, made after an old Icelandic embroidery which is preserved in the National Museum of Iceland. The yarn is coloured with traditional Icelandic herbal colours. The colours in the original embroidery have faded considerably over centuries.*

At the age of fourteen, he began to earn a living as a farm-hand and seaman. He was captivated by winter mornings on the western fiords, the melodies of the sea, the shifts in the weather, the mystical conceptions of folk belief, and other things which may appear mundane and dull to most of us ordinary people. Artists see so much that escapes the ordinary eye. This is pointed out by the painter Gunnlaugur Scheving, one of Ásgrímur's many admirers, in a little essay about Ásgrímur.[33]

After seven years of single-minded toil, Ásgrímur had amassed enough savings—200 krónur and two poorly fitting suits—to enable him to go to Copenhagen. He supported himself there by painting furniture, until he was admitted in 1900 to the Academy of Fine Arts in Copenhagen. After his stay at the academy and study trips abroad, chiefly to Italy and Germany, he returned to Iceland and began travelling around, eagerly painting what he saw. At that time he was influenced by various classical masters, the French impressionists, and especially Vincent van Gogh. He never tired of looking at van Gogh's paintings from Provence. Ásgrímur gradually gave up the dark, heavy colours of the nineteenth century for oil paintings and water-colours in brighter hues. Shades of blue, as well as green, brown, yellow, and red, were to be his favourite colours on the palette.

Through these paintings with Icelandic motifs he conveyed his romantic impression of the features that distinguish the grandiose Icelandic landscape. His paintings from Húsafell between Borgar-fjörður and Langjökull are good examples of this. His brush captures knotty, stunted birches on eroded red soil, against a background of mossy slopes and green meadow land, black expanses of lava and mountains, ice-blue lakes, and the white domes of the glaciers. He also loves to show how the wind plays with the leaves, how the shadows dance over the fields.

On other canvases we meet terrifying giants, wizards, and elves, creatures that we recognize from Icelandic folktales. They seem to grow out of the landscape. The people in these paintings are often fleeing from gruesome monsters. Alternatively, they can be running away from volcanic eruptions, when the earth's inner forces go berserk, with scarlet flames, boulders flung high into the air, gases, clouds of ash, and glowing streams of lava, menacingly creeping along and burning everything in their path.

But Ásgrímur could also immortalize motifs from the Icelandic sagas, as in 1903, when he applied for a travel grant from the Althing. On this occasion, according to an anecdote, he presented a painting for display in the Althing. Entitled *Lovely are the Slopes*, it showed Gunnar of Hlíðarendi with his horse. Ásgrímur was given the grant, although Hermann Jónasson, one of the members of parliament, remarked that Gunnar's horse on the painting had no bridle. Yet Hermann added with a smile that this gave a new explanation for Gunnar's return to Hlíðarendi. He had forgotten to bridle his horse, so he was forced to stay at home.

An Icelandic art historian has claimed that Ásgrímur was bound to the soil. This may be so. But he loved to listen to classical music: Bach, Mozart, Beethoven. He found room for a piano in his cramped home. When he depicted the creatures in folk belief, he let himself go. He gave his imagination free rein, forgetting drab, everyday reality. He showed this in his illustrations to thirty folktales in a book published in 1959, with a foreword by the literary scholar Einar Ólafur Sveinsson. Here we can see illustrations of such dramatic tales from Jón Árnason's collection as 'Búkolla', 'The Deacon of Myrká', 'Eyvindur of the Mountains', and 'The Night-Troll'.[34]

The tale of 'The Night-Troll' is about a troll who appears at the window of a girl who is alone at home with a baby in her arms. It is Christmas night, just before daybreak. The troll says:

Day is in the east,	*Dagur er í austri,*
My brave lass,	*snör mín, en snarpa,*
Dilly-dilly-do.	*og dillidó.*

The girl responds by pronouncing a spell. The troll disappears from the window. In the morning people found that a huge stone had appeared—the troll had been petrified by the rising sun.[35] Ásgrímur's drawing was reproduced in an ABC book and thus became one of his best-known works. It shows that the troll has precisely the characteristics that we would expect from one of his kind: strength, stupidity, and paganism, but also faithfulness. In fact, Icelandic has an adjective trölltryggur 'troll-true' to describe people who can really be trusted.

As a landscape painter, Ásgrímur was a pioneer. He revealed new ways of perceiving the Icelandic landscape, its beauty and its internal life. Like Einar Jónsson, he bequeathed all his works to the Icelandic people. They are preserved in a special museum in Reykjavík that bears his name. It is his old home—the one with the piano. He received many marks of distinction. In 1952 he was made an honorary member of the Royal Swedish Academy of Fine Arts.

Muggur

Originally many Icelanders probably had fairly vague notions about what the beings in the folktales looked like 'in reality'. To us, however, they appear real, since they have been painted and drawn with such conviction and power, not only by Ásgrímur Jónsson but also by Guðmundur Thorsteinsson, affectionately known as Muggur (1891–1924). These two artists have entered into the legends with such empathy that we, as it were, recognize the trolls; we feel that we have seen them ourselves.

During his years at the Academy of Fine Arts in Copenhagen, 1912–15, the talented and versatile Muggur suddenly produced his imaginative pictures of trolls. He had grown up in Bíldudalur by Arnarfjörður, in an environment filled with tales and superstitions. Among the servants in the home there was a woman whose special duty was to read stories aloud to the children, who thus became acquainted with the Icelandic sagas, the legends and the fairy tales. These stories and the landscape around Arnarfjörður were to mould Muggur's conceptual world.

Muggur was by nature humorous, often cheerful and relaxed, but he was also a weak-willed dreamer. He was inclined to abandon himself to a life of uninhibited bohemianism along with his fellow artists, the kind of life depicted in Henri Murger's novel and Giacomo Puccini's opera, *La Bohème*.

Muggur's life was brief. He died of tuberculosis at the age of 32. Yet he achieved so much in this short career. In 1920 he played the leading role in the Danish film *The History of the Borg Family*, based on Gunnar Gunnarsson's novel and partly filmed on location in Iceland. He founded an art school in Reykjavík, the first in Iceland, where one of his pupils was Gunnlaugur Scheving. During a summer in Siena he painted the altarpiece 'Christ Healing the Sick', a triptych which now adorns the church at the president's residence at Bessastaðir. The work was deposited there by the owner, the Icelandic Art Museum.

Just a few weeks before his death in a Danish sanatorium, Muggur summoned his strength to do a pencil-drawing. It shows a pretty little princess standing before a ghastly troll. The princess has got lost outside her castle park and wanders around in the wilderness, when she suddenly sees a terrifying monster in the shape of a man. With tears in his eyes and cupped hands, the monster falls on his knees before the fair princess. She looks up at him and asks softly, 'Is your name Troll?'[36]

Jóhannes Kjarval

The virtuoso landscape and portrait painter Jóhannes Sveinsson Kjarval (1885–1972) was a poor farmer's son from eastern Iceland. He worked hard at sea for many years before he had the chance to continue his education, first in London, then in Copenhagen. Halldór Laxness, who was quick to discover Kjarval, noted that Iceland is one of the few countries, perhaps the only one in the world, where young, ambitious men have to go to sea before they can afford to go to high school.[37]

As a very young man, he received his first guidance in Reykjavík from Ásgrímur Jónsson. In London he met the sculptor Einar Jónsson. Although Kjarval was later influenced during his long life by many different trends in art—romanticism, impressionism, expressionism, cubism, and abstract painting—he retained his freedom. He cannot be labelled as an exponent of any one artistic fashion. He gradually developed an independent style, a highly personal manner which he developed to mastery. The autumn of 1929 was an important turning-point in his life. He added new, imaginative elements to the traditional depiction of motifs. His paintings were to be characterized by dreamy romance and striking symbolism. He had two lyrical visions of the Icelandic landscape: one visible, one hidden. The latter is the home of the *huldufólk* whom we have met in Chapter 3.

In Kjarval's paintings after 1929—with motifs from places like

Þingvellir, Esja, and Álftanes—he often focuses his interest on colourful close-ups of lava formations, patches of moss, scattered rocks,
cliffs and gorges, hills and slopes. In this way he seductively brings
out both the rugged and the majestic, the visionary and yet down-to-
earth qualities of Þingvellir, the remarkable place which was once the
site of the Althing.

In this landscape we also meet the supernatural phenomena of
popular belief: elves and shield-maidens, hidden ships and secretive
fairies in their kingdom of boulders and cliffs. Kjarval had been
captivated by these creatures since his childhood. They are not depicted in a directly figurative way, but we still gain the impression that
they are moving in the landscape. It is animated.

It is not easy to describe in a few words what is typical of Kjarval's
paintings and drawings. They have to be seen, studied. Yet every
Icelander can immediately recognize his work, as most of us would
instantly recognize a painting by Rembrandt or van Gogh.

Kjarval's creative imagery is also evident in his poems. He was a
highly sensitive person. The painter was anxious to be taken seriously
as a poet too. He was fascinated by Jóhann Sigurjónsson's description
of life as music, to which he added: 'We are tones in an orchestra.'[38]

Kjarval was a pioneer. He trod new paths. With his chimerical art
he taught his fellow countrymen to see Iceland with new eyes. He was
also the country's most popular visual artist, perhaps because, in the
final phase of the struggle for independence, he—like Gunnlaugur
Scheving—was better than most at interpreting what is specifically
Icelandic. A retrospective exhibition of his paintings, arranged to
celebrate his seventieth birthday in 1955, attracted 25,000 visitors,
one-eighth of the population of Iceland at the time.

Since 1973, Kjarval's art has been on show in a special museum in
Reykjavík, known as Kjarvalsstaðir, which is also frequently used for
exhibitions of new Icelandic art and occasionally foreign art. Kjarval
is one of the Nordic artists who is represented at the Museum of
Modern Art in New York.

Gunnlaugur Scheving

This presentation of well-known Icelandic artists who have been in-spired by the native cultural heritage would not be complete without a consideration of the painter Gunnlaugur Scheving (1904–72), whose works are represented in several museums outside Iceland. He was born and died in Reykjavík. It was in the east country, however, that he grew up, in the good care of kind foster-parents. Gunnlaugur always spoke affectionately of them.

In this barren, sparsely populated district, there was plenty of room for hidden people and superstition. Fear of the darkness and anxiety about the unknown were a normal part of people's lives. The long winter evenings were spent reading the old sagas and the *rímur*-poems. Scheving also became familiar with the folk legends, these reflections of the experiences and dreams of past generations. He was fond of animals. He learned how to ride at an early age. He could sometimes see before him the elf-woman of the folksong, with her cow.

Scheving studied under Muggur and Einar Jónsson in Reykjavík before he went to the Academy of Fine Arts in Copenhagen. During his years there (1925–9) he was influenced by the cubists, particularly Paul Cézanne, Pablo Picasso, and Georges Braque. Picasso was his chief idol.

Gunnlaugur Scheving is best known for his monumental oil paint-ings in cubist style, showing Icelandic fishermen toiling for their daily bread. Down-to-earth realism in the style of the ancient Greeks and the Italian renaissance painters was always his guiding star. In the foreword to a little book on Ásgrímur Jónsson, he states without reserve: 'Nature does not only have its right in art. It is also a life-giv-ing force, in exactly the same way as abstract beauty is an indis-pensable condition for art.'[39] What helps to make these seascapes from the fishing stations of Grindavík and Hafnarfjörður so realistic is the fact that Scheving knew the craft of the seaman. He had been to sea. He knew what a fishing-boat looks like and how it is steered. He had seen weather-beaten Icelandic fishermen doing their work on board, while battling with the elements—fickle winds and rising wave-crests. He depicts the interplay between the sea with its shifting nuances of green and blue, the swaying deck, and the fishermen in their yellow oilskins.

Man is always at the centre of Scheving's work. The paintings convey a meaning with a broad scope in time and space. These earnest fishermen are like timeless heroes out of Greek mythology. Perhaps they are listening to the throbbing of the engine. Scheving compares it to the regular beats of the heart, or the recurrent theme in a symphony.

Art historians have wondered about the contrast between these realistic paintings of the sea and the atmosphere of dreamlike superstition that haunts Scheving's idyllic motifs from land. Here we see, for example, a stylized farmer's family with their cow, their guarantee of survival. Folklore takes over here, as in the oil paintings *Autumn Angel, Midwinter Night, Midsummer Night*, and *The Midsummer Dream of the Elf-Cow*.[40] But this contradiction is illusory. It is merely a reflection of two sides of the artist's mind.

The pastoral motifs in Scheving's art have their roots in his ability to live the past. Other expressions of his fascination with history are his paintings of the discovery and settlement of Iceland. In one of these we see Ingólfur Arnarson throwing the pillars of his high-seat overboard. Scheving illustrated two of the most popular Icelandic sagas, *Njáls saga* and *Grettis saga Ásmundarsonar*.

We obtain interesting insights into Scheving's explorations of the borderland between dream and reality in his drawings for an anthology of folksongs edited by Einar Ólafur Sveinsson under the title 'I Heard the Beautiful Voices'.[41] One of these songs is the children's prayer for the cows in the pasture, the 'Mary theme'. The children say the prayer while looking upwards, after which they make a sign of the cross in the air with the right hand. The prayer ends with the following verse:

Hail Mary, mother of God,
sit you down on a stone
and keep a good watch on my cows,
while I make my way home.

Scheving's drawing captures this motif perfectly: a treeless landscape with mountains on the horizon, and with the Virgin Mary in the foreground, sitting on a stone holding the baby Jesus in her arms, keeping watch over a cow that lies peacefully on the ground. Scheving has woven a bond between folk belief and the Icelandic landscape.

It is worth listening to the artist's own words. The following are extracts from a book in which Scheving talks with Matthías Johannessen.[42]

> MJ: Your descriptions of your childhood environment bear the stamp of folk legend. You must have become familiar with these legends at an early age.
>
> GS: Yes, for me they were a reality which I respected and feared. Once in winter, when I was alone in the living-room, I found an old whetstone. I threw it up in the air out of pure thoughtlessness, and as it landed on the floor I was seized by a terrible fear, because I immediately saw before me Thor's head with a bleeding wound in the crown. The whetstone was lodged right in the top of his head.

Gunnlaugur had thought of the tale of Thor's duel with the giant Hrungnir, in which a piece of the giant's whetstone pierced Thor's skull so that he fell forward on the earth. The whetstone still sits in Thor's head. Since then, it has been the rule that 'hones should never be thrown across the floor as, in that case, the hone is moved that is stuck in Thor's head'.[43]

> MJ: Isn't your big painting, which you call *Midwinter Night* (*Skammdegisnótt*), related to folk legends?
>
> GS: That may well be so. I can tell you how the painting came into being, so that you can draw your own conclusions. About twenty years ago, I was a guest on a farm one winter. In the night I heard that there were beasts on the other side of the board wall where I was sleeping. It was the rams, butting each other in the dark. That made me think of the time when people had cows under the floor. I had never seen that, but I had sometimes heard tell of it. And then I saw a picture before me: a cow bringing the light and heat of summer into the cold and severity of the winter's night. And I thought of the loneliness and fear of a human being during that long night. It struck me that the smell and the light of the cow could warm a woman who sat with her sleeping child, dreaming of the summer. The essential feature of all this was the cow's breath in the night darkness. I gave the painting a name at once. It wasn't really a name but a theme: 'the breath of the cow makes the child dream of a summer bird'. . . .
>
> MJ: Do you believe in elves—or in dwarves in rocks?
>
> GS: They belonged to a time a little after the onset of twilight on long winter evenings. I want them to exist. The elves are a symbol of what people wanted to be. They were generally pagans who stuck to old customs and respected the country's nature. They were devoted to

animals. They knew the art of patting a cow. Even the spider received its share of their love of nature. They did not want the beautiful hills, rocks, and other natural phenomena to be disdained or destroyed, for that was where they lived. They knew that intractability, stubbornness, and lack of fellow feeling were harmful. I think it is unlucky to go against the temperament of the elves. There are two reasons for this. Firstly, there is sound common sense in the elves' mentality. Secondly, the elves long preserved the memory of what had happened, whether good or ill. Otherwise, these beings are favourably disposed to mankind. They are guardian spirits (wights). Jónas Hallgrímsson says in his poem that when the dwarf has fled and the troll has died in his rock, then the people in the country have become 'a heavy-hearted people in trouble'.[44]

We glimpse a similar form of superstition in Halldór Laxness's *Ís-landsklukkan*. At the site of the assembly by Öxará, three women cleared of an accusation of crime meet an elf-woman dressed in black:

> The three companions looked in reverent silence at the elf-woman before them and were allowed to touch her. They wanted to do all that they could for her, since it is a tried and tested sign of luck to be good to the elves.

Einar Ólafur Sveinsson and other fiery spirits have expressed a hope that Iceland's native cultural heritage will continue to serve as a source of stimulus, an inspiring magic flute. This hope has been richly fulfilled. We may conclude by naming just a few of the acclaimed artists who have illustrated Icelandic legends in recent years: Eiríkur Smith, Gylfi Gíslason, Halldór Pétursson, Haraldur Guðbergsson, Hringur Jóhannesson, Jóhann Briem, Kjartan Guðjónsson, Tryggvi Magnús-son, and Þorbjörg Höskuldsdóttir.

Composers

The greatest and best riches in any
country is the people itself, those who
live there, think, and work.
Einar Benediktsson

Páll Ísólfsson

A central figure in Icelandic music was Páll Ísólfsson (1893–1974), an
organist of the highest order. In his musical style he carried on the
traditions of Bach, Brahms, and Reger.

Jón Þórarinsson

One of the disciples of Páll Ísólfsson is Jón Þórarinsson (born 1917).
In 1944–47 he studied at Yale University and the Juillard School of
Music in New York under the inspiring influence of Paul Hindemith.
Upon his return to Iceland he participated in the founding of the
Icelandic Symphony Orchestra. In 1950 he became its first Chairman.
He composed pieces of chamber music, such as the Clarinet Sonata,
and film music, including that for the film *Paradise Regained* after a
novel by Halldór Laxness. He has also written books, one on Páll
Ísólfsson, another on Sveinbjörn Sveinbjörnsson.

   Thus, Jón Þórarinsson has continued the pioneer work of Páll Ísólfsson.

Jón Leifs

Jón Leifs (1899–1968) spent most of his life as a composer in Germany, where he conducted orchestras and wrote about music. The
Nazis, however, took a dim view of him, since his first wife was
Jewish. In his native Iceland he also met some opposition, no doubt
because he was a rampant individualist who stubbornly followed his
own path.[45]

   Under the ineffaceable influence of Franz Liszt's *Faust* Symphony,
Jón Leifs composed *Söguhetjur* ('The Saga Symphony', op. 26). Here

he portrays in music five of the best-known heroes in the Icelandic sagas: Björn and Skarphéðinn in *Njáls saga*, Guðrún Ósvífursdóttir in *Laxdæla saga*, Grettir in *Grettis saga Ásmundarsonar*, and Þormóður Kolbrúnarskáld in *Fóstbræðra saga*.

Inspiration for his work comes from other sources too, Icelandic folk music and the *Elder Edda*. This is reflected in compositions such as 'Iceland Overture', 'Icelandic Folksongs', 'Three Eddic Songs for Voice and Piano', 'Love Songs from the Edda', and—after 1935—the three-part 'Edda Oratorio'. In this he has taken motifs from *Völuspá* dealing with the creation of the world, the life of the gods, Ragnarök and the rebirth of the world. After his return to Iceland he founded an association of Icelandic composers, Tónskáldafélag Íslands, and the Icelandic Performing Rights Society, STEF.

The complexity of Jón Leifs' personality reveals his kinship with the leading character in Romain Rolland's novel *Jean-Christophe*, a study of a German musician and his times. He is talented but easily clashes with the people around him. Moreover, Jón Leifs' music is generally abrupt and inaccessible, hard to play and anything but audience-friendly. It crackles. It creaks. It sparkles. It nevertheless has an almost magical attraction. It springs from the barren Icelandic landscape, from the fateful history of the Icelanders and the mysteries of the Eddic poems.

Jón Leifs' music initially failed to attract much interest in Iceland. It is all the more praiseworthy that efforts have been made to present his work abroad. His Concerto for Organ and Orchestra (op. 7) was performed for politely puzzled listeners at Wiesbaden in 1935 and to a hostile audience in Berlin in 1941. When it was revived by the Stockholm Philharmonic Orchestra in 1988, however, it was well received.

Jón Ásgeirsson

Jón Ásgeirsson (born 1928) is known for his opera *Þrymskviða*, based on the Eddic poem *The Lay of Þrymur*. It is about how Thor, disguised as the seductive goddess Freyja, visits the giant Þrymur and thereby retrieves his stolen hammer. Jón's ballet *Blindingsleikur* (Blind Man's Buff) takes its motif from an old folktale.

Jón Ásgeirsson shares Jón Leifs' pronounced interest in the native cultural heritage, which for both of them is synonymous with a living patrimony of Icelandic sagas and poems, passion hymns and old folk tunes. One such tune is the distinctive *Lilja*, based on the songs of praise and prayers to Mary written by the Augustinian friar Eysteinn Ásgrímsson (died in Niðarós in 1361).

The *Lilja* melody does not sound like traditional church music. It has its own mode. Jón Ásgeirsson has said that his orchestral work *Lilja* is based on his own meditations about the *Lilja* melody and its religious background. At the beginning and the end of the orchestral piece, which has been performed several times, bells are heard. The listener imagines that he hears the crystal-clear peal of a bell marking the start of the Sabbath. The monastery bell rings while the pious brother Eysteinn sits and confesses in poetry his faith in immortal values. One of these values for Eysteinn is the forgiving love that radiates for him through Jesus Christ and Mary, the mother of God.

Jón Ásgeirsson's sources of inspiration are said to include the passion hymns of the seventeenth-century priest Hallgrímur Péturs-son, the Icelandic sagas, the Eddic poems, and some of Igor Stravin-sky's ballets (*The Firebird, Petrouchka, The Rite of Spring*)—and perhaps also long strolls by the mostly deserted shores of Faxaflói bay. Here one can wind down and listen to the symphonic music of the sea in different movements. One can hear the lulling rhythm of the splash-ing waves, the rising and falling antiphonal surge in major and minor, the crescendo of the billows beating on the rocks.

Mining the Cultural Heritage

A chamber orchestra founded in Reykjavík in 1982, Íslenska hljóms-veitin, with its dynamic conductor Guðmundur Emilsson (born 1951), took a remarkable initiative in the spring of 1987. At his suggestion the orchestra took the first step in a project to hold twelve concerts in which a total of thirty-six works of art would be created: twelve poems, twelve pieces of music, and twelve sculptures. The idea, in other words, is to establish close collaboration between different practitio-ners of art, chiefly poets, composers, musicians, singers, sculptors, photographers, and film directors. To Guðmundur, such a combination is essential.

This bold project goes under the working name *Námur,* meaning 'mines'. The name in this context refers to a spiritual treasure of art and wisdom, like King Solomon's mines, the source of the great king's riches. The project has a common theme. It is to support Icelandic artists by directing their attention and that of the people to the national cultural heritage. The aim is to forge a link between contemporary art and this rich tradition. The idea is that all the nascent works of art should take their subject matter from different phases in Iceland's history: remarkable events or everyday life, storied heroes or simple farmers and fishermen. The works of art are to convey the harsh landscape, man's struggle with nature and with himself. The first concert was held in December 1987 and the second in April 1988. The ultimate goal is to present all thirty-six works of art again in the year 2000, when Iceland celebrates the millenary of the conversion to Christianity. The *Námur* idea was born out of discussions about how best to make this noteworthy commemoration into a culturally meaningful occasion.

The project can also be seen as a deliberate attempt by nationally minded Icelanders to support and preserve the native cultural heritage in an age of virtually insuperable foreign influence. In the sphere of music this is increasingly making itself felt in pop and rock music with English lyrics. It is obvious that this Anglo-American cultural influence is growing rapidly, having become particularly noticeable in the past decade. A rock concert in Iceland can now attract thousands of listeners.

Þorkell Sigurbjörnsson

The concert in Hallgrímskirkja in December 1987 assembled about eight hundred music-lovers, who came to hear the composition *Landnámsljóð* (Settlement Poem). The composer was Þorkell Sigurbjörnsson (born 1938).

Iceland is so small that an artist cannot afford to work as a narrow specialist. This society suits versatile musicians who can create and act in a variety of fields. Þorkell Sigurbjörnsson, for example, has appeared in several roles: as music teacher, as music critic, and as pianist. He is also a spokesman for Nordic collaboration in the sphere of music.

Atli Heimir Sveinsson

The concert in April 1988 was based on the poem 'Sturla' by Matthías Johannessen. It is about the historian Sturla Þórðarson, nephew of Snorri Sturluson and author of *Íslendinga saga* (part of *Sturlunga saga*), an account of Iceland's history in the thirteenth century. In a commentary on the poem, Matthías points out that this saga has helped to preserve Icelandic culture and the Icelandic language down to the present. He sees it as 'a signpost in the sea for those who have gone off course'. Matthías adds: Sturla has disappeared. The age of the Sturlungs is long past. But the memory of that time lives on. Like cotton-grass, it can be glimpsed in the darkness.

Matthías Johannessen's poem has inspired the composer Atli Heimir Sveinsson (born 1938) to a musical creation with the same title, a fine reflection of the message in the poem.

Atli has a broad register. He has also set to music poems from Jón Óskar's collection *Nóttin á herðum okkar* (Night on Our Shoulders). One of these poems, 'Vorkvæði um Ísland' (Spring Poem about Iceland), conjures up a vision of that wet June day at Þingvellir in 1944 when the rain 'poured over your shoulders and eyes and baptized you and the country'. These poems express a love like the Song of Songs that is Solomon's. They carry a message of tenderness, justice, and a better world. At a concert in Reykjavík in 1988, Atli Heimir's musical settings were rendered by the Swedish singers Ilona Maros (soprano) and Marianne Eklöf (mezzo-soprano).

Atli Heimir Sveinsson is a colourful personality of incredible versatility. In 1976 he was the first Icelander to receive the Nordic Prize for Composers, for a flute concerto. In 1982 his opera *Silkitromman* (*The Silken Drum*) was premièred at the Icelandic National Theatre. The opera has also attracted international acclaim, as has the television opera *Vikivaki*. His chamber opera *Le dernier amour du prince Genghi* is based on a novel by Marguerite Yourcenar, where the love motif is taken from an oriental tale. The libretto was written by the Icelandic poet Sigurður Pálsson (born 1948). The opera will be staged in 1993 by a French string quartet and other French performers under the direction of Jean Bernard.

On Good Friday 1988, passion hymns by Hallgrímur Pétursson were performed in the church named after the famous poet-priest, Hallgrímskirkja. It was Atli Heimir Sveinsson who put them to music, based on old hymn tunes from Rev. Bjarni Þorsteinsson's collection of folk tunes.

Jón Nordal and a New Generation

This selection would be incomplete without a mention of six more composers. Jón Nordal (born 1926) is widely admired for his orchestral works and for the Reykjavík Conservatory of which he has been director for several decades. Part of Jón's inspiration comes from the Icelandic landscape, peopled with the creatures of legend, as he has experienced it around lake Þingvallavatn. Hafliði Hallgrímsson (born 1941) is one of a new generation of Icelandic composers, who received the Nordic Prize for Composers in 1986. Karólína Eiríksdóttir (born 1951) has written an opera, *Någon har jag sett* (I Have Seen Someone), based on a collection of Swedish poems by Marie Louise Ramnefalk; it was first performed at Vadstena in Sweden in July 1988. The Austrian-born Páll Pampichler Pálsson (born 1928), who is one of the principle conductors of the Icelandic Symphony Orchestra, has composed a number of chamber, orchestral, and choral pieces. Hjálmar H. Ragnarsson (born 1952) has largely confined himself to the fields of chamber and choral music. Percussion music occupies a central place in the heart of Áskell Másson (born 1953). Two of his early compositions are based on the fairy tales of Hans Christian Andersen and the Brothers Grimm.

Notes to Chapter 4

1   The prize had previously been awarded to two Icelanders, to the novelist and children's writer Ólafur Jóhann Sigurðsson in 1976 and to the poet Snorri Hjartarson in 1981. These and many more writers are presented in *Iceland 1986: Handbook Published by the Central Bank of Iceland* (Reykjavík, 1987). In 1992 the prize was awarded to Fríða Á. Sigurðardóttir.

2   Albert Engström, *Åt Häcklefjäll* (Stockholm: Bonnier, 1913), part 1, p. 10.

3   Björn Th. Björnsson, *Seld Norðurljós* (Reykjavík: Mál og menning, 1982), p. 62.

4   See Chapter 3, 'Folk Belief and Folktales'.

5   Gunnar Gunnarsson, *Guest the One-Eyed*, trans. W. W. Worster (London: Gyldendal, 1920); *Seven Days' Darkness*, trans. Roberts Tapley (New York: Macmillan, 1930); *The Sworn Brothers: A Tale of the Early Days of Iceland*, trans. C. Field and W. Emmé (London: Gyldendal, 1920); *The Black Cliffs: Svartfugl*, trans. Cecil Wood (Madison: University of Wisconsin Press, 1967).

6   Gunnar Gunnarsson, *Ships in the Sky: Compiled from Uggi Greipsson's Notes*, trans. Evelyn Ramsden (London: Jarrolds, 1938); *The Night and the Dream*, trans. Evelyn Ramsden (New York: Bobbs-Merrill, 1938).

7   Guðmundur Kamban, *Hadda Padda: A Drama in Four Acts*, trans. Sadie Louise Peller (New York: Knopf, 1917).

8   Translated by Ruth Baer and Aline Burch as *Nonni and Manni: Lost in the Arctic, a True Story* (New York: P. J. Kennedy, 1958).

9   See Chapter 3, note 17.

10   The translations by Marshall Brement come from his *Three Modern Icelandic Poets: Selected Poems of Steinn Steinarr, Jón úr Vör and Matthías Johannessen* (Reykjavík: Iceland Review, 1985).

11   *Night Eyes and Other Poems* by Einar Bragi, trans. Patricia Aylett, Sigurður A. Magnússon, and Louis A. Muinzer (Advent Books, 1985).

12   *The Postwar Poetry of Iceland*, trans. with introduction by Sigurður A. Magnússon (Iowa City: University of Iowa Press, 1982), p. 65.

13   See Chapter 3, note 21.

14   See Peter Hallberg, *Halldór Laxness*, trans. Rory McTurk, Twayne's World Authors Series 89 (New York: Twayne, 1971).

15   Halldór Kiljan Laxness, *Independent People: An Epic*, trans. J. A. Thompson (London: Allen & Unwin, 1945); *World Light*, trans. Magnus Magnusson (Madison: University of Wisconsin Press, 1969); *The Atom Station*, trans. Magnus Magnusson (London: Methuen, 1961); on *Íslandsklukkan* see Chapter 1, note 66.

16   Kristinn E. Andrésson, *Íslenzkar nútímabókmenntir 1918–1948* (Reykjavík: Mál og menning, 1949), p. 199.

17   Sveinn Einarsson, 'Isländsk teater', *Gardar: Årsbok för Samfundet Sverige–Island i Lund–Malmö* 4 (1973), p. 6; *Íslenzk leiklist* I. *Ræturnar* (Reykjavík: Bókaútgáfa Menningarsjóðs, 1991).

18   See Chapter 2, 'The Icelandic Sagas', and the filmography in the Appendix.

19   Willard Fiske, *Chess in Iceland and in Icelandic Literature with Historical Notes on other Table-games* (Florence, 1905).

20   See also the brief discussion of chess in Chapter 1, 'Trade Monopoly and Natural Disasters'.

21   Our account is based mainly on Björn Th. Björnson's foreword to Carl Frederik Wilckens, *Thorvaldsen við Kóngsins nýjatorg: Endurminningar um daglegt líf*

Alberts Thorvaldsens, reminiscences of Albert Thorvaldsen's everyday life left by his private servant (Reykjavík: Setberg, 1978), pp. 7–30. In 1982 the Thorvaldsen Museum in Copenhagen arranged an exhibition of his works at Kjarvalsstaðir, the art museum of the city of Reykjavík. The catalogue included (pp. 19–29) an essay by Dr Kristján Eldjárn, 'Thorvaldsen og Ísland'.

22　*The Prose Edda of Snorri Sturluson: Tales from Norse Mythology*, trans. Jean I. Young (Berkeley: University of California Press, 1973), p. 29.

23　This was the first detailed census of its kind in Europe, and the entire material has been preserved; see *Iceland 1986*, p. 28.

24　Björn Th. Björnsson's foreword to *Thorvaldsen við Kóngsins nýjatorg*, p. 13.

25　Ólafur Kvaran, *Einar Jónssons skulptur, formutveckling och betydelsevärld*, diss., Lund University (Reykjavík, 1987).

26　See Chapter 3, 'Folk Belief and Folktales'.

27　On the tale of the night-troll, see below under 'Ásgrímur Jónsson'.

28　Björn Th. Björnsson, *Íslenzk myndlist* (Reykjavík: Helgafell, 1964), part 1, p. 66; Ólafur Kvaran, *Einar Jónssons skulptur*, pp. 100–4. The imagery was used in an article by the poet-priest Matthías Jochumsson.

29　Ólafur Kvaran, *Einar Jónssons skulptur*, pp. 134–5, 148–50, 237.

30　*Iceland 1986*, p. 295; cf. Sigurður A. Magnússon, *Northern Sphinx: Iceland and the Icelanders from the Settlement to the Present* (London: Hurst, 1977), pp. 197, 201.

31　Gunnar B. Kvaran, 'Le sculpteur islandais Ásmundur Sveinsson: Étude critique', diss. (Aix and Marseilles, 1986). See also Matthías Johannessen, *Sculptor Ásmundur Sveinsson: An Edda in Shapes and Symbols*, trans. May and Hallberg Hallmundsson (Reykjavík: Iceland Review Books, 1974); Björn Th. Björnsson, 'Den isländske skulptören Ásmundur Sveinsson' *Ord och bild* 65 (1956), pp. 273–84.

32　Tómas Guðmundsson, *Ásgrímur Jónsson: Myndir og minningar* (Reykjavík: Almenna bókafélagið, 1956), p. 25.

33　*Íslenzk list: Ásgrímur Jónsson*, foreword by Gunnlaugur Scheving and Bjarni Guðmundsson (Reykjavík: Helgafell, 1949).

34　Einar Ólafur Sveinsson, *Þjóðsagnabók Ásgríms Jónssonar* (Reykjavík: Bókaútgáfa Menningarsjóðs, 1959). See Hrafnhildur Schram and Hjörleifur Sigurðsson, *Ásgrímur Sveinsson* (Reykjavík: Lögberg, 1986), pp. 26–8.

35　The tale is retold by Jacqueline Simpson, *Icelandic Folktales and Legends* (London: Batsford, 1972), p. 82.

36　Björn Th. Björnsson, *Íslenzk myndlist*, part 1, p. 161; Björn Th. Björnsson, *Guðmundur Thorsteinsson Muggur* (Reykjavík: Helgafell, 1960), p. 159.

37　*Íslenzk list: Jóhannes Sveinsson Kjarval*, introduction by Halldór Kiljan Laxness (Reykjavík: Helgafell, 1950), p. 10.

38　Árni Sigurjónsson, 'The Literary Kjarval', in the catalogue to the Kjarval Centenary Exhibition (Reykjavík, 1985), p. 54.

39　*Íslenzk list: Ásgrímur Jónsson*, foreword.

40　Björn Th. Björnsson, *Íslenzk myndlist*, part 2, pp. 66–7.

41   *Fagrar heyrði ég raddirnar: Þjóðkvæði og stef*, ed. Einar Ól. Sveinsson (1942, reissued Reykjavík: Mál og menning, 1974).

42   Matthías Johannessen, *Gunnlaugur Scheving* (Reykjavík: Helgafell, 1974), pp. 105–7, 110–11.

43   *The Prose Edda of Snorri Sturluson*, p. 106.

44   This is a reference to Jónas Hallgrímsson's poem 'Gunnarshólmi'. The title alludes to a green oasis which existed in Jónas's time among the deserted sandy plains on the south coast of Iceland. According to the saga, it was there that Gunnar of Hlíðarendi looked up at the slopes. They seemed so lovely to him that he resolved to go home and not to go away. See Chapter 2, 'The Icelandic Sagas'.

45   For a presentation of Jón Leifs and other modern Icelandic composers, see Göran Bergendal, New Music in Iceland, trans. Peter Lyne (Reykjavík: Iceland Music Information Centre, 1991).

✦ Chapter 5 ✦

The Leap into the Present

Outline of Development, 1944–1992

Gaily and firmly it pealed,
the bell that once was cracked,
ringing in clearest tones
out over water and woods.

*From Halldór Laxness's poem 'Stóð
ég við Öxará', written on the occasion
of the proclamation of the Republic of
Iceland on 17 June 1944*

THE PROCLAMATION OF THE REPUBLIC from the Law-Rock at
Þingvellir on 17 June 1944 was the most distinct turning-point in the
history of Iceland.

In earlier epochs, changes had taken place at a relatively slow pace.
After the fall of the commonwealth in 1262, the Icelandic people did
not really lose their freedom until much later upheavals occurred: the
triumph of the Reformation in 1550, the imposition of a Danish trade
monopoly in 1602, and the absolute power of the Danish king, which
was confirmed in Iceland through the agreement in Kópavogur in
1662. In a similar way, when the Icelanders regained their independence, it was the result of a series of partial victories over a long
period. Important milestones were the restoration of the Althing in
1845, the constitution of 1874, the granting of limited home rule in
1904, and the Act of Union with Denmark in 1918, when the colony
of Iceland was transformed into a kingdom.

After 1944, however, development has proceeded at record speed. There have been thoroughgoing changes in virtually every area, as if a giant in seven-league boots had come to Iceland in 1944 and overturned everything: foreign and security policy, the law of the sea, the economy, technology, population, society, and culture.[1] What happened can be described as a leap into the present.

It is worth following the course of development in a few particular spheres. In this chapter we shall look at some of them in turn: security policy, membership of NATO, the agreement about the Keflavík base, the extension of fishery limits and the cod wars, and the move from the horse to the jet plane.

Security Policy: The First Steps

Some of the most dramatic events in the first years of Iceland's independence were enacted on the stage of security policy. Iceland took the step from neutrality to membership of NATO in 1949 and the defence agreement with the United States in 1951, revised in 1974 and supplemented in the 1980s with new agreements. This topic has been studied in depth by several analysts, and it was the subject of a doctoral thesis by the Icelander Elfar Loftsson.[2]

Let us examine the main trends in the development of security policy. A concise survey and a glance at the map—Iceland is located high in the North Atlantic, roughly half-way between Moscow and Washington, justifying the epithet 'the country between the superpowers'—will make it easier to understand the motives behind Iceland's post-war foreign and security policy.

The first coalition government (1944–7) in the newly founded republic was led by Ólafur Thors. The political parties had called a truce. External strains and patriotism united the Icelanders.

A little nation had become independent. Now it wanted to stand on its own feet and control the exploitation of the rich fishing banks along the coasts. With the 1941 defence agreement with the United States, Iceland had abandoned the permanent neutrality which had been proclaimed in 1918. But the Second World War ended in 1945. Iceland would have liked to see the departure of the numerous American soldiers. They spoke a foreign language and represented another culture, with partly differing values. They were no longer needed for the defence of the country. Their presence on Icelandic territory was therefore felt by many Icelanders to be a blow to their national pride and incompatible with the newly won independence.

This view may appear proper and natural. In Iceland's case, however, it turned out to be based on an illusion. The Second World War did not end with peace on earth. It was succeeded by a long series of armed conflicts and the cold war between East and West. This was mostly a consequence of the Soviet Union's deliberate expansion westwards: Stalin increased his empire with the incorporation between 1940 and 1945 of the Baltic states and large areas of other countries' territories, and between 1945 and 1948 he turned a number of Eastern European nations into Soviet vassal states. The cold war radically changed the situation of the Icelanders. Fresh in their memory were the events of 10 May 1940, when their country—neutral but defence-less—was occupied by British troops. This experience convinced the Icelanders once and for all that it is difficult for a small neutral country nowadays to remain aloof from a war, especially if the country in question is of strategic interest to the combatants and if it lacks its own military defence to boot. Since the British occupying troops were needed elsewhere after a year, they were replaced by American soldiers on 7 July 1941, following a defence agreement with the United States. The Americans built a few military bases in Iceland, including the one on the Keflavík promontory, about 50 kilometres south-west of Reykjavík.

After the end of the Second World War, then, Iceland faced a new threat. The country did not passively observe developments, however. It joined the United Nations Organization in 1946. Many people hoped that membership of the United Nations would solve Iceland's problems with the military bases, since the United Nations Security Council could ensure the safety of areas lacking their own military defence. That was what the optimists believed. The suspiciousness and discord within the United Nations showed that this hope was merely wishful thinking.[3]

Iceland was also drawn into cooperation with the other Nordic countries. This was gradually to comprise every conceivable area of society: culture, legislation, health and social welfare, the labour market, energy, communications, economy, technology, foreign policy, and so on. We can agree with a Swedish expert in his view that 'in terms of law, the Nordic states are much more united than the United States of America'.[4] Moreover, it was suggested that the Nordic countries should have a joint policy of non-alignment, similar to that of the inter-war years.

It was in this situation that Sweden took the initiative in the autumn of 1948 to negotiate with its neighbours, Denmark and Norway, about the possibility of forming a Nordic defence league which could be independent of the superpowers and free to pursue a policy of neutrality. Finland was prevented from cooperating after signing the Finno-Soviet Mutual Assistance Pact of April 1948. On other fronts, too, the advocates of a Nordic defence league were battling against the odds. The Danish and Norwegian governments did not believe in neutrality as a real option in security policy. They felt that they would be more safely protected against the expanding Soviet Union by guarantees from the USA.

One important factor in the stance of Denmark and Norway was their location by the Atlantic—with Iceland as a link in the chain of islands between North America and Europe, running from Newfoundland and Greenland to the Faroes and the British Isles. Apart from the geographical arguments, Denmark and Norway were swayed by the collective experience of the North Atlantic states of the war years, the demands of the Soviet Union in 1947 to have military bases on Spitsbergen, and the coup d'état in Prague in February 1948. The Swedish initiative failed for these reasons. Instead, Denmark and Norway were among the twelve states, along with Iceland, which founded the North Atlantic Treaty Organization in April 1949. Sweden, with its strong defence, stuck to its traditional foreign policy, that of non-alignment in peace with a view to neutrality in the event of war. Finland also chose to pursue a policy of neutrality, which was easier after the country joined the United Nations and the Nordic Council.

It should be pointed out that Iceland never took part in the negotiations about a Nordic defence league which collapsed in January 1949. The main reason was geographical. It was considered totally unrealistic that a Nordic defence league could encompass a country as distant as Iceland. The Icelanders have no military defence of their own. In view of the American-built airfield at Keflavík and the associated installations, it was felt that Iceland was closer to the American sphere of influence. Moreover, the Icelandic minister of foreign affairs, Bjarni Benediktsson, had been secretly informed in December 1948 by the American ambassador, Richard Butrick, of the plans to form a North Atlantic alliance in which Iceland would be offered membership.[5]

Although the Nordic countries took different paths as regards security policy, they were otherwise remarkably successful at preserving the spirit of cooperation, for example, in the consultations of the Nordic foreign ministers. This cooperation has been made both wider and deeper, with the founding of the Nordic Council in 1952. It was not until 1968, however, that the attractive Nordic House—a creation of the Finnish architect Alvar Aalto—was opened in Reykjavík.

This intensive cooperation between continental Scandinavia and the remote island in the North Atlantic rests on a firm basis. It has a long historical and cultural tradition. The Nordic peoples have a great deal in common: language, literature, history, customs, views of freedom and justice, democracy, and respect for the liberty of the individual.

This joint cultural heritage—especially the language, the poetry, and the Icelandic sagas—is genuine and palpable. It is ultimately these invisible bonds that bridge all distances. They make Nordic unity into a living reality. This is traditionally felt by the Icelandic people in particular.

US Demands for Military Bases and Grants of Marshall Aid

Some kings are good
and some are bad.

*Einar Þveræingur at the Althing
in the early eleventh century*

In the 1941 agreement on the defence of Iceland during the Second World War, the USA undertook to evacuate all troops 'immediately upon the termination of the present international emergency'.[6] The decision-makers in Washington were soon to regret this commitment. The realization of the growing strategic significance of Iceland made the USA reluctant to close its military bases in Iceland. In October

1945 the US government asked to lease the Keflavík base and two other bases for ninety-nine years. The Icelanders categorically refused. Gunnar Thoroddsen, representing the Independence Party, regarded the request as totally incompatible with Iceland's sovereignty. He said that the separation from Denmark would be of little value if independence were to be immediately circumscribed by the authorization of foreign military bases.[7]

Professor Gunnar Thoroddsen (died 1983) was an upright man with artistic talent. He was true to his patrimony, as a nephew of the principled freedom-fighter Skúli Thoroddsen. Many influential Icelanders shared Gunnar's view. It is convincingly expressed in Halldór Laxness's critical novel *The Atom Station*.

The American troops gradually left the country. Six hundred civilian American technicians were permitted to take their place at the Keflavík airfield, which the USA was allowed to use for civilian planes. This permission, valid for six years, was granted in 1946 in a technical agreement which led to the fall of the coalition government. The People's Unification Party–the Socialist Party, which had not been consulted in advance, left the government the following year.

In 1947 the last uniformed American personnel left the island. Iceland had officially got rid of all the soldiers. During the period 1947–51, however, American troop transports to Germany went via Iceland, under the direction of the Pentagon. It has therefore been asserted that the US military *de facto* never left Iceland. Apart from the transports, there was a continued American military presence, albeit in discreet form: 'The armed forces had changed into civilian clothes.'[8]

One American incentive was the Marshall Plan, named after the American Secretary of State, George C. Marshall, but officially known as the European Recovery Program. Between 1948 and 1953, Iceland received more Marshall Aid per head than any other state. The aid took the form of large sums of cash with which to buy American goods: about 30 million dollars as a gift and 5 million dollars as a loan. Iceland used this capital primarily to build two power stations (one on the river Laxá near Húsavík, the other at Sog south of Þingvallavatn) and the fertilizer factory at Gufunes near Reykjavík.[9]

Marshall Aid was welcome. But what was the donor's ulterior

motive? As a suspicious Trojan says in Virgil's *Aeneid*, 'Timeo Danaos et dona ferentes' (I fear the Greeks, even when they offer gifts).

Many Icelanders felt the same suspicion as Gunnar Thoroddsen did about the American demands for the bases. For centuries Iceland had been ruled by foreign monarchs. Should she now be dictated to by a superpower? What would happen to the new-found independence? The historically conscious Icelanders repeated the well-known account in Snorri's *Heimskringla* of how the Icelanders of the commonwealth once turned down an ominous proposal from the Norwegian king, Ólafur Haraldsson.

Through one of his liegemen at the Althing, the king offered to become the king of the Icelanders if they would be his subjects and friends. He asked them to give as proof of their friendship the offshore island or 'skerry' of Grímsey, north of Eyjafjörður. Many speakers at the assembly were in favour of granting the king's request. Finally Einar Þveræingur spoke, and his words swayed the general opinion. He was laconic. In a few much-quoted words he advised the Althing not to pay the king any 'land tax' or promise any other dues. 'And we would impose that bondage not only on ourselves but both on ourselves and our sons and all our people who live in this land; and that bondage this land would never be free or rid of. And though this king be a good one, as I believe he is, yet it is likely to be the case, as always hitherto, that when there is a change in the succession there will be some kings who are good and some who are bad.'[10]

Iceland Joins NATO (1949)

Not much time was to elapse before yet another event in the world—the coup d'état in Prague in 1948—further illustrated how difficult it was for small states to maintain their sovereignty and freedom. Influenced by the Prague coup, and perhaps more so by the change in Denmark's and Norway's security policy, Iceland joined NATO. The government's bill to this effect was adopted by the Althing on 30 March 1949, by 37 votes to 13 (ten members of the People's Unification Party–the Socialist Party, two Social Democrats, and one member of the Progressive Party).

The news of the impending decision provoked a general strike and riots in Reykjavík. An enraged crowd gathered at Austurvöllur, the square in front of the Althing. They broke windows in the chamber and threw in stones and eggs while the voting was in progress. The incident ended with the reserve police clearing the square with the aid of tear-gas and batons. Two police constables were seriously injured by the stone-throwing, and a dozen people received medical care for their wounds. A number of people were condemned to imprisonment for taking part in the attack on the Althing, but the sentences were never implemented.[11]

The decision of the Althing marked a watershed in the modern history of Iceland. It engendered a lasting bitterness in domestic politics, like a sore which has never completely healed. It should be borne in mind, however, that a clear majority of the Icelandic people are, and always have been, in favour of Iceland's continued membership of NATO.

Iceland signed the North Atlantic Treaty in Washington on 4 April 1949, and it was ratified by the Althing in July the same year.

The Keflavík Base (from 1951)

During the deliberations in Washington which preceded Iceland's membership of NATO, the American secretary of state emphasized that it would be 'out of the question that a foreign army or military bases were in Iceland in peacetime'. This pledge was regarded as an indispensable condition by Iceland.

Just two years later, however, the Keflavík base was re-established. On 7 May 1951 it was manned—in agreement with the Icelandic government—by about five thousand American soldiers. They arrived early in the morning, in noisy transport planes, which landed in a continuous flow at the international airport at Keflavík. The base was manned in accordance with a defence agreement between Iceland and the USA, which had been concluded just two days previously. This agreement of 5 May 1951 referred to the tension in the world after the outbreak of the Korean War. The preamble states that NATO 'has requested, because of the unsettled state of world affairs, that the United States and Iceland . . . make arrangements for the use of facilities in Iceland in defense of Iceland and thus also the North Atlantic Treaty area'.

According to the agreement, the number of personnel stationed was to be subject to the approval of the Icelandic government (article IV). There was to be no interference in internal Icelandic affairs (article V), and civil aviation operations at Keflavík Airport were to be wholly under the control of Iceland (article VI). The agreement could be terminated by either party after twelve months' notice (article VII).

The 1951 defence agreement, which was approved by the Althing after fiery debates, is still in force, but with the changes agreed by Iceland and the USA in a new agreement of 22 October 1974. This came about after the impressive victory earlier that year of the traditionally pro-NATO Independence Party, which increased its share of the votes from 36.2 per cent to 42.7 per cent.

The 1974 agreement contained the following clauses:

- The strength of the military personnel was to be reduced by 420, which meant a force of 2,900 soldiers.
- These American personnel were to be replaced by qualified Icelandic personnel as and when they became available.
- The US government would construct on-base housing for all its military personnel.
- Subject to the availability of funds, the United States would take measures to separate the civilian air terminal from military base facilities.
- Subject to the availability of funds and military requirements, the United States would cooperate in the construction of a new terminal complex with the necessary taxiways and ramp, access roads, and so on.
- The United States would help to upgrade the Keflavík airfield over a ten-year period to bring it into line with 'ICAO standards for Category II flight operations'.

The aims of the 1974 defence agreement between Iceland and the USA have been fulfilled point by point. The parties, for example, have implemented extensive construction projects. Keflavík received a new control tower at an early stage, described as 'one of the best in the world'. It came into use in July 1979. It is fully equipped to 'ICAO standards for Category II flight operations'. It is possible to land at Keflavík in all kinds of weather. Despite this advantage, NATO strategists have long expressed a desire for an alternative international airfield, to be located in northern Iceland.

It was not until 1987 that a new civil air terminal was inaugurated at Keflavík. Before this it was impossible to achieve a clear distinction between the military base and the older terminal, a cramped, barrack-like building. Ever since the Second World War, the military base and the civilian terminal had shared the same access road with a military guard at the entrance, and the same runways had been used by all aeroplanes. The result was that air passengers to and from Iceland had to pass through the base.

For this reason, the international airport at Keflavík made a curious impression for many decades: a civil air terminal in the centre of a huddle of military buildings, with Icelandic airport personnel here and American soldiers there. Travellers could see passenger planes lined up alongside sophisticated military aircraft from various NATO states—looking like easy targets for terrorist attacks.

The delay to the terminal project was due to domestic political dissension. The People's Alliance, which sat in two coalition governments between 1978 and 1983, was opposed to the project. The party's spokesman argued that the planned air terminal would be an over-dimensioned, unreasonably expensive showpiece.

After the election victory of the Independence Party in 1983, this party once again occupied the post of minister for foreign affairs, the first time for thirty years. (It had been occupied by Bjarni Benedikts-son, 1947–53; it was during his period of office that Iceland joined NATO and concluded the defence agreement with the USA.) On 5 July 1983 the new minister for foreign affairs, Geir Hallgrímsson, and the American ambassador to Iceland, Marshall Brement, signed an agreement, according to which the USA undertook to contribute funds for the construction of a new civil air terminal at Keflavík, separate from the military base. The terminal is designed for use as a military hospital in the event of war or emergency. The Icelandic government was to have the terminal built and to have the base modernized in consultation with the USA; the modernization was chiefly to take the form of new hangars, a new oil terminal in nearby Helguvík with docks and piers for 35,000-ton vessels, and new radar stations for improved surveillance of Icelandic airspace.

The new civil air terminal came into use in April 1987. It is named after Leifur Eiríksson, who discovered America. It is situated on the northern side of the airfield, completely separate from the military base. It is in every way a modern, comfortable, roomy building, with an area of 14,000 square metres. Architecturally, Flugstöð Leifs Eiríkssonar is a complete success. It is adorned with sculptures and works of art in glass, with some pieces by Leifur Breiðfjörð. It has large windows, through which travellers have a magnificent view of the surrounding lava fields. First-time visitors may think that they have landed on the moon. The basic black of the landscape is effectively relieved by patches of green or yellow-green moss, the shifting colours on the celestial palette, and a ring of mountains on the horizon, with snow-capped peaks for most of the year.

On leaving the lunar landscape around Keflavík and heading inland, one is quickly captivated by the scenery. It cannot fail to move the observer. Nowhere else in the world can the visitor experience such resplendent daylight as in Iceland. Probably few places on earth can match the beauty of a kaleidoscopic Icelandic summer landscape as it displays its flowering meadows and black lava fields in the crystal-clear air, with blue mountains and white-domed glaciers in the distance, and the sea shifting from deep blue to green.

On the subject of the discovery of America, three anecdotes deserve to be rescued from oblivion.

The Marquess of Dufferin and Ava, who visited Iceland in 1856, left us a famous account of his travels in these high latitudes. It may not always be historically accurate, but its qualities lie in the romantic charm and the ready wit of the Irish lord. During a banquet in Reykjavík, with 'a forest of glasses' on the table, the marquess toasted the ancient Icelanders in an exhilarated speech. He alluded to their discovery of America and mentioned, as if in passing, Columbus's visit.[12]

During a lecture tour of America, Oscar Wilde took offence at the Americans for various reasons. On his return to England he is said to have remarked, 'The Icelanders discovered America, but they were smart enough to lose it.'

The Icelandic poet Tómas Guðmundsson was once at Hotel Borg in Reykjavík as a guest of some American officers. He grew irritated at them and said: 'Do you know who discovered America?' They answered in chorus, 'Why, Columbus of course.' Tómas replied, 'No, we Icelanders did it. But we will never do it again.'

Delimitation at Sea: The Background

Iceland has been blessed by nature with exceptionally rich fishing waters. The island lies on a continental shelf which has some of the richest fishing banks in the world. Where the warm water of the Gulf Stream meets the cold currents of the Arctic Sea, the water temperature is ideal for the production of plankton. The marine biology here favours the reproduction of herring, cod, capelin, haddock, plaice, halibut, redfish (also known as rose-fish or ocean perch), and other fish species, as well as prawn, lobster, mussel, and other shellfish, not to mention large stocks of whale and seal.

In bygone days, these immense marine resources on the fishing banks that surround the otherwise mostly barren Iceland were used less by the Icelanders themselves than by other nations. For centuries the Basques, British, Dutch, French, Germans, and Norwegians—and to some extent also Faroe Islanders and other Scandinavians—have for preference exploited the distant fishing grounds off Iceland. One explanation for this was suggested in a note from the Danish minister of foreign affairs to his Dutch colleague in 1741:[13]

> The situation of the island of Iceland is known to everyone. Its cold climate allows no place for tilling the soil, and its inhabitants have only fishing as a means of subsistence. They use only small boats, in which they do not dare to venture far out to sea, and if the narrow zone of four miles had not been guaranteed to them . . . they would run the risk of dying of hunger.

In the seventeenth century the absolute king of Denmark issued various decrees granting Danish subjects a monopoly on all fishing and whaling around Iceland within an area which varied in size in different periods. From 1662 until 1859—even after the formal abolition of the monopoly—the zone encompassed sixteen nautical miles (1 nautical mile = 1,852 metres or 2,025 yards) from the coast. This was then reduced in stages, first to four nautical miles in 1859, then three in 1872—in other words, the expanse of water which could be controlled by a land-based cannon. Some states asserted a principle of international law, based on Roman law, about the freedom of the seas; this had been formulated by the Dutchman Hugo Grotius in his *Mare liberum* (1609), where he defended the right of the Netherlands to sail to India without impediment.

According to an opposing view, the principle of *mare clausum*, the ownership of the sea is vested in individual states. An expression of this is seen in the papal bull of 1493, by which the newly discovered colonies and the oceans were divided between Spain and Portugal, the leading maritime powers of the day.

Alongside these rival principles, states have maintained their right to territorial waters of varying extent. The united kingdom of Sweden-Norway, for example, had a four-mile limit. Of greater importance in practice was Great Britain's command over the North Sea and the North Atlantic. This is seen in an Anglo-Danish agreement of 1901 about a three-mile limit round Iceland and the Faroes and the closure to foreign fishermen of fiords with a maximum width of ten nautical miles. In this 'butter and ham agreement' Denmark recognized the three-mile limit in exchange for British undertakings to buy Danish agricultural produce. The agreement, which could only be revoked after a period of two years' notice, remained in force for about fifty years. It had devastating consequences for Iceland, since trawlers were already fishing along the seabed in those days. Iceland, still a Danish colony, was not consulted.[14]

The old European colonial powers were relatively quick to grant independence to their colonies after the Second World War. However, the old colonial exploitation of distant fishing grounds took much longer to eradicate. Britain recognized India and Pakistan as sovereign states in 1947, but it was only towards the end of 1976 that the last British trawlers left Icelandic fishing waters.

The protection of Iceland's territorial sea was the task of Danish vessels until 1918. In the inter-war years it was gradually assumed by Icelandic craft—*Þór*, *Óðinn*, and *Ægir*—until it came wholly into

Icelandic hands in 1940. Coastguard operations then were still ineffi-
cient. In practice, foreign vessels could fish in relative freedom, not
only in the open waters outside the three-mile zone but also sailing far
into the Icelandic fiords, regardless of their width. This took place
before the eyes of the Icelanders living on the coast, who may not have
been threatened by starvation but who at times—for example, during
the depression of the 1930s—did suffer from a shortage of food. Their
agricultural produce could sometimes be barely sufficient.

The Icelanders were known to say ironically that the foreign fishermen were sometimes so close to the coast that they could have taken
off their boots, waded ashore, and continued to fish in the farmers'
potato and turnip patches.

The Icelandic fishing banks were subject to over-fishing as early as
the 1930s. This had a serious effect on stocks of haddock and plaice.
The Second World War brought a much-needed respite from foreign
fishing, allowing stocks to recover. Just after the Second World War,
however, fishing was resumed on an even more intensive scale. The
Icelandic stocks were continuously over-fished in the period 1945–75.
The same period saw the coming of new technology: fishing vessels
equipped with hydro-acoustic sounding and detection devices, on-
board freezing plants, and ultra-efficient catching gear. With narrow-
mesh trawls they could operate like vacuum cleaners sucking fish from
the sea. Up until 1959, foreign vessels caught about half of the total
catch of demersal fish in the waters around Iceland.[15]

Profits were high, but they did not last long. Of the three varieties
of herring that traditionally occurred around the coasts of Iceland, two
disappeared almost completely: the Atlantic-Scandinavian herring
which spawns in Norway and the Iceland herring which spawns on the
south coast of Iceland in the spring. The third variety, the Iceland
herring which spawns on the south coast of Iceland in the summer, has
begun to recover in recent years. What remained were the valuable cod
stocks, but these too have been reduced to a dangerously low level.

Since fishing and fish produce have accounted for an average of 75
to 90 per cent of Iceland's exports for decades, thus being vital for the
survival of the country, the Icelanders were endangered by this development. In 1952 the government of Iceland pointed out in a statement
to the United Nations Commission on International Law that 'the

fishing grounds are the *conditio sine qua non* of the Icelandic people for they make the country habitable'. The threat to the Icelandic people was unequivocal and unendurable. It continued to grow in the post-war years. It is against this background that we must view the Icelanders' tenacious struggle to get rid of the British, German, and other foreign fishermen from the Icelandic fishing grounds. Already in 1948 the Althing passed a law (no. 44) on the scientific conservation of fisheries in the waters of the continental shelf.

Scarcely any Icelandic law can have been as far-sighted as this one from 1948. It has been invoked as support for most of the state measures to protect the fish stocks and their spawning grounds on the Icelandic fishing banks. It has also been invoked every time Iceland has extended her fishing limits. The law of 1948 was an important foundation for the Icelanders after the Second World War, when they carried their struggle for independence out to the seas.

Success in this struggle required more efficient coastal surveillance, a doubling of the Icelandic fishing fleet between 1945 and 1948, and internal unity. Whereas the issues of security policy from 1949 (NATO membership and the Keflavík base) deeply divided the Icelandic people, the question of fishing limits generally had the effect of uniting the political parties.[16] They have all had the same goal: to achieve the greatest possible fishing territory for Iceland.

The New Law of the Sea and the Cod Wars

A decisive factor in the success of Iceland's struggle was the new view of the law of the sea which was asserted just after the Second World War by the USA, some Latin American republics, and other states in the Third World. Iceland shaped her policy on the law of the sea in keeping with this development. One incentive was President Harry S. Truman's declaration in 1945 about the right of the United States to the continental shelf, that is, the exclusive right to the use of the seabed and its resources off the American coast, to a depth of 200 metres. The Latin American states of Argentina, Chile, and Ecuador demanded territorial seas reaching as far as 200 nautical miles from the coast.[17]

A stubborn struggle began between states with opposing interests (broadly speaking, old colonial powers versus coastal states in the

Third World) and between supporters of conflicting principles of international law. States which had a long history of fishing far away from their own waters pleaded for the preservation of agreements on three-mile limits and the principles of the freedom of the high seas and traditional fishing rights. These principles clashed with the right of a coastal state to exert exclusive jurisdiction over its own natural resources within a reasonable distance from the coast. To put it another way: how far out to sea does a coastal state have jurisdiction, and where does the free sea begin? Where should the boundary between the two be drawn?

This clash of principles has been analysed by Hannes Jónsson. He describes the outcome of the British-Icelandic cod wars as 'the triumph of the *Progressive* over the *Colonial* school of thought on the Law of the Sea'.[18]

Iceland played a leading role in this conflict between two views of the law of the sea. The Icelanders pointed out that the then existing law of the sea did not protect the coastal states' assets in the sea and on their continental shelves. One of the main purposes of a new law of the sea should be to give this protection to the coastal states. Growing support for these arguments came from the Third World, Latin America, and later the entire 77-state group (mostly developing countries). Unlike the Latin American countries, Iceland made a distinction between the concepts of *territorial sea* and *exclusive economic zone* (an area of the sea where the existing resources are under the jurisdiction of the coastal state). This distinction was later to be codified in the United Nations Convention on the Law of the Sea, which was signed at Montego Bay in Jamaica on 10 December 1982. It has been ratified by Iceland.[19]

Iceland's first step towards the extension of her territorial waters had been taken in 1949, with the revocation of the 1901 agreement about the three-mile limit. This took effect in 1951. The fishing limits were then extended in four stages:

in 1952 to   4 nautical miles;
in 1958 to   12 nautical miles;
in 1972 to   50 nautical miles;
in 1975 to 200 nautical miles.

The United Kingdom, West Germany, Belgium, and the other NATO states were not slow to react. The toughest opposition came from the British. They had already been exploiting the Icelandic fishing banks in the fifteenth and sixteenth centuries, when they had fought five cod wars with the Hanseatic League.[20] The British, believing that they had a traditional right to fish off Iceland, also invoked the principle of the freedom of the seas.

In 1952, when Iceland extended her fishing limits to four nautical miles, calculated from straight baselines, she was able to refer to a precedent for the calculation of the baselines. The Court of International Justice at the Hague had ruled in 1951 in the Anglo-Norwegian fisheries case. The Hague Tribunal had taken into consideration the Norwegian archipelago with its relatively shallow fishing banks located between the skerries; these had been used from time immemorial by Norwegian fishermen as a source of livelihood. The court therefore ruled that special regard should be given to the geographical, economic, and historical factors which spoke in favour of applying the Norwegian principles. The special interests of Norway as a coastal state were thus deemed to be of greater relevance than the fishing interests of other states.[21]

The British reaction to the four-mile Icelandic limit came quickly. A ban was imposed on the landing of Icelandic fish at Grimsby and Hull. Britain had long been a major market for Icelandic fish. (It had, incidentally, helped the British people to survive during the Second World War.) The boycott was intended to deal a devastating blow to Icelandic fish exports. The result was the opposite. The Icelanders, who had supplied fresh fish to the British market for decades, now began instead to expand their deep-freezing facilities. In a short time this increased both employment in the industry and export earnings for frozen and salted fish products. These were successfully sold to new markets: the USA, the USSR, and various states in Eastern Europe. These Icelandic measures dampened the effect of the British boycott. Since it did not bring the intended results, the ban was lifted after four years.

Fleets of trawlers from both Western and Eastern Europe caught fish on an industrial scale in the 1950s. With their fine-meshed nets, they efficiently scoured the floor of the North Atlantic. Catches were of record size, but they took a heavy toll on the Icelandic fish stocks, which risked extermination. The economically valuable cod was particularly endangered. The four-mile limit was seen to be an insufficient shield against over-fishing.

The situation for the Icelanders was threatening. They turned in their need to the United Nations. The United Nations Commission on International Law took its time—far too long in the opinion of the Icelanders. The Commission, which had been studying the complex problem of the law of the sea since 1949, declared in a report to the United Nations General Assembly in 1956 that 'International law does not permit an extension of the territorial sea beyond 12 miles'. The Commission, however, did not put forward any concrete suggestions about either the width of the territorial sea or about fishing limits beyond the territorial sea. The issue of a review of the law of the sea was referred instead by the General Assembly to the 1958 Conference on the Law of the Sea in Geneva.

At this first conference on the law of the sea (the second was held in 1960 and the third in 1974–82), a number of far-sighted proposals were put forward. Gunnlaugur Þórðarson, for example, argued—chiefly on historical grounds—that Iceland should be recognized as having territorial waters of 16 nautical miles calculated from straight baselines and a continental shelf zone of at least 50 nautical miles reckoned from the baselines.[22]

Canada suggested a 12-mile fishing limit reckoned from the baselines of the coastal state. Iceland supported the Canadian proposal, as did the majority of the countries represented at the conference. It was therefore carried in the plenary session by 37 votes to 35, with 9 abstentions. But the majority was not big enough for the proposal to be adopted as a binding convention. According to the procedural rules of the conference, this would have required a qualified majority, two-thirds of the delegates.

A political scientist who has studied the proposals about territorial waters and fishing zones put forward at the first Geneva conference—including proposals from India, Mexico, the Soviet Union, Colombia, and the USA—has argued that the result can nevertheless be described as a breakthrough for new ideas. He says that the Geneva conference 'wrote the epitaph' to the three-mile limit. A majority of states asserted that a coastal state should be entitled to some form of 12-mile limit.[23]

This meant that Iceland could expect almost worldwide support for her next move. Later the same year, the Icelanders turned from words to actions. With effect from 1 September 1958, a 12-mile fishing limit was proclaimed. Iceland's allies in NATO protested vehemently. The British went furthest. They immediately sent warships to Icelandic waters. British trawlers fished under their protection within the 12-mile limit for three years. This was the first conflict involving warships to be enacted on the Icelandic fishing banks, but it was not the last. So began the 'cod wars'.

The first cod war led to a number of incidents. The most critical situation came when the British captured some Icelandic coastguards who had boarded a British trawler. The British set them ashore in a rowing-boat close to the Keflavík base.[24] The first cod war ended with a compromise in 1961. The British recognized the Icelandic 12-mile limit. In return, Iceland granted the British limited rights to fish within the zone for a further three years. The Icelandic government at the time, which was to remain in power for an unusually long period (1959–71), granted yet another concession. Disputes about an extension of Iceland's fishing limits were to be referred to the Hague Tribunal at the request of either one of the parties. This concession was criticized in the Althing by the left-wing parties, since in their view Iceland should be recognized as having jurisdiction over the whole continental shelf.

The left-wing government which took office in 1971 under the leadership of Ólafur Jóhannesson was also united in its opposition to this clause in the 1961 agreement. They maintained that it had been accepted by Iceland under duress—the presence of British warships. Moreover, there were now 'changed circumstances' in the matter of the law of the sea and in the economic situation. Iceland was therefore no longer bound by the clause.[25] Over-fishing by foreign trawlers in Icelandic waters was invoked as a justification for the extension of the fishing limit to 50 nautical miles, with effect from 1 September 1972. This meant that Iceland unilaterally revoked the agreement of 1961. Britain and West Germany refused to accept the 50-mile limit. In the same year they brought a suit against Iceland at the International Court of Justice in the Hague. The tribunal instructed the parties to take steps to ensure that British and German trawlers could catch certain annual quotas in Icelandic waters.[26] Iceland, however, refused to appear before the court. 'Nations do not let their survival depend on an international judgement,' said a spokesman for the Icelandic government. Some of the opposition, who had been in power when the 1961 agreement was concluded, claimed that it would have been more proper for Iceland to argue her case before the Hague Tribunal.[27]

During the second cod war which now followed, lasting for just over a year, ships of the Royal Navy were once again sent to Iceland. This led to a few perilous incidents. British warships deliberately rammed the small Icelandic coastguard vessels on several occasions. Then the secret Icelandic weapon was deployed. The Icelanders used special shears to cut the wires that held the British trawlers' nets. The Icelandic vessels were also fitted with 25 mm cannon dating from the turn of the century. Like the shears, they are now museum exhibits.

There was an unexpected pause in the second cod war after the volcanic eruption on Heimaey in the Vestmannaeyjar group of islands on 23 January 1973. Iceland at once concentrated all resources on evacuating the islanders and stemming the flow of lava over Heimaey, Iceland's most important fishing harbour. Much of the town of Vest-mannaeyjar, including the harbour entrance and the church, was saved from destruction, as if by a miracle. The work of reconstruction got under way quickly. Iceland received generous assistance for this from many quarters, particularly from the other Nordic countries.

The fisheries dispute took a serious turn again in May 1973, when British frigates began to operate inside the 50-mile zone. This led to rammings and other serious incidents, for which both sides were to blame. Iceland was waging an unequal struggle at sea. This inferiority, however, was offset to some extent by purposeful propaganda and a diplomatic offensive waged on many fronts. Expressions of this were a protest lodged with the United Nations Security Council, separate fishery agreements with Belgium and Norway, official visits to the Soviet Union and Poland, and energetic moves within NATO. A revo-cation of the defence agreement about Keflavík was on the agenda.

Iceland went even further than this. On 27 September 1973, when the second cod war had been in progress for a year, the Icelandic government declared that it would sever diplomatic relations with Britain if the Royal Navy did not withdraw its warships from the 50-mile zone within a certain time. The British stepped down in the face of this threat. The warships were withdrawn. Then the prime ministers of the two countries—Ólafur Jóhannesson and Edward Heath—sat down together at the negotiation table. Their discussions in London resulted in an agreement. This allowed a limited amount of British fishing within the 50-mile limit for the next two years.

In terms of international law, 1974 was a mixed year for Iceland. On the one hand, the Hague Tribunal had pronounced a verdict according to which the extension of the fishing limits to 50 nautical miles was illegal. On the other hand, it was in that year that the Third United Nations Conference on the Law of the Sea began in Caracas. It was immediately obvious there that time was working in favour of the Icelanders, and against the view *de lege lata* expressed by the Hague Tribunal.

Back in March 1970, all the coastal states in South America except three (Colombia, Venezuela, and Guyana) had proclaimed jurisdictional zones of 200 nautical miles for the study, use, conservation, and administration of natural resources off their own coasts. Their arguments were the same as Iceland's.[28] In other words, the demands of the coastal states for recognized economic zones of 200 nautical miles had widespread support. This support was so great that they could probably expect binding rules of international law concerning such zones.

The news from Caracas came at a good time for the Independence Party, which won the general election in 1974, partly on the pledge to extend the fishing limits to 200 nautical miles.

In accordance with this pledge, Geir Hallgrímsson's government proclaimed a 200-mile exclusive economic zone on 15 October 1975. This was recognized on certain terms by West Germany and other states, but not by Britain. The British trawlers returned to their old catching-places within the 200-mile zone. So too did the British warships, which—according to Icelandic sources—again deliberately manoeuvred in such a way as to ram or collide with the Icelandic coastguard vessels, although their own ships were damaged by the collisions as well. The response of the Icelanders was to cut the wires of forty-six British and nine West German trawlers.

The third cod war once again raised the political temperature between Iceland and Britain. Talks in January 1976 between the two prime ministers—this time Geir Hallgrímsson and Harold Wilson—achieved nothing. The incidents on the Icelandic fishing banks became more serious.

This was the last straw for the Icelanders. On 1 February they broke diplomatic relations with Britain. The allies of the two states in NATO were anxious to bring this untoward conflict to an end, in view of the strategic importance for NATO of the Keflavík base. Concern about the base and the possibility of Iceland leaving NATO had also been evident in the previous cod war.[29] Norwegian mediation in the spring led to an Anglo-Icelandic agreement on 1 June. British fishing was permitted within the 200-mile zone for six months. The agreement was in reality a British capitulation. On 1 December 1976, the British trawlers sailed out of Iceland's exclusive economic zone for the last time.

The British surrender in Oslo was due to changes in the law of the sea. When it became clear that more and more states were considering introducing 200-mile economic zones, the British were forced to do the same. They had to implement the extension when the European Economic Community, of which Britain was a member, decided to proclaim a common economic zone of 200 nautical miles on 1 January 1977. With this prospect in view, the British had no choice but to negotiate with Iceland, whatever the price. They had to stop waging a hopeless war.

Iceland was soon to achieve full international recognition for her claims. This came within the framework of the Third United Nations Conference on the Law of the Sea. After eight years of discussion, the states arrived at the convention that was signed at Montego Bay in 1982. This provides that a coastal state is entitled to:

(i)   territorial waters extending for 12 nautical miles calculated from straight baselines (articles 2–3);
(ii) an exclusive economic zone of 200 nautical miles calculated from the baselines (articles 55–57);
(iii) sovereignty over its continental shelf as defined in article 76 of the Convention on the Law of the Sea.[30]

Cod Wars, Iceland, and NATO: A Retrospect

The three cod wars fought between 1958 and 1976 never led to armed conflict in the traditional sense, no more than subsequent dramatic incidents in Cyprus and the Aegean involving the two NATO states of Turkey and Greece. The situation in the stormy North Atlantic, with the might of the Royal Navy against the five or six small vessels of the Icelandic coastguard and the half-dozen Iceland aircraft, showed a lack of balance bordering on the absurd. It calls to mind the little shepherd boy David in his duel with the Philistine giant Goliath.

Undaunted Icelandic seamen under the command of skilled captains such as Guðmundur Kjærnested, Höskuldur Skarphéðinsson, and Þröstur Sigtryggsson won a place in the hearts of the Icelandic people. They became national heroes. Everyone looked up to them.

One of these naval heroes, who cut the wires of British and German trawler nets right under the noses of British warships, was Þröstur Sigtryggsson, who was captain of the coastguard vessel *Ægir*. Þröstur cut wires with great gusto, showing both courage and quick wit. Like the cunning Odysseus, he used every imaginable trick with great success. He has recounted his exploits in an interview book entitled 'The Joking Sparrow'.[31]

A few examples of Þröstur's tactics come from exploits performed in late 1975 and early 1976. A British frigate had followed the *Ægir* along the east coast of Iceland down towards Reyðarfjörður. The *Ægir* took shelter in the fiord during a storm, to await better weather but also to shake off the unwelcome escort. As the frigate cruised past the fiord along the 12-mile limit and its officers were toasting the New Year, the *Ægir* took the opportunity to switch off its normal signal lamp. Þröstur mounted the sort of lanterns used by cargo boats. He then sneaked out of the fiord in the shelter of darkness and snow showers. He dodged the frigate's radar. He was also lucky enough to avoid discovery by a British Nimrod plane. Heading north in windless weather and copious snowfall, he then surprised three trawlers calmly fishing near Langanes. They escaped at the last minute by hauling in their nets. Then the *Ægir* lit its proper signal lamp. A British frigate arrived on the scene and pursued the *Ægir* in to the 12-mile limit at Langanes. The British thought that they had been dealing with two Icelandic coastguard vessels.

A few days later, the *Ægir* set out again to try to baffle the British and take their trawlers by surprise. With his radar switched off, Þröstur followed the Icelandic cargo ship the *Fjallfoss* inside the 12-mile limit. He was using the same signal lamp as the *Fjallfoss* as she headed south along the east coast, past Vopnafjörður. Close to the Glettinganes lighthouse the *Fjallfoss* left the 12-mile boundary and sailed right through a group of trawlers. The *Ægir* followed after at a distance of one hour. Once again Þröstur was lucky. A sudden snow shower saved him from discovery by a British helicopter. Shortly afterwards he surprised the trawlers. They were not expecting any coastguard vessels in the vicinity. At intervals of just just seven minutes the *Ægir* cut the wires of two trawlers—an Icelandic record. Two hours later, the *Ægir* was able to cut the wires of two more trawlers.

With stratagems like this, the *Ægir* was repeatedly able to sneak up on unsuspecting trawlers. The weather could be atrocious, with coal-black fog and no visibility, but this made no difference. Nothing could stop him. Swiftly, almost like the ghostly *Flying Dutchman*, Þröstur manoeuvred the *Ægir* back and forth on the seas.

Like a latter-day Scarlet Pimpernel, Þröstur played hide-and-seek with well-armed, well-equipped British frigates. They sought him everywhere but rarely found him—usually only when he wanted to be seen.

Þröstur sometimes felt sorry for the commanders of the British frigates. They were well trained. They were seasoned seamen. But they had to show restraint in the face of the Icelandic coastguard vessels. Their hands were tied by strict instructions from London: Iceland was after all a NATO ally. They had weapons but were not allowed to use them. They reminded Þröstur of a boxer who enters the ring without boxing gloves.

There were some serious incidents. One of them, which indirectly caused a death, was the result of a collision in 1973 between the *Ægir* and the British frigate *Apollo*. Each side believed the other to be at fault when collisions occurred. In fact, damage to both sides was paid by the British, since the coastguards were insured in London. These incidents, however, never got entirely out of hand.[32] For this reason the cod wars never escalated into armed conflicts; they were fought using commercial and political weapons. In the first cod war, Iceland refused to attend a NATO meeting in London in 1959, and the Icelandic ambassador was called home for lengthy consultations.[33]

The leaders on both sides showed restraint. A contributory factor here was no doubt the signals from Washington and other NATO capitals. Iceland's threat to withdraw from NATO was never expressed directly, but the NATO governments were all aware of the possibility. It was always in the air.

To the extent that reports from the cod wars in the North Atlantic eventually became front-page news in *The Times* and other newspapers—in competition with reports from trouble spots in other corners of the world—Iceland's struggle attracted the attention of the world. Moulders of public opinion began to win sympathy for the little island nation's struggle for survival. Demonstrations were arranged in a number of capital cities to manifest support for Iceland. Politically and strategically, and in terms of the law of the sea, the Icelanders held all the trumps. They also knew how to play their cards.

Time worked in favour of the Icelandic people, who defended themselves with such single-minded enthusiasm and national unity against the encroachment of foreign warships. At the same time, the British realized that theirs was a hopeless struggle. The Suez crisis of 1956 had transformed the proud Great Britain into a second-class power.

Trained British diplomats were quick to realize this. One of these was the British ambassador to Reykjavík at the time of the first cod war, Sir Andrew Gilchrist. He has recorded his recollections of this period in his entertaining book, *Cod Wars and How to Lose Them.*[34] He tells how he himself was the victim of a demonstration outside the British ambassador's residence. He reacted by treating his staff and three newly arrived British journalists to champagne. He sat down at the piano and played a piece by Bach and then, attired in his Scottish kilt, he played a reel on his bagpipes. Highly imaginative versions of this episode have circulated. They were embroidered on by the journalists who were present, and later appeared in the book *Anatomy of Britain.*[35]

Sir Andrew undoubtedly has a sense of humour. But he is also a realist. He makes several thought-provoking reflections. A couple of them may be quoted here, since they shed light on what the cod wars were really about and why they ended the way they did.

The use of Royal Navy warships in the first cod war was a fundamental error. The measure was without effect and self-defeating. It is therefore remarkable that the British government should have resorted to the same mistaken gunboat diplomacy in virtually identical situations in 1972 and 1976. Military action by warships was of course possible in theory. In practice, however, it was out of the question for many reasons, chiefly because of the Keflavík base, which was vital for the USA and NATO. In Gilchrist's words, the American troops on the base were 'in effect hostages to the Icelanders for good behaviour by the British'. The Americans were always tormented by concern about the possibility of losing this strategically important base.

Gilchrist also points out that Iceland was one of the states which, under the Geneva conference of 1958, had tried to obtain the international recognition of 12-mile zones for coastal states, which the British opposed. The failure to achieve agreement in Geneva led to a lack of clarity about what the law was. The Icelanders were able to take advantage of this: later, in the absence of internationally recognized regulations, they were able to extend their fishing limits in stages to 12, 50, and 200 nautical miles.

Gilchrist has a high opinion of the legal talent and political wisdom of the Icelanders who were involved. One of them was the expert on the law of the sea, Ambassador Hans G. Andersen. According to the then Secretary General of NATO, the Belgian Paul-Henri Spaak, Andersen was 'remarkable for his legal expertise, but even more outstanding for his obstinacy'.[36] Gilchrist agrees in this verdict. In his view, this Icelander exceeded in obstinacy both John Foster Dulles and Molotov. 'Dulles was subject to sudden impulse, and Molotov could sometimes spring a prepared surprise; Hans Andersen was obstinacy pure and undefiled. He deserves well of his country.'[37]

Sir Andrew shows here his sense for *le bon mot*. Critics have said that the comparison is lame. Dulles and Molotov were leading statesmen, whereas Andersen was merely an official carrying out the instructions of his government. On the other hand, it is known that a few Icelandic officials did play a crucial role during the cod wars. In some

situations their influence was decisive. One of these officials was Hans
G. Andersen.[38]

Population Growth

The population of Iceland has more than doubled in the last half-century. In round figures, the population in 1940 was 121,000, while in
early 1992 it was about 260,000. The countryside has been depopulated as a result of migration to the towns. About 91 per cent of the
Icelandic people now live in built-up areas, 58 per cent of them in the
south-western corner with Reykjavík and the surrounding towns.

This is an extremely large population growth, as can be seen from
a comparison with the other Nordic countries, which have a similar
cultural and economic standard. There are considerable differences
within Scandinavia in the natural population growth—that is, the
excess of births over deaths per 1,000 inhabitants—in 1970, 1980,
1989, and 1989. This is clear from the following table, which has been
compiled by the Statistical Bureau of Iceland (Hagstofa Íslands) on
the basis of the *Yearbook of Nordic Statistics* and other sources.[39]

	Excess of births over deaths per 1,000 inhabitants				Population growth per 1,000 inhabitants			
	1970	*1980*	*1988*	*1989*	*1970*	*1980*	*1988*	*1989*
Denmark	4.6	0.3	0.0	0.4	6.9	0.3	0.1	1.1
Finland	4.2	3.9	2.9	2.9	−2.6	3.5	3.2	3.7
Norway	6.4	2.4	2.9	3.4	5.7	3.3	5.3	2.9
Sweden	3.7	0.6	1.8	2.8	9.6	1.8	5.3	8.0
Faroes	13.7	9.9	9.3	–	4.0	8.3	3.1	–
Greenland	18.5	12.8	14.2	–	13.0	17.5	12.0	–
Iceland	12.4	13.1	11.4	11.3	5.6	10.9	17.5	7.2

Population growth stagnated during these years in Denmark, Finland,
Norway, and Sweden, whereas in all the western Nordic countries—
the Faroes, Greenland, and Iceland—it has remained remarkably high.
The increase is particularly striking in the case of Iceland. The curve
for excess of births over deaths, however, is now pointing downwards
throughout Scandinavia, including the western Nordic countries.

What is the reason for the divergent demographic trend in these
western countries between 1970 and 1988? According to an Icelandic

textbook in history, experts believe that these three islands in the North Atlantic take a different course from normal industrial states, since fishery and other primary production are such an important part of the livelihood of the islanders. This is thought to create a stronger link between man and nature than in other countries, which is reflected in a higher birth rate than elsewhere.[40]

At first sight this hypothesis may appear plausible, but it is not wholly convincing. There are surely many other theories. A number of factors interact in a complex way to favour population growth in these western islands: the geographical location, history, economic development, and the relative calm in what are still fairly tradition-bound societies.

In the case of the Icelanders we may also mention such factors as their go-ahead spirit and faith in the future, their ancient culture and strong national consciousness, and their self-esteem. Besides this there is the strong family spirit, the respect which women enjoy in society, and the fact that children are generally welcome in Iceland. It does not matter much whether a child is born in or out of wedlock.

Iceland offers a special favour with its beautiful landscape and its pure air, the saga atmosphere, the pyrotechnic colours and the tremulous light. Icelanders love to tour their own country. Wonderful excursions can be experienced—when the weather permits.

Foreigners are often ignorant about Iceland. This may be exemplified in a little anecdote. An Icelander once met a Frenchman who led a hectic life in Paris and who had no children. He had never been to Iceland and had not the faintest idea about its culture. He said to the Icelander, 'I can understand that you Icelanders have so many children and that you play so much chess. You have nothing else to do on the long winter evenings when you want a bit of fun.'

From Horse to Jet Plane

It really is like riding on the moon.
Albert Engström, Åt Häcklefjäll

The Icelandic Horse

The 100,000 of us who live in or near Reykjavík today live in a modern city consisting mostly of self-contained houses of concrete scattered over a wide area. There is no railway, no underground, no trams. But there are buses and cars. Along with the USA and Sweden, Iceland has the world's highest number of cars per inhabitant. The population of 260,000 owns around 121,000 cars. Year by year, day by day, we have grown accustomed to hearing and seeing aeroplanes taking off and landing in rapid, noisy succession at an airfield in the middle of the city. It is too small for the traffic, and although it is said to be safe, it looks risky to have a busy airfield located between the sea and the city centre, dangerously close to the Althing, the Cathedral, the government departments, and the surrounding houses. It was constructed around 1940 by the British occupying forces, who gave more consideration to strategic than to environmental aspects. When planes take off, they almost brush the roofs of the houses, before they quickly disappear as little spots among the banks of cloud or into the azure skies.

Cars, aeroplanes, pop and rock music, advertising, television and radio are everyday features of our modern life, but we find it difficult to realize that this entire urban environment is not much more than fifty years old.

It is even harder to take the imaginative leap a thousand years back in time, to the Viking Age, when Iceland was a commonwealth. How did people in those days live?

One thing is certain. During the long journey from Norway, Ingólfur Arnarson and later colonists had cramped conditions on their high-prowed ships. Like Noah in his ark, they had to find room for the horses, cows, pigs, and sheep they needed to survive in the new virgin country.

One of the most important of these domestic animals was a breed of small but powerfully built horse with a long, thick tail. These beasts showed their capacity to tolerate all kinds of weather. An Iceland horse can stay outdoors even in severe winters. Hair growth varies with the season; it is long and shaggy in winter but short in summer. The Iceland horse—sometimes known as the Icelandic pony—is tough, strong, and equipped with an instinctive ability to find its bearings and negotiate the often rugged terrain of Iceland. Another distinctive feature of the Iceland horse is its different gaits. Depending on the nature of the terrain, it can walk, trot, amble, gallop, and *tölt*, a typically Icelandic gait which is extremely comfortable for the rider; the footfalls are like those for walking, but the speed is roughly the same as trotting.[41]

In the age of the commonwealth, the settlers would ride to the assembly at Þingvellir when the year neared the high summer. The commonwealth had its legendary heroes, but without their horses they would have been unable to carry out their exploits.

The medieval Icelanders valued their horses highly. This is evident from *Hrafnkels saga Freysgoða*: the powerful priest-chieftain Hrafnkell gave his god Freyr a half share of his most prized possessions, including his stallion, Freyfaxi. Hrafnkell had made a solemn oath. He would kill anyone who rode Freyfaxi without his permission. When his shepherd Einar once broke the ban, it led to a bitter, violent feud between two kindreds.[42]

Archaeological finds in Norwegian graves from the Viking Age show that the Iceland horse belongs to an ancient race. It died out in other parts of Europe but survived in the isolation of Iceland, where it has adapted to the colder winters which have followed a deterioration in climate.

When the Thirty Years War was raging in Europe, riding was a privilege reserved for warriors and noblemen. Not so in Iceland. Here the farmers rode their horses. They took advantage of the orientation skills of the Iceland horse. A farmer could ride to the nearest village to fetch provisions, which could well include *brennivín*, the Icelandic aquavit. It did not matter if he drank himself senseless. All he had to do was mount his horse, which would calmly carry him home. Farmers fitted pack-saddles to their horses to bring in the hay from the enclosed homefield or from more remote grasslands. Thanks to the horse, they could solve all their transport problems. The lack of roads, however, made horse-drawn vehicles out of the question.

We have a description of a horseback journey to Hekla, undertaken in 1772 by an Anglo-Swedish exploration party consisting of some distinguished visitors: Daniel Carl Solander, a disciple of the great Swedish botanist Linnaeus; his patron Sir Joseph Banks; and Uno von Troil, later Archbishop of Uppsala.[43]

During the twelve-day trip to Hekla, the travellers followed a route well-known to tourists today. They rode to the site of the assembly by Þingvallavatn, past the hot springs at Laugarvatn, past the original Geysir (which then spouted water to a height of 92 feet), to the bishop's see of Skálholt. The travellers, exhausted from their ride, were able to rest under eiderdowns in the bishop's residence. Before they started the actual climb up the volcano, they rode over lava fields covered with ash and expanses of 'flying sand'. On one occasion, von Troil felt as if he was riding through an Arabian desert.

A century later, another English visitor, John Coles, was initially horrified at the sight of the horses on which he was expected to tour Iceland:[44]

> They looked for all the world like a collection of costermongers' ponies, and contained among them some of the ugliest beasts that I have ever seen. I thought, however, that they might only be the pack animals, and therefore asked for the riding horses; when these were pointed out to me, I felt by no means cheered. . . . I ventured to express my misgivings to Geir Zoëga, who only smiled at my fears, and declared that they were really good horses, well able to carry a heavier man than myself, and indeed he was quite correct in saying this, for a better little beast for fording a river or going over bad and dangerous ground than my ugly wall-eyed horse, if he was only allowed to have his head and go his own way, could not be wished for.

An earlier Scottish visitor, Sir George Steuart Mackenzie, was equally impressed by the sure-footedness of the Iceland horse:[45]

> In going through a bog, an Iceland horse seems to know precisely where he may place his foot in safety, and where he cannot venture to pass. If in doubt, he will feel the ground with his foot before he attempts to place his whole weight upon it. If convinced that there is danger, neither

coaxing nor whipping will induce him to go forward. When left to
himself he will find his way, and carry over his burden in safety. It
sometimes happens, though very seldom, that in traversing an extensive
bog a horse will sink to his belly, but he soon extricates himself with
apparent ease.

The Icelandic terrain certainly required horses as sure-footed as this.
Where there were roads at all, they were, in the words of Halldór
Laxness, made by horses' hooves and not by human hands.[46] The horse
remained indispensable well into the twentieth century.

Iceland in the old days had no roads worthy of the name. There were
only bridle-paths, and these were snowed up in winter. People had
therefore built cairns along stretches of road in uninhabited terrain.
These helped to orient the postman as he walked up hill and down dale,
or waded through mountain streams and rivers, with his face lashed
by whirling snow, gusts of wind, and rain. Before dusk he would reach
an isolated farmstead with the eagerly awaited letters. Without the
cairns he might never have reached his destination.

Icelandic shipping and foreign trade in the nineteenth century were
mostly in the hands of foreigners. The Icelanders generally made their
living from farming with primitive implements and fishing in small
boats near the coast. Even rich farmers and rural officials lived in
houses with turf roofs. The houses of the poor were built entirely of
turf, but more prosperous farms had a wooden gable for the entrance.
Houses of this type are preserved as museums at Glaumbær in Skagafjörður and Laufás in Eyjafjörður.

The only fireplace was in the kitchen. Other rooms in the house were
not heated, apart from the *baðstofa*, which was high up so that the heat
from the kitchen rose towards it. *Baðstofa* originally means 'bath-
room' or 'sauna', but it came to be used as a living-room and bedroom.
Sometimes the cows were housed under the *baðstofa*. The better
houses were often panelled with wood on the inside. The hearth was
on the kitchen floor, with a smoke-hole in the roof above it. This hole
also admitted light. The houses were surprisingly warm but smoky and
badly lit. They provided the ideal atmosphere for the evening vigils
(*kvöldvökur*), of the kind immortalized by the Danish painter Heinrich
August Schiøtt (1823–95). Everyone would listen to the house-father
as he read aloud, while the women busied themselves with carding,

Evening vigil in the baðstofa, *as visualized in this imaginative drawing by the French artist Auguste Mayer.*

spinning, and knitting, and the men carved or repaired tools. Several generations lived together in the same house.

From a distance these houses looked rather like grassy mounds. The people who emerged from them looked to foreign visitors like underground creatures.

There were also plenty of small turf-built churches. Some of them are still in use, for example, the one at Víðimýri in Skagafjörður in northern Iceland, built in 1834. The churches sometimes had bells on the gable. Some churches—such as the one on the island of Viðey near Reykjavík—were so small that they held no more than fifty people. One of them has been described as 'the smallest house of God in the world'. In the church at Víðimýri the pews were placed on each side of an aisle. The men sat on the south side and the women on the north. Each parishioner had a pew to suit his social status.

It has been said that the coming of turf churches of this kind was a sign of decline in the centuries of poverty, when the Icelanders could not afford to build wooden churches. It is likely, however, that turf churches were built right from the introduction of Christianity. This theory is supported by archaeological finds of the remains of a small turf church in Greenland. It dates from the time when Greenland was converted.[47]

Around the turn of the century, in other words, Icelandic society still had an almost medieval character. For centuries it had been a patriarchal society which had changed very little. But change was on the way. It was essential. The country was unable to feed all its people. At the end of the nineteenth century, this drove one-fifth of the population to emigrate to America.

The transformation took place in the course of the twentieth century, mostly as a consequence of the economic crisis of the 1930s and the subsequent upswing during the allied occupation of Iceland. The fishermen acquired their own trawlers, while the farmers abandoned their scythes, rakes, and spades for tractors with reapers and ploughs.

Let us try to imagine the herring-fishing station of Siglufjörður in northern Iceland as it looked in August 1939. The small houses clung to the steep slopes above the harbour, in the shadow of the high mountain. Prosperity depended on whether or not the herring came. In the countryside around the village the farms had many draught-horses but only a few tractors and cars, which jolted along on the atrocious dirt roads riddled with holes. People lived a threadbare existence. Poverty was widespread after the depression of the 1930s. Social welfare was still imperfect. All food which had to be imported—fruit, vegetables, and colonial produce—was in short supply.

A young woman, looking like the proud Salka Valka in the novel by Laxness, sits on a jetty in the harbour. She gazes out over the water, which just now is as smooth as a mirror. She sees the flocks of screeching gulls and the steep cliffs surrounding the narrow fiord. She dreams of travelling out to see the world. A passenger boat belonging to the Icelandic Steamship Company puts out from the biggest jetty. As it sails out it stirs up the water of the fiord. She watches as it makes its way out towards the open sea. Perhaps she ought to have been on board? What if she cleaned enough herring so as to be able to afford to take the next boat? But there will be no more boats. A few weeks later, a world war starts. Iceland is virtually closed off from the outside world until the summer of 1945.

When the Second World War ended, the independent republic of Iceland made the jump from the horse direct to the jet plane. It was a swift, revolutionary step. There was no time for the intermediate stage of railways. Nor would they have suited Iceland, for various reasons. The population doubled. The structure of society was shaken up as trade expanded and communications grew in intensity. The new age brought trawlers, cargo boats, and other vessels, cars, buses, aeroplanes, and helicopters. Using statistical evidence, we shall examine how Icelandic communications have developed.[48]

Communications by Sea

In 1991 the Icelandic merchant and fishing fleet comprised a total of 1,155 vessels with a gross register tonnage of 184,000. Much of this tonnage consists of fishing vessels. There are both hyper-modern giant ships for industrial fishing and a large number of small craft under 10 tons. On the other hand, the cargo fleet is not big. It transports only about half of Iceland's imports and two-thirds of the exports. Oil and petrol are brought to Iceland in foreign tankers. Until 1984, transports by ship of military equipment and other supplies to the Keflavík base were entirely in the hands of Icelandic shipping companies. Since 1984, however, some of these transports have been taken over by Rainbow Navigation, an American competitor.

Nature has blessed Iceland with many fine harbours, such as those in Reykjavík and Vestmannaeyjar. The entrance to the harbour in the biggest of these islands, Heimaey, was improved in a miraculous way by the volcanic eruption of 1973. The south coast, however, is rather inaccessible by sea because of the lack of good harbours. It is a low, shallow delta coast. Huge expanses of sand and lava extend all the way to the south and south-east shores. Between them flow all the glacial rivers that drain Mýrdalsjökull and Vatnajökull, Europe's largest glacier. One of its peaks, Hvannadalshnúkur, reaches a height of 2,119 metres above sea level.

The first person to gain an unfavourable impression of the south coast of Iceland was a man in the shape of a whale. This was the warlock sent by the king of Denmark to reconnoitre the country. According to the saga, the warlock could see nothing along the south coast but sand and vast deserts. His reconnaissance was unsuccessful, and King Haraldur had to abandon his plans for an invasion of Iceland.[49]

The spring tide depth of berths in Reykjavík harbour is at least 8 metres, while the depth in the harbour at the large aluminium smelter at Straumsvík—on the road from Reykjavík to Keflavík—is at least 12 metres at spring tide. There are great differences between high and low tide—in some places as much as 5 metres.

Iceland's location in the middle of the North Atlantic leaves it particularly exposed to bad weather. Cold polar air over northern Canada (Newfoundland and Labrador) and Greenland is constantly mixed with warm air from more southern parts of the Atlantic. This clash of cold and warm air masses leads to incessant troughs of low pressure. They move quickly over the Atlantic, usually from south-west to north-east. When they pass over Iceland they cause sudden changes in the weather: temperature differences, precipitation, strong winds, and occasionally violent storms. Hour by hour, day by day, these changes are continually forecast on radio and television. Icelandic meteorologists do not have an easy task, although their computer equipment is said to be top modern.

The consequences are obvious. During the space of twenty-four hours all types of weather may be experienced. Foreign tourists—when complaining, for example, about an unexpected shower of hail or sleet—are often told by the Icelandic guides: 'Just wait a minute for the sun to reappear.' And this is in fact literally the case. In the highlands and in the north, snow may fall in almost any season, though in summer it is unlikely to remain long.

There are few places in the world where storms can blow up with such unexpected force as in the waters around Iceland. Locally violent storms (within fiords, bays and valleys), not recorded on the computerized weather-charts of large ocean-areas, may build up at an extraordinary speed—at times within five to ten minutes. Even in recent years many ships have foundered on the sharp cliffs or the treacherous submerged rocks. Two shipwrecks may be mentioned here; the first has a legendary dimension, while the other is a deeply poignant tragedy.

At Skeiðarársandur, a desolate, inhospitable stretch of the sandy south coast south of Vatnajökull, a Dutch East Indiaman was stranded in the middle of the seventeenth century. The ship had been carrying

Near the main University of Iceland building the visitor may come across this memorial stone portraying Charcot together with an inscription in Icelandic. It reads in translation: 'Dr. Jean Baptiste Charcot, born in Paris 15.7.1867, lost with his ship, the Pourquoi pas?*, against the rock Þormóðssker 16.9.1936. He loved Iceland. There the memory of him and his ship will live on for ever.'*

a precious cargo. For decades, Icelandic treasure-hunters have been digging in search of the 'golden ship', in the hope of being able to raise another jewel of nautical history, like the *Mary Rose* in England or the *Wasa* in Sweden.

A tragic shipwreck occurred in Faxaflói, the bay north-west of Reykjavík, one September night in 1936. A worn-out French exploration ship, the *Pourquoi Pas?*, with forty souls on board, was wrecked that night. A sudden hurricane, with gusts of wind reaching speeds—unusual for the time of year—of 120 kilometres per hour, drove the ship against a hidden rock. With her old steam engine coughing, she sprang a leak and foundered quickly. The leader of the expedition was the famous polar researcher and physician, Jean Baptiste Charcot (1867–1936). He had given the ship its name, meaning 'Why not?', as a response to irritating objections to the sailing profession. It was he who led the first French expedition to the Antarctic, where an island bears his name, Charcot Island. He also made research trips to Jan Mayen in 1912 and Rockall in 1921. He had visited Iceland fourteen times.

Doctor Charcot was a humanitarian and an animal-lover. His last act, just before the ship sank, was to enter his cabin, where he took up a bird. It was a lesser black-headed gull which he had found injured in Greenland and rescued. He quickly returned to the deck, where he released the gull. It immediately stretched its wings in flight and rose free on the winds, while the breakers pummelled the ship, crushing it against the rock.

The only surviving Frenchman told how the proud old sailing ship could not withstand the hurricane. Waves as tall as houses had led to incorrect navigation. The captain saw faint signals from a lighthouse but he mistook its position.

The Icelandic senior physician, Doctor Bjarni Jónsson, has described how, as a young man, he helped to embalm the bodies of thirty-nine drowned Frenchmen. They were lined up shoulder to shoulder on the floor of the morgue. Just a few days earlier, they had been cheerfully strolling around the streets of Reykjavík. Bjarni writes that he never had such a harrowing experience before or since.[50]

An Icelandic film with the French actor Pierre Vaneck in the leading role as Doctor Charcot was made in 1991. Entitled *Svo á jörðu sem á himni* (*On Earth as in Heaven*), it was directed by Kristín Jóhannesdóttir, who has studied film in Paris. This well-acted film has won prizes, and deservedly so. It is an unforgettable panegyric to Jean Baptiste Charcot, who died a hero's death in Faxaflói. Before setting sail, he said to an Icelandic friend, 'This will be the last voyage for the *Pourquoi Pas?* The ship has grown old and tired. So have I.' He was quite prepared to spend his last days in Iceland.

Times have changed. There are now about 145 lighthouses around Iceland. Thanks to them, a ship approaching the coast can always see the flashing signals from a lighthouse. Additional aids to navigation are radio beacons, radar, and loran. Ships and aircraft also have continual access to weather forecasts. The Icelandic meteorologists have satellite pictures of the entire North Atlantic, and their computerized data have become increasingly reliable, especially in the last ten years.

The Road Network

Iceland has a small population (about 260,000) for its area (103,000 km^2). The climate is fickle. On the same spring or autumn day, it is possible to experience rain and sunshine, winds and calm, snowstorms and summer warmth. The landscape is often rocky. It is criss-crossed by countless mountain streams and rivers. The terrain makes it expensive to build and maintain roads. This explains the poor quality of the roads outside the Reykjavík area. They are generally substandard, with a devastating effect on cars.

Iceland changed from left-hand to right-hand traffic in 1968.

In recent years the main roads have been gradually improved and asphalted in places. About half of the ring road around Iceland has a permanent surface.

The ring road was inaugurated on a summer day in 1974. Over 50,000 Icelanders that summer met at Þingvellir to celebrate the 1,100th anniversary of the discovery and settlement of Iceland. The event took place on one of the hottest, sunniest days for many years. The main speakers were the Nobel Prize winner Halldór Laxness and the archaeologist Dr Kristján Eldjárn, who was then president. The Althing announced that it was allocating a large sum of money to fight soil erosion, Iceland's most serious environmental problem. The inauguration of the ring road was the other great event that summer.[51] It was the result of magnificent work by Icelandic engineers. They had finally managed to build sturdy bridges over the torrential glacial rivers in the south-eastern corner of the island. These rivers have been difficult to bridge because they treacherously change their course. Moreover, the ring road can always be destroyed by a glacial outburst, a sudden rush of water from a glacier.

The most difficult stretch of road to build was along the banks and bridges south of Breiðamerkurjökull. This is a *skriðjökull*, from which parts of varying size break loose and float away as icebergs.

Breiðamerkurjökull is drained to the sea by a short glacial river. Before it reaches the sea, the glacier forms a peaceful lagoon (Jökulsárlón) filled with shining white icebergs. This is the haunt of countless plaintive-eyed seals, who become inquisitive if one whistles to them or holds up a pastel-coloured object. This lagoon is an El Dorado for tourists. It must be seen. It must be experienced. In sunny weather it offers the most marvellous views: nature's own symphony of tones and chords of colours and enchanting effects of light.

Aviation

Most Icelandic roads are, as we have seen, of a very poor standard. To make them worse, many are blocked by snow for long periods in winter. It is therefore essential that the country has a well-developed system of domestic aviation.

For a long time, Iceland had two major competing airlines, Iceland-air (Flugfélag Íslands) and Icelandic Airlines (Loftleiðir), offering scheduled flights to a variety of cities in North America and Europe. They took advantage of Iceland's geographical position to attract touchdowns at Keflavík with the prospect of stopovers for sightseeing in 'a different country'. Having two large airlines was undoubtedly a remarkable achievement for so small a nation with its limited economic resources. In 1973 these companies were amalgamated into Icelandair (Flugleiðir), which now competes with foreign aviation companies, at present SAS and Lufthansa.

Icelandair receives no state or municipal subsidies. Its operations have been generating a profit for years, giving good dividends to the shareholders.

In recent years Icelandair has renewed its entire fleet, buying big Boeing planes for the international routes and Fokker F50's for domestic traffic. The new Boeing planes are not only an effective weapon in the struggle for passengers on the international routes. They also mean relatively low running costs. The Icelandair planes that fly to and from the USA are in use 16–17 hours a day. This high utilization of the planes results in relatively low overheads. The transatlantic traffic has another advantage. Many transit passengers spend a few days in Iceland, contributing to the country's revenue from tourism.

From the economic point of view, domestic aviation is of some concern, especially as regards flights to small, isolated places. This traffic is unprofitable, but it is vital for the inhabitants of these places. By keeping the domestic lines open, Icelandair is performing a splendid service for the people in the sparsely populated parts of the country.

Air traffic is expanding. A new use in recent years is for exporting some kinds of fish and shellfish.

The base for international flights is the large airport at Keflavík, while domestic flights use the airfield in Reykjavík. In the rest of the country there are plenty of other airfields of varying quality. Many visitors to Iceland are fascinated—for example, when coming in to land at Keflavík—to see Iceland from the air. It is a fabulous sight.

One of the authors of this book, Esbjörn Rosenblad, was invited by the Icelandic coastguard to take part in a four-hour inspection flight in their Fokker plane. This happened in November 1981, on a day of clear sunshine and good visibility. It was a fascinating experience in many ways. The plane flew in a broad arc over the sea to the west of Iceland. It maintained an average speed of 350 km/h and a height of 400 metres. Beneath us we could see a large number of fishing vessels (all of them Icelandic). They were trawlers of various kinds and boats with long lines, fishing for cod, redfish, and herring. Seagulls circled around the boats, looking to us like small insects.

Just west of the Gulf Stream we observed a thin ice-floe, which grew more compact in the direction of Greenland, and icebergs reaching heights of ten to twenty metres. At the north-west corner of Iceland we saw fairly flat, snow-clad mountains rising steeply out of the sea.

Towards the end of this short winter day we headed back to the airfield in Reykjavík. As the sleepy sun sank in the ocean, twilight drew its veil over the land and the waters. The fishing vessels lit their lanterns. They shone like glow-worms in the gathering winter darkness.

Satellite Telecommunications

At Úlfarsfell in Mosfellssveit near Reykjavík, the Icelanders have built a tracking station for the exchange of telephone, telegraph, telefax, and television signals with other countries via the INTER SAT satellite. This station, which is called Skyggnir (the all-seeing), was opened in 1980. In other words, this was the year when the Icelanders took the step into the space age and were able to benefit from modern facilities for international telecommunications.

Television programmes are sent via Skyggnir by way of London to and from television stations in the rest of the world. Before 1980, the programmes had to be transported by air to Iceland. Needless to say, this took time. Thanks to Skyggnir they are now dispatched in a matter of seconds.

Radio, Television, and Daily Newspapers

With its sparse population, Iceland today needs to be held together by radio and television. All the Icelanders can be reached at the same time by news, weather forecasts, announcements, and advertising.

There have been nationwide radio broadcasts since 1930, and television since 1966. Colour television did not come until 1975. To begin with, there was only one channel for radio and one for television, both state-owned. The television was closed on Thursdays to give the staff a day off.

New legislation allowed the establishment in the autumn of 1986 of private radio and television. There are now several radio stations and two television channels. The television-free Thursdays, which many people appreciated, are now but a memory. Advertising has been permitted for many years on both radio and television. On certain conditions, people are allowed to put up dishes to receive satellite television.

The press in Iceland, as elsewhere in the world, has experienced setbacks in recent years, with smaller newspapers being forced to close down. Apart from a few party newspapers with a weak economy and low circulation, the picture is dominated by two nationwide dailies, both of which call themselves politically independent. One of them is *Morgunblaðið*, the morning paper with an average circulation of 51,000, and the other is the evening tabloid *Dagblaðið-Vísir*, with a circulation of some 40,000.

Iceland as a Tourist Attraction

Iceland is attracting more and more tourists. In 1950 there were only about 4,000, but in 1990 the figure had risen to 142,000. The flow of tourists breaks records every year. About 35 per cent of the visitors come from the other Nordic countries, 46 per cent from the rest of Europe (mainly Germans and British), and 17 per cent from North America. Ranked in order of their country of origin, the tourists come from the USA, Germany, and Sweden, followed by Denmark and Britain. Most of them arrive at Keflavík by air. Some tourists prefer cruise ships or the Faroese car ferry, the *Norrøna*, which brings them to the little town of Seyðisfjörður on the east coast.

More than half of the visitors come to Iceland between June and August, whereas only a few choose the dark winter months with their rain, snow, and storms. This imbalance is a source of concern for the Icelandic tourist trade, with its big new hotels and restaurants.

For accommodation, visitors can choose between luxury hotels or the boarding schools throughout the country which are turned into cheap tourist hotels in the summer. You can also spend the night in a tent or on a farm. Warm and waterproof clothes are recommended. You can plan your trip with the aid of a map, tourist brochures, and a guidebook.[52] If you are travelling on your own, do not forget to visit the Information Office for tourists at 2 Bankastræti in Reykjavík or other tourist offices elsewhere in the country.

It is fascinating to explore Iceland. It offers such attractions as bathing in hot springs (30–35°C) or in the geothermally heated waters of open-air swimming-pools (20–25°C), riding, golf, fishing for salmon and trout in rivers and lakes, and expeditions into the wilds.

The visitor to Iceland encounters different landscape, a different environment, and different conditions. Some things may take the traveller by surprise and even cause difficulties for those who are not properly prepared. If you are not used to gravel roads, you must drive carefully after you leave the tarmac behind. When driving in the interior, one must also bear in mind that it is forbidden to drive off the marked tracks. Tourists are well advised to go on organized tours and benefit from the commentary of a registered Icelandic guide.[53]

Although there are many interesting things to be seen in Reykjavík, most of the main tourist attractions are found in the uninhabited areas. When travelling, you often find yourself suddenly on the very edge of a high bird-cliff where you can see puffins or guillemots. You may cross geothermal areas with boiling geysers or bubbling mud-pools. You may cross sharp lava rocks to reach a glacier. You can climb high peaks or steep ravines to view the desert of black sand or the green expanses of grassland below. In Iceland the grass and the flowers have especially bright colours because of the perpetual daylight in the summer.

This island of ice and fire, this land of poetry and saga has much to enchant the visitor, especially the landscape. It inspired the romantic Lord Dufferin to the following lyrical description of the beauty that met his eye as his schooner yacht *Foam* cruised in towards Reykjavík:[54]

> The panorama of the bay of Faxa Fiord is magnificent—with a width of fifty miles from horn to horn, the one running down into a rocky ridge

of pumice, the other towering to the height of five thousand feet in a pyramid of eternal snow, while round the intervening semicircle crowd the peaks of a hundred noble mountains. As you approach the shore, you are very much reminded of the west coast of Scotland, except that everything is more *intense*, the atmosphere clearer, the light more vivid, the air more bracing, the hills steeper, loftier, more tormented, as the French say, and more gaunt; while, between their base and the sea, stretches a dirty greenish slope, patched with houses which themselves, both roof and walls, are of a mouldy-green, as if some long-since inhabited country had been fished up out of the bottom of the sea.

The effects of light and shadow are the purest I ever saw, the contrasts of colour most astonishing,—one square front of a mountain jutting out in a blaze of gold against the flank of another, dyed of the darkest purple, while up against the azure sky beyond, rise peaks of glittering snow and ice.

Notes to Chapter 5

1   A summary of the course of development can be found in *Iceland 1986: Handbook Published by the Central Bank of Iceland* (Reykjavík, 1987), pp. 53–4.

2   Elfar Loftsson, *Island i Nato: Partierna och försvarsfrågan*, Göteborg Studies in Politics 9 (Göteborg: Författares bokmagasin, 1981). See also Benedikt Gröndal, *Iceland from Neutrality to NATO Membership* (Oslo: Universitetsforlaget, 1971); Björn Bjarnason, 'The Security of Iceland', *Cooperation and Conflict* 3/4 (1972); Þór Whitehead, 'Lýðveldi og herstöðvar', *Skírnir* 152 (1976); Hannes Jónsson, 'Utanríkisstefna Íslands lýðveldistímabilið og mótun hennar', *Andvari* 1986.

3   Heimir Þorleifsson, *Frá einveldi til lýðveldis: Íslandssaga eftir 1830* (Reykjavík, 1973), p. 283.

4   Owe Rainer, *Makterna* (Stockholm: Norstedt, 1984), p. 66.

5   Frantz Wendt, *The Nordic Council and Co-operation in Scandinavia* (Copenhagen: Nordic Council, 1959), pp. 233–4; Benedikt Gröndal, *Iceland from Neutrality to NATO Membership*, pp. 41–3; Elfar Loftsson, *Island i Nato*, pp. 147–9.

6   Elfar Loftsson, *Island i Nato*, p. 132.

7   Heimir Þorleifsson, *Frá einveldi til lýðveldis*, p. 283.

8   Sigurður A. Magnússon, *Northern Sphinx: Iceland and the Icelanders from the Settlement to the Present* (London: Hurst, 1977), p. 143.

9   Bragi Guðmundsson and Gunnar Karlsson, *Uppruni nútímans: Íslandssaga frá öndverðri 19. öld til síðari hluta 20. aldar* (Reykjavík: Mál og menning, 1986), p. 338.

10 Snorri Sturluson, *Heimskringla: History of the Kings of Norway,* trans. Lee M.

Hollander (Austin: University of Texas Press, 1964), p. 395 (ch. 125 of *Ólafs saga helga*).

11 *Uppruni nútímans*, p. 340; Heimir Þorleifsson, *Frá einveldi til lýðveldis*, p. 288.

12 Lord Dufferin, *Letters from High Latitudes* (London: Murray, 1857), p. 60.

13 Charles de Martens, *Causes célèbres du Droit des Gens* (Paris and Leipzig, 1827), p. 396; quoted from Gunnlaugur Thordarson, *Les Eaux territoriales d'Islande en ce qui concerne la pêche* (Reykjavík: Hlaðbúð, 1958), p. 133.

14 Gunnlaugur Thordarson, *Les Eaux territoriales*, pp. 7–14, 131–9; *Uppruni nútímans*, p. 347; Hannes Jónsson, *Friends in Conflict: The Anglo-Icelandic Cod Wars and the Law of the Sea* (London: Hurst, 1982), pp. 31–5.

15 Leading article in *Morgunblaðið*, 17 May 1988, 'Landgrunnslög—verndun fiskimiða' (The Law of the Continental Shelf—Protecting the Fishing Grounds); Hannes Jónsson, *Friends in Conflict*, pp. 209–10.

16 One exception was the feud about Iceland's refusal to appear before the Hague Tribunal, 1971–2.

17 Gunnlaugur Thordarson, *Les Eaux territoriales*, p. 14.

18 Hannes Jónsson, *Friends in Conflict*, pp. 196–207.

19 *Iceland 1986*, p. 130. The text of the Convention was published in 1985 by the Icelandic Ministry of Foreign Affairs.

20 See Chapter 1, 'Reformation and Cod Wars'.

21 *The Anglo-Norwegian Fisheries Case* (Judgment of 18 December 1951, International Court of Justice Report 116). For a summary see Karin Hjertonsson, *The New Law of the Sea: Influence of the Latin American States on Recent Developments of the Law of the Sea* (Stockholm: Norstedt, 1973), pp. 160–2.

22 Gunnlaugur Thordarson, *Les Eaux territoriales*, pp. 139, 142.

23 Morris Davis, *Iceland Extends its Fisheries Limits: A Political Analysis* (Oslo: Universitetsforlaget, 1963), pp. 80–88. The tendency was clear; at the 1960 conference in Geneva, a joint proposal from Canada and the USA was supported by an even greater number of states (54 to 28, with 5 abstentions), but still not with the necessary qualified majority.

24 Heimir Þorleifsson, *Frá einveldi til lýðveldis*, p. 294.

25 R. P. Barston and Hjálmar W. Hannesson, 'The Anglo-Icelandic Fisheries Dispute', *International Relations* 4:6 (1974), pp. 564–6, 571.

26 Hjertonsson, *The New Law of the Sea*, p. 136.

27 Heimir Þorleifsson, *Frá einveldi til lýðveldis*, p. 296.

28 Hjertonsson, *The New Law of the Sea*, pp. 36, 104.

29 Benedikt Gröndal, *Iceland from Neutrality to NATO Membership*, p. 59; Hjertonsson, *The New Law of the Sea*, p. 137; cf. Heimir Þorleifsson, *Frá einveldi til lýðveldis*, p. 300.

30 *Iceland 1986*, p. 130.

31 Sigurdór Sigurdórsson, *Spaugsami spörfuglinn* (Reykjavík: Örn og Örlygur, 1987), pp. 94–121.

32 Ibid., pp. 100–4.

33   Benedikt Gröndal, *Iceland from Neutrality to NATO Membership*, p. 59.

34   Sir Andrew Gilchrist, *Cod Wars and How to Lose Them* (Edinburgh: Q Press, 1978), pp. vii, 100, 104, 106, 110.

35   Anthony Sampson, *Anatomy of Britain* (London: Hodder and Stoughton, 1962), p. 305.

36   Paul-Henri Spaak, *Combats inachevés* (Paris: Fayard, 1969), part 2, p. 137, quoted from Gilchrist, *Cod Wars and How to Lose Them*, pp. 104–5.

37   Gilchrist, *Cod Wars and How to Lose Them*, p. 105.

38   Davis, *Iceland Extends its Fisheries Limits*, pp. 75–6.

39   Hagstofa Íslands based its table on the following sources: *Yearbook of Nordic Statistics* (Nordic Council); *Yearbook for Population Research in Finland* (Population Research Institute, Helsinki); *Befolkningens bevægelser* (Danish Central Statistical Office); the United Nations *Demographic Yearbook*; *Recent Demographic Developments in the Member States of the Council of Europe*; and two publications of Hagstofa Íslands, *Hagtíðindi* and *Mannfjöldaskýrslur*.

40   *Uppruni nútímans*, pp. 313–4.

41   Sigurður A. Magnússon, *Northern Sphinx*, pp. 238–9.

42   *Hrafnkel's Saga and Other Icelandic Stories*, trans. Hermann Pálsson (Harmondsworth: Penguin, 1971).

43   Uno von Troil, *Brev om Island*, ed. Einar Fors Bergström, Skrifter utgivna av Samfundet Sverige–Island 3 (Stockholm: Hökerberg, 1933), pp. 21–2.

44   John Coles, *Summer Travelling in Iceland; Being the Narrative of Two Journeys across the Island by Unfrequented Routes* (London: Murray, 1882), p. 11. Coles consistently misspells Geir Zoëga as Gier Zoega.

45   Sir George Steuart Mackenzie, *Travels in the Island of Iceland during the Summer of the Year MDCCCX* (Edinburgh, 1811), p. 137.

46   Halldór Laxness, *Íslandsklukkan*, 3rd ed. (Reykjavík: Helgafell, 1969), p. 94.

47   Þór Magnússon, 'A Showcase of Icelandic National Treasures', *Iceland Review* 1987, pp. 38, 77.

48   *Iceland 1986*, pp. 183–8.

49   *Ólafs saga Tryggvasonar*, ch. 33. See Chapter 3, 'Folk Belief and Folktales'.

50   Bjarni Jónsson, *Morgunblaðið*, 13 September 1986; the article was also translated into French.

51   Sigurður A. Magnússon, *Northern Sphinx*, p. 142.

52   See, for example, Peter Kidson, *Iceland in a Nutshell* (Reykjavík: Iceland Travel Books, 1974); Don Philpott, *The Visitor's Guide to Iceland* (Ashbourne, Derbyshire: Moorland, 1985); David Williams, *Iceland: The Visitor's Guide* (London: Stacey International, 1986); Tony Escritt, *Iceland: The Traveller's Guide* (Harrow: Iceland Information Centre, 1990).

53   Icelandic tourist guides are trained for two terms at the Tourist Guide School of Iceland under the direction of Birna G. Bjarnleifsdóttir.

54   Dufferin, *Letters from High Latitudes*, pp. 38–9.

❧ Chapter 6 ❧

Iceland Today

How Iceland is Governed

The Icelandic Constitution

Tout seroit perdu si le même homme,
ou le même corps des principaux, ou
des nobles, ou du peuple, exerçoient
ces trois pouvoirs: celui de faire des
lois, celui d'exécuter les résolutions
publiques, et celui de juger les crimes
ou les différends des particuliers.

Charles de Montesquieu, De l'esprit
des lois

ACCORDING TO THE CONSTITUTION OF 17 June 1944, which has
since been revised four times (in 1959, 1968, 1984, and 1991), Iceland
is a republic with a constitutional form of government (article 1).
Parliamentarism was introduced in principle in 1903 when Iceland was
granted limited home rule, and it was fully implemented in conjunction with the Act of Union of 1918. It is based on customary law but
is not expressly confirmed by statute.

The constitution assumes a tripartite division of power in the spirit
of the French political philosopher Montesquieu.[1] Since 1874, the
doctrine of the strict separation of the powers, each one sovereign
within its own sphere, has served as a model for the Icelandic form of
government. Yet it is not implemented in the constitution of 1944. This

was instead shaped in conformity with parliamentarism. This means, as we know, that the majority in a legislative parliament (in this case the Icelandic Althing) has the decisive power. Without the support of a parliamentary majority, the executive (in this case an Icelandic government) cannot exercise power. Formally (according to article 2), *legislative* power lies with the Althing and the president of Iceland. The same article states that *executive* power is exercised by the president and other government authorities in accordance with the constitution and the other laws of the country. *Judicial* power is exercised by the courts.

Other provisions in the constitution concern the president and the government, the Althing, the courts, the Lutheran state church, and human rights.

The president (who may be a man or a woman) is not responsible for official presidential actions, exercising office through his or her ministers (articles 11 and 13). The president stands above politics. The president is the head of state, a personification of the entire people.

In practice, executive power is exercised solely by the government and legislative power solely by the Althing. Since 1991 this has consisted of a single chamber with sixty-three members.

The courts work on two levels: a supreme court in Reykjavík and district courts of first instance. Judges are appointed for life and cannot be dismissed except by a court judgement (article 61). According to customary law, Icelandic courts can declare that a statute is unconstitutional. They thus have the right to try new laws.[2]

The shape of the Icelandic form of government is thus based on centuries of development and long-nourished dreams of freedom. The Icelanders have emphasized the need for a strong central government (the lack of which proved fatal to the Icelandic commonwealth), independent courts, and an elected parliament. Since its first meeting at Þingvellir in 930, the Althing has been the cornerstone of the democratic institutions of the Icelandic people.

The concept of the Althing concurs with the ideas expressed by the French philosopher and political theorist Jean-Jacques Rousseau. His major work, *Du contrat social* (1762), is based on the theory that society arose through a contract between individuals. Rousseau's ideas were recognized in the Declaration of the Rights of Man in Paris in

1789, which asserted that 'the source of all sovereignty lies essentially in the people'. Democracy—government of the people, by the people, for the people—is the foundation of the Icelandic state. The Icelandic people have the right to establish their own constitution and to choose their own form of government.

The Office of President and its Occupants

The significance of the presidency for the Icelandic people is fully understandable if we look back to the situation in 1918. In that year the country was declared to be a free and sovereign kingdom in personal union with Denmark. But the head of state was a foreigner. Of course it was an unforgettable and festive occasion when the king deigned to visit his distant kingdom. Christian X (1870–1947) and Queen Alexandrine were highly appreciated by the Icelanders for their nobility of character. Yet even under the reign of Christian X, the Icelanders could not help thinking that they had spent centuries under the rule of foreign monarchs.

For the Icelanders, the kingdom was a reminder that they had still not achieved full independence. The dream they yearned for was to get rid of the monarchy. They wanted to found a republic. They wanted a president elected by the people. He would be a confirmation of the successful outcome of the protracted struggle for independence; through his non-political position, he would symbolize the unity of the country.

That day came on 17 June 1944. The Republic of Iceland was proclaimed at Þingvellir. Iceland received her new constitution at the same time. It closely followed the constitution of 1920. The word 'king' was replaced by 'president'. The latter was to be elected by the people for four years at a time through a direct secret ballot (articles 3–8). Otherwise the president has roughly the same position and functions (articles 9–30) as the constitutional monarchs in Scandinavia.

The president's functions include, for example, signing statutes (in emergencies also provisional laws, when the Althing is not in session—article 28), decrees, appointments, and treaties. He has great power during government crises. The party leaders negotiate the formation of a new government under the president's supervision. He can thus influence the outcome. Normally, in view of the division of the parties, he has to try to arrive at a coalition which can enjoy the support of a majority in the Althing.

The president opens and closes parliamentary sessions, presides over cabinet meetings, and represents Iceland during state visits and other official events. In addition, he closely follows state business and takes part in various cultural occasions.

The office of president has been held by four persons:

(1) the diplomat Sveinn Björnsson, 1944–52, who was regent 1941–4;
(2) the politician Ásgeir Ásgeirsson, 1952–68, who was educated as a theologian but never ordained;
(3) the archaeologist Dr Kristján Eldjárn, 1968–80;
(4) the former director of Iðnó, the Reykjavík Civic Theatre, Vigdís Finnbogadóttir, 1980–.

Vigdís was the first woman in the world to be appointed head of state through a general election. By virtue of her personality she has won widespread respect and admiration as president, both at home and abroad.

Since the foundation of the republic, it has been accepted practice for a president who intends to seek re-election after a four-year period to be automatically returned without opposition. This has become something of an unwritten law. In accordance with this practice, Vigdís Finnbogadóttir was appointed for a second four-year period in 1984. In 1988, however, she unexpectedly found that she had a rival candidate—the first time that the prevailing practice was challenged. She was opposed by a housewife from Vestmannaeyjar, Sigrún Þorsteinsdóttir, who was able to stand after scraping together the 1,500 signatures which are required for a presidential candidate according to the constitution (article 5). She thus forced a presidential election.

Sigrún is closely connected to the little Human Party (Flokkur mannsins) which received 1.6 per cent of the votes in the 1987 general election, thus failing to win any seats in the Althing. She said that she had nothing personal against Vigdís, but she wanted to strengthen the office of president. It should, in her opinion, be occupied by a strong leader. The office should be more than an ornament, 'a splendid feather in the nation's cap'. The president should be able to exercise political power and work to protect human rights. The president should be free to obstruct the passing of a law if it is felt to be in breach of human rights or to jeopardize the living conditions of the people. In such cases the president, with the support of the constitution (article 26) should be able to refuse to sign a statute passed by the Althing. Although it may come into force, it should be referred to the people in a referendum as soon as circumstances allow.

Vigdís Finnbogadóttir has opposed any such idea, with reference to previous practice and to her view of the president's position as head of state. As a private person, the president may not always be pleased with all the decisions of the Althing, but a president should never go against the elected parliament. No president has ever done so during the many years that have elapsed since the foundation of the republic. Referendums on disputed issues would lead to political disintegration and general division.

Another aspect of this fundamental constitutional issue is that the president is elected by voters from all the political parties. They rely on him or her not to intervene in the issues that happen to be dividing the nation. The president is elevated above all the tumults of domestic politics. The president is the link that holds all the people together.

The presidential election of 25 June 1988 was dominated by the voters' interest in these questions of principle about the power and position of the president. Should the president remain non-political and exercise office as a symbol of national unity? Or should he enjoy political power on the scale of, say, the president of the United States? What would be the consequences of adopting the latter alternative?

The application of article 26, which has hitherto been a dead letter in the constitution, would in the opinion of many have serious repercussions. It would probably lead to divisive power struggles between the president and the Althing, and frequent referendums on the Swiss model.

Before the election, the issue was the subject of penetrating analysis on television and in other news media. It became clear that not only experienced political scientists and politicians like the then prime minister, Þorsteinn Pálsson, but also 'the man in the street' were generally satisfied with the present system, which has been shaped by the Icelanders themselves. People agreed that things were all right as they were. There was a long tradition of not caring about the political views of a presidential candidate. The Icelanders preferred to elect presidents who had made themselves known through their cultural work. They had chosen non-political presidents with a distinctly humanist image, such as Kristján Eldjárn and Vigdís Finnbogadóttir. Moreover, many had expressed their undisguised admiration for Vigdís. They praised her sense of responsibility, her sound judgement, and her strong commitment to culture, combined with her pleasant manner and winning smile.

Against this background, the outcome of the election was a foregone conclusion: an overwhelming victory for the sitting president. Vigdís received 92.7 per cent of the votes, against 5.3 per cent for Sigrún Þorsteinsdóttir. This was a record in the modern history of Iceland and a personal triumph for Vigdís herself. The people paid their tribute to a popular president.

Since the presidential election of 1988, it has appeared desirable to revise the Icelandic constitution in at least two respects. To begin with, the population has more than doubled in the period 1944–92. A candidate for president should therefore be expected to collect much more than the present 1,500 signatures. Raising the minimum number of nominating voters could restrict the number of candidates, as well as emphasizing the importance of the office of president for the Icelandic people.

Secondly, it might be justified to adopt the French system of a presidential election in two rounds. This could ensure—in the event of many candidates standing for election—that the president who was finally elected would enjoy the support of a clear majority of the voters.

Vigdís herself has advocated this reform. In 1980 she was elected by a tiny majority. She received only 33.8 per cent of the votes. She had three rivals. The state arbitrator, Guðlaugur Þorvaldsson, polled 32.3 per cent of the votes. The remaining votes were divided between the politician Albert Guðmundsson and the ambassador Pétur Thorsteinsson.

Vigdís Finnbogadóttir was re-elected in 1992 for a fourth four-year term as president of Iceland.

The Althing and Constituent Representation

Iceland is divided into eight constituencies. The members of the Althing are elected for four years by proportional representation. The Althing has 63 seats. The number was previously 60, but this was increased in 1984 through an amendment to the constitution (article 31). There were simultaneous changes concerning suffrage (article 33) and eligibility for election (article 34). The voting age was lowered from 20 to 18.

The ceaseless flow of migration to the south-west corner of Iceland (the capital Reykjavík and the Reykjanes peninsula) and the declining population in the rest of the country have meant that the sparsely populated countryside is over-represented in the Althing. This has been at least partly rectified by changes in constituent representation and the introduction of nine additional mandates with no geographical ties.

These rules testify to a never-ending struggle for influence in the Althing, a tug of war between the inhabitants of the densely populated south-western corner and the people in the rest of Iceland. The aim is to achieve fair representation for the electorate.

Political Parties

The Icelandic political parties and the way they cooperate differ greatly from the general pattern in Western Europe.

This difference is easy to see but difficult to explain. The causes may be historical, social, and economic. Among them we may mention the long struggle for independence, the inherited national spirit, the strong family ties, and the pronounced individualism of the Icelanders. They like to manage their lives with the aid of the family, relatives, good friends, and neighbours, but without the interference of the authorities. Most Icelanders (80–85 per cent) own their own homes, and about 35 per cent live in one-family houses.[3] These homes are generally better equipped and furnished, and above all more spacious than dwellings in Scandinavia. Direct taxes are lower than in the other

Nordic countries, but there is a greater span between high and low income brackets. In addition, there are other typically Icelandic factors such as high private consumption and a comparatively small public sector, combined with—as a rule—full employment and a standard of living that is one of the highest in the world. Icelandic welfare is vulnerable, however. It is based on fishing, which is sensitive to market fluctuations, and related to this is the problem of inflation, which has proved difficult to combat.

Icelandic party politics cannot easily be fitted into the normal left–right pattern. The watershed in Icelandic politics is not really between left and right but rather between parties which stand for traditionally Icelandic values and parties which seek to open the country more to the surrounding world.

The *Progressive Party* is traditionally a rural party, supported by the farmers. In recent years they have also made gains in the towns. They still represent the interests of farmers, of small rural industries which use agricultural produce as their raw materials, and particularly the profitable fisheries in the fishing stations around the coast. The Progressive Party's spokesmen for these sparsely populated districts claim that too large a share of the profits from fishing is unfairly raked in by entrepreneurs in the Reykjavík area. Some of the party's sympathizers are opposed to membership of NATO, and even more wish to close the Keflavík base.

The *People's Alliance* is a wage-earners' party, but it also has sympathizers among the farmers. Its members are firmly opposed to NATO and the base. But it would be too simple to say that this is because they are 'communists'. Their attitude is just as much based on their patriotism. The party has many supporters among the so-called intellectuals, who are generally very nationally-minded in Iceland.

The *Independence Party,* which is the biggest in Iceland, is supported by a variety of groups: private entrepreneurs, white-collar workers, trade union people, and other wage-earners. Many of these voters own their own homes. Many of the members are united by the fact that they earn their living in 'the modern sector' with its foreign connections. The same applies to the *Social Democratic Party* (or Labour Party), whose members are often employed in industry. This explains the community of interests between these two parties. Another common denominator for the Independence Party and the Social Democratic Party is that they both support NATO membership and accept the Keflavík base as a necessary evil.

To simplify matters somewhat crudely, it can be said that Iceland's political life is characterized by the tension between, on the one hand, the Independence Party and the Social Democratic Party as representatives of the modern sector, and on the other hand, the representatives of the traditional sector in the Progressive Party and the People's Alliance. The internationally oriented parties win most of their supporters from the modern industrial sector. They work mostly to secure full employment and efficiency in business and industry. The 'nationalist' parties are more interested in regional policies.

Within each group there are left–right divisions of a kind, but in today's Icelandic society it is generally true to say that these divisions are not as significant as the opposition between the representatives of the traditional and the modern sectors.

The period 1944–87 saw the occasional emergence of some small parties. These usually sprang up overnight and disappeared almost as quickly. In general, however, political life in Iceland has been dominated by the four parties or groupings mentioned above, with the following share of the votes:

- The conservative-liberal Independence Party (Sjálfstæðisflokkur-inn), with its voters mostly in the densely populated south-west. Average share of the votes: about 40 per cent.
- The traditionally agrarian Progressive Party (Framsóknarflokkur-inn), with close ties to the Icelandic cooperative movement, Samband (SÍS). Average share of the votes: about 25 per cent.
- Socialist parties, including the radical left-wing People's Alliance (Alþýðubandalagið), also with rural supporters. Average share of the votes: 15–20 per cent.
- The Social Democratic Party (Alþýðuflokkurinn), with most of its support in the towns. Average share of the votes: 10–15 per cent.

The voting figures are averages for the period 1944–87, but they show a remarkable stability in the support for the traditional parties. This is probably due to the fact that Icelandic electors are creatures of habit.[4]

In the past they would rarely consider changing to another party. They were loyal to a party once they had chosen it.

This pattern was broken, however, in the 1987 general election, although there had previously been signs of increased mobility among the electorate—perhaps due in part to the impact of television. Many viewers now vote for a person rather than for a party. In any case, Icelandic voters today do not show the same party loyalty as before. The sudden change in the 1987 election was a result of two concrete events. One was the split in the Independence Party. Just a month before the election, the seasoned politician Albert Guðmundsson broke away to form the Citizens' Party (Borgaraflokkurinn). Albert had once been a professional footballer in Italy and France; finally, he became Icelandic ambassador in Paris. The success of his Citizens' Party was short-lived, however; it failed to survive the 1991 election. The same cannot be said of the other new party of the 1980s, the *Women's Alliance* (Samtök um kvennalista). They have proved that they are able to attract and hold voters. They won three seats in the 1983 election, six in the 1987 election, and five in 1991.

The success of the Women's Alliance, which must be unique in the western world, has several causes. To begin with, it is generally considered that women have been a neglected group in Icelandic society in at least three respects. Few elected representatives in local and national politics have been female, even though women have been entitled to vote and be elected since 1915. On the labour market, women have been a low-income group. To make matters worse, they have been badly hit by the shortage of nursery schools for the children—a particularly serious problem for the large number of unmarried mothers (the largest proportion in the western world)—and the high housing costs. In addition, their work in the home has not been valued highly enough. The large women's demonstration in Reykjavík in 1975 was a clear and widely supported protest against the prevailing inequality.

The women who represent the Women's Alliance in the Althing have convincingly shown the need for reforms. They have also maintained that women 'acquire a world of experience peculiar to themselves. To protect and foster life is viewed as the major principle of their being, considerations different from those that chiefly weigh in the world of men.'[5]

Male values have dominated for centuries. The views of women are entitled to the same esteem as those of the men. This at least was the way women reasoned in the days of the commonwealth. Women then were respected. They were appreciated. The men listened to them. We see this in the Icelandic sagas.

Since the Second World War, the Independence Party has consistently advocated foreign investment in Icelandic industry and defence cooperation with the West (membership of NATO and the manning of the Keflavík base). The same line has generally—but not always—been argued by the Social Democratic Party and a majority of the Progressive Party. Criticism of the Keflavík base has often been vociferous, not least in 1956, just before the Hungarian crisis in the autumn of that year, and under the 'left-wing' government of 1971–4. Despite this, membership of NATO has always been supported by parties which have together been able to muster at least 75–80 per cent of the votes in the Althing. The main opposition to Iceland's present security policy comes from the People's Alliance. They campaign for a neutral Iceland with small domestic industries.

It should be noted that the People's Alliance has taken part in left-wing coalitions in 1978–9, 1980–3, and 1988–91, even though none of these governments has had the evacuation of the Keflavík base on its platform. The Women's Alliance has the same 'army out!' attitude as the People's Alliance; the women reject all participation in military alliances.

The following table shows the state of the political parties in 1992, with the percentage polled in the 1991 general election and the number of seats held in the Althing by each party:

	%	no. of seats
Independence Party	38.6	26
Progressive Party	18.9	13
People's Alliance	14.4	9
Social Democratic Party	15.5	10
Women's Alliance	8.3	5
three small parties	4.3	0
total	100	63

Governments and Prime Ministers

Iceland is overwhelmingly dependent on fish and fish products, which account for 70–80 per cent of export values. With the prices for these exports being extremely sensitive to fluctuations in the trade cycle, it is understandable that Iceland has repeatedly found herself in economic crisis. This has taken the form of recurrent peaks of inflation and an excess of imports over exports, frequent devaluations, large foreign debts, repeated strikes and unrest on the labour market. Another source of concern is the difficulty of uniting opposing parties in strong coalition governments. Some coalitions have been short-lived.

From 1944 until the present day (1992), no political party has ever had an absolute majority in the Althing. Of the seventeen governments since the proclamation of the republic, all have been coalitions, except for three minority governments, 1949–50, 1958–9, and 1979–80.

The decisive factor in the formation of governments has generally been the parties' stances on security policy, the methods of combating inflation, fish quotas, taxes, tariffs, and other economic matters. Problems of regional policy have also played a role in conjunction with the growth of the south-western corner of Iceland at the expense of the rest of the country. Another issue has been whether the establishment of energy-intensive industries in Iceland should be undertaken in collaboration with multinational companies. An example of this is the aluminium smelter at Straumsvík on the road from Keflavík to Reykjavík. This, the biggest industrial plant in Iceland, is owned by the Swiss Alusuisse group and its Icelandic subsidiary ÍSAL.

This problem of large-scale industries and international investments of capital has fostered party-political differences similar to those raised by the security issue. Broadly speaking, it is the pro-NATO parties (the Independence Party, the Social Democratic Party, and parts of the Progressive Party) which have been in favour of foreign investment. The opposition has come from opponents of the Keflavík base within various parties and more particularly from the People's Alliance.

These issues around which the parties try to form coalition governments do not usually lead to the left–right groupings that are characteristic of many democratic countries. As we have seen, this is a distinctive feature of Icelandic politics. The government which built up the newly independent republic (1944–7), for example, was based on cooperation between the Independence Party, the Social Democratic Party, and the Socialist Party. The two-party government which was in power from 1959 until 1971 (an Icelandic record), with the ambition of reconstructing trade and industry, likewise paid no regard to traditional left and right blocs; it was a coalition of the Independence Party and the Social Democratic Party. In both cases the Progressive Party was bypassed, but they have otherwise taken part in the majority of Icelandic governments since the war. Since 1956 the Progressive Party has shown itself prepared to collaborate with the People's Alliance. The expression 'left-wing government' has been used to designate every Icelandic coalition which has not included the Independence Party. In five governments, however, the Independence Party has found a willing partner in the Social Democratic Party.

Gunnar Thoroddsen's government of 1980–3 was something of a political hybrid. It was based on a small group from the Independence Party along with the Progressive Party and the People's Alliance. Gunnar Thoroddsen was deputy chairman of the Independence Party. The opposition—the majority of the Independence Party—was led by the party chairman Geir Hallgrímsson, along with the Social Democratic Party. Despite this remarkable situation, the Independence Party survived the temporary split and remained a united party.

A detailed account of developments in domestic Icelandic post-war politics would be beyond the scope of this book. The composition of Icelandic governments since 1959, along with the names of the prime ministers and their political affiliation, can be seen in the following table:[6]

1959–1971 Independence Party and Social Democratic Party	1959–1963 Ólafur Thors (Ind.) 1963–1970 Bjarni Benediktsson (Ind.) 1970–1971 Jóhann Hafstein (Ind.)
1971–1974 Progressive Party, People's Alliance, and Hannibal Valdimarsson's Liberal and Left Alliance	Ólafur Jóhannesson (Prog.)

1974–1978
Independence Party and Progressive   Geir Hallgrímsson (Ind.)
Party

1978–1979
Progressive Party, Social Democratic   Ólafur Jóhannesson (Prog.)
Party, and People's Alliance

1979–1980
Social Democratic Party (minority   Benedikt Gröndal (Soc. Dem.)
government)

1980–1983
A group from the Independence Party,   Gunnar Thoroddsen (Ind.)
Progressive Party, People's Alliance

1983–1987
Progressive Party and Independence   Steingrímur Hermannsson (Prog.)
Party

1987–1988
Independence Party, Progressive Party,   Þorsteinn Pálsson (Ind.)
and Social Democratic Party

1988–1991
Progressive Party, Social Democratic   Steingrímur Hermannsson (Prog.)
Party, and People's Alliance

1991–
Independence Party and Social   Davíð Oddsson (Ind.) '
Democratic Party

Ecological Problems

. . . hardy patches of growth in the
country's defiant resistance to the
sand-chafing wind of destruction. . . .
And all the vegetation blows away.
What remains is a light-brown pillar
of dust in the air, nothing more.
Nothing but the all-powerful
wilderness.

Thor Vilhjálmsson, Grámosinn glóir

Environmental problems are of momentous consequence for the survival of our planet. One aspect of our abuse of the environment is the

ruthless industrial exploitation in the developed countries, with the consumption of the earth's limited resources and with land and sea being devastated by toxic emissions. Another aspect can be seen in the developing countries, with the felling of the rain forests and the spoiling of cultivable soil, combined with starvation, unprecedented population growth, poverty and repression, disease and armed conflict. All this serves to remind us that the present threat to the environment is global. Distances are shrinking in the age of the jet plane and television satellites. State boundaries mean nothing in the era of nuclear power and poison-spreading large-scale industry. This planet is a whole; no one can hide in his own corner. We are all in the same boat, Iceland too.

The atomic bombs dropped on Hiroshima and Nagasaki in August 1945 were the first warning signal. The meltdown in the nuclear reactor at Chernobyl in 1986 was another *mene tekel* written on the wall. The whole world is affected by holes in the ozone layer in the stratosphere, or by the general depletion of the ozone that surrounds the globe and protects us from ultraviolet radiation. The ozone layer is endangered mainly by chloro-fluorocarbons (CFCs). The continued emission of CFCs is therefore synonymous with playing Russian roulette with the future of mankind.

Today's threat to the environment is global. It menaces all life on this earth.

The Icelanders are well aware of the existence of problems caused by the abuse of the environment. They attach growing importance to ecological and conservational issues. *Vistfræði* or ecology—the study of the interaction of organisms with one another and with their physical surroundings—has become more than an empty, fashionable word. Ecological awareness is rather a commandment, a guiding star, a beacon in the darkness.

Soil Erosion

The most serious environmental problem in Iceland is soil erosion. The landscape today makes this patently obvious. It is virtually treeless. With a few exceptions, vegetation finds it difficult to survive in these ecologically unfavourable surroundings. It is circumscribed by huge glaciers drained by violently rushing rivers, which occasionally change their courses, and recurrent volcanic eruptions—on average twenty a century in historical times—bringing flows of glowing hot lava, showers of fluorine-rich ash, and sulphurous mists. Under the glaciers (which cover about 11 per cent of the area of Iceland) and on the sterile plains of lava (covering about 10 per cent of the country) there stretch seemingly endless expanses of desert and semi-desert, made up of gravel, stone, volcanic ash, and sand. The vegetation that can survive here is exposed to sharp fluctuations in temperature, snow, rain, and piercing winds which make the topsoil whirl. Another threat comes from grazing animals, particularly sheep. The result can be seen at a glance. The Icelandic landscape strikes the observer by its naked-ness, the absence of fixed points for the eye, the scarcity of trees. All that exists are stunted birches, which are the subject of a joke: 'If you get lost in an Icelandic forest, just rise and look around.'[7]

It is easy to point to the causes. To begin with, it takes a long time for humus to form and vegetation to colonize it. An illuminating example comes from the world's youngest island, Surtsey, creation of the fire-god Surtur. This rose out of the sea in 1963–7 after a series of volcanic eruptions. Surtsey is a gold-mine for scholars who want to study how life arises.

A modern problem is the damage to the Icelandic highlands caused by unthinking tourists. A great danger comes from those who tour the country by car or bus, without qualified tourist guides. Icelanders often have negative experiences of foreign chartered buses with foreigners at the steering-wheel, arriving by car ferry at Seyðisfjörður on the east coast. This criticism is justified. Throughout the highlands it is possi-ble to see the tracks of buses, jeeps, motorcycles, and ordinary cars. Most of the tourists' litter, with the exception of the plastic, decom-poses through time. But the deep tracks left by a single jeep on roadless terrain in an oasis between two expanses of sand can take years for nature to wipe out. Tourists, Icelanders and foreigners alike, should therefore always stick to marked tracks. Traffic in the summer should be under constant surveillance, for example by plane.

Serious concern has been expressed over foreign tours with char-tered buses and jeeps driven by foreigners. They often arrive early in the spring, when no Icelandic guide would think of driving in the central highlands. The ground is wet in spring, and the sprouting vegetation can easily be destroyed by heavy vehicles. The damage is enormous. Foreigners who are not used to such conditions are advised to participate in tours organized by Icelandic tourist bureaux, escorted by qualified guides.

Another reason for the vulnerability of the Icelandic vegetation is that the topsoil contains a very low proportion of humus-binding clay. This makes the soil loose and porous. It has low resistance in harsh weather, an easy victim to abrasion by wind and water. This applies especially to dry areas where the soil contains large amounts of sand and volcanic ash.

Iceland is located just south of the Arctic Circle, which runs through the island of Grímsey off the north coast. Reykjavík is at roughly the same latitude as Fairbanks in Alaska and Arkhangelsk in Russia. In the central highlands the temperature falls quickly and vegetation declines. The upper limit for a continuous vegetation cover is on average no more than six or seven hundred metres above sea level, and the upper limit for trees and shrubs is no more than 250–300 metres above sea level.[8]

As long as Iceland remained a virgin island with no grass-eating mammals, an ecological balance was maintained. The destruction of the soil by volcanic eruptions, rain, snow, and wind was offset by the factors favouring the formation of humus and vegetation. In addition, palaeoclimatologists reckon that the climate was relatively mild. So it appears to have been when the Vikings discovered the island in the second half of the ninth century. About 65 per cent of the country had vegetation cover in those days. At least 25 per cent was covered with birch woods, with a variety of downy birch (*Betula pubescens* ssp. *tortuosa*), occasional stands of rowan and dwarf birch (*Betula nana*), and various willow species of the genus *Salix*. According to *Land-námabók*, the Swedish Viking Garðar Svavarsson noted that the country was wooded between the mountains and the coast. The trees bound the humus. They protected the underlying vegetation and the soil.

With the arrival of the colonists, however, the ecological balance was disturbed. The quickly growing population chopped down the woods. Trees and bushes were used for firewood, charcoal, and timber. The driftwood that could be found on the coast did not go far to meet the needs. Sheep and horses over-grazed the grass. Nature's gifts were thoughtlessly exploited, so that the vegetation cover became thin or non-existent. The topsoil was loosened and blown or washed away. Catastrophic soil erosion (*uppblástur*) began.

The situation was made worse by a deterioration in the climate. A lasting cold spell—the little ice age—set in around 1600. Moreover, there were repeated volcanic eruptions. The worst one came in 1783, when Laki, just west of Vatnajökull, spread ash over almost all of Iceland. This poisoned the soil so that over half the livestock died and the population was decimated through hunger.

The wasting of the soil has continued at an ever-increasing rate in the twentieth century. Sandstorms rage from time to time. Soil erosion has destroyed about 3,000 hectares of soil annually, an area over twice the size of the island of Heimaey (1,340 hectares). This figure does not represent the annual average in modern times, but is an estimate of the total erosion since the settlement. The problem is still acute. In dry summers it can happen that whole clouds of loose soil are whirled away with such intensity that they darken the sky and almost hide the sun. All that remains is sterile land, looking as if it had been sand-blasted.

As a result, the vegetation cover of Iceland is reduced to about 25 per cent of the area of the country. Only about one per cent is wooded.

The Icelanders were long powerless in the face of this destruction. It was as if they were panic-stricken. They thought that it was beyond human might to prevent this attack by the forces of devastation. Some farmers built ramparts of stone or timber to protect their crops against the sandstorms. But this was in vain. Their efforts were of little or no use. They may well have imagined that, when they screwed up their eyes and looked at the swirling sandstorms, they could make out terrible trolls. Their struggle must have appeared as hopeless as that of Cervantes' noble Don Quixote, the 'knight of the sad countenance', who took windmills for giants and attacked them with his lance.

It finally became clear to the Icelanders that soil erosion could only be stopped if the government took action. In 1907, when Hannes Hafstein was Minister for Icelandic Affairs (the first Icelander in this post), the Althing passed its first law on the organized battle against soil erosion.

One of the main causes of the problem has been the large number of freely grazing animals, mostly sheep but also horses. The first measure was therefore to enclose certain areas where grazing was to be prohibited. These areas were sown with European lyme-grass (*Elymus arenarius*) and later a species of lupin from Alaska (*Lupinus nootkatensis*). Lyme-grass is a hardy Icelandic plant, also found on sand-dunes in Britain and Scandinavia. There is no more effective means of binding sand. The Alaskan lupin, which was introduced to Iceland in 1945, is also said to be perfect for Icelandic conditions. It has spread quickly in the landscape, helping to fertilize the soil for other herbs. Its lovely blue flowers brighten hills and fields, giving them lustre, a new life. The introduction of the Alaskan lupin was a stroke of fortune, a welcome addition to the Icelandic flora, although even this flower has its critics.

It is well known that some species of lupin contain substances which can cause disease in grazing animals. Trial cultivation of Alaskan lupin in Iceland since 1976, however, suggests that it is not harmful to animals. They eat it only during the spring, when it is not poisonous, but avoid it in the summer, when it flowers and tastes bitter. On the other hand, it has proved to have several excellent qualities. It has been praised for its vigour and for the way it functions as a 'living fertilizer factory', in that the bacteria that thrive on its aerial roots absorb nitrogen from the air.

The Icelanders are nevertheless cautious, for ecological reasons. They are at present confining the cultivation and use of Alaskan lupin to certain enclosed areas where it has proved particularly useful. It is sown there along with sand-binding lyme-grass, grass-seed, and fertilizer.[9]

Since the 1950s, sowing has been done by way of tractors or aeroplane. The work is under the auspices of a state authority, the Soil Conservation Service of Iceland (Landgræðsla ríkisins). Its operations are unfortunately restricted because of insufficient funds—although the resources allocated by the Althing in the jubilee year of 1974 brought a ray of hope. Many people would like to see more money being invested in this effort. Some of the professional pilots, for example, sow grass-seed without payment. There are active ecological movements, such as Landvernd (National Reclamation and Conservation Federation, formed in 1969) and Líf og land (Life and Land). The latter has been led since 1987 by the actress Herdís Þorvaldsdóttir. The ecological spokesmen campaign for a reduction in stock-breeding and more fences to check the movement of livestock. Another important measure is forest plantation, whether under government auspices or on a voluntary basis, with the Skógræktarfélag Íslands (Icelandic Forestry Association) leading the way. Planted trees include foreign species such as Alaskan poplar, spruce, pine, and Siberian larch. By and large, the plantations have been sucessful. It is hoped that the introduced species will both benefit and embellish the Icelandic flora.

The aim is to restore the vegetation cover that has blown away and the forests that have vanished. It is difficult to predict the outcome of this struggle. It may take a long time. An enormous task of halting extensive active erosion and restoring eroded areas and degraded vegetation lies ahead. However, the fight is being waged. Approximately two per cent of Iceland has been fenced off by the Soil Conservation Service to prevent livestock from grazing in areas that have suffered severe erosion. The vegetation has recovered considerably within these protected areas and in other places where grazing intensity has been reduced.

Many Icelanders dream of regaining as much as possible of the grasslands lined with birch which greeted the Viking settlers 1,100 years ago. To achieve this, today's Icelanders must make a giant effort, or, in their own words, *lyfta Grettistaki* 'perform a Grettir lift', a feat comparable to the exploits of the saga hero. Enclosed areas in various parts of the country were planted in 1990 with some three million trees, to be followed in 1991–2 by four million trees annually. The work goes on. There are plans to plant more and more trees along with the continual sowing of lime-grass, lupin, grass-seed and fertilizer, and the building of new ramparts and fences to protect the growing vegetation.

President Vigdís Finnbogadóttir has formulated the watchword for continued work in this sphere: 'We must go on, look beyond the garden around our own house, create an attitude which will make the nation see the entire country as its own garden.'

Travellers to Iceland are generally impressed by the single-minded efforts of the Icelanders to stop soil erosion, and to restore the vegetation, in particular in order to reforest their country. Trees are being planted near Þingvellir for a so-called friendship forest, financed by contributions from foreign visitors to Iceland.

Noise and Litter

Soil erosion overshadows all other environmental problems. This does not mean that the other problems are negligible. We recognize some of them from elsewhere in the western world. One problem is the noise generated by modern society: aeroplanes and motor vehicles, piercing loudspeakers blaring out pop and rock music. In 1987 representatives of all the parties in the Althing advocated introducing legislation to deal with the problem.

Another source of concern is how to dispose of the growing mountain of waste. Towns and countryside also face the problem of litter, in the form of empty beer-cans, plastic, glass, paper, and the like. This disfigures streets, squares, beauty spots, and the picturesque shores of Iceland. The numerous beer-cans are due to the sale of beer, which was legalized on 1 March 1989, after being prohibited since 1915. People eagerly looked forward to the day when proper beer (as opposed to the low-alcohol variant) could be bought in the state monopoly shops and restaurants. Some 340,000 cans of beer were sold on the first day. The event was followed by news-hounds from television companies, who had previously visited Reykjavík to report on chess matches, cod wars, and the summit meeting of Reagan and Gorbachev. Most beer-cans, thankfully, are returned for the deposit; they have not become a serious environmental problem. A deposit is payable on all single-use soft-drink containers.

Air and Water Pollution

Other problems are caused by air and water pollution. Their common denominator is that they are all of the same type as comparable problems on both sides of the Atlantic, although they affect Iceland on a smaller scale. One reason for this is Iceland's reassuring distance from western industrial centres. Another is that Iceland uses environment-friendly sources such as hydroelectric power and geothermal energy.

Houses are heated by district central heating in the form of geothermal water. This is a clean method. Back in the early 1930s, however, visibility in Reykjavík was clouded by smoke; it hung stubbornly over the town on windless days. When the reeking boilers, fired by imported coal, were replaced by long pipelines carrying hot water from native springs, the change was dramatic. Today's visitor to Reykjavík is fascinated by the generally smokeless air and the crystal-clear visibility (although we shall see an exception below).

Ingólfur Arnarson called the place 'Reeky Bay' when he saw the steam issuing from the hot springs in Laugardalur valley. Women continued to wash clothes there until the 1930s. The word *reykur* in Reykjavík and other place-names refers to 'steam', but in other contexts it means 'smoke', the sort produced by fire and burning tobacco, or exhaust fumes from factories and motor vehicles. The related word *reek* means 'smoke' in Scots dialects, and—as any Scot knows— Edinburgh is referred to as 'Auld Reekie'.

Iceland in the 1990s, however, has one of the world's highest car densities. Motorists can now choose between leaded and unleaded petrol. Car exhaust fumes give great cause for concern. They reach levels that are only 10 per cent below the threshold value which the Icelandic Ministry of the Environment considers hazardous. The fumes emitted by cars and factories poison the air. From a vantage point at Valhúsahæð in Seltjarnarnes, about three kilometres from the old centre of Reykjavík, there is a view in every direction. Close at hand is a bay with ultramarine, sometimes cobalt-blue or green-tinged water. It is bordered by Esja and other mountains, usually capped with snow. At a distance of 120 kilometres, the shining white cap of Snæfellsjökull rises over the sea. Yet this wonderful vision can be spoiled in calm weather, when a yellow, grey, or bluish haze can be seen hovering over Reykjavík. The reason that this haze is seldom visible is that calm weather is a rare phenomenon in Iceland. Otherwise, one can easily agree with Albert Engström in his enraptured description of the magnificent panorama, when his ship had 'cast anchor on the world's most beautiful roadstead'.[10]

Air pollution is also caused by emissions from factories, chiefly from the aluminium smelter at Straumsvík, just south of Reykjavík, the ferrosilicon plant at Grundartangi by Hvalfjörður, 100 kilometres by car from Reykjavík, the fish-meal factories, and a fertilizer factory on the outskirts of Reykjavík.

Yet another source of anxiety is water pollution. Problems are evident in northern Iceland. Many Icelanders worry about developments in the river Laxá and the world-famous, ecologically sensitive Mývatn ('Midge Lake'). This is the main breeding place in northern Europe for ducks, with at least fifteen species and a total of some 10,000 pairs. It is also a playground for wild geese, waders, swans, and smaller birds such as Slavonian grebe (*Podiceps auritus*), whimbrel (*Numenius phaeopus*), and red-necked phalarope (*Phalaropus lobatus*). The lake is infested with midges and other insects. There are plenty of char, brown trout, and stickleback. Mývatn is shallow, generally not more than 1–3 metres. It is sunny and full of nutrients. The fauna on the bed consist of midge larvae, worms, and small crustaceans that live on the remains of rotting plants, bacteria, and diatoms.

Mývatn is incised by bays. Its many islands and peculiar lava formations remind the visitor that this lake is located in a volcanic area. There were eruptions here in 1724–9 and more recently the Krafla eruptions of 1975–84. In the midst of all the devastation, Mývatn appears like a miracle of creation, a bright, magical spark of life. It is a precious spot, both for scientific research and as a tourist attraction.

Well into the twentieth century, settlement around Mývatn was based on the traditional sheep farming, trout-fishing, and collecting of duck eggs. Since 1950 the situation has changed. Tourism and industry have become the main sources of livelihood. Population has grown. Human interference has had an unfavourable effect on the lake. A textbook example of this was the import of mink in the 1930s. These escaped from captivity and soon gave rise to a colony of bird-eating wild minks. Environmental balance has been affected by a combination of factors, including the growth in tourism and—perhaps most of all—the construction in 1966–8 of a diatomite factory. This is located on a shore of the lake, near the geothermal power station of Krafla. Production in the factory is wholly based on the occurrence of natural resources in the vicinity: the diatomaceous deposit which is pumped up from the bottom of the lake, and the geothermal steam emanating from a borehole in the nearby high-temperature area of Námaskarð.

The pumping of diatomite (or kieselguhr) has disturbed the ecological balance in Mývatn, most visibly in the northern part of the lake near the factory, because it has grown deeper and the bottom has become partly uneven in the dredged areas and attracted increased quantities of nitrogen in particular, but also phosphorus. The latter is freed from the mud on the bottom during pumping, discharged from the factory in the wastewater, and returned via the groundwater to the lake. In addition to direct effects on depth and bottom characteristics where dredging has taken place, the diatomite dredging appears to have had an indirect effect on the bottom characteristics of a large area outside the dredged trenches, in the north basin of the lake, where a layer of sand with a thickness of 0.5 to 1 centimetre has formed in recent years on the bottom. The greater depth of the lake means that food on the bottom has become inaccessible to ducks and other waterfowl. The swarms of midges that hatch in the spring have diminished in recent years. Stocks of duck and trout are declining, presumably because of shortage of food. Experts conclude that the feeding conditions for most species of waterfowl have deteriorated. Further research will follow.[11]

The diatomite factory will probably continue its operations for some time. It generates income and jobs in an area where work is otherwise scarce. In the long term, though, scientists fear that there is a risk that the birds and fish will disappear from Mývatn or be drastically reduced in numbers.

The diatomite factory has always been a thorn in the flesh for Icelandic environmentalists. They were splendidly successful in preventing the construction of a big power station in the salmon-rich river which drains Mývatn, and which forms magnificent cataracts where it enters the sea. Nearby is the famous farm of Laxamýri, birthplace of the poet Jóhann Sigurjónsson. The river is rightly named Laxá, 'Salmon River'. Some shrub-clad islets just above the cataracts provide a habitat for eider ducks.

Albert Engström waxes lyrical in his description of the bird-life of Laxá:[12]

> I have never before or since seen a river with so many birds in the water and on the banks. There was a furious life, flight, swishing of wings. There were ducks of various kinds and goldeneyes. The river flowed in rather sudden twists, and it appeared like an esplanade for birds. They

flew at a rushing speed. And on the shores, hundreds of mothers walked with their young in rows, waddling and safe.

Other environmental problems come from sewage and fish farming. As a rule, sewage from towns is untreated. It flows or is pumped directly into the sea. Measurements made just outside Reykjavík and the northern town of Akureyri (with about 15,000 inhabitants) show high contents of bacteria, despite the tidal currents four times a day in the salt water. It is said not to have had any effect on fish stocks yet. It can, however, become an acute ecological problem, for instance, in deep fiords with relatively stagnant water. A concrete example is Eyjafjörður with the town of Akureyri at the end of the fiord. Icelandic fishermen are now fishing far away from the coast to avoid these waters.

Yet the Icelanders are well on the way to solving this problem. Reykjavík and the neighbouring towns, for example, have initiated measures which will follow a plan of action during the 1990s. Sewage will be channelled into modern treatment plants. The treated water will be pumped three or four kilometres out to sea in pipelines.

Concern is felt about the ecological imbalance caused by fish farming, a livelihood which attained great economic importance in the 1980s. Fish are hatched in large pools on land or in cages sunk in the sea. In both cases they discharge large amounts of nutrients in the form of phosphorus and nitrogen compounds. About 90 per cent of these are then blended with the freshwater or saltwater, either directly or via the fishes' excrement.

An equally unexpected and unwelcome problem entailed by the cultivation of salmon in the sea (ocean ranching), according to some hypotheses, concerns environmental and hereditary factors. Some scientists are afraid that salmon-breeding may backfire. If a cultivated salmon is allowed to escape from its cage, whether accidentally or deliberately, it normally swims into the nearest salmon river. Cultivated salmon are gradually blended with the strains of salmon that have migrated up rivers from time immemorial. The latter are often incredibly strong. There are examples of Icelandic salmon jumping up five-metre-high waterfalls. The problem is that cultivated salmon lack the instinct of natural salmon to return—after one or two years in the sea—to the river where they were spawned. Cultivated salmon have been environmentally influenced for life in a cage and not in a flowing river. Moreover, they are usually not so strong. This makes it difficult for them to survive. Scientists still do not know very much about the salmon which are a hybrid of cultivated and natural strains. But it is feared that these hybrids may be genetically inferior. They do not know how to behave in what are for them alien surroundings. They may not find their way to the right river. There is a risk that, in the long term, natural salmon stocks can be damaged by cultivated salmon. According to measurements made in 1989, cultivated salmon accounted for 30 per cent of the salmon stocks in Elliðaár, the river that flows through Reykjavík. More research into this subject is in progress.

Some people regard these fears about fish farming as exaggerated. It may also be said in passing that the economic outlook is good for fish farming in various forms, such as hatching fish in cages and releasing the fry in estuaries. According to experts, there is a bright future for this business, especially in the still unpolluted waters around Iceland. This may be so. It nevertheless seems clear that ecological consideration requires us to set up limits for the degree of human interference with nature. We must have some regard for the ingenious laws of nature herself. They have been tried and tested by time. The conclusion is obvious: fish farmers and salmon fishermen, on the open sea, in the rivers, and by the coast, should—in their own interests— take adequate measures to safeguard the stocks of wild salmon. Mankind should not forget that the riches of the oceans, the lakes, and the rivers are the gifts of creation to mankind.

The fishery authorities in Iceland are aware of the importance of these ecological problems. In 1988 they issued regulations with a view to preventing diseases in fish and the mixture of different stocks of salmon. Inspection mostly takes the form of marking. This encompasses 10 per cent of the fish that are bred in cages and some of the fry that are released in estuaries to migrate to the sea and be caught when they return to the same estuary.

Potential Threats to the Environment

Winds occasionally bring pollution all the way from central Europe. Is there a risk that this will increase?

Luckily for Iceland, the air that is blown here is mostly clear. It comes with beautifully pure winds from polar areas—such as the North Pole, Jan Mayen, Greenland, and Labrador—where there is no pollution.

If we look into the future and try to see round the corner, we cannot avoid wondering about the danger of oil slicks and radioactive emissions. What would happen to the Icelandic fishing grounds if a supertanker full of oil were shipwrecked off the coast of Iceland? And what would happen if a nuclear submarine ran aground on the Icelandic fishing banks?

In Chapter 8, 'Iceland and the Riches of the Sea', we shall return to the threats to the marine environment. Because Iceland is so heavily dependent on its fisheries, and because pollution recognizes no boundaries, the risk of ecological imbalance could be devastating. In that chapter we shall also highlight the problem of seals and whales.

The Icelanders and Their Language: An Island in a Sea of English

If the Icelanders lose their language,
they will cease to exist.
Einar Ólafur Sveinsson

For a small island people, the national language—the ability to communicate in speech and writing—is an inalienable heirloom. It is their very life. This at any rate is the case for the few Icelanders. The population of Iceland at present (1992) is about 260,000. Outside Iceland there are only a few thousand people who speak Icelandic, mostly in countries like Canada, the USA, Sweden, and Denmark.

The language has always been the be-all and end-all of the Icelanders.

The foundation was laid in the ninth and tenth centuries, when Scandinavians, chiefly from three districts in western Norway (Sogn, Fjordane, and Hordaland) settled in Iceland. The mixture of western Norwegian dialects spoken by the colonists soon took on its own distinctive features. It took shape during the age of the commonwealth, when the Icelanders developed their own language. They used it to write down the unique sagas and the Eddic and skaldic poems which had previously been handed down orally from generation to generation. The importance of the language was further emphasized during all the centuries when the country was under the rule of foreign monarchs, when the Icelanders read the old sagas, poems, and the Bible, sang hymns and the highly popular *rímur*-ballads,[13] all in the vernacular. This has continued into our own times, when Halldór Laxness and other inspired Icelandic storytellers and poets still put Iceland on the world map, linguistically and culturally.

What does language mean for a people's cohesion? An example of its ability to hold a nation together comes from Romanian. This distinctive member of the Romance family of languages—an eastern outpost in a sea of Slavonic—has its roots in the Latin which the emperor Trajan's legions and Roman colonists spoke in the Balkan province of Dacia from around AD 100. This eastern variant of Latin was soon cut off from Rome and western Latin. It was displaced as a literary language by other languages until the nineteenth century, when the Romanian language was used as an instrument for national revival.

The Concise Oxford Dictionary defines nation as 'a community of people of mainly common descent, history, language, etc.' This agrees well with the definition of *þjóð* in an Icelandic dictionary: 'a large group of people usually with a common language and culture, sometimes a common historical heritage and memories, mostly living in a continuous territory with mutual internal economic ties'.[14]

It will be seen that the Icelanders put language and culture before descent. They have good reason for doing so. Let us therefore take a look at the Icelandic language. We shall briefly try to chart its origin, development, distinctive features, and vocabulary, as well as its situation today and its chances of surviving in a computer age when English appears to be all-conquering.

The Icelandic Language: A Rich and Well-Preserved Heritage

In the so-called Dark Ages, when the Germanic migrations helped to bring down the Roman Empire, everyone in Scandinavia—except the aboriginal peoples—spoke a common language with minor regional differences. In the Viking Age this Common Scandinavian or Proto-Norse language split into two main groups: East Norse and West Norse. The East Norse group has evolved into today's Swedish and Danish. The West Norse group comprises Norwegian, Faroese, and Icelandic. It was also formerly spoken in other Viking colonies in Greenland and in coastal regions of Ireland, England, Scotland, in the Hebrides, the Orkneys, and the Shetlands.[15]

The contours of a distinct Icelandic language began to emerge as early as the tenth century. As the western Norwegian dialects on which it was based began to undergo changes, the languages diverged. For example, Norwegian lost an initial *h-* before *l, n,* and *r,* whereas the Icelanders preserved this consonant cluster: compare Icelandic *hlutur* 'lot, share, thing' with Norwegian *lott,* Icelandic *hnot* 'nut' with Norwegian *nøtt,* Icelandic *hringja* 'to ring' with Norwegian *ringe.* (Note that English has undergone a similar change; the Anglo-Saxon forms of these words were *hlot, hnutu,* and *hringan.*)

Norwegian was to undergo fairly radical changes, whereas Icelandic—a decidedly conservative language—has not witnessed any great changes except in pronunciation. There have been considerable sound changes, especially affecting the vowels. Icelandic has retained the stress on the first syllable of a word; there are no exceptions, not even in borrowed words. The grammar has also preserved its complex system of inflections—reminiscent of that in German and Latin—along with its sentence structure. The vocabulary is also virtually intact.

It is this Icelandic conservatism in grammar and vocabulary, together with the sound changes, which make the language very difficult for speakers of Norwegian, Swedish, or Danish. On the other hand, it is much easier for Icelanders to understand one of these languages. Having learned Danish in school, they can easily pick up the other Nordic languages (but not, of course, Finnish, which is totally unrelated).

Icelandic, in other words, is a peculiar language with an archaic structure. This does not mean that it is cumbersome and starchy. On the contrary. It is in many ways expressive, flexible, subtle, and with a rich vocabulary.

There is a simple explanation for the large treasury of words.

Icelandic has room for both old and new. Not only has it retained almost all of the ancient vocabulary; it has also been augmented with new words. These include not only borrowed words but also an incredible amount of new coinages and compounds, which the Icelanders have created and continue to create in pace with new technology and the terminology of the information age. These native formations often replace foreign loan-words, which find it difficult to be incorporated in the Icelandic language.

The conversion of Iceland to Christianity left its mark on the language in the form of early loan-words. Examples like *kirkja, biskup, prestur, munkur, engill,* and *djöfull* scarcely need to be translated. Although they ultimately derive from Latin and Greek, most of them came via Old Saxon or English. Direct loans include the words *páskar* 'Easter', *kerti* 'candle', *altari* 'altar', *guðspjall* 'gospel', and *blessa* 'to bless'. That the art of writing came via England is shown by the borrowing of the word *bókfell* 'parchment' from Old English *bôcfell,* literally 'book-skin', and the adoption of the Anglo-Saxon consonants *þ* (for the 'th' sound in *thing*) and *ð* (for the voiced equivalent in *other*). It may surprise English-speaking people to learn that these typically Icelandic letters come from their own language, or that Old English had a word spelled *þing* which, exactly like the Icelandic equivalent, could denote a 'meeting' or 'court', as well as a 'matter' or 'thing' discussed at such an assembly.

Later foreign influences came from the courtly language of the French, as in the word *kurteisi* 'courtesy'. The word *letur* 'graphic sign' derives from Old French *lettre* (Latin *littera, litera*). Danish or Low German gave the words *púði* 'cushion', *rúða* 'window-pane', *fag* 'subject, profession', *forsóma* 'neglect', *hartnær* 'almost', and little everyday words like *kannski* 'perhaps', *strax* 'at once', *bara* 'only, just', and *takk* 'thanks'. Typical international loan-words which are more recent additions to the Icelandic vocabulary are *prófessor, tóbak, píanó,* and *ópera*. They are all declined according to Icelandic inflectional patterns, and all are stressed on the first syllable.

Modern Icelanders often use many ancient expressions unreflectingly. We may consider two examples. Newspaper reports often use the saying *hann bar sigur af hólmi,* meaning 'he was victorious'. The literal sense is that 'he carried victory from the islet'. It derives from the time when a duel (*hólmganga*) was fought on an islet or in some comparable enclosed space. The imagery of the old idioms is often graphic. In the old days, people used to sneak up on seals out on rocks or skerries and stun them with a club. They were knocked unconscious. The verb for this was *rota*. Nowadays, if someone is sleeping so soundly that he or she cannot be woken, it is said that the person *sefur eins og rotaður selur* 'is sleeping like a stunned seal'.

The Icelandic language lacks distinct dialects. Its uniformity is remarkable, especially if we compare the dialectal diversity of, say, England, where there are great differences in vocabulary and pronunciation, making it easy to identify where a person comes from. The absence of such dialectal differences in Iceland is due in part to the isolated location of the country and the mobility of the population. Although Iceland has always been sparsely populated, with people living in isolated farmsteads, the farmers and shepherds of bygone days had a strong family feeling. They maintained contacts with kinsmen and friends. They rode on their horses to pay frequent visits to each other. People from all corners of the country met at the Althing each year. This functioned as a meeting-place where news was spread, sagas were told, and old friends met.

But why was the language able not only to escape dialectal diversity but also to remain so faithful to tradition? The main reason for this is probably to be found in the close bonds between the spoken and the written word. The sagas which had been passed on orally were put into writing as early as the twelfth and thirteenth centuries. Instead of listening to them, the Icelanders could read them. Literature in the vernacular thus became a guiding principle for the entire people.

Almost ever since Iceland was Christianized, the clergy preached in Icelandic, and the popular hymns of the poet-priest Hallgrímur Pétursson were sung in the vernacular. It was also a stroke of luck that the Bible was translated into Icelandic as early as 1584. This translation, known as the 'Guðbrandur Bible', and the sagas were read in most Icelandic homes. Thus, the close links between speech and literature never ceased. They held firm because the Icelanders have always been a book-loving nation. This explains why modern Icelanders can read their classics, the Icelandic sagas, without difficulty. They read them with pleasure. An Icelandic clergyman has said that he does not only read his evening prayers; he likes to round off his reading with a saga, before he falls asleep. A few years ago, when the people were celebrating the memory of Leifur Eiríksson and his discovery of America, the then mayor of Reykjavík, Davíð Oddsson, read aloud an extract from *Grænlendinga saga*. This description of the discovery was committed to parchment in the thirteenth century. Yet it was clear that no one among the thousands of listeners—not even the small children—had any difficulty in understanding the centuries-old language of the saga. An Icelander can read the medieval sagas with almost as much ease as he reads his daily paper.[16]

The recitation of the saga by the mayor of Reykjavík invites the following comparison. We know that the globe-trotting Pope John Paul II sings the mass in Latin and English, in the Vatican and around the world. But who can imagine the mayor of Rome addressing a crowd from a rostrum among the ruins of the Forum Romanum, and reading aloud the sonorous Latin of Caesar's *De Bello Gallico*?

Latin is no longer a living language; Icelandic has not died yet. On the contrary, it shows great vitality. It is also anchored in a traditional naming system, with patronymics ending in *-son* and *-dóttir*. These patronymics are preceded by all the ancient forenames that occur in the Icelandic sagas. Assume, for example, that a man called Egill Ásmundarson has two children to whom he gives the names Grímur and Auður. The son *is called* Grímur and he *is* Egilsson. The daughter's name is Auður, who happens to be Egilsdóttir, and she continues to be 'Egill's daughter' even when she marries. It is wrong to call her Mrs Egilsdóttir; if any title is used, she is Frú Auður. (Compare the title of an English knight; Mr Gilchrist was dubbed 'Sir Andrew'.)

The systematic use of Christian names prevails in Iceland. The telephone book lists all subscribers under their forenames. The same rule applies in national registration (and in the index to this book), even for the minority of Icelanders who have special family names, such as Nordal, Laxness, Hagalín, Brekkan, Blöndal, or Kvaran.

The peculiar position of the Icelandic language brings both advantages and disadvantages for its speakers. One inconvenience for them is that they have to learn other languages at an early age, if they are not to be isolated from the surrounding world. The only people with whom they could communicate would be the 45,000 or so Faroe

Islanders, who speak a closely related language. Although the two languages differ in pronunciation, their vocabulary is largely the same. Faroese and Icelanders can understand each other's written languages without much difficulty. In the Nordic House in Tórshavn, capital of the Faroes, Icelandic and Faroese actors staged a joint performance of Ibsen's *A Doll's House* in April 1984. It was produced by Sveinn Einarsson, former director of the Icelandic National Theatre. The play was later performed in the Reykjavík Civic Theatre by the same actors. Although they spoke their respective native languages, they could understand each other well after two weeks' rehearsal. The Icelandic audience, however, had some difficulty in understanding the Faroese actors because of their pronunciation.

The advantage of retaining an archaic language is a source of spiritual strength for the Icelanders. They have direct contact with the written language of past generations.

Threats to the Language in the Past and in the Computer Age

Two phases in Icelandic history have seen serious threats to the position of the native language. The first was the influence of Danish after the Reformation. This reached its peak around 1800. Linguistically speaking, Reykjavík was then a half-Danish town. The Danish philologist Rasmus Christian Rask (1787–1832), who spent the years 1813–15 in Iceland, feared that the Icelandic language would die out in Reykjavík within a hundred years. He thought that it could survive in the countryside for another couple of centuries.

Rasmus Rask was a great friend of the Icelanders and their language. One of his main efforts to conserve it was, as we have seen, the foundation of an Icelandic literary society.[17] It still publishes the journal *Skírnir.* Rask was hailed in an anonymous Icelandic poem of praise:

> Though loyal to his fatherland,
> a score of tongues he spoke;
> but greatest was the love he felt
> for Iceland's speech and folk.

In 1987 a seminar was held in Reykjavík to mark the bicentennial of Rask's birth. It was emphasized that his inspiring struggle to protect the Icelandic language has an urgent message for modern-day Icelanders. They face a new threat to their language, which in this computer age is more serious than anything experienced in the past.

The two threats to the language cannot really be compared. The influence of Danish in Rask's time was largely confined to the towns and the state officials. The influence of English today affects the entire country and reaches the whole population.

The mass media—chiefly programmes in English on satellite television, as well as English-language radio stations and videos, films and advertising, pop music and magazines—subject the Icelandic people to an incessant flow of Anglo-American language and culture. Icelandic children have a growing vocabulary of English words before they reach school age. Foreign linguistic influence has become increasingly obvious in Reykjavík in recent years. Shops, hotels, restaurants, pubs, and cafés often have English names. (Spanish, French, and Italian names are also becoming common as Icelanders travel more.) English rock music is heard in more and more places, even at public baths and other municipal institutions.

In the long term, this foreign influence—especially the invasion from space—threatens Icelandic language and culture, the things that make Iceland an independent nation.

Let us look more closely at the influence of the English language, with its effect on children and young people in particular. Television and radio stations broadcast a huge number of English-language programmes around the clock. The percentage of Anglo-American films and series is growing all the time. Icelandic newsreaders, reporters, debaters, politicians, and other figures in the mass media often speak a slovenly language, peppered with English loan-words. Videos are almost all in English, as are advertisements and pop songs. English can be heard, mostly in a noisy variety, in shops, restaurants, and even in the streets. English words are incessantly pounded into the ears of the listeners.

It used to be self-evident for Icelanders to cherish their native language, and for public notices to be in Icelandic. Not so now. Icelandic banks, for example, often use stamps with English text, such as 'May' and 'August'. There are road signs saying not only 'Stop' but also 'City Center'.

Deficiencies in pronunciation and vocabulary are often blamed on teachers, who often receive scant appreciation for their work. The teachers themselves claim that they are underpaid. People with high academic qualifications often leave the teaching career for this reason. Teachers of Icelandic point out that their swim against the current is becoming more difficult all the time. The influence of the English language seems to be unstoppable. According to some teachers, if it goes so far that the children become bilingual, there is reason to fear for the long-term survival of Icelandic.

Iceland is surrounded by examples of dead or dying Celtic and Norse languages. The Gaelic languages, comprising Irish, Manx, and Scots Gaelic, have been superseded by English, the language of the powers that be, except in shrinking marginal areas. Gaelic, a symbol of Irish freedom, survived the coming of the Vikings and also for a time the English. But the ruthless repression of Oliver Cromwell's troops began the process that led to the decline of the native language, which is now spoken by a very small minority on the west coast.

The philologist Einar Ólafur Sveinsson has described the threat from English to a number of island peoples in the North Atlantic. The inhabitants of Shetland and Orkney now speak only English. Norn (cf. Icelandic *norrænn* 'Nordic' or 'Norse'), the Scandinavian language that was once spoken there, became extinct after the Reformation. No one can understand it any more. The place-names, which are almost all of Norse origin, have become corrupted and incomprehensible. The islanders have tried to get back to their roots, but in vain. Their numbers have dwindled, and they have become impoverished. Many have solved their problems by emigrating. The Faroe Islanders were once exposed to a similar menace. In the nineteenth century, however, they were able to save their nationality by developing a written language in which to preserve their treasury of native poems and ballads.

Einar Ólafur sums up the seriousness of this threat: 'If the Icelanders lose their language, they will cease to exist.'[18]

Measures to Safeguard the Icelandic Language

Icelandic linguistic purists—with President Vigdís Finnbogadóttir at their head—are well aware of the existence of the threat from the

English language. The best way to honour Rasmus Rask and his work, they say, is to make a fresh effort to protect and preserve the Icelandic language. The purists have formulated some guiding principles. Icelanders are recommended to avoid loanwords. Instead they should follow the pattern of speech which is used in Iceland by ordinary, intelligent people, in Old Icelandic literature, and by the best modern Icelandic writers.

Suitable measures would include more tuition in Icelandic in the schools, obligatory Icelandic subtitling of foreign television programmes and films, and the continued creation of native equivalents for new foreign terms, to be published regularly in dictionary form. These neologisms, which are characteristically known as *nýyrði* (literally 'new words'), are based on native roots and inflected according to Icelandic rules. It is hoped that these measures can eliminate the use in speech and writing of English loan-words in fields such as science and technology.[19]

No equivalent to the Académie française has ever been founded in Iceland, but there have been organized efforts on a more modest scale. One such came in 1919, when the Association of Engineers set up a special committee on words (Orðanefnd). It included Guðmundur Finnbogason (1873–1944), head of the National Library of Iceland and school reformer, and Sigurður Nordal (1886–1971), the linguistic and literary scholar. Decades later, in 1951, this work was assumed by the Dictionary Committee of the University of Iceland. Since 1964 responsibility for language purism has been in the hands of the Icelandic Language Committee.

Linguistic purists in the Scandinavian countries have regular consultations, since they all have the same goal: to preserve the linguistic heritage and prevent the thoughtless use of foreign words and forms. Iceland was visited in 1989 by members of the Swedish Academy, who discussed Icelandic language and literature with, among others, Vigdís Finnbogadóttir and Halldór Laxness. The permanent secretary of the Swedish Academy, Professor Sture Allén, declared that a knowledge of Icelandic culture can increase the Swedes' appreciation of their own cultural heritage.

Both before and after the foundation of the committee on words in 1919, the Icelanders have faced the problem of how to coin Icelandic terms for new phenomena. There have to be words for things like steam engines, trawlers, telephones, computers, and jet planes. The Icelanders solve this problem with elegance, inventiveness, and playful imagination. They create new words. Alternatively, they adapt existing words, giving them new meanings. They combine old words in new senses. *Sími,* an old word meaning 'thread, cord' (with distant cognates in Indo-Iranian), was revived to be used for the telephone; it was originally called *talsími* 'speaking cord', while the telegraph was called *ritsími* 'writing cord'. Incidentally, this word *sími* 'thread' also appears in Old Persian, which is reminiscent of our common Indo-European heritage, illustrated by words such as 'father' (*pitar*) and 'mother' (*matar*). *Vél,* which in Old Icelandic meant an 'artifice, cunning device, trick', was given the new sense of 'machine, engine'. The steam engine was christened *gufuvél* 'vapour device' and the aeroplane became a *flugvél* 'flying device'. The Icelanders, having developed a taste for this game, have given new meanings to a host of other old words. Another more common method has been to create compounds. The word *fræði* 'wisdom, knowledge', for example, is used to form transparent equivalents to English words in *-ology*. Meteorology is called *veðurfræði* 'weather-lore', and psychology is *sálarfræði* 'soul- or mind-lore'. *Tölva,* the Icelandic word for 'computer', is a blend of *tala* 'number' and *völva* 'seeress' (known from the seeress's prophecy in the Eddic poem *Völuspá*); the neologism thus conjures up the uncanny intelligence of the machines while also revealing the cleverness of the person who coined it. Let us look at some other examples of the creativity with which the Icelanders have found new words for new things and new ideas:

English	*Icelandic*	*literal meaning*
antipathy	andúð	against-mind
car	bifreið	moving carriage
compass	áttaviti	direction-shower
composer	tónskáld	tone-poet
container (freight)	gámur	glutton
demonstration	kröfuganga	demand-walk
design	hanna	do something with skill
discuss	rökræða	talk of arguments
echo	bergmál	rock-speech

electricity	rafmagn	amber-power
fantasy	hugarflug	flight of mind
galosh	skóhlíf	shoe-guard
geothermal energy	jarðhiti	earth-heat
gymnastics	fimleikar	nimble games
helicopter	þyrla	whirler
heresy	trúvilla	faith-error
hurricane	fellibylur	felling gust
individual	einstaklingur	single person
inflation	verðbólga	value swelling
inspiration	innblástur	in-blowing
interview	viðtal	talk-with
jet plane	þota	rusher, whistler
library	bókasafn	book collection
locomotive	eimreið	steam-carriage
margarine	smjörlíki	butter-like
microscope	smásjá	small-watcher
missionary	trúboði	faith-preacher
optimism	bjartsýni	bright sight
passport	vegabréf	road-letter
pension	eftirlaun	after-pay
pessimism	svartsýni	black sight
petroleum	steinolía	stone-oil
photocopy	ljósrit	light-script
photograph	ljósmynd	light-picture
procession	skrúðganga	finery-walk
production	framleiðsla	leading forth
radar	ratsjá	finding-the-way watcher
radio	útvarp	out-cast
reactor	kjarnakljúfur	nucleus-splitter
secretary	ritari	writer
skyscraper	skýjakljúfur	cloud-splitter
space-craft	geimfar	vessel in space
supersonic	hljóðfrár	sound-swift
surgical operation	uppskurður	cutting open
sympathy	samúð	together-mind
telefax	myndsendir	picture-sender
telescope	sjónauki	sight-increaser
television	sjónvarp	sight-cast
territorial water	landhelgi	land sanctuary (inviolability)
theatre	leikhús	play-house
trawler	togari	one who hauls
tropics	hitabelti	heat-belt
underpants	nærbuxur	near-trousers
video	myndband	picture-tape

These neologisms usually catch on quickly in schools and the mass media. This may sound surprising. One explanation for the success of native coinages over foreign words is that published lists of newly formed Icelandic words are carefully scrutinized by favourably disposed teachers, newspapermen, debaters, and other moulders of public opinion.

The whole of Europe, indeed the whole world, is exposed to the massive influence of Anglo-American language and culture, via satellite television, video, and computers. Many languages are trying to mitigate the effects of this invasion from space, but few can have been as successful as Icelandic. There are two obvious reasons for this success. To begin with, the Icelanders are fully aware of the threat. They have a basically positive attitude to linguistic purism. Pride in their own language is a part of their general national consciousness. It reflects their pride in their country. Secondly, the population is small and homogeneous, making it easier to achieve linguistic uniformity and consensus.

Let us compare Iceland with another small sovereign state, the Grand Duchy of Luxemburg. Of the population of 370,000 (in 1990), roughly 30 per cent are foreigners. The spoken language in Luxemburg—which is wedged in between Germany, France, and Belgium—is a Moselle Franconian dialect of German called Luxemburgish, but this is not used for writing. The written languages are German and French, but French is the only official language. Luxemburg is an industrial state and a strong financial centre. However, it has not yet a university of its own, whereas the University of Iceland was inaugurated on 17 June 1911, the centenary of the birth of the national hero, Jón Sigurðsson.

Iceland's Economy and the Surrounding World

It is, generally speaking, expensive to
be an Icelander.

Halldór Laxness

The epigraph above is a statement made by Halldór Laxness during a reception in Stockholm in 1955, when he was there to receive the Nobel Prize for Literature. A reporter posed an acid question: is it not expensive to drive a luxurious car on the dirt roads of Iceland? The reporter was aware of the author's radical left-wing views and also of the pleasure he took in the benefits of the affluent society, such as owning a Cadillac.

Halldór Laxness saw the sting in this question, which was followed by an embarrassed silence. Yet his sense of humour and his gift for repartee saved the situation. 'It is, generally speaking, expensive to be an Icelander,' he said with a twinkle in his eye and a friendly smile. This disarming reply relieved the atmosphere. At the same time, Laxness drew the listeners' attention to the difficulties of a small nation in today's changeable world.[20]

A Small Nation Largely Dependent on Fishing

In Iceland, the fishing industry is the
number one bread-winner of the
nation.

Sigurður Markússon

It is not difficult to see the nature of the economic and commercial problems that confront the Icelanders. They are, it is true, one of the best-educated peoples in the world. They have achieved a high standard of living, generally full employment, and a well-developed welfare society. They enjoy high technical standards, and they can take advantage of the country's prime natural resources: the all-important fish, and energy in the form of hydroelectric power and geothermal heat. They inhabit a large island (the second largest in Europe after Great

Britain), but the population is undeniably small—only about 260,000. Moreover, Iceland is poor in minerals, and the climate restricts the scope of agriculture. The survival of the Icelanders is therefore still largely dependent on some of the oldest trades in the world: fishing and food preparation. Since the 1970s, fish and fish products have accounted for an average 75 per cent of Iceland's goods exports. In 1990 the proportion was 76 per cent.

It goes without saying that it is insecure to base a whole nation's economy on a one-sided dependence on fishing, a fickle source of income, sensitive to market fluctuations and changes in nature. There can suddenly be large catches. They can disappear just as suddenly. World prices rise and fall in pace with supply and demand. A textbook example was the collapse of the Icelandic herring fishery in 1967–8, which happened to coincide with a drastic fall in fish prices. In retrospect, we can also observe that the decades after the Second World War have struck one blow after the other to Iceland. With its open economy, this country has suffered more than highly industrial countries, which have been able to fall back on a more all-round industrial base.

The Icelanders are well aware that this dependence on fish is their Achilles heel. They have tried to escape this vulnerability. Their primary approach has been to follow a path which is natural for them. With the aid of invested capital from abroad, they have utilized some of Iceland's enormous renewable energy resources and created energy-intensive industries based on them. Particularly determined efforts in this field were made by the two-party government (the Independence and Social Democratic parties) which held power from 1959 to 1971.

As a result of such endeavours in the energy sector, Iceland has acquired factories producing, for example, aluminium, ferrosilicon, and diatomite (kieselguhr), as well as for the production for domestic consumption of fertilizer, cement, rockwool, and salt. Aluminium already accounts for about 10 per cent of goods exports. The aim is to triple production capacity over the next few years, which would require constructing new power stations. The efforts have thus met with a fair degree of success, although the exaggerated expectations of the Icelanders, especially as regards the exploitation of geothermal energy, have not yet been fully met. The optimists expected a quicker rate of development. The reasons for the delays have been of many kinds: technical problems in combination with economic considerations and domestic politics. Negotiations with foreign investors have concerned such matters as risk-taking and profitability, the shares to be owned by the Icelandic state, and investment terms: taxation, duties, environmental interests, and so on.

The new large-scale industries give jobs to only a small fraction of the Icelandic workforce. On the other hand, the production of industrial goods (about half of these being aluminium) accounted for an average of 22.8 per cent of the value of export commodities. One thing is certain: Iceland is on the right path.

A survey of Icelandic industry in the early 1990s shows that, apart from the energy sector (which we shall consider separately in Chapter 9), Icelandic industry has the following main branches: fishing, fish processing, fish farming, manufacturing, tourism, and agriculture.[21]

Fishing

Icelandic waters yield catches of demersal fish (species from the sea-bottom), such as cod, haddock, halibut, redfish, saithe, plaice, and catfish. The Icelandic fishermen also catch pelagic species (those living near the surface), chiefly the smeltlike capelin, blue whiting, and herring, of which two stocks spawn off the coast of Iceland and one off the coast of Norway), and shellfish such as prawn, lobster, and scallop.

By far the greatest earnings come from the cod fishery. It was with good reason that the three fishery disputes with Britain were called the 'cod wars'. Cod is followed in value by catches of shellfish, redfish, haddock, halibut, and saithe. Good income is also to be had from capelin and herring, when these pelagic species come. The coming of the herring was once a dramatic event in an Icelandic fishing station. Halldór Laxness has described it in a famous short story entitled 'Saga úr síldinni' (A Tale of the Herring).

The mostly ultra-modern Icelandic fishing fleet includes a growing number of freezing ships. These floating factories, known in fishing parlance as freezer-trawlers, freeze the fish on board and normally land their products in Iceland. The frozen products, together with the products of the local freezing plants, are then exported to various parts of the world by freezer vessels or in freezer containers on board container vessels. The fresh fish comes from the wetfish trawlers and other fishing boats. Some of it is exported iced in containers, but most of the fresh fish is used as raw material for the local freezing plants and the local saltfish producers. Britain and Germany are the main markets for fresh fish.

It may be said in passing here that whaling in Iceland—despite everything that has been written on the inflamed topic—has always been insignificant. In 1985, the last year of commercial whaling, it accounted for only one per cent of the total export of commodities from Iceland. Whaling for scientific purposes was discontinued in 1990.

Fish Processing

Technologically advanced fish factories can be adapted as needed for different methods of preparing fish: freezing, salting, or drying. The factories use production lines which are increasingly controlled by computers, electronics, and other modern technology.

Technical development has been incredibly swift in recent years. Most of the work was formerly manual, but now fish are processed automatically in large factories. Despite increased production and reduced manpower, the Icelanders have been able to maintain the quality of their products.

Fish Farming

In collaboration with Norway, Sweden, the USA, and other countries, Iceland invested large sums of money in fish farming in the 1980s. Salmon, rainbow trout, brown trout, sea trout, and char are bred in pools on land or in cages in the sea. As a rule—when cold winters do not interfere—the fish are bred in highly favourable conditions, since Iceland has fresh spring water and unpolluted seas.

The ecological problems associated with fish farming have been considered earlier in this chapter.

Manufacturing

Apart from the energy-intensive industries mentioned above, the past few years have seen the growth of more and more small to medium-sized manufacturing industries. They turn out a wide range of products: from fishing equipment and export packaging to boats, instruments, and engines. The woollen industry has achieved fame for its warm garments, such as caps, scarves, and Icelandic sweaters.

Tourism

Iceland, as we have seen in Chapter 5, is attracting tourists in ever larger numbers. They bring a welcome contribution to the balance of payments, and stimulate the burgeoning hotel and restaurant trade.

Agriculture

About one-fifth of the total area of Iceland is estimated to be suitable for agriculture and its ancillary occupations. Only 6 per cent of this is cultivated. The rest is used for pasture or is undeveloped. Iceland is self-sufficient as regards meat, dairy produce, and eggs. The small number of Icelandic farmers is constantly declining. They also pursue ancillary occupations, such as gardening, fishing, fish farming, fur farming, and raising pigs and hens.

We should not forget that Iceland lies just below the Arctic Circle. On the other hand, it does have a never-ending supply of geothermal energy, which is used to heat greenhouses and open-air swimming-pools. This means that a visitor in mid-winter may be lucky enough to pick roses or eat bananas in a greenhouse and then take a dip in the nearest pool.

Economic Growth Combined with Employment, Living Standards, and Social Security

The Icelandic economy calls to mind a painting by Rembrandt, where dark shadows serve to emphasize the bright features in the field of vision.

The head of Janus in ancient Rome was depicted with two faces. An analysis of the Icelandic economy must also consider its two faces.

One represents the dark side: strikes, inflation, and growing foreign debts. Looking back at the economy since 1930, we see how it has gone up and down like a roller-coaster. The considerable reserves of currency built up during the Second World War melted away in 1945–7 like snow in the spring sunshine. In the decades that followed, economic development has constantly soared and plummeted in rapid succession. For example, after a protracted boom, the Icelandic economy was hit fairly abruptly in 1989–92 by a sharp recession. The main reason was the falling catches of cod. Ever since the record year of 1950, cod stocks have continually declined. According to a recent forecast, catches of cod must be reduced by 40 per cent in 1993. It is easy to see what this would mean for the Icelandic economy. The precious cod normally accounts for about a quarter of Iceland's export earnings. The reduced cod catches led to a negative trade balance, a budget deficit, bankruptcies (for salmon farmers and others), and growing unemployment (1.5 per cent in 1991, rising to 3 per cent in early 1992). This recession forced government cutbacks with a view to reducing the costs of social welfare, schools, and higher education. The crisis accentuated the problem of Iceland's one-sided dependence on the fishery sector.

The other side of the Janus face has sunnier features. For the Icelandic economy as a whole (ignoring the recent global recession) they include economic growth combined with virtually full employment, a high standard of living, the security of living in a developed welfare state, and low inflation. Using official Icelandic statistics,[22] let us look more closely at the brighter side of the Icelandic economy.

Since 1945, the Icelandic labour market has been predominantly characterized by full employment. Registered unemployment over the past decade, calculated on a yearly basis, has been on average less than one per cent, much lower than the average for the OECD countries. The Icelandic people have been almost completely spared from unemployment throughout the post-war period.

Despite all the instability occasioned by changes in the economic cycle, Iceland has achieved strong growth and increased prosperity in the past half-century, when the population has more than doubled. Icelandic economists have calculated that the gross domestic product (GDP) for the period 1946–84 rose by an annual average of 4.2 per cent. Between 1970 and 1988, the increase was as high as 4.9 per cent, which may be compared with the mean for the OECD countries—3 per cent. The forces stimulating this economic growth have been rising export values combined with large capital investments and increased private consumption.

Capital investments have comprised power stations based on hydro-electric and geothermal energy, factories, greenhouses, fish farms, and other projects in the expanding energy sector, communication facilities, airfields, harbours, lighthouses, roads, streets, and bridges. To this we may add the public sector investments in hospitals, schools, universities, churches, old people's homes, administrative buildings, leisure and sports centres, and so on, and private sector investments in housing in particular. In the period 1980–8, housing accounted for an annual average of 22.3 per cent of all investment.

Right from their arrival at Keflavík, many visitors to Iceland are surprised by the amount of building in progress. They compare Reykjavík to the Klondike, and liken the scattered housing in the suburbs to Mediterranean villages, where white houses with flat roofs overlook open bays with the deep blue or blue-green mirror of the sea, with the horizon between sky and sea consisting of a non-Mediterranean element in the lava-black cliffs, crowned even in summer with patches of shining snow.

The Icelandic people have also managed to attain a high level of prosperity. Measured in terms of the number of cars, telephones, televisions, video cassette recorders, radios, household appliances, doctors, or hospital beds per thousand inhabitants, or in terms of the size and comfort of their homes, the standard of living enjoyed by the Icelanders is one of the highest in the world. In no other country is infant mortality so low, and few countries in the world have as high a life expectancy for new-born babies as Iceland.

Another distinctive feature is that private consumption in Iceland is higher than in any other Nordic country, as is the average housing standard. Between 80 and 85 per cent of the Icelanders own their own homes, and about 35 per cent live in single-family houses. In the Reykjavík region, however, the proportion of people living in single-family houses is 'only' 25 per cent.[23]

The public sector is relatively small; in 1988 it accounted for 37.3

per cent of the gross domestic product. This is rather surprising, since the Icelandic state provides social welfare on a par with that of the rest of Scandinavia. Since 1936, social insurance has covered virtually all Icelanders who need help as a result of accident, disease, old age, invalidity, and unemployment. The system has been expanded to include family allowance, housing allowance, maternity and parental allowance, and study loans.

Despite all this, then, Iceland has a relatively limited public sector. This is said to be due to a number of interacting factors. These include the lack of defence expenditure, low unemployment, a system of private pension funds, and a population of low mean age. The population pyramid still has a broad base, while the top, consisting of people aged 65 and over, is relatively narrow (10.7 per cent on 31 December 1990).

Inflation: On the Way to Balance

Iceland, as we have just seen, has achieved a high degree of economic growth, employment, standard of living, and social welfare. Yet this prosperity rests on a shaky foundation. The instability reveals itself every now and then in sudden peaks of inflation with subsequent import surpluses, unrest on the labour market, bankruptcies, frequent devaluations of the Icelandic króna, and a tendency to incur growing foreign debts.

For about fifty years, Icelandic governments have repeatedly tried to check the stubborn inflation. They have used weapons such as price controls, wage freezes, the prohibition of index-linked wages, and other interventions in price mechanisms. A system of price-equalization reserves has been used on a limited scale in the fishing industry. Icelandic governments have occasionally been able to curb inflation, but it has always returned sooner or later. It is impossible to dam a swift river if one does not block its tributaries.

Iceland's economic vulnerability has been accentuated time and time again because it has such a small domestic market and has such a one-sided dependence on fishing. For these reasons, inflation works as a vicious circle.

Let us follow the typical rise and course of an Icelandic price and

wage spiral. Higher prices for fish and fish products on foreign markets, combined with good catches, bring sudden increases in income
for people in the fishing industry (shipowners and seamen, industrial-
ists, fishery workers) and, like a chain reaction, for all wage-earners
in Iceland. Higher purchasing power leads to increased demand for
goods and services. This is reflected in inflated prices for goods across
the board—although less so for imported goods, since the pace of
inflation is usually slower in neighbouring countries. Close on the
heels of this development comes a superheating of the labour market,
with pay rises and wage drift. The inflationary avalanche slides on.
Domestic production costs soar. Exports stagnate, while the volume of
imports swells. The trade balance is upset by the excess of imported
goods.

The situation becomes untenable for the employers. Then, on top of
everything, the fish market declines. Earnings from the fishing industry fall. Catches can also be reduced. The discrepancy between debits
and credits widens. Pay cuts for the wage-earners are out of the
question. Borrowing entails considerable expense.

In this crisis there is always a ready way out. This is to lower the
exchange rate for the Icelandic króna in relation to foreign currencies.
A devaluation turns the situation around for the fishing industry. The
fish industry gains some breathing-space. Yet the favourable effects of
devaluation are often diluted after a while because Iceland is so
dependent on imported goods. Devaluation automatically makes it
more expensive to buy imports, such as fuel for the trawlers. Prices
rise. Wage-earners demand and receive higher wages. Production costs
increase. Soon the only solution is a new devaluation. But devaluation
is often an ineffective weapon, since it does not solve the long-term
problems. If it is not accompanied by other measures to curb prices, it
is merely like an anaesthetic which temporarily relieves the patient's
pain without curing the disease.

Despite this inherent difficulty, the Icelanders have frequently been
forced to manage with the aid of devaluation. The inflationary spiral
has occasionally escalated to high levels. In 1983 it reached a peak of
84.3 per cent. In subsequent years it hovered around an annual average
of 20–30 per cent.[24]

As regards the economy, then, uncertainty about the future is the constant companion of every Icelander. It follows him like a shadow. It is therefore understandable that there were many Icelanders during and after the Second World War who were profoundly suspicious of bank savings. They preferred to place their savings in real estate and capital goods. Rather than watch inflation eat up the money they have saved, they have bought houses, cars, furniture, works of art, and modern gadgets.

After index protection of lending and borrowing against inflation was permitted in 1979, however, there was a noticeable increase in bank savings. In 1979 bank deposits accounted for 24.4 per cent of the gross domestic product, a figure which had risen to 37.1 per cent in 1990. This shows that the Icelanders now have greater faith in inflation-protected savings in banks and savings associations.

Happily, Iceland seems to be successfully combating inflation. In 1991 it averaged only 4.8 per cent. At the moment of writing (1992) there is practically no inflation.

External Debt

In the period 1960–88, Iceland's foreign debt swelled, and with it the cost of debt service (interest and repayments), as follows:[25]

Year	Net external debt as a percentage of GDP	Debt service as a percentage of export revenue
1970	21.1	10.1
1975	36.1	14.5
1980	27.9	13.5
1985	52.8	19.9
1988	41.7	17.3
1989	47.4	19.3
1990	47.4	20.1

Almost half of these debts are due to capital investments in the energy sector: hydroelectric power, geothermal energy, and energy-intensive industry. They are expected to bring profits in the long term and hence improve Iceland's ability to repay external loans. This ability increased significantly in the 1980s, albeit not wholly in pace with foreign borrowing.

Main Features of Trade Policy

Fisheries, freezing plants, and other fish factories dominate the Icelandic economy. The base is otherwise narrow. Most industrial goods and raw materials, fuel oil, colonial produce, and grain have to be imported. Moreover, Iceland has a very small domestic market. The country is therefore dependent on foreign trade, which must function smoothly without technical impediments such as tariffs and customs formalities, import duties, taxes, and import bans. The value of exports and imports accounts for about 40 per cent of the gross domestic product.

In other words, it is in Iceland's interest to pursue liberal trade policies and to work internationally to foster free trade. Iceland joined the European Free Trade Association (EFTA) in 1970 and signed a free trade agreement with the European Economic Community in 1972. Iceland participates in such international bodies as the Organization for Economic Cooperation and Development (OECD), the General Agreement on Tariffs and Trade (GATT), the International Monetary Fund (IMF), and the International Bank for Reconstruction and Development (the World Bank).[26] Within Scandinavia it is a member of the Nordic Council and the Nordic Investment Bank.

The main goal of Iceland's liberal trade policy has long been to ensure a market for fish and fish products abroad. This was the main reason for joining EFTA. The Icelanders joined although they were aware that membership would mean considerable economic difficulties for some of the small domestic companies—for example, those producing textiles and garments, furniture, and food—which had previously been shielded from foreign competition. It was the same reason that lay behind the free trade agreement with the European Community. On the whole, the political parties have unanimously supported this trade policy. However, Iceland's membership of EFTA was hotly debated in the late 1960s. The People's Alliance voted against membership, and the Progressive Party, while also critical, abstained. Since then, on the other hand, these parties have not opposed Icelandic membership of EFTA. It may also be mentioned that these two parties strongly opposed the liberalization of trade which took place in the early 1960s, carried through by the coalition government of the Independence Party and the Social Democratic Party.

Besides trading with the countries of Western Europe, Iceland maintains vigorous trading links with the USA and Japan (a recent major customer). The former Soviet Union was traditionally a good market for Icelandic fish.

The British ban on the landing of Icelandic fish in Grimsby and Hull in the early 1950s, and the decision of Nigeria to stop buying dried fish in 1982 are both good examples of the way unilateral trade restrictions imposed by foreign countries can damage the Icelandic economy. This has also suffered as a result of other kinds of action, such as foreign over-fishing off the coast of Iceland before and after the Second World War, the rise in oil prices in the 1970s, and the international recessions in 1949–52, 1982–3, and the 1990s.

Crises and drastic changes like these have often hit Iceland hard. Yet the country is able to adapt quickly to new situations. Iceland has been able to find new trading partners, for example, during the cod wars. Another measure which we have seen is devaluation, sometimes combined with price and wage freezes. Thanks to these trade and economic policies, the fishing fleet and the fish industry have generally been able to cope with crises. In social and economic terms, however, these measures have created considerable unrest on the Icelandic labour market—especially in the small fishing stations around the coast—and repeated peaks of high inflation. Strikes have been more common in Iceland than in most industrial countries, and until recently the inflation rate has been much higher than in Western Europe, Canada, and the USA.

Outlook for the Future

International development suggests that the world in the 1990s will be carved up between three large trading blocs, with the European Community, the USA, and Japan as the main actors. What will happen to the states outside these blocs? Will they become insignificant pawns in the power game played by the mighty triad?

When assessing the outlook for the future, it is interesting to observe that Iceland's foreign trade in the 1980s became increasingly concentrated in Western Europe, the European Community and the other EFTA countries. In the 1970s about a third of all Icelandic exports still went to the USA and a significant proportion to Eastern Europe. For various reasons, however, such as competition from Canada, the low value of the dollar, and stagnation in Eastern Europe before the collapse of the communist regimes, these markets declined in importance for Iceland. At the same time, Western Europe has become more and more attractive.

In 1990 the European Community and EFTA together accounted for 76 per cent of Iceland's goods exports and 66 per cent of its imports. The European Community's share was 68 per cent of the exports and 50 per cent of the imports. The conclusion is obvious. The process of integration with Western Europe is all-important for Iceland.

With its population of 260,000, Iceland is a dwarf in comparison with the 320 million inhabitants of the giant European Community. The coming of a single market at the end of 1992—perhaps the embryo of a European Union—with free movement of goods, services, capital, and labour will confront Iceland with a multitude of problems, chiefly concerning the economy and foreign policy. It will also affect a number of other areas: language and culture, the environment, the labour market, social welfare, communications, education, research, technology, and aid to developing countries.

Will Iceland in future be an isolated outpost beyond the European pale? Or will the citizens of the European Community still regard the Icelanders as Europeans, albeit in EFTA clothes? What is the future of EFTA as most of its members now apply for membership of the European Community? It is easier to pose questions than to provide answers.[27]

One answer, for the time being at least, is the agreement on a European Economic Area (EEA) signed by the member states of the European Community and EFTA. This means that most of Iceland's fish exports to the European Community will be exempt from duty. In January 1993 Iceland decided to join the EEA.

Icelandic membership of the European Community seems to be a matter of doubt. At the time of writing, no party supports an application for membership. The reasons for this were spelled out by the former prime minister, Steingrímur Hermannsson, at an EFTA meeting in Oslo on 14–15 March 1989:

> We can never surrender unconditionally to any supranational authority. We can never relinquish our sovereignty or our right to make the decisions needed to ensure our livelihood and our independence. We shall always have independent disposition over our natural bounties. They constitute the very foundation for our existence.

Steingrímur is among the fiercest opponents of applying for membership of the European Community. Some other politicians are more open to the possibility of Icelandic membership in the future.

Iceland's policy in this matter is partly based on its struggle for independence, on the three cod wars fought between 1958 and 1976, and on the strong will of the Icelandic people to preserve their language, their cultural heritage, and their distinctive nationality.

It is inevitable that there will be difficulties in adapting to changes in the surrounding world. We may nevertheless hope that the process of integration will usher in a bright future for the economy of Iceland and its links with the rest of the globe.

The Cooperative Movement in Iceland

The cooperative movement works for the general good. We must therefore continue energetically to develop the strength of the movement. Let us remain optimistic and keep our high aims. 'Will-power draws half the load.'

Erlendur Einarsson, Managing Director of Samband, 1955–86, in his first report to the Annual General Meeting of the Federation of Iceland Cooperative Societies, 1956

The cooperative movement in Iceland has a long history. The first cooperative society—Kaupfélag Þingeyinga in northern Iceland—was founded in 1882, thirty-eight years after the first cooperative store had been opened in 1844 by some English flannel weavers in Rochdale. That first cooperative society consisted of farmers. It was later followed by similar associations. The pioneer years of the 1880s must have appeared hopeless at times. Yet the farmers survived despite what looked like insuperable obstacles: the opposition of powerful Danish merchants, severe winters, storms, drift-ice from the North Pole, and the unprotected harbour of Húsavík where it was difficult to moor a boat. But the farmers stuck together and refused to give up.[28] They followed principles similar to those of the Rochdale pioneers: (1) open, voluntary membership; (2) democratic management; (3) the division of surplus profit among the members in proportion to their purchases; (4) limited capital interest on the members' investments in the enterprise; (5) cash trading; (6) political and religious neutrality; (7) educational work among the members.

A precursor of the Rochdale weavers was the British philosopher and social reformer Robert Owen (1771–1858). He was born of poor parents but worked himself up to prosperity as a young man, managing a cotton spinning mill. He wrote many works in which he tirelessly advocated improved conditions for workers. One measure in this was the founding of consumer associations. Owen's ideas reflected the spirit of the age. At almost the same time, the German social theorist and scientist Ferdinand Lassalle (1825–64) was pleading in Breslau and Berlin against the *laissez-faire* doctrines of the Manchester school and in favour of workers' cooperatives with state credit. Long before this, similar visions had been formulated by a French count, the social philosopher Henri de Saint-Simon (1760–1825).

So much for the international roots of the Icelandic cooperative movement. At the end of 1991, there were 26 active cooperative societies in Iceland. Membership totalled some 26,000 people, or about 10 per cent of the population.

The most important cooperative in industrial terms is to be found in the town of Akureyri in northern Iceland: Kaupfélag Eyfirðinga (KEA), which runs several businesses and industries in the area, such as a dairy, a slaughterhouse, meat processing plants, and fish factories. KEA also runs a coffee-roasting factory and a chemicals factory.

The Icelandic cooperative movement has two distinctive features. First, the local cooperatives include both consumers and producers. The producers include not only farmers and fishermen but also companies in the fish industry. Second, the local cooperatives are supported by one political party in particular—the Progressive Party, an agrarian party in the centre of the political spectrum.

Samband

In 1902 the local cooperatives were organized under an umbrella organization, the Federation of Iceland Cooperative Societies (Samband íslenzkra samvinnufélaga, abbreviated as SÍS and known colloquially as Samband). For decades Samband—with its affiliated companies—was Iceland's largest enterprise. Having long been a major power factor in the Icelandic economy, it was hit by a series of financial setbacks in the 1980s.

The Federation was reorganized in 1990 so that its operative divisions were restructured as joint-stock companies. In 1991 these new companies achieved total sales which were 7.2 per cent more than the 1990 sales of the corresponding divisions within Samband. The intention was that Samband would remain a majority shareholder in all six of the new companies. At Samband's Annual General Meeting in 1992 this idea was abandoned. The meeting resolved that a distribution of ownership was the most desirable form, with no single party owning more than one-third of the stock in any single company. As this publication goes to press, Samband is negotiating with its main banker in Iceland on an extensive sale of shares and fixed assets. Both Samband and the bank stress that the point is that Samband has enough assets to cover its debts. It is, however, a foregone conclusion that Samband's ownership in the new companies—as well as in other affiliated companies—will be drastically reduced.

Samband has founded a college at Bifröst in Borgarfjörður, on the way from Reykjavík to Akureyri. This college provides higher education in business administration, as well as holding short courses. In 1991 Samband donated its share in the college to a foundation that is now responsible for the opeartion of the college. The reader will remember that Bifröst 'the moving bridge' was the name of the rainbow in Snorri's *Edda*; it led from earth to the fortress of the Æsir in heaven.[29] The colours of the rainbow are used by the International Cooperative Alliance and in international cooperation in general.

Samband and the local cooperatives state their aim as being to further the prosperity of their members. Their targets are:

direct:	to keep prices of consumer goods low
	to keep prices of the members' own products high
indirect:	to create jobs
	to maintain the infrastructure in sparsely populated
	areas through customer service
	to support cultural activity

Evaluation

How do the results obtained by the cooperative movement match the targets? Opinions on this differ. Icelandic analysts are nevertheless unanimous in praising the cooperative movement for the decisive influence it has had in developing the country's agriculture, fisheries, and small industries. Towards the end of the nineteenth century Iceland was in a state of abject poverty, where the farmer-fishermen waged an unequal struggle against foreign merchants. In this struggle they found a welcome ally in the cooperative movement.

The Icelandic cooperative movement today has not only lost most of its former power. It also faces a typically modern problem. Some members feel that it is difficult for them to influence decisions in the movement. The distance between the management and the grass roots can appear great. People are aware of the problem and try to improve the situation by providing better information and maintaining direct contact with the ordinary members.

We have seen the steady rise of Samband. However, in recent years we have witnessed its sharp decline, followed in 1992 by the sale of most of its shareholdings. In the limited companies, the business survives, but Samband's ownership has either been eliminated or substantially reduced.

Notes to Chapter 6

1   The epigraph to this section is taken from Montesquieu's *De l'esprit des lois* (1748). He describes the separation of the powers as a sound constitutional

principle and a guarantee against repression. He contrasts it with the deterrent example of the Ottoman Empire, where the three powers were all vested in the sultan. See also Ólafur Jóhannesson, *Stjórnskipun Íslands* (Reykjavík: Hlaðbúð, 1960), pp. 79–87.

2   *Iceland 1986: Handbook Published by the Central Bank of Iceland* (Reykjavík, 1987), p. 110.

3   Ibid., pp. 248–9.

4   Heimir Þorleifsson, *Frá einveldi til lýðveldis: Íslandssaga eftir 1830* (Reykjavík: Bókaverzlun Sigfúsar Eymundssonar, 1973), p. 249.

5   *Iceland 1986*, p. 120. On the 1991 general election see Gunnar Helgi Kristinsson, 'The Icelandic Parliamentary Election of April 1991: a European Periphery at the Polls', *Scandinavian Political Studies* 14:4 (1991), pp. 343–53.

6   Ibid., p. 124.

7   The fact that Iceland has long been like this is shown by William Jackson Hooker's description in *Journal of a Tour in Iceland in the Summer of 1809* (London, 1813), vol. 1, p. 295: 'we previously touched upon the borders of some brush-wood, which here bears the name of a forest . . . the tallest [trees] did not exceed three feet or four at the utmost'.

8   See Eyþór Einarsson, 'The Flora and Vegetation of Iceland,' brochure published by Icelandair; he notes, however, that 'there are places in the interior regions where continuous vegetation may be found as high as at the altitude of 1200 m and Birch shrub as high as 550 m'.

9   Andrés Arnalds, 'Ecosystem Disturbance in Iceland', *Arctic and Alpine Research* 19:4 (1987), pp. 508–13; Sveinn Runólfsson, 'Land Reclamation in Iceland', *Arctic and Alpine Research* 19:4 (1987), pp. 514–17. Andrés Arnalds, 'Conservation Awareness in Iceland', *the 7th International Soil Conservation Conference Sydney 1992—People Protecting Their Land*, pp. 272–275.

10   Albert Engström, *Åt Häcklefjäll* (Stockholm: Bonnier, 1911). Compare Lord Dufferin's description of Faxaflói in Chapter 5, 'Iceland as a Tourist Attraction'.

11   Committee of Experts for Lake Mývatn Research, *Effects of the Operations of Kisilidjan Inc., on the Lake Mývatn Biota: Committee Report* (Reykjavík: Ministry for the Environment, 1991). See also David Williams, *Mývatn: A Paradise for Nature Lovers* (Reykjavík: Örn og Örlygur, 1988).

12   Engström, *Åt Häcklefjäll*, part 1, p. 108.

13   On the rímur see Chapter 2, 'The Icelandic Manuscripts'.

14   *Íslensk orðabók handa skólum og almenningi*, ed. Árni Böðvarsson, 2nd ed. (Reykjavík: Bókaútgáfa Menningarsjóðs, 1983), s.v. þjóð.

15   Einar Haugen, *The Scandinavian Languages: An Introduction to Their History* (London: Faber, 1976), p. 332. A brief account of the Icelandic language can be found in *Iceland 1986*, pp. 55–65.

16   Marshall Brement, *Three Modern Icelandic Poets: Selected Poems of Steinn Steinarr, Jón úr Vör and Matthías Johannessen* (Reykjavík: Iceland Review, 1985), p. 13.

17   See Chapter 1, 'The Struggle for Independence', 'The Beginnings'.

18   Einar Ólafur Sveinsson, 'Um íslenzkt þjóðerni', in his *Við uppspretturnar* (Reykjavík: Helgafell, 1956), p. 22.

19   Regarding Icelandic linguistic purism and Icelandic neologisms, see Halldór Halldórsson, 'Icelandic Purism and Its History', *Word* 30:1–2 (1979), pp. 76–86; Halldór Halldórsson, *Íslenzk málrækt* (Reykjavík: Hlaðbúð, 1971); *Iceland 1986*, pp. 55–65.

20   Gylfi Þ. Gíslason, *The Problem of Being an Icelander Past, Present and Future* (Reykjavík: Almenna bókafélagið, 1973), p. 7.

21   *The Economy of Iceland, June 1992* (Reykjavík: Central Bank of Iceland, 1992).

22   The statistics come from Þjóðhagsstofnun (National Institute of Economics); *Iceland 1986*, pp. 32, 195–205, 247–9; and later statistics. Cf. *OECD Economic Surveys: Iceland 1988/1989*. Details of home ownership among Icelanders come from a consumer survey conducted in 1985–6 by the Statistical Bureau of Iceland.

23   *Húsnæðiskönnun 1988*, a study of housing undertaken for Húsnæðisstofnun ríkisins (State Housing Authority) by the Department of Political Science at the University of Iceland.

24   Statistics provided by the Statistical Bureau of Iceland show that inflation in Iceland during the past five decades was on average as follows: 12.6 per cent in 1940–50, 6.6 per cent in 1950–60, 11.9 per cent in 1960–70, 33.1 per cent in 1970–80, and 33.5 per cent in 1980–90.

25   Statistics have been provided by the Central Bank of Iceland.

26   *Iceland 1986*, pp. 232–4.

27   See the following articles by the political scientist Gunnar Helgi Kristinsson: 'Iceland: Vulnerability in a Fish-based Economy', *Cooperation and Conflict: Nordic Journal of International Politics* 12:4 (1987); 'Iceland's Interests and Options in Europe', in *Facing the Change in Europe: EFTA Countries' Integration Strategies*, ed. Kari Möttölä and Heikki Patomäki (Helsinki: Finnish Institute of International Affairs, 1989); 'Iceland', in *The Wider Western Europe: Reshaping the EC/EFTA Relationship*, ed. Helen Wallace (London: Pinter Publishing for The Royal Institute of International Affairs, 1991), pp. 159–78.

28   Thorsten Odhe, *Iceland—the Co-operative Island* (Chicago: Cooperative League of the USA, 1960), pp. 49–52.

29   The abbreviation 'hf.' stands for *hlutafélag* 'share company'. It is a compound of *hlutur* 'lot' and *félag* 'business partnership, company'. English *fellow* is borrowed from the related Old Norse word *félagi* 'companion', originally someone who lays down money (fee) in an undertaking.

30   See Chapter 2, 'Snorri's Edda'.

⁂ Chapter 7 ⁂

Iceland in the Global Context

The Starting Position

THE WINTER SUN AT ICELAND'S latitude is an unforgettable sight as its oblique, fiery rays sink into the surging waters of the Atlantic, while a crescent moon, or a full moon with a cold halo, shines with its borrowed light. The sun is a vision of a ball of fire, and the moon calls to mind a Chinese lantern of pure, glistening gold. Both take up their places in the firmament, before the star-studded night sky sweeps its dark mantle over the frozen ground. Day follows night in time's eternal cycle. Let us, too, take a few giant steps in time. The swiftness of thought can bring us from the era when the Eddic poems were composed and the Icelandic sagas narrated, to the present day. We leave behind us both anonymous and named skalds. We leave behind us such inspired Icelandic historians as Ari fróði and Sæmundur fróði, Sturla Þórðarson and his uncle, Snorri Sturluson. They captivate the reader. They enchant us in the same way as Homer with his *Iliad* and *Odyssey*, those immortal epics about the Greeks' ten-year siege of the walled city of Troy, and the return of Odysseus; after seemingly endless wanderings, the cunning hero finally comes home to his faithful Penelope, waiting on the rocky island of Ithaca.

The present day is different. News of world events now comes straight into our living-rooms. As habitual newspaper readers, radio listeners, and television viewers, we are constantly assailed by reporters anxious to catch our attention with the latest headline, and the pictures that flash before us on our television screens. Today we can have more than our fill of the never-ending flow of news. We may even be tempted to switch off our radios and television sets, to stop listening, to close our eyes. Some of the reports make us uneasy: great powers and powers which dream of greatness arm themselves and fight their battles, directly and indirectly; terrifying scenes of civil war and terrorist attacks. In our computer age we have perfected technology, but many countries are governed by autocrats who are far from perfect. Arthur Koestler has rightly described man as 'an intellectual giant but a moral dwarf'.

Questions of foreign affairs and security policy, of course, are primarily the responsibility of politicians and diplomats, as well as being topics for journalists and newsreaders to cover in their reports. Yet in modern-day democracies they concern us all. The international situation must be incessantly analysed. The pattern of security policy must be continually dissected. In our times of revolutionary changes, it makes sense to keep oneself informed, not to forget the world around us. In this respect, we should not act as Zeus, when he fell asleep during a critical phase of the siege of Troy. He was lured into doing so by Hera. And so, deep in peace, thundering Zeus 'slept on Gargaron peak, conquered by Sleep and strong assaults of Love, his wife locked in his arms.'[1]

As we write these lines, the world has undergone dramatic changes. It is easier to judge past events in the light of history than that which is happening at present. However, one might be tempted to compare the impact of the changes of recent years with other turning-points in history. The future may be hopeful, but it is highly uncertain. The cold war is over, nuclear arms are being drastically reduced, and after the collapse of the Soviet Union only one true superpower is left. This chapter will mostly review issues of Icelandic foreign and security policy in the cold war context. Let us begin by looking at the strategic location of Iceland, what it meant during the cold war, and what it may mean in future.

Iceland's Strategic Position and its Consequences

'Geography has not lost its importance, and Europe has not lost its position as the most important reference area for the security problems of the Nordic countries.' These are the words of Urho Kekkonen, President of Finland, in a speech delivered in Stockholm on 8 May 1978, when he revived the 1963 suggestion about a nuclear-free zone in Scandinavia.

When considering military geography, we must remember that Iceland is located in the middle of the North Atlantic. Reykjavík, the northernmost capital in the world, lies roughly half-way between Moscow and Washington.

In terms of population, Iceland is a mini-state, with about 260,000 inhabitants. In terms of area, however, it is fairly large, 103,000 km^2, and if we include the 200-mile exclusive economic zone, 758,000 km^2. Iceland, in other words, comprises a large and thinly populated area, which requires a strong defence for its protection. Yet Iceland is one of the few states in the world which does not have its own military defence. Nor has it ever had one.

From the Second World War, Iceland was a focal point of strategic interest. Superpowers found it increasingly important to control the shipping routes over the North Atlantic, and especially the waterways north of the Arctic Circle, on either side of Iceland. The surveillance of these passages is best managed from Iceland. The location allows supervision of all the warplanes, warships, and submarines that traffic the area.

Iceland therefore deserved the epithet of 'the country between the superpowers'.[2] Far northwest of Iceland is the United States base at Thule in Greenland. To the east—in the perpetually ice-free waters north of the Kola Peninsula—lie the naval bases around Murmansk, formerly Soviet, now Russian. A weakness of these bases is that the passages from the Kola Peninsula to the Atlantic, via the Barents Sea and the Norwegian Sea, pass over three suboceanic ridges: first the one stretching from the North Cape to Spitsbergen, then the ridge from the Lofoten Islands to Jan Mayen, and finally, the ridge that extends from Greenland via Iceland and the Faroes to Scotland, known as the GIUK (Greenland–Iceland–United Kingdom) gap.

Not surprisingly, NATO has been eager to keep an eye on the passage of submarines over these 'thresholds'. The Soviet Union was equally anxious to achieve mastery of these channels. An Icelandic expert on security policy has underlined the significance of Iceland as 'the key to the defense of the North Atlantic'.[3]

It is the exposed strategic position of Iceland which explains the course taken by the country on security policy: joining NATO in 1949 and signing the defence agreement with the USA in 1951 (renewed and revised in 1974) which led to the American manning of the Keflavík base.[4]

For the security of Iceland, there was scarcely any realistic alternative to membership of NATO and the retention of the Keflavík base. NATO strategists see the base as a vital link. In an armed conflict, the NATO bases in Iceland would be of immeasurable value both for safeguarding shipping over the Atlantic and for conducting effective anti-submarine operations. In peacetime it is important as a point of support for reconnaissance flights. Probably nowhere else in the world have the Americans sighted as many Soviet planes as during these flights. After Mikhail Gorbachev came to power in the Kremlin in 1985, however, the number of Soviet planes flying over Icelandic airspace was significantly reduced.

Although NATO does not pay Iceland anything for the right to maintain a military base on its territory—the primary contribution of the Icelandic people to the joint NATO defence—it is obvious that the Keflavík base brings economic benefits to Iceland. It is also clear that it entails a number of indirect advantages. Among them are the use of a large, modern, well-equipped international airport for civil aviation, conveniently located near the capital,[5] landing rights for Icelandic airlines in the USA, and probably other benefits on the political-economic level, not to mention income for Icelandic companies and private persons, especially those living near the base. It is a factor in the generation of employment.

Many people regard the base as a necessary evil. Yet it is evident that Icelanders, in their heart of hearts, feel a sense of discomfort. What nation would like to have foreign soldiers billeted on its own soil, just fifty kilometres from the capital?

The Icelandic people, with their remarkable cultural and historical background, are fervently patriotic. Regardless of which party they support, the nationally conscious Icelanders often feel that the American presence at Keflavík is in many ways a threat to their linguistic and cultural identity, for example, through the American television programmes formerly broadcast from there, and through the low-quality radio programmes still poured out from the base. Opponents of the base are concerned about this undesirable cultural influence.

The other NATO states long regarded Iceland as a reluctant ally. They compared her with a sleeping partner, sitting on the key to the North Atlantic. Iceland is and remains unarmed. Since the mid-1980s, however, Iceland has made a greater contribution to NATO. On the one hand, the Icelanders have worked single-mindedly for disarmament and détente between East and West. On the other hand, they have civil experts collaborating in the NATO defence. In Reykjavík the Ministry of Foreign Affairs has established a well-manned defence division which cooperates with the defence ministries of the other NATO states and the Keflavík base. In the NATO headquarters in Brussels, Iceland is represented by a defence attaché with military training. Other contributions are made by the Icelandic experts who look after the radar and communication facilities.[6]

Police, Coastguards, Civil Defence

Although the sovereign state of Iceland has no military defence of its own, it is not wholly defenceless in peacetime. The state has at its disposal civil authorities—police, coastguards, and civil defence—with the powers to combat crime, terrorist outrages, and encroachment on Iceland's exclusive economic zone. In addition, the country has its national rescue service and other voluntary organizations ready to assist in the event of disaster.

Life-saving measures are necessary in Iceland more often than in many other countries. They can be necessitated by volcanic eruptions, earthquakes, violent winter storms, and serious avalanches. Landslides or heavy avalanches have at times come close to burying small Icelandic coastal towns and fishing stations. Fearless and defiant, they cling to steep mountain slopes or nestle at the foot of black lava cliffs.

In addition, Iceland—as we shall now see—is on the way to taking over radar surveillance of its own airspace.

Radar Surveillance of Icelandic Airspace: Development and Modernization

Radar is the eyes of the defence.

The surveillance of the airspace over and around Iceland was formerly undertaken by AWACS (Airborne Warning and Control System) planes from the military base at Keflavík and two radar stations in southern Iceland. These were built in 1958. One is located in the south-west at Miðnesheiði near Keflavík, the other in the south-east at Stokksnes by Hornafjörður. Their antiquated equipment was unable to cover the whole of northern Iceland; this was therefore an 'open area', which was under radar surveillance only when the AWACS planes were in the air.

The incomplete surveillance of the airspace meant that Soviet fighters were sometimes able to fly in over Iceland unseen. One way to manage this was to come in low, under the radar. Since they ignored treaty law on making their presence known to Icelandic air traffic control, they were a conceivable danger to civil planes. When these unannounced fighters appeared on the radar screens, the base was swift to respond. It would send up F15 Eagle planes to identify the encroachers.[7] Protection against surprise attacks—like the Japanese attack on Pearl Harbour in 1941—was also provided by specially reinforced aircraft carriers, fuelled from subterranean oil-tanks.[8]

On the basis of agreements concluded between Iceland and the USA in the period 1981–5, it was decided that the deficiencies in surveillance would be remedied by modernizing air defence and radar facilities.[9] Two new radar stations have been built in northern Iceland. One is at Bolafjall, to the west-north-west of the little town of Bolungarvík, in the north-west corner of Iceland—where it resembles a jawbone pointing towards Greenland; the other is at Gunnólfsvíkurfjall on the Langanes promontory in the north-east corner of Iceland. In addition, the old radar stations in southern Iceland are being modernized. These four stations will be linked through a joint communications centre at Keflavík airport, to coordinate and control the system. It is planned to have the communications centre operating by 1995, but the four radar stations are already in operation.

Each of the two new radar stations in northern Iceland is housed in a building covering an area of about 1,500 square metres, with a 27-metre-high radar dome. From a distance they look like giant, shining golf balls. They have ultra-modern equipment, selected after tenders submitted by NATO member states. The buildings have been made as wind- and waterproof as possible, which is essential in view of the winter storms. They have been built at heights of 600–700 metres above sea level, which means that they command magnificent views over the mountains and the sea. Motorists can reach them by specially constructed roads with hairpin bends. Environmental protection has been a guiding star, but some mishaps have occurred.

Apart from the technical and strategic benefits to the USA and NATO, with better control over the GIUK gap, Iceland also derives obvious advantages of a technical kind, particularly the much improved safety of civil aviation, both domestic and international.

The four radar stations and the Keflavík communications centre have a range of about 250 nautical miles. In other words, it extends beyond Iceland's exclusive economic zone, reaching eastern Greenland to the west.

Using special apparatus, Iceland's coastguard is expected to keep all the ships within the exclusive economic zone under radar surveillance. Other expected advantages for Iceland will be improved reports on weather and ice.

The idea was that the construction expenses for this project will be met by the NATO Infrastructure Programme, while the USA will cover the running costs. The Icelanders, however, will manage the operation and maintenance of the radar stations. Icelandic technicians, who number about forty, are being specially trained in the USA and at home so that they can gradually take over the entire responsibility for operations. At the same time, they can acquire detailed knowledge of radar, telecommunications, computer technology, and programming.

The work of radar surveillance is carried on under the supervision of an Icelandic Radar Agency, Ratsjárstofnun, which was established in 1987.

In this way Iceland makes an active contribution to the joint NATO defence.

Aims of Icelandic Foreign Policy

La liberté consiste à pouvoir faire tout
ce qui ne nuit pas à autrui.

Déclaration des droits de l'homme et
du citoyen, adopted by the French
National Assembly in 1789

This revolutionary definition of liberty in the Declaration of the Rights of Man—the right to do anything that does not harm others—would hardly have found favour with the Florentine political philosopher Machiavelli (1469–1527), with his experience of ruthlessly cunning Renaissance princes. On the other hand, it would certainly be endorsed by the unarmed, peace-loving people of Iceland. It is therefore a suitable motto for this section.

When Steingrímur Hermannsson began his second period as prime minister in 1988, the foreign policy of his government was spelled out by the minister of foreign affairs in a declaration that began as follows: 'The aim of Iceland's foreign policy is to strengthen the independence of the country and to safeguard its interests in international affairs. This will be pursued through active participation in international co-operation.'[10] The subsequent government under Davíð Oddsson proclaimed the same aims.

In practice, this has meant that Icelandic foreign policy, ever since the country joined NATO in 1949, has followed three long-term lines: (1) international cooperation within the framework of the United Nations and other international organizations such as OECD, GATT, EFTA, and the Council of Europe; (2) Nordic cooperation, one of the cornerstones of Icelandic foreign policy; (3) in the field of security policy, activities associated with membership of NATO and more recently the Conference on Security and Cooperation in Europe (CSCE).

These main lines in the course of Icelandic foreign policy have been firmly anchored for over forty years. What about the other aspects of foreign policy? Some issues have now been left behind. No state, for example, now questions Iceland's rights to a 200-mile exclusive economic zone. On the other hand, radical changes in the world in recent years—from Gorbachev's rise to power in the Kremlin, with the upheavals in Eastern Europe and the disintegration of the Soviet Union, the breakthrough in negotiations about reductions to the huge arsenals of nuclear and conventional arms held by the military blocs, increased threats of environmental disaster, the growth of the European Community, and the incessant famines in the Third World—have highlighted new issues. Icelandic foreign policy in recent years has been focused on East–West relations, with the summit meeting in Reykjavík being the start of the thaw, Iceland's desire for disarmament at sea and more efficient environmental protection, Iceland's foreign trade and cooperation with developing countries, and the application of the defence treaty with the USA. Let us look at each of these areas in turn.

The Thaw between East and West: Summit Meeting in Reykjavík

The Icelanders want an agreement.
The walls of suspicion between East
and West are crumbling.

Mikhail Gorbachev at Reykjavík in
1986 before the meeting with Reagan

At the start of the 1980s, the outlook on the future that prevailed in Iceland, as elsewhere, was one of widespread unease and pessimism. The cold war between East and West, the arms race, the balance of terror with modern nuclear bombs capable of effecting many times the destruction and radiation caused by the bombs that fell on Hiroshima and Nagasaki in 1945, and the poisoned atmosphere between the superpowers—constantly nourished by fear and mutual suspicion—all this provoked nightmares. Was the twilight of the gods at hand?

Towards the end of the 1980s, however, we seemed to be justified in having a brighter view of the future. It was as if a spring breeze were refreshing the world. In the Soviet Union a hopeful change of system was bringing reform, pointing the way to a brighter future for the whole of humanity. For Mikhail Gorbachev, it appeared as if *per-estroika* (restructuring) and *glasnost* (openness) were more than empty slogans. We were encouraged by news of cordial summit meetings, agreements leading to disarmament, the end of a number of wars in Asia and Africa, and the liberation of the peoples of Eastern Europe. People were strengthened in their faith in the United Nations as an organization for maintaining international peace and security. It can be reshaped into something more than what it undeniably is as well: 'a mirror of world politics.'[11]

It really appears that we have witnessed a turning point in history, a thaw between East and West. There is a great deal of truth in the view that it can be dated to the coming of a new generation in the Kremlin, which brought Gorbachev to power in 1985, and his series of meetings with the American presidents Ronald Reagan and George Bush. At the suggestion of Gorbachev, and thanks to preparations accomplished in record time by the Icelanders (who were given only ten days' notice), his meeting with Reagan was organized in Reykjavík on 11–12 October 1986. To Höfði, the old, white, haunted house by the Faxaflói bay, came the distinguished guests in their long motorcades, accompanied by their aides, interpreters, bodyguards, and a swarm of armed security men and news reporters. Much of Reykjavík was closed off, with policemen at every street corner and on the roofs around Höfði. Helicopters circled in the sky, and Icelandic coastguard vessels cruised in the bay. The city was silent, as if dead. The streets were virtually empty. Almost everyone was sitting in front of a television set, waiting for news. The air was tense with excitement. It was almost unbearable. Some prayed reverently for peace, while others brooded with anxiety. Reykjavík was adorned with flagpoles bearing the standards of the USSR, the USA, Iceland, and Reykjavík, the latter with the emblem of the city. This symbolizes Ingólfur Arnarson's high-seat pillars. According to *Landnámabók*, Ingólfur threw them overboard when his ship was near a promontory on the south coast of Iceland. They are said to have floated ashore at the place which is now called Reykjavík. A miniature of this flag and a statue by Ásmundur Sveinsson decorated the room where the leaders of the superpowers discussed the problems of the world.

At the opening ceremony of the Althing on 10 October, the day before the summit meeting, President Vigdís Finnbogadóttir said: 'It is a noteworthy fact of history that, at the same time as Iceland is ceremonially opening her parliament, our nation has been honoured by the selection of Iceland's capital as the place where the leaders of the superpowers will meet to moderate their differences and disputes.'

Vigdís said that the Icelandic Althing—the oldest parliament in the world—was originally a meeting place for wrangling kindreds and districts, since the power of laws and reason is greater than that of the sword. She then said, 'It is the sincere hope of all of us that this Icelandic heritage will accompany the superpowers' choice of meeting place, and that they will here place in the scales the weight that leads to peace and disarmament.'

The president concluded by expressing her certainty that Iceland's prestige would be enhanced by hosting the meeting. 'The good reputation of a peace-loving people is now resounding all over the world.'[12]

Just before the discussions began, a number of newspapermen and photographers were allowed into Höfði. On this occasion Gorbachev said to Reagan, 'The Icelanders we met yesterday tried with very good reason to convince me that we should reach some sort of agreement with you, Mr. President. I then asked them if they had said the same thing to you, Mr. President. Their answer was yes.' Reagan replied, 'I am always hopeful.'[13] The two statesmen smiled amicably and shook hands. The meeting had got off to a promising start.

The end of the meeting came as something of an anticlimax. Grave, tired, and tight-lipped, the superpower leaders left Höfði. They seemed disappointed. They had not reached an agreement. Admittedly, they had managed to specify the remaining points of dispute. It also turned out that they were able to agree on many issues, especially a reduction in medium-range and intercontinental missiles in Europe and Asia. But they did not make it all the way. At that time they could not resolve their conflicting views on America's strategic defence initiative, the planned system to shoot down intercontinental missiles in space.

On the other hand, it was patently clear that Gorbachev and Reagan were both aiming for an agreement. Before their departure from Iceland they announced that they would have another meeting where they would try to resolve the outstanding differences. Moreover, it was clear that the two men enjoyed each other's company.

It later turned out that the two leaders had in fact come further in their extensive discussions than either of them had dared to dream. There were more talks in Höfði than planned, and they were longer than scheduled. The meeting had meant a breakthrough. The ice was broken, and a thaw seemed near.[14]

The Icelanders were praised for their good organization, their amiable hospitality, and the efficiency with which they had arranged everything. No unpleasant incidents disturbed the meeting in Reykjavík.

It is said that the summit meeting signified the third discovery of Iceland. The first discovery was by Ingólfur Arnarson 1,100 years ago. The second was by the allies in the Second World War. With the meeting of Gorbachev and Reagan in Reykjavík, Iceland was discovered overnight by the whole world.

Disarmament at Sea and Environmental Protection

Environmental destruction knows no
frontiers.

*Jón Baldvin Hannibalsson in a speech
to the Althing, 1989*

In his speech to the Althing on 24 April 1989, the minister of foreign affairs, Jón Baldvin Hannibalsson, pointed out the decisive role played by the presence or absence of trust between states. Suspicion and fear lead nations to arm themselves. Mutual trust is one of the necessary conditions for states to cut down their armaments. Unilateral disarmament would be naive. Other prerequisites for disarmament are multilateral action, control measures, and consideration for the vital security interests of individual states.

The survival of the Icelandic people depends on shipping in the North Atlantic routes and fishing off the coast of the country. The sea must not be polluted through nuclear accidents, oil spills, or radioactive waste. It had been estimated, according to Jón Baldvin, that 30 per cent of the world's nuclear arms were deployed on warships and submarines. A reminder of this danger came from recent accidents involving Soviet submarines in the Baltic Sea and the western part of the Barents Sea.

For these reasons, Iceland and the other Nordic countries attach priority to environmental protection, especially at sea. Iceland is prepared, according to Jón Baldvin, to do all in its power to shield itself against the consequences of ecological disasters. To this end, the ministries of foreign affairs and justice confer with the Icelandic police authorities, the coastguard, the civil defence, and the National Institute of Radiation Protection.

A special Ministry of the Environment was created in 1990.

Foreign Trade

The EFTA member Iceland, with its heavy dependence on the fluctuating world market for fish, faces many potential problems as the European Community becomes a single market at the end of 1992. In an increasingly integrated Europe, with free movement of goods, services, capital, and labour, Iceland must ensure that it can sell its fish and fish products without impediment. As part of the bargaining between the EC and EFTA to create a European Economic Area, Iceland therefore negotiated the right to free trade in its exports to the EC.

Membership of the European Community would be a last resort for Iceland. The Icelanders cannot tolerate the thought of opening their exclusive economic zone to EC trawlers. They cannot forget that they only became masters of their own zone after three cod wars with Britain.[15]

Iceland emphasizes the interplay of trade and defence. The survival of the NATO member Iceland ultimately depends on its fisheries and its fish exports. The Icelanders refer to the undertaking of the twelve states which signed the North Atlantic Treaty in 1949, that they 'will seek to eliminate conflict in their international economic policies'.[16]

Foreign trade has become an important aspect of Icelandic foreign policy. This is clear to all the organizations and private persons who have anything to do with the country's exports. Matters concerning foreign trade are handled by a special division of the Ministry of Foreign Affairs. Problems in trade policy have been discussed in a previous chapter.[17]

Cooperation with Developing Countries

When calculated as a percentage of the gross domestic product, Iceland's aid to developing countries is undoubtedly on a modest scale, especially when compared with the other Nordic countries. In 1988, for example, it made up 0.06 per cent of the GDP, whereas in Norway the figure was 1.12 per cent, in Denmark 0.89 per cent, in Sweden 0.87 per cent, and in Finland 0.59 per cent. Iceland aims to increase its share in stages to 0.7 per cent of the GDP.[18]

Of the aid to developing countries paid by Iceland, about half is multilateral and the other half bilateral. The multilateral aid is given as contributions to various agencies of the United Nations and to Nordic cooperative projects in Africa (in countries like Malawi).

The bilateral aid is intended to establish development cooperation with some of the poorest nations of the world. Iceland wants to help them to help themselves. This can take the form of Icelandic expertise in exploiting marine resources or geothermal energy. Countries which have benefited from this include Cape Verde, the island state off the African coast, and Namibia. Iceland offers these countries cooperation in the true sense of the word. One precondition for Icelandic aid is that the receiving state contributes money, equipment, and labour. They cannot be simply passive recipients of gifts in the form of money or necessary but unproductive disaster relief. They must learn new methods. They must be activated. They must be made interested, able to take initiatives and responsibility on their own. The Icelandic experts can then withdraw.

Iceland's cooperation in fisheries with Cape Verde, which began in 1980, is based on this philosophy. For many years it was concentrated on the research ship RS *Fengur*. The name of the ship was a happy choice: Fengur, one of Odin's many bynames, means 'gain' or 'catch'. The name was bestowed with good intentions. On board the *Fengur*, people from Cape Verde and Iceland have together discovered previously unknown stocks of demersal fish in the waters around the group of islands. The Cape Verde Islanders have also learned how to go about catching fish with their own vessels. They have bought eleven boats from the Netherlands, mostly intended for catching tuna. The Icelanders declare that the Cape Verde Islanders were willing and quick to learn how to fish using modern techniques.

Iceland is also supporting a women's association in Cape Verde. The aim is to train women for gainful employment.

Another Icelandic effort which is also appreciated is the United Nations University Geothermal Training Programme in Reykjavík.[19] Its purpose is to give a grounding in geothermal know-how to students from developing countries with volcanic areas, so that they can return to their homelands with an ability to exploit the benefits of geothermal energy. One such country is Kenya.

The Application of Iceland's Defence Agreement with the USA

Every now and then, criticism is levelled at Iceland's membership of NATO and the defence agreement with the USA. This policy has nevertheless been the prerequisite for continued independence for a country that lacks its own military defence.

Iceland's contacts with the Keflavík base are largely without friction. This is guaranteed by a variety of practical arrangements. The entrance to the civil air terminal is separate from the military base. American personnel live within the base and are not allowed to wear uniform when outside the base on furlough. The American television broadcasts have been blocked so that they can only be seen locally. Television broadcasts reaching beyond the base area were prohibited in 1974; this cultural policy was the outcome of several years of debate.

Iceland's links with the military base and its personnel are nevertheless a delicate matter in domestic politics. Statements by leading Americans can easily be interpreted as unwarranted interference in Icelandic affairs. If the American admiral in Keflavík makes a speech he must be careful in what he says. The American ambassador in Reykjavík must likewise weigh every word.

The troops at the base comprise about three thousand American soldiers. In addition, there is a unit of the Dutch air force and officers from various NATO countries (in 1992 Canada, Denmark, the Netherlands, Norway, and Britain). Administrative duties, service, and construction work also require American civilian personnel and about a thousand Icelanders.

NATO's defence planning presupposes that, when war breaks out or threatens to break out, reinforcements can be moved from the USA to Keflavík at very short notice. The Icelanders therefore understand that the defence forces in the USA and limited troop units from the USA must from time to time carry out manoeuvres in the base area and thus acquaint themselves with the Icelandic terrain. Every manoeuvre requires the consent of the Icelandic minister of foreign affairs.

Although cooperation with the base is mostly harmonious, the Icelanders have occasionally been outraged by disturbing incidents. One such was the 'Rainbow affair' a few years ago. The formal cause was an American law of 1904, according to which military equipment sent from the USA to American bases must be transported on American ships. The Americans invoked this old law, even though it had been enacted in completely different circumstances. It was used as a justification for letting the lion's share of goods transports to the Keflavík base be taken over by the American company Rainbow Navigation Inc. Icelandic vessels shipping fish and fish products to the USA were excluded from this work, and so had to return to Iceland empty. Two Icelandic shipping companies—Eimskip hf. and Hafskip hf.—suffered significant losses as a result.

A heated phase of the Rainbow affair came in 1985, when the company's *Rainbow Hope*, on arrival at the harbour in Njarðvík, was subjected to a rigorous customs inspection. This was carried out on the direct instructions of the minister of finance, Albert Guðmundsson. He said that the American defence forces did not have the right to import fresh meat to Iceland, since this is strictly prohibited by the 1928 law on measures to prevent foot-and-mouth disease; this scourge had formerly taken a heavy toll of the Icelandic stocks of sheep.

Albert's action was endorsed by the Chief Veterinary Officer, who declared that the importation of meat by the defence forces was a clear breach of the 1928 act. Albert was also warmly supported by the Icelandic news media. The newspaper *Nýi Tíminn*, for example, wrote that the American soldiers were not too good to eat Icelandic lamb.

The Rainbow affair was later settled in a friendly spirit. Anxiety and discontent have been provoked again, however, by oil spills in conjunction with American construction work: in 1987 at Ytri-Njarðvík near Keflavík, and in 1989 at the new radar station at Bolafjall in north-west Iceland.

On the other hand, the Icelanders have welcomed the improved radar surveillance of their airspace. As we have seen, the operation and maintenance of the new radar stations are gradually being taken over by specially trained Icelandic specialists. In this sphere of technology Iceland is thus assuming an important role.

The Support of the Electorate for Icelandic Foreign Policy

In a democracy, security and defence policies are naturally always dependent on the views of the political parties. The policies are ultimately determined by the ideological attitudes of the parties and by their willingness to grant money for defence or—in the case of Iceland—for other purposes, such as guarding its exclusive economic zone. In a dictatorship, on the other hand, defence policies are not dependent on such considerations. Dissenting political parties are not tolerated. The dictator need not care about the views of the silent masses. Normally, however, not even a dictator is totally indifferent to the facial expressions of the people around him.

To put it somewhat crudely, then, one may say that every state—regardless of its form of government—pursues foreign politics as part of its domestic politics. It may seem superfluous to point out this link between foreign policy and domestic opinion. Suffice it to say that a detailed analysis of a country's domestic politics can help to explain the course of its foreign politics: the policies pursued in the past, those currently being pursued, and those which we have reason to expect in the future.

Icelandic Political Parties

This link between political parties and the defence of a country has been analysed in an interesting way for Iceland by the political scientist Róbert Árnason. His study covers the period 1945–80.[20] Although it does not extend to the present day, it is still readable. It is a useful retrospect. If it is supplemented with details from the 1980s and 1990s, one can obtain a rounded picture of the attitudes of the political parties to the course of Icelandic foreign politics.

Membership of NATO

Three of the parties represented in the Althing at present (1993)—the Independence Party, the Progressive Party, and the Social Democratic Party—support Icelandic membership of NATO. During the forty-odd years that have passed since Iceland joined the alliance, not one government has requested to leave it. During this long period the pro-NATO parties have always had a safe majority in the Althing. In view of the relative stability of party support, it would require radical changes for this majority to disappear.

The People's Alliance, on the other hand, maintains that any military threat to Iceland is a consequence of NATO membership. It is precisely this membership which increases the risk of Iceland being attacked in the event of war. The political platform of the People's Alliance holds that Iceland should: (1) withdraw from NATO; (2) revoke the defence agreement which grants the USA the Keflavík base; (3) remain unarmed; (4) pursue a policy of neutrality. The Women's Alliance, which is also supported by many men, is divided on the issue. In the 1987 election a small majority (56 per cent) of their voters was in favour of NATO membership.

The Keflavík Base

During the cold war, the presence of the Keflavík base was strongly supported by the Independence Party and just as vehemently opposed by the People's Alliance. A clear majority of the Women's Alliance (65 per cent in the 1987 election) opposed the base.

The Icelandic Electorate

The views of the Icelandic electorate have been the subject of scientific study by another Icelandic political scientist, Ólafur Þ. Harðarson. His findings are based on opinion polls conducted after the general elections of 1983 and 1987, inquiring into attitudes to: (1) membership of NATO; (2) the Keflavík base; (3) leasing the base.[21]

Membership of NATO

Of the voters who expressed their views, there was a broad majority in both 1983 and 1987 in favour of NATO membership—about 80 per cent. It was considered necessary for the defence of Icelandic independence.

The Keflavík Base

Support for the Keflavík base dropped from 64 per cent in 1983 to 55 per cent in 1987. At the same time, a growing number of Icelanders feel that the question of the base is unimportant. The proportion of voters with this opinion rose from 15 per cent in 1983 to 26 per cent in 1987.

This turn of the tide in popular opinion has been explained as being due to a number of stumbling-blocks in Iceland's relations with the USA . Ólafur points out such examples as Icelandic whaling, the meat imports by the American defence forces, and the take-over of ship transports by American companies, taking this source of income from the Icelandic companies which had previously handled these transports.

Opposition to the base was also widespread while Iceland was fighting the cod wars with Britain.

Leasing the Base

The demand that NATO should pay for the privilege of leasing the land where the Keflavík base stands was originally put forward by the Icelandic broker Aron Guðbrandsson (1905–88). Aron was a well-known, well-off, and well-liked citizen of Reykjavík. He argued his views, generally known as 'Aronskan', in the newspapers, and he has many supporters, 'Aronistar'. They made up 68 per cent of the electorate in 1983 and 64 per cent in 1987. Aron's opponents point out that the granting of the Keflavík base is Iceland's primary contribution to NATO's defence. To lease it would mean that Iceland could lose some of her freedom of action.

Conclusion

*With laws shall our land be built up
but with lawlessness laid waste.*

In a speech to the United Nations General Assembly in 1986, the former Icelandic minister of foreign affairs, Matthías Á. Mathiesen, retold an episode from Homer's *Iliad*, about the passivity of Zeus in the fight between Sarpedon and Patroclus during the siege of Troy.[22] Just as the gods and mortals of antiquity obeyed certain rules of conduct, Matthías implored the leaders of the powerful nations to show restraint in their conduct, disregarding their own short-term interests and instead taking the whole of humanity into consideration.

The Icelandic minister of foreign affairs was right. The gods themselves sometimes took part in the battles before the gates of Troy, it is true, but despite their partiality they showed exemplary *sophrosyne* 'moderation'—part of the heritage of Athens and Sparta.

We children of a later age, as Matthías said to conclude his speech, should consider the wisdom in *Njáls saga*, where the eponymous hero says: 'With laws shall our land be built up but with lawlessness laid waste.' Or in Icelandic: 'Með lögum skal land byggja en ólögum eyða.'[23]

The proverb 'With laws shall our land be built up' is an ancient expression of a common Nordic view of justice. It was known throughout Scandinavia in the Middle Ages. It was written down in two of the medieval legal codices of Sweden (for Uppland and Hälsingland), in Denmark (the law of Jutland), in Norway (the law of Frostathing), and in the Icelandic codex *Járnsíða*, the law that applied from 1271 to 1280, before *Jónsbók* was adopted.[24]

Iceland nurtures her share of the ancient Nordic tradition of law and liberty with closely related customs and statutes. Iceland has contributed to the codification of the new law of the sea which emerged after the Second World War. This was validated in the United Nations Convention on the Law of the Sea.[25] In the same spirit, as we have seen, prime goals of Icelandic foreign policy have been the improvement of East–West relations, disarmament at sea, environmental protection, and liberalized foreign trade.

The end of the 1980s saw a dramatic thaw in the cold war. Mutual suspicion, fear, and the arms race gave way to trust, measures to create confidence, and a desire to cooperate on reducing arms. A new historical era began in 1989, when the redrawing of Europe's political map began. Gorbachev's visit to the Pope showed the desire of the USSR to ensure the collaboration of the Vatican in the reshaping of Europe.[26] The peoples of the former Soviet Union were once again granted democracy and human rights. The barbed wire of the Iron Curtain was cut. People broke holes in the Berlin Wall, which quickly collapsed. It was transformed with unexpected speed into a monument to an odious period of repression. Tourists flocked to Berlin to take home pieces of concrete as souvenirs of the 'wall of shame'.

There were other signs of the times. At Christmas 1989, Beethoven's Ninth Symphony was broadcast by television from a peace concert in East Berlin. It was played by an orchestra with members from both parts of Germany. In times of revolution and upheaval, as we have learned from history, setbacks and troubles can never be ruled out. Nor, unfortunately, can the apparently endless series of armed conflicts. We may nevertheless hope that the winds of change which began to blow over Eastern Europe in the late 1980s will be overwhelmingly favourable. One thing is certain. The American–Soviet summit meeting in Reykjavík with its atmosphere of reconciliation—the Reykjavík spirit—was undoubtedly a turning-point. It was the start of a constructive dialogue between East and West. This meeting between Mikhail Gorbachev and Ronald Reagan was well stage-managed. It was also something of a triumph for the state authorities and diplomats who represented Iceland.

The détente between East and West, the fall of the communist dictatorships, and the consequences of this development—such as the liberation of the Baltic states and the peoples of Eastern Europe—were encouraging news. We must nevertheless feel concern about the chaotic situation in the East, and the violent forms taken by the disintegration of the Soviet Union[27] and Yugoslavia. Ethnic and religious conflict has led to war. Starvation, poverty, and flows of refugees are inevitable consequences.

Another source of unease is what will happen to all the unemployed experts in nuclear arms. At present (1992) the nuclear arsenals of Russia, Belarus, Ukraine, and Kazakhstan are not under the joint command of the Commonwealth of Independent States, so we cannot ignore the risk of nuclear arms proliferating.

In this situation, it is essential for Iceland to retain security in NATO and an unchanged defence agreement about the Keflavík base. An Icelandic expert has concluded that Iceland has 'no reason to change its security arrangement during the present transitional period in East–West relations'.[28] The bilateral defence cooperation between Iceland and the United States will continue to be one of the main pillars of foreign policy. However, parallel with the changes discussed above, Iceland should expect a reduction in the significance and activities of the Iceland Defence Force in the next few years.

Situated between continental Europe and America, Icelanders feel a sort of divided loyalty. It has been pointed out that Iceland's ambiguous position in the global context reflects its geological situation:[29]

> The remarkable natural formation of Þingvellir, Iceland's thousand-year-old assembly place, where chieftains and free men gathered to make laws and judge cases, mirrors in many ways the situation in which the little Nordic island state finds itself today as well, in a Europe which is rapidly changing.
>
> Right through Þingvellir there runs the boundary between two continental plates which have given rise to the country. One is very slowly moving west towards North America, and one is moving in the direction of Europe, eastwards.
>
> This natural phenomenon is echoed in an interesting way in Icelandic security policy, which traditionally stands on two legs—one American, and one European; the latter is often associated with the cultural Nordic community that is manifest in inter-Nordic cooperation and supported by the strong Nordic sense felt by the average Icelander.

Notes to Chapter 7

1   Homer, *The Iliad*, trans. Robert Fagles, book 14, 'Hera Outflanks Zeus' (Harmondsworth: Penguin, 1990).

2   This term was coined in an analysis of Iceland's strategic importance by Lars Hultkrantz and Svante Johansson, *Island mellan supermakterna* (Stockholm: Oktoberförlaget, 1977).

3   Gunnar Gunnarsson, *The Keflavík Base: Plans and Projects* (Reykjavík: Icelandic Commission on Security and International Affairs, 1986), p. 14; 'Isländsk säkerhetspolitik', in *Säkerhetspolitik i Norden*, ed. Nils Andrén (Stockholm: Försvar och säkerhetspolitik, 1984). See also Albert Jónsson, *Iceland, NATO and the Keflavík Base* (Reykjavík: Icelandic Commission on Security and International Affairs, 1989); Björn Bjarnason, 'L'Islande et l'Alliance', *Revue de l'OTAN* 34:1 (1986), pp. 7–12.

4   See Chapter 5, 'Security Policy: The First Steps'.

5   See Chapter 5, 'The Keflavík Base (from 1951)'.

6   Paul Giniewsky, 'L'Islande: l'allié désarmé de l'OTAN', *Rivista di Studi Politici Internazionali* 221 (1989), pp. 37–46.

7   'Íslenskir starfsmenn taka við ratsjárstöðinni á Miðnesheiði', *Morgunblaðið*, 6 April 1989; Gunnar Gunnarsson, *The Keflavík Base*, p. 32.

8   Gunnar Gunnarsson, *The Keflavík Base*, pp. 5–6.

9   This account is based on a technical report, the annual reports to the Althing by Icelandic ministers of foreign affairs, articles in *Morgunblaðið*, and details supplied by Icelandic authorities.

10   Speech to the Althing by Jón Baldvin Hannibalsson, 24 April 1989.

11   Torsten Örn, *FN—världspolitikens spegel* (Stockholm: PAN/Norstedt, 1969).

12   Quoted in *Morgunblaðið*, 12 October 1986.

13   Ibid.

14   See Patrick Glynn, *Closing Pandora's Box: Arms Races, Arms Control, and the History of the Cold War* (New York: BasicBooks, 1992), pp. 349–51, 'The Reykjavik Drama'.

15   See Chapter 5, 'The New Law of the Sea and the Cod Wars'.

16   North Atlantic Treaty, Washington, DC, 4 April 1949, article 2.

17   See Chapter 6, 'Outlook for the Future'.

18   Jón Baldvin Hannibalsson's report to the Althing, April 1988, p. 10.

19   See Chapter 9, 'Geothermal Energy'.

20   Róbert Árnason, *Political Parties and Defence: The Case of Iceland 1945–1980* (Kingston, Canada: Queen's University Centre for International Relations, 1980).

21   Ólafur Þ. Harðarson, *Viðhorf íslendinga til öryggis- og utanríkismála* (Reykjavík: Öryggisnefnd, 1984); *Íslendingar og öryggismálin 1983–1987* (Reykjavík: Öryggisnefnd, 1989). Exactly the same voters who were questioned in 1983 were interviewed once again in 1987; this method shows whether and in what way the subjects had changed their stance on the issues.

22   *The Iliad*, book 16.

23   *Njal's Saga*, trans. Magnus Magnusson and Hermann Pálsson (Harmondsworth: Penguin, 1960), ch. 70. Every Icelander knows the saying 'Með lögum skal land byggja'; the words can be read on every police car and on the Icelandic policemen's caps.

24　*Brennu-Njáls saga*, ed. Einar Ól. Sveinsson, Íslenzk fornrit 12 (Reykjavík: Hið íslenzka fornritafélag, 1954), footnote on p. 172.

25　See Chapter 5, 'The New Law of the Sea and the Cod Wars'.

26　For centuries, papal nuncios and legates have made themselves known as good negotiators and well-informed reporters. The Vatican established diplomatic relations with all the Nordic countries except Finland in 1982; diplomatic relations with Finland go back to 1966.

27　Marshall Brement, *Reaching out to Moscow. From Confrontation to Co-operation* (New York: Praeger, 1991).

28　Gunnar Gunnarsson, 'Continuity and Change in Icelandic Security and Foreign Policy', *Annals of the American Academy of Political and Social Science* 512 (November 1990).

29　Larscrik Häggman, 'Islands kluvenhet', *Hufvudstadsbladet*, Helsinki, 5 July 1992.

ᵈᵉᶜ Chapter 8 ᶜᵉᵈ

Iceland and the Riches of the Sea

When all is said and done, life is
mostly stockfish and not daydreams.

Salka Valka to the idealist Arnaldur,
whom she loved, in the novel by
Halldór Laxness

Masters of Their Own House

Il ne revient jamais. Une nuit d'août,
là-bas, au large de la sombre Islande,
au milieu d'un grand bruit de fureur,
avaient été célébrées ses noces avec la
mer.

Pierre Loti, Pêcheur d'Islande

THESE WINGED WORDS BY PIERRE LOTI are carved on a high stone
in the old cemetery of Reykjavík. The stone with its inscription in
French and a free Icelandic translation—'a token of friendship and
admiration for France'—was raised by the Icelandic people to honour
the memory of the polar explorer Jean Baptiste Charcot and his companions. They drowned when their sailing ship, the *Pourquoi pas?*,
was wrecked in 1936 during a hurricane in the Faxaflói bay, north-west
of Reykjavík.[1]

This shipwreck was not unique. Countless fishermen and seamen
have perished in the dangerous waters around Iceland. It still happens
all too often that even ships with modern equipment are wrecked in

sudden storms. One thing should be made clear, however. Few states take more pains than Iceland in the matter of safety at sea and the well-being of the fishermen. This is seen both in the way the fishing vessels are equipped and in the way the fishermen are trained.

Drowning accidents were once much more common, since most Icelandic farmer-fishermen had only deckless rowing-boats in which they fished near the coast. Everyone worried about the unpredictable sea. Little more than a generation ago, an Icelandic fisherman's wife would not dare to argue or quarrel with her husband before he set out to fish. She was perpetually anxious that they would never see each other again. It was important that they should not part as enemies.

Despite all the dangers, the Icelanders constantly put out to sea, to supplement their meagre diet with fish. In times of crop failure it was vital to have fresh, salted, or dried fish as an important supplement to the daily bread.

But the Icelanders were not the only people exploiting the rich fishing banks around their coasts. They have been visited and plundered by foreigners from many nations. We may remind the reader of the five cod wars about fishing off Iceland fought at the end of the Middle Ages between England and the Hanseatic League, and Iceland's three cod wars with Britain in the period 1958–76. These ended, as we know, in a total victory for Iceland, which declared an exclusive economic zone of 200 nautical miles on 15 October 1975. Iceland's claim was gradually recognized by the affected states, both *de facto* and *de jure*. The legal status was codified by the Third United Nations Conference on the Law of the Sea, which resulted, after long deliberation, in the 1982 Convention on the Law of the Sea, signed at Montego Bay.[2]

The full scope of Iceland's success is seen in the following table, which shows that the Icelandic fishing limits have been extended many times over during the second half of the twentieth century:

3 nautical miles	1901–1952	24,500 km^2
4 nautical miles	1952–1958	42,900 km^2
12 nautical miles	1958–1972	69,800 km^2
50 nautical miles	1972–1975	216,000 km^2
200 nautical miles	1975–	758,000 km^2

This means that Iceland in 1975 had won jurisdiction over an area of the sea more than thirty times greater than it had until 1951, when the Anglo-Danish agreement about the three-mile limit ceased to apply.

A 200-Mile Exclusive Economic Zone

The rules concerning Iceland's 12-mile territorial water, the 200-mile exclusive economic zone, and the continental shelf are stipulated in an act of 1 June 1979 (no. 41). According to this law, Iceland's territorial sea extends 12 nautical miles calculated from baselines drawn between 38 specially enumerated points, including the island of Surtsey (which rose from the sea south-west of Vestmannaeyjar in 1963), the low-water line at Kolbeinsey and the outermost points and rocks of the island of Grímsey, both north of Iceland, and Hvalbakur east of Iceland (article 1). The act also declares that Iceland's sovereignty includes this territorial sea, the seabed below it, and the airspace above it (article 2).

Within the 200-mile exclusive economic zone (article 3), Iceland has sovereign rights to the extraction of resources and other economic exploitation (such as energy production by water, currents, or winds), as well as jurisdiction over: (1) building; (2) scientific research; (3) the conservation of the marine environment. Activities in the exclusive economic zone must take place 'in accordance with international agreements to which Iceland is a Party' (article 4). These include the Convention on the Law of the Sea with its provisions about the conservation and exploitation of species which migrate between zones (article 64) and marine mammals such as seals and whales (article 65). Iceland also has sovereignty over the extraction of resources within its continental shelf (articles 5 and 6).

Between Iceland on the one hand and Greenland and the Faroes on the other hand, the Icelandic exclusive economic zone and the continental shelf are demarcated where necessary by a median line (article 7). It should be noted that the article does not mention either Jan Mayen or Rockall—two potential bones of contention, as we shall see below.

It is Iceland's responsibility to take measures to protect the marine environment against pollution and other damage (article 8).

Finally, the law declares that scientific research within Icelandic territorial waters, the exclusive economic zone, or the continental shelf requires approval from the appropriate Icelandic authority (article 9) after application six months in advance (article 10).

Surtsey and Kolbeinsey

The little islands of Surtsey and Kolbeinsey are both important as baseline points. One wonders whether their existence is connected to the eternal struggle between the gods and the fire-giant Surtur. The name Surtur calls to mind his blazing sword. These rocky islands have risen hissing from the sea, out of the grasp of the sea-god Ægir, his wife Rán, and their nine daughters, the waves.

According to *Svarfdæla saga*, the events of which took place in the tenth century, Kolbeinsey takes its name from a man called Kolbeinn who lived in northern Iceland. He had come into conflict with his kinsman Uni. Everyone was against Kolbeinn. He grew so furious, according to the saga, that 'he rushed away to a ship and sailed out to sea. He was shipwrecked on the rock that lies north of Grímsey. Kolbeinn was killed there. The island is named after him. It is called Kolbeinsey.'[3]

In the old days, people went to Kolbeinsey in springtime, in fishing-boats with eight oars, to collect eider-down and to catch seals and birds. The seals were so unafraid, it was said, that men could catch them with their bare hands. Tradition has handed down a story about three brothers who sailed there in foggy weather in 1580. The fog made them sleepy. Or could it have been magic? In any case, they could not stay awake. Finally, the fog lifted. The sun burst forth in the west. To the east they could see something white, which they at first took for the sail of a ship. But they suddenly saw that it was the highest mountain on Kolbeinsey, which was completely white with cliff-birds and a cover of cotton-grass.[4]

But Surtsey and Kolbeinsey are incessantly at the mercy of the violent onslaught of the waves. Blocks of rock frequently come loose. Present-day Kolbeinsey has been described as a bare rock or a skerry. At the time when the three brothers sailed there, the island is alleged to have been much larger. By 1978, however, it had shrunk to only 42 37 metres and a height of 5.4 metres above the sea.

Geologists predict that, within fifty years, Kolbeinsey will have been completely broken down by waves and ice. Today it is still visible as a dark rock.

Denmark refuses to recognize Kolbeinsey as a basis for calculating an exclusive economic zone or a continental shelf, since it is an uninhabitable rock in the sea which can have no independent economic life of its own.[5] The Icelanders reply that other states have long recognized Kolbeinsey as a basis for calculating the exclusive economic zone. They are nevertheless concerned that Kolbeinsey will gradually become smaller and eventually be swallowed up by the sea.

What will happen if Kolbeinsey disappears? The Icelanders, not wanting to stake everything on one uncertain card, have begun to take preventive action. In 1989 they built a concrete landing-place for helicopters on Kolbeinsey. They also intend to install a radar reflector and instruments for meteorological, geological, and other measurements.

While the colonization of Surtsey by moss, herbs, low shrubs, insects, birds, and occasional mammals gives us a vision of the origin of life on earth, the creation process, in the ocean around Kolbeinsey we see a different world, rare and quite unlike what we see on land. In 1988 a manned German mini-submarine explored these depths in conjunction with Icelandic scientists. No one had done so before. South of Kolbeinsey, they discovered a few sulphurous geothermal areas, 100–200 metres under the surface, with a much richer and more varied flora and fauna than anyone would have dared to imagine. They also found micro-organisms which thrived in the hot springs at a temperature of 180°C. Before this, it had been thought that the highest temperature endured by biological life was 110°C. As the scientists eagerly took samples for testing, their little submarine was shaken by the currents from the hot springs.[6]

Coastguards and Foreign Fishermen

As we have seen, Iceland's 200-mile exclusive economic zone covers an area of 758,000 km^2. This area is about 7.5 times greater than the land territory of Iceland (103,000 km^2). We may compare the size of Iceland's exclusive economic zone with that of the Baltic Sea, which is about 400,000 km^2. In other words, the Icelanders have a huge area of the sea to administer, preserve, and supervise.

Iceland's coastguard (Landhelgisgæsla Íslands) was founded in 1926. It comes under the authority of the Ministry of Justice. Its duties are stated in Act 25 of 1967. One main task is to supervise fishing within Iceland's exclusive economic zone. The supervision includes checking catch quotas, protecting spawning places, and inspecting fishing equipment. The coastguard's sphere of responsibility also includes a number of other duties, such as sea rescue, salvaging wrecked vessels, bringing aid to isolated places, taking part in hydrographical surveying and research in marine biology, disarming mines, and assisting in civil defence.

To discharge these duties, the coastguard has at its disposal three small but instrumentally well equipped vessels, *Týr, Ægir,* and *Óðinn* (all famous from the cod wars with Britain), two helicopters of French manufacture, and a Dutch Fokker plane. While the cod wars were in progress, the coastguard employed about 200 people. Afterwards the force was reduced to around 120. The personnel are civilians, but the director has had military training. Since Iceland has no military defence of its own, its coastguard, police force, and civil defence are of considerable significance.

Thanks to modernized radar surveillance of the airspace over and around Iceland, which is managed by four radar stations and a joint communications centre at the international airport at Keflavík, the coastguard is expected in the future to benefit from radar surveillance over all the ships within the exclusive economic zone.

Nowadays, no foreign vessels have fishing rights in Iceland's exclusive economic zone, except for a small number of Belgian and Faroese vessels.[7] They have been allowed by agreement to catch limited annual quantities. These are relatively small for the Faroes and even smaller for Belgium.[8]

The fishing quotas granted to Belgium should be seen as a symbolic thanks to that country for having recognized Iceland's extended fishing limits as early as the start of the 1970s.

Iceland grants slightly larger quantities to the Faroes. The most vociferous criticism of this comes from the Icelandic fishermen's and seamen's organizations, those who are professionally concerned. Yet many Icelanders fully understand the Icelandic generosity towards the people of the Faroes. Their attitude on this issue is often: 'I don't see the Faroese as foreigners, but as friends and kinsmen.'

It is not irrelevant to examine the grounds for this attitude. Both Iceland and the Faroes were colonized in the ninth and tenth centuries. Most of the settlers came from Scandinavia. The majority sailed to Iceland, but some stayed in the Faroes. This means that Icelanders and Faroe Islanders have a great deal in common. They have close historical, linguistic, and cultural ties. They also share their position as 'mini-nations' with a similar economy and similar problems. It is not surprising that they feel a strong mutual affinity. For the Icelandic man in the street, then, it is natural to show generosity to the Faroese neighbours.

In addition, as we shall see in the section on Jan Mayen, there is an agreement between Iceland, Norway, and Greenland regarding capelin. The agreement grants the parties limited mutual fishing rights in each other's zones.

Cooperation with Other Coastal States

The nations by the northern seas must increase their cooperative endeavours in cultivating, protecting and exploiting the riches of the seas, and strengthen their political cooperation and economic bonds. They must negotiate and seek an amicable solution to their differences.

Eyjólfur Konráð Jónsson, member of the Althing, in a lecture in 1986

Ever since the colonists from Scandinavia settled Iceland 1,100 years ago, its inhabitants have been linked to the rest of the world by the sea. The sea and its riches have become the destiny of the Icelanders, an essential condition for their survival and their present welfare. The yields of agriculture have mostly been poor, and the country's energy resources have only been seriously exploited in our own times.

It was thus a decisive success for the Icelanders when they won full international recognition for their exclusive economic zone of 200 nautical miles. They have controlled this enormous expanse of sea since 1976.

Yet the Icelanders then did not just become 'masters of their own house'. They also shouldered the full responsibility for protecting the fish stocks and other resources within the 200-mile limit from over-fishing and extermination. They have to be tended and utilized, in a rational and scientific way. Research is conducted under state auspices by the Marine Research Institute, as well as by fish laboratories and institutes for quality control of fish products. The scientists have their say first. Then the government implements Iceland's fishery policies, which are based on quotas. That is the principle.

After the size of the fish stocks and the expected reproduction capacity have been estimated by the Marine Research Institute, the Ministry of Fisheries sets the annual maximum quotas for different species of fish allocated to each fishing vessel.[9] There are other measures to be taken, chiefly the protection of areas visited by fish for spawning, prohibition against catching fish under a certain size, and instructions about minimum sizes for the mesh in nets and trawls.

But this is not enough. Outside the exclusive economic zone, the stocks of fish—such as cod, salmon, capelin, and herring—which wander with the ocean currents are endangered by over-fishing by foreigners. This is a very real threat. It has occurred in all the points of the compass:

- *in the north*, around Jan Mayen and eastern Greenland, in the form of capelin fishing;
- *in the south*, in the form of Russian factory-ships catching redfish and other species on the fishing banks of the Reykjanes Ridge;
- *in the east*, in the form of alleged poaching of salmon from the North Atlantic stock;
- *in the west*, in the form of fishing by the European Community along the coasts of Greenland.

In other words, the Icelanders have the constant problem of foreign fishing outside the exclusive economic zone. This anxiety is the reason for their claims to jurisdiction both in the north (the Norwegian island of Jan Mayen) and in the south (the Reykjanes Ridge and its offshoot towards Rockall). The problem to the north has been solved by agreements with Norway, one in 1980 concerning fisheries and the continental shelf, one in 1981 about the delimitation of the continental shelf between Iceland and Jan Mayen.

The oceanic salmon is protected by the 1982 Convention on North Atlantic Salmon. This was the first multilateral convention to be established in Iceland. It therefore justifies the name of the 'Reykjavík Convention', as Iceland's leading expert on international law said with a smile when it was signed.

Other multilateral conventions of relevance for Iceland are the United Nations Convention on the Law of the Sea, the 1980 agreement about fishery collaboration in the North-East Atlantic, and the 1978 agreement about fishery collaboration in the North-West Atlantic.

Virtually all the ocean between Norway and Canada is divided up between the coastal states which have exclusive economic zones and continental shelves there. The question has arisen about the principles which should be followed for the delimitation of these zones (article 74 of the Convention on the Law of the Sea) and shelves (article 83). In some cases, such as Rockall, it has proved difficult to negotiate agreements about where the boundaries should run. One alternative is to use the resources jointly; this kind of cooperation has been applied in the case of Jan Mayen.

Since the cod wars have ended and Iceland has been recognized as having jurisdiction over a 200-mile exclusive economic zone, it is now possible to analyse the law of the sea in the North Atlantic. The *de facto* application of the law is still taking shape, however, which means that any picture that is painted needs to be constantly retouched.

Jan Mayen

The volcanic island of Jan Mayen lies in the Arctic Sea, some 550 kilometres north-north-east of Langanes in Iceland, at a latitude of 71° north. Its area is 372 km^2.

Jan Mayen is called after the Dutchman who sailed there in 1614. Yet it is not likely that he was the first to discover the island. Scholars think that an island which was discovered and given the name of

'Svalbard'[10] in 1194 is identical with Jan Mayen. The discovery is described in the saga of Guðmundur Arason, Bishop of Hólar (born 1161): 'King Sverrir was crowned. Svalbard was discovered. Guð-mundur Arason was then aged 33 winters.'[11] Svalbard is also mentioned in *Landnámabók*. The distance calculated (four days' and four nights' sail) indicates, according to some historians, that the narrator is referring to Jan Mayen.

Icelanders undertook or planned journeys to Jan Mayen in the nineteenth and twentieth centuries. One trip there was made in the war year of 1918, when timber was in very short supply; the crew of the *Snorri* found plenty of driftwood on the island.[12]

A manned Norwegian weather station was set up on Jan Mayen in 1921. In 1929 the island came under Norwegian sovereignty. Before this, three Icelandic prime ministers had pointed out that Iceland had certain interests in the island (such as collecting driftwood and data for weather forecasts). The conclusion was drawn by Prime Minister Jón Þorláksson in his far-sighted letter of 27 July 1927. He wrote:[13]

> In so far as there can be any talk of using the island for other interests, the Icelandic government wishes to reserve the rights of Icelandic citizens on an equal footing with those of the citizens of any other state.

In 1979 the Norwegian government announced that it was planning to proclaim a 200-mile exclusive economic zone around Jan Mayen, to protect the resources of the fishing banks around the island. At that time the waters were particularly rich in capelin, but fishing was free for all states in the open seas around the island, which had territorial waters extending only four nautical miles. Within an exclusive economic zone it would be possible for Norway to find suitable ways to prevent over-fishing: quotas and rules about control, inspection, and the obligation of fishing vessels to notify their presence.

Iceland could well understand that the Norwegian plans were justified. Iceland, however, made two legal claims: an undiminished exclusive economic zone around Iceland and equality with Norway in the area around Jan Mayen.

Iceland adduced a number of arguments in favour of its claim:

1. Jan Mayen is located on Iceland's continental shelf.

2. Every geological map calls this area the Icelandic Plateau. The depth here is generally at most 1,000 to 2,000 metres.

3. The suboceanic gap between Norway and Jan Mayen, on the other hand, is about 3,500 metres deep.

4. The economic factor: fishing is of overwhelming importance for the livelihood of the Icelandic people. This was also the dissenting opinion of Judge Padilla Nervo, who supported the Icelandic demands in the Fisheries Jurisdiction Case (United Kingdom of Great Britain and Northern Ireland v. Iceland).[14]

5. The marine biological factor: The capelin around Jan Mayen migrates from Iceland in summer and returns in winter. It is Icelandic in the sense that the present stocks around Jan Mayen, according to fishery experts, have their spawning grounds off the south coast of Iceland.

6. Historical claims in the light of Icelandic documents: apart from all the above arguments, the Icelanders referred to a file concerning Jan Mayen found in the National Archives in Reykjavík, with documents from the 1920s, including the letter from Jón Þorláksson.

Iceland did not challenge the wording of the Norwegian act of 27 February 1930 (section 1), which stated that 'the island of Jan Mayen is a part of the Kingdom of Norway'. The Icelanders observed that, although there is a manned weather station on the island, it has no inhabitants who live off the island's resources. Jan Mayen may be 'more than a rock' and 'a fairly large island (*allstór eyja*)', but in normal conditions it would hardly be considered habitable.

The Jan Mayen affair highlighted at least three issues in international law:

• Does the possession of Jan Mayen give Norway the right to proclaim an exclusive economic zone around the island (article 121 of the Convention on the Law of the Sea)?

• What is to be the law as regards the extraction of resources in the sea and on the seabed around a small island with no economic life of its own, if this island belongs to one state but lies on the continental shelf of another state?

• In this case, according to what principles should an exclusive economic zone around Jan Mayen be delimited from the zones around Iceland and Greenland (article 74)?

The Jan Mayen question was thus a complex problem with implications for security policy. Both Norway and Iceland were anxious to arrive at an understanding. There was never any prospect of a 'capelin war'. On the contrary: the negotiations were conducted in a friendly spirit. Iceland gained a hearing for its claim to an undiminished 200-mile exclusive economic zone including the area adjacent to Jan Mayen. The catch of capelin was divided so that Iceland received 85 per cent, against only 15 per cent for Norway.[15]

The Icelandic–Norwegian agreement of 1981 concerning the continental shelf was based on the recommendations of a conciliation board consisting of three experts on the law of the sea.

The conciliation board started from the assumption that, in terms of international law, Jan Mayen must be considered to be an island with a right to its own territorial sea, its own exclusive economic zone, and its own continental shelf. At the same time, the board referred to the norms of the Convention on the Law of the Sea which are to be applied when drawing boundaries between the exclusive economic zones (article 74) and continental shelves (article 83) of adjacent or opposite states. The board also referred to the reasoning of the International Court of Justice in the North Sea Continental Shelf Cases.[16]

'The three wise men' arrived at a Solomonic solution. Iceland and Norway should jointly exploit the natural resources of the continental shelf just south of Jan Mayen. If oil or gas is found in this area, the prospecting oil company will receive 50 per cent of the income, with the remainder to be divided equally between Iceland and Norway.

Geological studies on and around Jan Mayen show that the entire Jan Mayen Ridge consists of sedimentary rocks, which can in theory contain gas and oil.

Rockall

There may also be oil deep in the older layers of rock in the Hatton-Rockall area. This is the conclusion of Icelandic geologists after preliminary measurements of sediments in 1989.

Rockall—a granite rock located about 400 kilometres north-west of

Ireland and 300 kilometres west of the Scottish island of St Kilda—
was claimed by Britain in 1860. The upper part of the rock is covered
with the white droppings of breeding seabirds. The rock, which rises
21 metres above the sea, stands out like a ship with swelling white
sails. Like Kolbeinsey, Rockall is an example of the kind of rock
(Icelandic *klettur*) defined in article 121:3 of the Convention on the
Law of the Sea. To speak of 'the island of Rockall' is thus a contradiction in terms.[17]

Since 1980 Iceland has claimed parts of the Hatton-Rockall shelf.
These claims were made concrete in 1985.[18] Denmark has also claimed
part of this shelf on behalf of the Faroe Islands.

Other interested parties are Britain and Ireland. These two states
have signed an agreement about sharing the seabed between them.

Iceland's claim—in accordance with article 76 of the Convention
on the Law of the Sea—comprises 350 nautical miles of the continental shelf on the Reykjanes Ridge and its offshoot (in the west as far as
the boundary of Greenland's exclusive economic zone), and also the
parts of the shelf around Hatton-Rockall which are outside the exclusive economic zones of Denmark, Britain, and Ireland. The Icelanders
maintain—on geological and other grounds—that these parts of the
Hatton-Rockall shelf are the natural prolongation of Iceland's land
territory and continental shelf.

In support of their claim, the Icelanders say that they can draw a
continuous line south, straight through the disputed area, to mark the
slope of the Icelandic continental shelf. It would not be possible for
the British or Irish to draw a continuous line, since the 2,500-metre-
deep Rockall Trough separates the Rockall area from the British Isles.
The Rockall Trough is a rift valley formed 200 million years ago.
Geologically speaking, then, the Rockall area is not part of the British
Isles.

Britain has categorically opposed the Icelandic claim to parts of the
Hatton-Rockall shelf. In the British view, the lack of any geological,
geomorphological, or geographical connection between Iceland and
this shelf area means that there is no valid basis for the Icelandic claim.

There are thus two diametrically opposed views.

The discussion about Rockall and Kolbeinsey has gone on for some
time. We may safely agree with the seasoned diplomats who predict

that the evaluation of the rival claims to the Hatton-Rockall shelf area will keep international lawyers fully occupied for many years to come.

The Icelandic government has tried to break the deadlock by suggesting that boundary negotiations should be conducted at a high level. Alternatively, the four affected coastal states could try to arrive at a compromise by which they can jointly conduct research and exploit the natural resources of the Rockall area.[19] The Icelanders have invoked the model of the settlement concerning Jan Mayen. The Icelandic expert on the law of the sea, Hans G. Andersen, has described this as 'unique in the history of international law'.

The Polar Zone and the North-East Passage

The polar explorer Vilhjálmur Stefánsson (1879–1962)—known for his expeditions to the Eskimos at the estuary of the Mackenzie River in Canada's Northwest Territories, to the Colville Delta on the north coast of Alaska, to Coronation Gulf, Wrangel Island, and other Arctic regions, and for his hypothesis about the blond Eskimos in northern Canada—was born in Canada of Icelandic parents.

The Icelanders continue to take a keen interest in the polar areas of the North Atlantic. Each generation takes up the torch. As regards polar research today, the searchlight is pointed at sea ice (drift-ice, pack-ice, icebergs, vast areas of ice) and theories about how temperatures in the polar zone affect the climate in Iceland.[20]

In 1982 the Icelandic meteorologist and expert on sea ice Þór Jakobsson was the only foreigner to take part in a Soviet expedition by ice-breaker along the east coast of Greenland. His report on the expedition led him to hear of an inspiring mission. Could the North-East Passage—the sea route between the Atlantic and the Pacific north of Europe and Asia and through the Bering Strait—be used in summer as an international trade route? The trip from London to Tokyo via the North-East Passage (7,000 nautical miles) would be only half as long as the route via the Cape of Good Hope (14,200 nautical miles). It would also be shorter than the routes via the Panama Canal (12,400 nautical miles) and the Suez Canal (11,000 nautical miles).

What had been a bold, outstanding achievement for the Swedish polar explorer Adolf Nordenskiöld (1832–1901) could now be technically possible, thanks to powerful ice-breakers and reports of ice via satellite. Moreover, we may assume that the ice-sheet north of Asia will become thinner as a result of global warming, the so-called greenhouse effect of environmental pollution. Perhaps a shipping route via the North-East Passage could be commercially viable. If so, what role can Iceland play?

On 8 October 1987 an international conference on 'The Arctic Sea Route' was held in Reykjavík.[21] The conference got off to a flying start. One week earlier, Mikhail Gorbachev made a speech in Murmansk, in which he in principle opened the North-East Passage to foreign ships assisted by Soviet ice-breakers. The wording of the speech recalled the conciliatory 'Reykjavík spirit' which characterized the summit meeting between Gorbachev and Reagan at Höfði in October 1986.

At first sight this idea may appear unrealistic, but surely nothing is impossible for mankind in the space age. The Russians sent up their first Sputnik in 1957. Just twelve years later, in 1969, the Americans took their first steps on the moon. Before the expedition, the astronauts had prepared themselves by training in the lava landscape of Iceland. But that is a different story.

As regards the North-East Passage, developments have been promising. Since the 1987 conference in Reykjavík, there has been steady progress in promoting the idea of a commercial transarctic sea route during the four months of the year when heavy ice in the Arctic is very much reduced. This possibility has been further discussed at international conferences, and a limited interest has been maintained by Icelandic authorities and politicians.

An important change concerns the great interest shown by the Russians in offering services to countries willing to try the 'Northern Sea Route' between the North Atlantic and the Pacific. On 14 September 1990 the Soviet Minister of the Merchant Marine approved 'Regulations for Navigation on the Seaways of the Northern Sea Route'. Since 1991 ice-going cargo vessels have made a few trips from Murmansk to the Pacific by way of the Northern Sea Route.

Developments are proceeding rapidly. At the invitation of the Government of Canada, eight Arctic states (including Iceland) have started to explore the possibilities of establishing an inter-governmental coɔperation procedure organized as an Arctic Council. The first meeting for this purpose took place in Ottawa in 1992.

Nothing, however, will promote the use of the Arctic Sea Route as effectively as continued research in the area, in the fields of geophysics, biology, and sociology alike. Since the end of the Cold War there have been some delays in the research activities of scientists of the former Soviet Union. On the other hand, increased possibilities of cooperation between scientists of all nations will in a few years fulfil the hope of great progress in northern studies.

Many international projects in the Arctic are under way or being planned. Three examples may be mentioned: (a) the diverse 'Arctic Climate System Study' organized by the global network the World Meteorological Organization of the United Nations; (b) the more concentrated Nansen Centennial Arctic Programme initiated by Norway; (c) an interesting research project planned by the Commonwealth of Independent States, named 'The Influence of Changes in the Arctic Environment on Global Processes'.

Threats to the Marine Environment

Have we just seen the tip of the
iceberg?
*Magnús Jóhannesson, Director of
Shipping*

Pollution Knows No Boundaries

The clear air of Iceland is famous for its freshness. The water in the ocean currents around the fishing banks has been shown by tests to be incredibly clean—a prime sales argument for Icelandic fish. Iceland lies far from the industrial centres of the western world. It has no oil refineries, just a few industries, and a relatively small merchant fleet. The population is small. They mostly use environment-friendly sources of energy such as hydroelectric power and geothermal energy.

Despite—or perhaps because of—this, the Icelanders are concerned about anything which can pollute the sea or spoil the air. They have started to combat pollution on the home front. Their research and inspection efforts comprise hazards such as factory emissions and car exhaust fumes,[22] heavy metals in the manufacture of aluminium and ferrosilicon,[23] bans on the import and use of PCBs, and nutrient excesses caused by fish farming. In addition, they have taken action to pick up oil residues, plastic waste, and lost fishing gear.

Most of their anxiety, however, is caused by the sort of pollution which comes from outside Iceland, knowing no boundaries. One such problem is the contamination of the sea by radioactive matter and persistent organic substances, especially because of the rather strong currents from other oceans and pelagic fish wandering with the currents.

In 1986 the disaster at the Ukrainian nuclear power station of Chernobyl made people aware of the dangers. It showed that nuclear accidents can cause long-term damage to the economic life and environment of distant countries. Radioactive fallout from Chernobyl descended over large areas of continental Europe. There was much less fallout over Iceland, partly because of the distance, partly because the weather was in Iceland's favour at the time. Yet the North Atlantic is constantly being crossed by nuclear-powered submarines carrying nuclear arms. Frequent submarine accidents should serve as a warning signal.

Another headache for Iceland is the shipping of radioactive substances, oil, and dangerous chemicals. Transports like these should be undertaken with the maximum of caution. Supertankers full of oil are not welcome in the Arctic Sea, where the flora and fauna are particularly sensitive. The low temperatures delay the evaporation of floating oil.

Even for distant Iceland, then, it is urgent to prevent other nations from dumping oil and radioactive waste in the sea, for example, from nuclear power stations and reprocessing plants for reactor fuel, such as the one planned at Dounreay in Scotland. Radioactivity, oil, and toxic industrial waste follow the ocean currents along the coast of Norway to Spitsbergen. They then head west towards Greenland and follow the east coast of Greenland south towards Icelandic waters. The poisons are diluted on this long journey. Radioactivity in the sea north of Iceland is only a hundredth of what it is in the North Sea.

The National Institute of Radiation Protection (founded in 1967) has carried out regular studies of radioactivity. This has been measured in rainwater, grass and moss, and in foodstuffs such as meat, fish, and milk. Natural gamma radiation from the ground is very low in Iceland, since the bedrock is mainly basalt and other volcanic rock.

Transports by ocean currents usually take four to six years to reach Iceland from the North Sea. There is nevertheless a risk that poisonous substances in the North Sea can be brought to Iceland much more quickly by shoals of pelagic fish, such as blue whiting and herring. In view of the direction of currents in this part of the North Atlantic, an oil spill from Jan Mayen could be disastrous for the Icelandic fisheries, the life-blood of the Icelandic people.

The Icelanders observe what has happened in the North Sea and its coastal areas in recent years. They are worried that the environmental damage will be worse in the future. Have we just seen the tip of the iceberg? Since its foundation in 1929, the Directorate of Shipping has been responsible for the protection of the Icelandic waters from pollution. The Director of Shipping, Magnús Jóhannesson, points out that we know far too little about the long-term damage to life in the sea caused by such persistent substances as PCBs, DDT, and dioxins. These hazardous substances are carried by air from continent to continent and are precipitated in cool climates. They are amassed in large quantities over the polar areas. The effects of these poisons may not be discovered until it is too late to prevent the damage. It is therefore necessary to arrive at internationally agreed demands for a reversed burden of proof in these matters. This would mean that no substances may be discharged at sea unless it has been proved that they do not cause pollution of any kind.

Iceland is therefore whole-hearted in her support of demands for firm measures against environmental destruction. Iceland has established a special 'pollution zone'. It covers the entire continental shelf area outside Iceland's exclusive economic zone—south towards Rockall—which Iceland claims. [24]

Ecological Disturbances

Iceland's continental shelf and the fishing banks there provide a habitat for a wide range of marine life. There are rich stocks of fish from 150 different species, such as cod, haddock, halibut, and herring, and shellfish such as prawns and Norway lobsters. There are fair numbers of fin whales, sei whales, and minke whales (all baleen whales), and an estimated 50,000 common seals and 10,000 grey seals. All these fish, crustaceans, and mammals compete with each other and with huge flocks of sea birds for the food in the ocean.

Around the coasts of Iceland it is common to see clumps of seaweed which have floated ashore. They give only a hint of the range of nutrition that is found in the sea. The lowest nutrient in the food chain consists of microscopically small algae (plant plankton) which live on minerals and other inorganic substances in the water. Some algae are luminous, producing a phosphorescent glow known as sea-fire. The Icelandic waters contains tens of millions of tons of algae.[25] They are the basis of all life in the sea, starting with the equally microscopic crustaceans (animal plankton) which live on the algae. This plankton is eaten by, for example, herring and capelin, which are then eaten by bigger fish, seals, and whales. Plankton thus feeds higher forms of life in a long chain. At the bottom of the sea, demersal species like cod feed on crustaceans, starfish, sea-urchin shells, worms, molluscs, and other delicacies.

The currents that flow around the coasts of Iceland are of crucial importance for all life in the sea. Warm water, with a high salt content and a deep blue colour, is brought from the Caribbean Sea by the Gulf Stream. It flows through the Gulf of Mexico (hence the name), along the east coast of North America, where it joins the North Atlantic Drift to be carried across towards Europe.

The branch of the Gulf Stream which mellows the climate of Iceland flows around the south and west coasts. In the north it meets cold polar currents from eastern Greenland and the Arctic Sea.

The temperature of the water in the sea is not constant. It changes from time to time as a result of the fluctuating strength of the various currents. In years when the cold masses of water predominate and approach the coast, the quantity of algae falls, and with it the supply of small crustaceans. The shortage of food then reverberates up the food chain, affecting the fish, mammals, and birds at the top.[26]

In other words, the ecological balance in the sea is sensitive. It can also be upset by human interference, such as over-fishing with fine-meshed trawls, which sweep the bottom of the sea like vacuum cleaners, completely devastating the fish stocks. They also kill small fish.[27] Moreover, excessively large catches of one species can affect the supply of fish of other species. In the period 1980–2, for example, the stocks of capelin fell by about 90 per cent. The serious aspect was that cod stocks declined at the same time by about 25 per cent, since capelin is an important part of the diet of the cod.

For marine biologists, then, it is increasingly important to find out who eats whom in the sea, when, in what quantities, and in what circumstances.

According to marine biological research, both seals and whales are large-scale consumers of food. Seals swallow enormous quantities of commercially valuable fish, including cod fry, small cod up to the age of four, saithe, halibut, and catfish. Besides, the seals spread intestinal worms to these fish, which is a serious economic problem for the fishing industry and a worry for those who sell Icelandic fish to foreign markets.

The marine biologists draw two conclusions. Firstly, it is important when establishing fishing quotas to take into consideration the entire complex interplay between different fish species and mammals, and the total yield of the sea's resources. Secondly, it is essential to conserve all the species and to be sensible about the way they are exploited. If the Icelanders fail to do so, their country's resources will be reduced, and they will have a smaller inheritance to hand on to coming generations.

Icelandic Whaling

There was plenty of everything. . . .
Whales often got stranded.

Egils saga Skalla-Grímssonar, ch. 29

Historical Background

When Flóki Vilgerðarson, Skalla-Grímur, and other Scandinavians settled by the fiords of Iceland, they noticed the occurrence of whales,

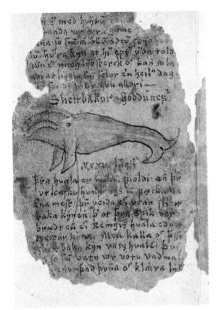

*To the left, the blue whale (*balaenoptera musculus*). To the right, the sperm whale (*physeter macrocephalus*). — Photos from illustrations in medieval Icelandic manuscripts, which are preserved in the National Library of Iceland. The Latin names of these whales are recorded in the Systema Naturae of 1758 by the Swedish scholar Carl von Linné.*

not infrequently whales which got stranded. Several Icelandic sagas tell of this.[28] The most striking feature of these old accounts is the way people quarrelled about how stranded whales were to be divided. Ever since the colonization (*landnám*) of Iceland, whale meat has been a part of the Icelandic diet. Sometimes the disputes led to killings. In the legal codex *Jónsbók*, which was drawn up in 1281 by the lawman Jón Einarsson at the behest of King Magnús lagabætir (Magnus the Law-amender), king of Norway, there is a special section on the procedure for establishing ownership of harpooned and stranded whales.[29]

Icelandic waters have traditionally harboured large stocks of whale. They have been decimated by foreign whalers but are now recovering. Towards the end of the 1980s, according to careful counts, there were still relatively high numbers of whales in these waters. These colossal beasts are part of the riches of the sea. The blue whale, which has been a protected species around Iceland since 1959, can reach lengths of nearly 30 metres and weigh up to 150 tons. It is the biggest animal that has ever lived on earth. The sea around Iceland also has about ten other species of whales which can be described as frequent, besides which it is visited occasionally by a few species from both arctic and warm seas.[30]

It is understandable that whales have always captured the imagination of the Icelanders. In *Konungs skuggsjá* (*The King's Mirror*), a thirteenth-century Norwegian handbook for princes, we read that there is nothing in the waters around Iceland as memorable and renowned as the whales. Their existence was associated with a great deal of folklore. Whales occur in some Icelandic legends.[31]

The Icelanders themselves claim that before 1948 they mainly caught whales for local or domestic consumption (except for certain commercial whaling by Norwegian ships in the years 1935–9 at Tálknafjörður in the north-west corner of Iceland). Whaling on a large scale was once pursued around Iceland—as around the Faroe Islands, Spitsbergen, and in the other oceans of the world—but by foreign fishermen. First came the Basques, then the British, the Dutch, and from the end of the nineteenth century also the Norwegians. The whale-blubber was boiled to produce train-oil, which was used to light the streets of European towns and Icelandic homes, where reeking train-oil lamps spread their flickering light. The horn-plates[32] of baleen whales were used to stiffen ladies' dresses and make them stand out; crinolines are a typical example of the whims of fashion which have from time to time afflicted free-born animals and birds.

With the advent of steam, mechanized harpooning techniques (an explosive harpoon was designed in 1868), and whale-ships with processing plants for boiling the blubber, whaling degenerated. It became an unrestricted slaughter. This led to a number of protest meetings in Iceland. In 1915 the Althing prohibited all whaling.[33] Thus Iceland at an early stage became one of the leading nations in conserving whale stocks which had been subject to over-exploitation.

The Present Day

After the Second World War the Icelanders began to catch whale themselves. Commercial whaling was pursued from 1948 to 1985, and whaling for scientific purposes from 1986 to 1989. This was criticized by international environmental organizations such as Greenpeace and Sea Shepherd. The Icelanders, however, claim that the whaling was done on a strictly regulated scale and in consultation with the Scientific Committee of the International Whaling Commission (IWC). Large whales (fin whales and sei whales, along with sperm whales) were harpooned from four specially equipped ships. They operated in deep waters off the west coast of Iceland, but within the present 200-mile exclusive economic zone. The ships towed the harpooned whales to a land-based processing plant at Hvalfjörður north of Reykjavík. This fiord has taken its name from the whales that have been seen there since the first settlement of Iceland. The smaller minke whales were caught from ordinary small fishing vessels.

Iceland's catch for 1979 was 440 large whales. By 1989 this figure had been reduced to 68 fin whales. The reduction was the result of a decision by the IWC to introduce a moratorium, a temporary ban on commercial whaling in the period 1986–90. The Icelanders made no reservations against the IWC decision, which they respected. Iceland, however, exercised the right established by the International Convention for the Regulation of Whaling, allowing the signatory governments to authorize whaling for scientific purposes.[34]

This scientific whaling—including extensive measures to count, photograph, and mark whales—was conducted between 1986 and 1989 under the auspices of the Marine Research Institute, Reykjavík, in consultation with the IWC and in collaboration with marine biologists from other states. The aim was to increase knowledge about the size of the Icelandic whale stocks, their age, reproduction, migrations, and the conditions for their existence. Many research ships and aeroplanes took part in the research. The results have shown that the two species—fin whales and minke whales—which were caught in the largest numbers after the Second World War still seem to be in a healthy state. Estimates show that the stocks in the area between Greenland, Iceland, and Jan Mayen number 15,000–16,000 fin whales and around 28,000 minke whales.

Since 1990 until this year (1992), no whales have been caught in Icelandic waters, not even for scientific purposes.

Icelandic Whaling: Opponents and Supporters

The endless debate about whaling has generated more heat than light. The opposing parties find it difficult to arrive at a common language free of emotion. They would benefit from a proper study of each other's arguments.

Representatives of environmental movements around the world have pointed out that whaling has been a tragic business ever since the seventeenth century. It has been condemned as 'one of many deterrent examples of the way mankind has failed to husband the earth's living resources.' In many oceans, whaling has led to the near-total elimination of some species, such as the Greenland whale and the blue whale. Most species have been reduced to a few per cent of their original numbers. Global stocks of the biggest whale, the blue whale, according to a cautious estimate, have been reduced from around 200,000 to 2,000–4,000 individuals. Man may believe himself to be wise but does not always act in accordance with the designation *Homo sapiens.* At present the situation is different for different species of whale. According to the conservationists, some species, like the Greenland whale and the sperm whale, are threatened with extinction. Others ought to be given a chance to recover. The whale stocks should be seen as a living natural resource which the whole world owns in common. The environmental movements do not believe in any talk of whaling for scientific purposes. They regard this as hypocrisy.

Among those who advocate a ban on whaling, there are people—including a few Icelandic animal-lovers and conservationists—who say that it is cruel in principle to kill whales and other large mammals. Other opponents of whaling stress the alleged lack of reliable data on the size of whale stocks and the conditions necessary for their existence.

The supporters of Icelandic whaling warn against generalized conclusions. They naturally agree with the environmental movements that the whale stocks must not be exterminated. But they refer to scientific studies from 1986 to 1989 which show that the survival of most whale species in Iceland's part of the North Atlantic is still not at risk. No one in the Scientific Committee of the IWC would claim that the whale stocks around Iceland are threatened with extinction.

The overwhelming majority of the Icelandic people concur in the view that the whale stocks around Iceland—just like the fish stocks—are a natural resource which can and should be exploited if the catch is carefully limited by quotas. Moreover, the Icelanders are concerned that an end to whaling may have troublesome consequences. It will eventually lead to a growing stock of whales. These are large-scale consumers of food, mostly in the form of plankton and krill, as well as capelin, herring, and cod. Disproportionately large stocks of whales and seals could therefore lead to unwanted disturbances to the ecological balance and have a detrimental effect on the Icelandic fisheries.

Whales are a part of the marine ecological system. This also includes other resources, especially the fish stocks, which are the basis for the survival of the Icelandic people. Any significant growth in the number of whales may have a long-term effect on this vital ecosystem.[35]

Iceland Leaves the International Whaling Commission

The Icelandic government has declared its withdrawal from the International Convention for the Regulation of Whaling and also from the IWC, with effect from 30 June 1992. The declaration points out that the IWC has frequently disregarded the advice of its own Scientific Committee. This has serious consequences for Iceland. 'The economic and social fabric of this island nation is overwhelmingly dependent on the health and productivity of the surrounding marine environment. Whales have an important ecological role in the Icelandic exclusive economic zone; they consume more than the amount of seafood that our fishermen harvest. Whales must, therefore, be treated in the same manner as other resources, subject to the same management principles.'

Iceland has not yet decided to resume whaling, but has participated in the establishment of a regional organization for the effective conservation and rational management of whales and seals in the North Atlantic. Other full members of this regional organization are the

Faroe Islands, Greenland, and Norway. Their aim is to safeguard the future of the marine mammal stocks in the north-eastern part of the Atlantic Ocean. At the same time, regulated harvesting will be allowed under scientific control only, and the needs of the northern fishing communities will be taken into account.

Conclusion

The chasm between the opposing views of the big international environmental movements and the coastal nations in the North-East Atlantic—the Faroes, Greenland, Iceland, and Norway—appears to be incapable of being bridged. The situation is a stalemate. It has been so for years. Rudyard Kipling's winged words come to mind:[36]

> Oh, East is East, and West is West and never the twain shall meet.

In the long term, however, this prediction has been shown to be incorrect. Or rather, Kipling has been misinterpreted. In the subsequent lines he goes on to show that people *can* bridge the distances:

> But there is neither East nor West, Border, nor Breed, nor Birth,
> When two strong men stand face to face, though they come from the ends of the earth!

Feelings of hostility and alienation can be surmounted. Research and increased insight create room for broad-mindedness and forbearance. We may hope for a future when there will be greater mutual understanding between the environmentalists and the island nations of the North Atlantic who depend for their living on the bounties of the sea. As regards most of the overall environmental issues, their values do in fact coincide.

Notes to Chapter 8

1   See Chapter 5, 'Communications by Sea'.

2   See Chapter 1, 'Reformation and Cod Wars', and Chapter 5, 'The New Law of the Sea and the Cod Wars'. See also Hannes Jónsson, *Friends in Conflict: The Anglo-Icelandic Cod Wars and the Law of the Sea* (London: Hurst, 1982), pp. 178–87.

3   *Svarfdæla saga*, ed. Jónas Kristjánsson in *Eyfirðinga sögur*, Íslenzk fornrit 9

(Reykjavík: Hið íslenzka fornritafélag, 1956). There is as yet no English translation of this saga. Other toponymic explanations have been suggested for Kolbeinsey: the name Kolbeinn, like other place-names in *Kol-*, has been interpreted as 'dark, straight cliff'.

4   Jón Árnason, *Íslenzkar þjóðsögur og æfintýri*, reissue in 6 vols. (Reykjavík: Þjóðsaga, 1961), vol. 2, pp. 127–8.

5   Article 121:3 of the Convention on the Law of the Sea states: 'Rocks which cannot sustain human habitation or economic life of their own shall have no exclusive economic zone or continental shelf.'

6   Report in *Morgunblaðið*, 14 June 1988, entitled 'Þetta var önnur veröld, engu lík' (This was a different world, not like any other).

7   Hannes Jónsson, *Friends in Conflict*, p. 187.

8   The following details have been provided by the Ministry of Fisheries on fishing quotas granted to foreign vessels: *Belgium* (three trawlers), 1,701 tons in 1991, 548 tons of this being cod. *Faroes* (vessels with long lines and hand lines), 6,500 tons of demersal fish in 1992, 1,000 tons of this being cod. The last season in which Norwegian vessels were granted fishing rights was 1989.

9   When setting fish quotas, the Ministry of Fisheries usually bases its decisions on the recommendations of the marine biologists, but for reasons of regional politics or economics the scientific advice is not always followed fully.

10   *Svalbarð,* or derivatives of it, is a common farm-name in Iceland, meaning a 'cool edge'. When applied to Jan Mayen, it probably refers to the ice-capped volcano Beerenberg (2,340 m). Svalbard is also another name for Spitsbergen.

11   *Biskupa sögur* II, *Guðmundar saga Arasonar*, ed. Guðni Jónsson (Reykjavík: Íslendingasagnaútgáfan, 1953), ch. 23; see also *The Book of Settlements: Landnámabók*, trans. Hermann Pálsson and Paul Edwards (Winnipeg: University of Manitoba Press, 1972), p. 16.

12   This and other details in this section mostly come from Sigurður Líndal's *Island og det gamle Svalbard* (Reykjavík, 1980).

13   The letter from the Icelandic government was reproduced in bill no. 27 of 1928 to the Norwegian parliament, concerning the incorporation of Jan Mayen into Norway. This was a *de facto* recognition by Norway of the Icelandic reservation.

14   *International Court of Justice Reports* 1973, pp. 37–40. Cf. Björn Bjarnason, 'Noen islandske synspunkter i Jan Mayen-saken', *Internasjonal Politikk* 4 (1979).

15   A modified version of the agreement, taking into account the interests of Greenland in the area, was signed in 1989. It grants Iceland 78 per cent of the capelin catch, as against 11 per cent each for Norway and Greenland. This agreement was renewed with minor changes in 1992.

16   *International Court of Justice Reports* 1969, p. 51.

17   English popular etymology would probably interpret Rockall as 'all rock'. In fact, the name is a compound of the Old Norse words *rok* 'storm' and *karl* 'man'. The Icelanders sometimes use *karl* to refer to a lone rock rising high out of the sea.

18   Icelandic Regulation dated 9 May 1985, *Stjórnatíðindi* B 19.

19   Letter from Steingrímur Hermannsson, prime minister of Iceland, to Margaret Thatcher, prime minister of the United Kingdom, 24 February 1989.

20   Markús Á. Einarsson, 'Climate of Iceland', chapter 7 in vol. 15 of *World Survey of Climatology* (Oxford: Elsevier, 1984), pp. 673–97.

21   The proceedings of the conference were published as *The Arctic Sea Route* (1987); see p. 121. Cf. the International Conference of the Arctic and Nordic Countries on Coordination of Research in the Arctic (Leningrad, 12–15 December 1985), the Swedish *Ymer* expedition of 1980, published as *Expedition Ymer-80*, vol. 101 of *Ymer* (1981), and *Arctic News-Record: Polar Bulletin* 7 (1991), no. 5.

22   See Chapter 6, 'Ecological Problems'.

23   See Chapter 6, 'Iceland's Economy and the Surrounding World'.

24   Gunnar G. Schram, *Verndun hafsins, hafréttarsáttmálinn og íslensk lög* (Protection of the Sea, the Convention on the Law of the Sea and Icelandic Law) (Reykjavík: Bókaútgáfa Orators, 1988).

25   'The quantity of algae is so great that there are instances of 90 million algae being found in just one litre of sea water.' Ingvar Hallgrímsson, 'Lífið í sjónum', in *Náttúra Íslands*, 2nd ed. (Reykjavík: Almenna Bókafélagið, 1981), p. 440.

26   Ibid., pp. 439–47. See also *Iceland 1986: Handbook Published by the Central Bank of Iceland* (Reykjavík, 1987), pp. 147–8.

27   See Chapter 5, 'Frontiers at Sea: The Background'.

28   See, for example, *Landnámabók*, *Egils saga*, *Fóstbræðra saga*, and *Grettis saga*.

29   *Jónsbók*, ed. Ólafur Halldórsson (Copenhagen, 1904), ch. 62, 'Um festing á hval'. King Magnús lagabætir (1238–80) was son of King Hákon Hákonarson 'the Old', who had brought Iceland and Greenland under his rule.

30   Details provided by the Marine Research Institute. See also Jóhann Sigurjónsson, Þ. Gunnlaugsson, and M. Payne, 1989. 'Nass-87: Shipboard Sightings Surveys in Icelandic and Adjacent Waters June–July 1987', *Report of the International Whaling Commission* 39 (1989), pp. 395–409.

31   *The King's Mirror*, trans. Laurence Marcellus Larson (New York, 1917). See also Chapter 3, 'Folk Belief and Folktales'.

32   The commonly used word 'whalebone' is scarcely adequate; a better term is 'baleen-plate', to describe the series of thin, parallel horny plates through which baleen whales consume food, not using any teeth. Although Aristotle described the dolphins not as fish but as mammals, whales were generally referred to as 'whale-fish' until the Swedish botanist Carolus Linnaeus (Carl von Linné) classified whales as mammals in his *Systema Naturae* in 1758.

33   See Trausti Einarsson, *Hvalveiðar við Ísland 1600–1939* (Reykjavík: Bókaútgáfa Menningarsjóðs, 1987), and Lúðvík Kristjánsson, *Íslenzkir sjávarhættir* 5, with a summary in English (Reykjavík: Bókaútgáfa Menningarsjóðs, 1986).

34   'For purposes of scientific research', article VIII of the International Convention for the Regulation of Whaling (1946). The sperm whale has been declared a protected species since 1983. This toothed cetacean, according to Icelandic

marine biologists, is polygamous, mating in warm waters, presumably north of the Equator. A large number of males are left without partners and migrate northwards. It was these solitary males, mostly aged 21–30, which were caught in Icelandic waters. They were probably not necessary for the survival of the sperm whale stocks.

35   Extract from a letter of 13 April 1989 from the Icelandic embassy in London to The Sunday Times.

36   Rudyard Kipling, *The Ballad of East and West* (New York: Manfield & Wessels, 1899).

❧{ Chapter 9 }❧

Volcanoes and Their Effects

Iceland: A Volcanic Island in the Atlantic

I will venture to pronounce, that
Iceland has been formed by eruptions
of fire.

Uno von Troil, Letters on Iceland

UNO VON TROIL'S ABSORBING DESCRIPTION of Iceland's 'fire-spouting mountains' and 'hot spouting water-springs' is one of countless examples of the power of the Icelandic landscape to etch itself indelibly in the memory of every traveller to Iceland. The Swedish theologian was blinded by the beautiful sight of the waters and steaming springs of Laugarvatn—a lake to the west of the sulphur-reeking volcano Hekla, 'abode of the damned'—gleaming in the morning sun:[1]

> The morning was uncommonly clear, and the sun had already begun to gild the tops of the neighbouring mountains; it was so perfect a calm, that the lake on which some swans were swimming was as smooth as a looking-glass; and round about it rose, in eight different places, the steam of the hot springs, which gradually disappeared high up in the air.

Albert Engström is also lyrical when, panting with satisfaction and dripping with sweat after climbing along black lava tracks and an uncannily steep crater wall, he finally looks around from the summit of Hekla:[2]

> The vision is crystal-clear—not a cloud in the sky! Half of Iceland lies like a sunlit relief map below us, around us.
> The glaciers glisten in the sun. The silver ribbons of rivers vein the

enormous expanses, green fields and hills shine like patches of life in the landscape, deserts spread out their dead surfaces.

'Glacier' is the usual translation for the word *jökull*, although many of the Icelandic glaciers are technically ice-caps. About 11 per cent of the surface of Iceland is covered with glaciers, including Vatnajökull (8,300 km²), Langjökull (953 km²), Hofsjökull (925 km²), Mýrdalsjökull (596 km²), Drangajökull (160 km²), and Eyjafjallajökull (77.5 km²). Vatnajökull is the biggest glacier in the world outside the Arctic regions.

Under Vatnajökull's glistening expanses of snow and ice lies Grímsvötn, an active volcano. There are likewise active volcanoes under, for example, Öræfajökull, Eyjafjallajökull, and Mýrdalsjökull (with the volcano Katla). When these volcanoes erupt, parts of the glaciers melt. This causes huge amounts of water to flow towards the sea. This kind of glacial outburst is known as *jökulhlaup*—even in English geophysical terminology. The most famous of the slowly sliding Icelandic glaciers (*skriðjöklar*) are Breiðamerkurjökull and Skeiðarárjökull, both on the southern edge of Vatnajökull. On their way to the sea, they both form lagoons of icebergs calved from the glaciers. Sometimes they are drained by glacial outbursts.

It is with good reason that Iceland has been given names like 'the land of contrasts' and 'the land of fire and ice'.[3] It is in fact one of the most volcanic countries in the world—Iceland, which shakes and trembles when the chained Loki violently jerks his fetters. On the central plateau there are over a hundred volcanoes which have not erupted in the past thousand years, and about thirty still active volcanoes such as Hekla, Öræfajökull, Eyjafjallajökull, Katla, Askja, and Krafla. The most active of the Icelandic volcanoes, measured in terms of the number of eruptions, are Grímsvötn, Hekla, Katla, Askja, and Krafla.

The town of Vestmannaeyjar on the island of Heimaey off the south coast of Iceland has enjoyed long prosperity thanks to the fishing. It is built on the slopes of the 'extinct' volcano Helgafell. The description proved to be illusory on 23 January 1973. After a few earth tremors the day before, that night saw the start of a violent, fiery eruption (Icelandic *eldgos*, literally 'fire-gush') which lasted for several months. The flow of lava threatened the houses and the fishing harbour. By the early summer, when the outburst finally stopped, a third of the town had been covered with lava and ash.

The view from Reykjavík offers many wonderful sights. To the south-west, in the same direction as Keflavík, the horizon displays the characteristic silhouette of the mountain Keilir. It was created during the Ice Age out of tuff and breccia (hyaloclastite) by a volcanic eruption under the ice. The perfect conical shape of Keilir is reminiscent of the highest mountain in Japan, Fujiyama.

Volcanic eruptions and earthquakes are a part of the destiny of the Icelandic people. In historical times, eruptions of varying intensity have occurred on average every five years. The whole island has been built up of volcanic material consisting of lava, stone, gravel, sand, and ash. Parts of Iceland are frequently shaken by earth tremors. Catastrophic earthquakes occur at longer intervals than the volcanic eruptions. Some of the worst earthquakes devastated large areas of southern Iceland in 1784 and 1896.

Geologists predict new earthquakes in southern Iceland. Volcanoes can also erupt at any time. Will the next eruption be at Askja, Katla, or Hekla? Eruptions and earthquakes mostly come unexpectedly, or at least without many advance warnings. The 1973 eruption on Heimaey is a good example of this.

A third of all the lava that has covered the earth's surface since the Middle Ages has erupted in Iceland.[4] This estimate, however, does not include submarine eruptions. According to a recent geological hypothesis, these are much more extensive than those on the land surface, and mostly associated with the large crustal plate boundaries.

On the geological time-scale, which is counted in billions of years, Iceland is one of the youngest countries on the planet. It was created when the huge land-mass of Eurasia-America was split. The Eurasian Plate was separated from the North American Plate, and Norway from Greenland. In the North Atlantic, where the plates are diverging, Iceland rose from the sea as a ridge. The splitting process has been going on for 50–60 million years, and for the last four million years the rate of divergence has been on average 2 cm/year.[5] This may seem trifling, but one should consider that it means a difference of 2 metres in 100 years, and 20 metres in 1,000 years. One effect is volcanic eruptions with glowing flows of magma from the interior of the earth.

This occurs at vents and fissures which the geologists call volcanoes, after the Roman god of fire and smithcraft, Vulcan, the counterpart of the Greek Hephaestus.

Geologists assume that some Icelandic *central volcanoes* split laterally along linear fissures. This means that lava can spout up from right under the volcano or tens of kilometres from it. Krafla is an example of a volcano with a system of fissures.

In the latter part of the Tertiary Period—from 20 to 2 million years before the present—Iceland had a warm climate. During part of this period, its flora was similar to the subtropical vegetation of Florida today. The Tertiary was followed by the Quaternary, the period in which we now live. During the last one million years of the Tertiary and the Quarternary until ten thousand years ago, the ice age reigned. During this ice age recurrent glaciations almost entirely covered Iceland with continuous ice sheets in alternation with warmer spells. These are called glacial and interglacial periods.

The last Ice Age came to an end about 10,000 years ago. The glaciers are a reminder of that time. In this land of ice and fire, the glaciers frequently compete for space with geothermal springs. In the mountain area of Kverkfjöll, on the north side of Vatnajökull, the tourist can enjoy a hot bath inside an ice cave right under the glacier.

Zones of active volcanism cover some 29 per cent of the area of Iceland. They are concentrated in belts along the Icelandic segment of the Mid-Atlantic Ridge. These zones run diagonally through Iceland from the Reykjanes peninsula and Vestmannaeyjar in the south and south-west, through the Krafla area north-east of lake Mývatn in the north, and on to the coast.

Iceland has been described as 'the only country in the world where a mid-oceanic ridge sticks out of the sea'.[6] The country is still being formed and renewed. The underwater eruptions of 1963–7 which produced the island of Surtsey were a dramatic testimony to this, witnessed by the world via film and television. Further testimony came from the Vestmannaeyjar eruption of 1973. We follow this volcanic activity with never-ceasing amazement. We observe it with our own eyes. We can see volcanoes, furiously spouting geysers, and bubbling springs of hot water. In the centre of Reykjavík, the geothermal heat steams out of pump-holes and water-pipes, almost under our feet. The primeval forces of nature feel uncannily close, even if they have been tamed by modern technology.

It was therefore a natural choice to site the Nordic Volcanological Institute in Reykjavík.

Volcanoes in Literature

What were the gods wroth over then,
when the lava on which we are now
standing was burning here?

Snorri goði

Volcanic eruptions are not a common motif in Icelandic poetry and sagas. One example which the reader will no doubt remember occurs in *Völuspá* (*The Seeress's Prophecy*), the poem which begins the *Elder Edda*; this describes Ragnarök in a stanza that conjures up a picture of a volcanic eruption.[7]

The Althing which assembled in the high summer of the year 1000, in front of the law-rock by lake Þingvallavatn, had to decide whether the Icelandic people would continue to worship the Æsir or adopt the cult of the White Christ. According to the account in *Kristni saga*, the thing-men debating the matter were disturbed by the news of 'earth-fire' at Ölfus, to the south of the lake. This was probably a volcanic eruption at Hengill or Skálafell, near a heath now overgrown with moss and heather, Hellisheiði. From there the lava flowed down towards the plain around Ölfus and Hveragerði.

The heathen contingent at the assembly interpreted the eruption as a sign of the gods' displeasure over this new-fangled Christianity. But Snorri, one of the priest-chieftains (*goðar*), was not short of an answer: 'What were the gods wroth over then, when the lava on which we are now standing was burning here?'[8]

According to the geologist Kristján Sæmundsson, this lava is about 9,000 years old. In other words, it was 8,000 years old when Snorri posed his rhetorical question.

Landnámabók lists the first settlers of Iceland and the areas which they colonized. One of the *landnámsmenn* was Þórir Grímsson. He sailed to western Iceland, where he settled in an area north of Borgar-fjörður, with its distinctive meadow land and bogs—preserved in the place-name Mýrar ('Mires')—and south of the mountainous peninsula with Snæfellsjökull. He claimed land between the mountains and the shore by the river Kaldá. He was described as a great chieftain (*höfð-ingi mikill*).

During an evening walk to the mouth of the river, the aged Þórir had a magical, mysterious experience. When Þórir was old and blind, he went out late one evening and saw a huge evil-looking man come rowing into the estuary of the river Kaldá in an iron boat.[9] The man walked up to a farm known as Hrip and started digging in the ground there, beside the gate to a milking fold. At night a volcanic eruption began there. It produced the lava that is now called Borgarhraun. There stood the farm where the crater is now.[10]

A witty French contribution to this topic came from the pen of Jules Verne (1828–1905) in his adventure *Journey to the Centre of the Earth*.[11] The journey is undertaken by Professor Lidenbrock of Hamburg. He is presented as a geologist and mineralogist, a learned but selfish man. He looks like a six-foot centaur. By deciphering a remarkable runic parchment, this veritable polyglot has found out that a crater in the extinct volcano of Snæfellsjökull leads to the centre of the earth.

Members of Paul Gaimard's scientific expedition carrying torches, as they walk deep down in the dark cave of Surtshellir. Drawing by the French painter Auguste Mayer.

With his nephew and an Icelandic guide named Hans, the German professor climbs down into the crater. After a journey full of surprises, they return to the surface, where they wonder where they are. In Iceland? On Jan Mayen? In the Malay Archipelago? No, they are in the middle of the Mediterranean, on Stromboli, near the volcano Etna. Hans then collects his wages, says 'Farewell', and returns to Reykjavík.

It appears likely that Jules Verne got the idea for his novel, which appeared in 1867, from a description of Iceland published in Paris in 1839–52. This was the work of the French physician and scientist Paul Gaimard (1790–1858), with evocative drawings by the painter August Mayer (1805–90).[12] The exotic quality of Iceland must have appealed to Jules Verne, and we may guess that the drawings set his imagination working. Those from the Surtshellir cave certainly call to mind the leading characters in the novel as they boldly descend into the crater on their way to the centre of the earth.

Surtshellir lies on a lava plain in western Iceland, just west of Eiríksjökull and north of a mountain called Strútur. The cave itself— like Surtsey, Iceland's youngest island, another creation of the fire giant Surtur—is 1,600 metres long. Folktales depict it as a haven for fugitives, cattle thieves, and outlaws. With a little fantasy it is not hard to imagine that the cave leads far down. Why not to the centre of the earth?

Volcanic Eruptions in Reality

One of the world's most disastrous eruptions in historical times occurred in 1883, on the volcanic island of Krakatoa in the Sunda Strait between Sumatra and Java. It is estimated to have killed some 40,000 people. It was a violent eruption in every way. When the gas exploded, the noise was heard as far away as Hong Kong and Australia, and two-thirds of the island was blown away. This was followed by a pillar of ash which covered everything in darkness. Particles of ash were spread round the globe, and huge tidal waves were blown up. All over the world, a red glow could be seen at sunset, as the oblique rays of the sun broke through the ash particles.

Terrible destruction has also been wreaked by Iceland's volcanoes.

Since the discovery and settlement of Iceland, Katla has spouted fire about twenty times (the latest being 1918) and Hekla 17 times (the latest in 1947–8, 1970, 1980–1, and as recently as 1991). This century the volcanoes Askja, Grímsvötn, and Krafla have also reminded us that they are not extinct. Krafla, near Mývatn in northern Iceland, attracted particular attention; it had been dormant since the 'Mývatn fires' in the eighteenth century, but in the period 1975–84 it erupted nine times. Showers of volcanic ash and glacial outbursts from Öræfajökull in 1362 and 1727 destroyed the once-rich agricultural land at the foot of the glacier. Extensive damage was caused in eastern Iceland in 1875 when Askja erupted violently; the resulting cloud of ash spread all the way to the Baltic Sea.

The eruptions of the eighteenth century were particularly severe. They began with the eruption of Öræfajökull in 1727 and the Mývatn fires, which burned from 1724 until 1729. The greatest damage was caused in 1783 by the violent eruption of Lakagígar, near the glacier river of Skaftá. The effects of the poisonous mist have been mentioned in a previous chapter.[13]

In the wake of all these natural disasters—including the 1784 earthquake in southern Iceland—there followed ineluctably a Ragnarök-like destruction in the shape of massive flows of lava, volcanic ash, toxic mists spreading sulphur and fluorine, glacial outbursts, sudden cold spells, and storms.

For anyone travelling through the interior of Iceland, the result is almost frighteningly obvious. We see a landscape with little or no trees or vegetation. It is characterized by glaciers and volcanoes, bare deserts of stone, gravel, or sand, sterile expanses of lava. Much of Iceland's surface—especially the areas around Vatnajökull, including Öræfajökull and Skeiðarárjökull—have this unmistakable hallmark. It is a wasteland. Underneath tall, steep glacier margins with their many foaming waterfalls, we gaze out over seemingly endless deserts, crossed by rushing glacier rivers. In the shadow of the glaciers we can admittedly find the odd farm, such as Skaftafell, Svínafell, and Hof, defiantly clinging high up on the slopes. The farms, with their small green fields and modest clumps of trees, look like oases. They do not detract from the overall impression. We find ourselves in a remote wilderness, a place of great natural beauty. It fully deserves the name *öræfi*, the Icelandic word for unpopulated wasteland.

When the eruption began on Heimaey, one of the islands in the Vestmannaeyjar group, on 23 January 1973, threatening the town of Vestmannaeyjar with its five thousand inhabitants, the entire population was evacuated the same night by fishing-boats and aeroplanes. Luckily, the weather that night was exceptionally good since a storm had just died down. Moreover, because of the storm, the whole fishing fleet had been moored in the harbour. Besides rescuing people, the operation salvaged livestock, cars, furniture, and other movable property. Anything that could be saved was removed. Lava poured copiously out of a newly formed crater. It flowed closer to the town each day. The showers of ash falling on the houses grew thicker and thicker, just as they did over Pompeii and Herculaneum after the eruption of Vesuvius in AD 79. The volcano rumbled. A blinding fire in the sky could be seen at a great distance. On the mainland, which is about twelve kilometres north of Heimaey as the crow flies, it could be seen from Hellisheiði, an upland heath between Reykjavík and the south coast.

The Icelanders were never panic-stricken. They seldom lose their composure. People in Iceland are used to sudden snowstorms, cloudbursts, and other bad weather. Moreover, only ten years earlier, the islanders had witnessed the eruption of Surtsey, just 15 kilometres from Heimaey. (When Surtsey erupted, the geologist Trausti Einarsson predicted that the same thing could happen on Heimaey. At his suggestion, the Icelandic civil defence drew up an evacuation plan for Heimaey.) Now, instead of watching from the stalls, the citizens found themselves on the stage. Deep down they were full of anxiety and consternation, as they saw the volcanic ash and lava burying their homes. They were all in a state of dread.

In this situation there were Icelanders who put their faith in divine providence. One of these was Gunnlaugur Þórðarson (born 1919), a doctor of law, humanist, and art collector. On the third day of the eruption he went to Vestmannaeyjar with the two paintings of Gunnlaugur Scheving[14] that he liked best. He put them in front of the altar in the chancel of the church, Landakirkja, as a sort of talisman. He fervently prayed that this sanctuary of the Lord might be saved. Two months later, a 'fire service' (*eldmessa*) was held in Landakirkja. The flow of lava did indeed stop a little way from the church. Faith is important for those who believe. The power of faith can move mountains. After the service in Landakirkja, the lava continued to flow with undiminished force. It destroyed many houses. But the church still stands.

The act of taking the Scheving paintings to Landakirkja reminded the Icelanders of two remarkable events, both associated with the disasters of the eighteenth century. At the time of the Mývatn fires, a river of lava flowed threateningly in the direction of the church in Reykjahlíð. Strangely, the lava stopped at the last minute. At a distance of just a few metres, it piled up around the church and the cemetery, which were completely surrounded by the glowing lava. This miracle is mentioned in an official report, with the statement that 'it still testifies today to the wonderful protection of the Almighty'.[15]

A closely related phenomenon occurred during the eruption of Lakagígar in 1783, when the flow of lava was one of the greatest in the world this millennium. The church at Kirkjubæjarklaustur and the whole settlement around it was threatened by the huge flood of lava from these 'Skaftá fires'. It was relentlessly nearing the church. In this fateful hour, the pastor of Kirkjubæjarklaustur, Jón Steingrímsson, assembled the parishioners for a fire service in the church. Jón and his congregation had their prayers answered. The flow of lava, which had been approaching at full speed that morning, stopped.[16] This earned Jón the name of 'fire-cleric' (*eldklerkur*).

The age of miracles is not over for those who believe.

Earthquakes

Iceland is a geophysical laboratory.
Markus Båth, Professor Emeritus of seismology at Uppsala University

Earthquakes generally happen in a matter of seconds, with little or no advance warning. They are most common in volcanic areas. They make themselves felt as shakes, tremors, and jolts, probably caused by plate movements in the earth's crust or stresses caused by volcanic activity.

The most disastrous earthquakes in historical times, calculated in terms of the number of people killed, have occurred in China, followed by Japan, Italy (the city of Messina in Sicily), and Peru. One of the most famous was the earthquake in Lisbon in 1755. Shortly after the destruction of the Portuguese capital, the French philosopher Voltaire wrote the didactic poem 'Le Disastre de Lisbonne'. In it he protested against exaggerated optimism and ridiculed the blind faith in this world as the best of all possible worlds. Two of the most thoroughly investigated earthquakes took place in San Francisco in 1906 and 1989. The great earthquake of 1906 and the subsequent fires ruined much of the city.[17]

In Iceland, as we have seen, the Eurasian and North American Plates are moving away from each other. As a consequence of this and the accompanying stresses built up in the crust, earthquakes occur in certain parts of the country. Both earthquakes and eruptions may occur throughout the volcanic zones, but there are also zones of particular earthquake activity in the southern lowlands and the adjoining Reykjanes peninsula and in the coastal regions of north-eastern Iceland.

The greatest damage has been caused by earthquakes that have afflicted the southern Icelandic lowlands. The most violent reached 7.1 on the Richter scale. A study by Icelandic scientists suggests that periods of serious earthquakes recur in this region at average intervals of 140 years. The last period was around the turn of the century (1896–1912). According to this theory, then, we may expect the next period around 2040, plus or minus several decades. Whatever the date, the next major earthquake is expected to come in the south of Iceland.[18]

How powerful will this earthquake be? According to historical seismic statistics, it is likely that an earthquake of 6 or more on the Richter scale will occur in the southern seismic zone within the next twenty years.

Earthquakes of similar strength can also occur along the north coast. The biggest of these, however, happen off the coast. This means that earthquakes have not caused as much damage here as in southern Iceland.

How would an earthquake affect Reykjavík? Most of the houses there are solid concrete buildings. Many of them stand on rock. Houses like these are said to withstand even serious earthquakes. The greatest risk is for houses resting on props. Also in the danger zone are buildings with shops or large office premises on the ground floor, with large, high, open rooms lacking stable dividing walls. A powerful earthquake could destroy the ground floor, causing the upper floors to collapse. Other endangered buildings would be those built on soft ground and also multi-storey blocks. The latter are still not so numerous in Reykjavík, where the tallest building was once christened 'the house on the prairie' by a Finnish ambassador.

Other potential risks are that electricity transmission lines from power stations can fall. Since the telephone network would presumably be put out of operation, a radio network with 130 stations is being built up all over Iceland to be used in an emergency.

The scientists who have studied these risks use a variety of methods and instruments to try to identify signs of an impending earthquake. They can, for example, measure changes in stress in the earth's crust and minor tremors caused by these. Other advance warnings can be discovered by studying changes in groundwater level, electrical disturbances, and changed radon content in the water that assembles in boreholes. In the short term, abnormal behaviour by animals also appears to be a useful sign in predicting earthquakes. The Icelanders can also learn a great deal from the geophysical experiences of the earthquakes in San Francisco in 1906 and 1989.

Intensive seismic data collection in the southern lowlands began in 1986 as part of a joint Nordic research project. The aim is to reduce the risks in the event of an earthquake and to improve the techniques for predicting earthquakes.[19]

Geothermal Energy

Some hot springs are used for dyeing,
and they could most likely be put to
other uses as well.

*Prediction made by Uno von Troil in
1772 after a tour of Stóri Geysir and
other 'hot spouting water-springs'*

Iceland's Natural Resources

Apart from some occurrences of sulphur, salt, and diatomite, Iceland
is judged to lack exploitable mineral resources of any significance. In
a previous chapter we have mentioned that the entire Jan Mayen Ridge
north of the Icelandic mainland consists of sedimentary rocks, which
could in theory contain fossil fuels (coal, crude oil, and natural gas).
Icelandic geologists have also investigated deep-lying layers of the
seabed to the west of the granite rock of Rockall. Preliminary prospecting has been conducted in these areas on the fringe of Iceland's
exclusive economic zone, the first of which is located on the northern
continental shelf, the other on the natural prolongation of the continental shelf to the south; so far, however, this has been without success.[20]

Iceland is thus, at least at first sight, poor in minerals. On the other
hand, it has been blessed by nature with resources of a different kind:
areas suitable for agriculture or animal husbandry, mostly along the
indented coastline, the fish stocks on the rich fishing banks along the
coasts, and energy in the form of hydroelectric power and geothermal
heat. Nor should we forget the Gulf Stream.

These energy resources are constantly being renewed in nature's
eternal cycle. This applies not only to the water in rivers and lakes,
which are constantly being refilled by precipitation. In volcanic areas,
rainwater and meltwater from the glaciers trickle through cracks in the
bedrock, down to layers of lava and rock which are still hot after
volcanic activity. There the water is heated to high temperatures, after
which it is sent back up to the surface, sometimes under considerable
pressure. We see it in the form of hot springs (Icelandic *hverir*),

bubbling hot water, steam, or geysers hurling cascades of boiling hot water high into the air.

Expert calculations and the use of new technology show that this country possesses virtually inexhaustible and still scarcely exploited energy sources for domestic consumption. There is room for considerable expansion in future. As regards energy, then, Iceland is well endowed by nature. One consequence of this is that the Icelanders have still not given any serious thought to alternative sources of energy, such as the inherent power of tides, winds, and waves. These energy sources are potentially significant but not so commercially attractive.

Geothermal Energy: Resources and Expansion

Geothermal energy is usually classified according to the temperature of the borehole. Roughly speaking, 'low temperatures' are those under 150°C, while 'high temperatures' are those over 150°C. In Iceland the high temperature areas can be found in two partly parallel volcanic zones, which run diagonally through the country from the Reykjanes peninsula and Vestmannaeyjar in the south-west to the area around the volcano Krafla and the town of Húsavík in the north-east, a little south of the Arctic Circle. These are parts of the volcanic Mid-Atlantic Ridge which extends all the way down the Atlantic Ocean.

There are nineteen *high-temperature areas* covering a total of 600 square kilometres. Their location is shown on a map among the colour plates, reproduced here by kind permission from the book *Energy Resources and Dams in Iceland* (Reykjavík, 1989).

Perhaps the most talked-about power station in Iceland is the geothermal station of Krafla near lake Mývatn, south of Húsavík. It was designed in 1974 for a capacity of 60 MW (megawatts). The output at present is still only about half of this, around 30 MW. The reason is that some parts of the geothermal area are still contaminated by harmful volcanic gases produced by the eruptions. The Krafla project, in other words, illustrates the latent risk associated with energy extraction in high-temperature areas. It might have been possible to obviate this risk by more careful investigation of the geological and vulcanological conditions in this area.

A significant share of the extractable geothermal energy, however, can be found in precisely these high-temperature areas, which are mostly volcanically active. Other power stations in these areas which have been highly successful are those at Bjarnarflag, Svartsengi, and Nesjavellir. As at Krafla, however, it is always necessary to take some chances.

Most of the exploited geothermal energy comes from *low-temperature areas*. These can be found in most parts of the country, but chiefly on the fringes of the volcanic zones.

In both high- and low-temperature areas, the Icelanders generally have to drill holes to a depth of 1,000–2,400 metres. This is enough in most parts of the country to reach supplies of hot water. They are used—as we shall see shortly—mainly to heat houses. This form of district central heating is exemplified by the plants in Reykir and Reykjavík, which have long served the people of Reykjavík and neighbouring towns.

The consumption of hot water is constantly increasing. A much-needed addition to the supply has been obtained from a new geothermal power station. This is Nesjavellir by lake Þingvallavatn, east of Reykjavík. Since 1990, when operations began, hot water has been pumped in steel pipelines all the way to Reykjavík, through rugged mountain and heath terrain. The station now has an output of 150 MW of thermal energy. Together, these plants provide about 142,000 people—more than half the population of Iceland—with heat for their homes.

Hot-water boreholes are often surrounded by huge clouds of steam. They evoke scenes from Dante's *Divina commedia*, with its visions of hell, purgatory, and paradise. The imagination is fired, for example, by the pillars of steam that rise above the geothermal power station of Svartsengi. This is located on the Reykjanes peninsula, between the fishing villages of Grindavík and Keflavík. The plant produces both electricity (11 MW) and hot water (125 MW). The hot water is piped to neighbouring municipalities to heat houses, and to the airport and military base at Keflavík.

The Icelanders are proud to show off Svartsengi. Both technically and architecturally, this geothermal power station is a complete success. It lies west-south-west of Reykjavík, in a geologically much calmer area than Krafla, which has been dogged by misfortune. In the area around Svartsengi there are about thirty volcanoes, but only five of these have erupted since Iceland was settled.

Experts at the Nordic Volcanological Institute in Reykjavík assess the risk of new eruptions in the Svartsengi area as small. Geological conditions on the site were one factor in the localization of the power station. The decisive factor, however, was the short distance to densely populated areas.[21]

The wastewater from the power station is rich in sulphur, salt, and silica. It is pumped out into an aquamarine lagoon with a temperature of about 35°C, which is surrounded by clouds of steam. This 'Blue Lagoon' (Bláa lónið) in the middle of the black lava plain has proved— at least temporarily—to have a healing effect on people suffering from psoriasis, rheumatism, sciatica, eczema, and other complaints. It is therefore visited by sick people from many countries.

Complete healing is not achieved in respect of psoriasis, but this illness is likely to be mitigated, particularly if the Lagoon baths are combined with radio-therapy. Systematic research is going on.

The Utilization of Geothermal Energy

Heating Homes

I found time . . . to visit the wonderful hot springs and the glasshouses they are made to serve. I thought immediately that they should also be used to heat Reykjavík, and tried to further this plan even during the war. I am glad that it has now been carried out.

Winston Churchill's account of a visit to Iceland in August 1941

The Icelanders actually started to drill for hot water for Reykjavík back in 1928. Drilling was first undertaken at the hot springs in Laugardalur, which is now the site of the largest swimming-pool in Iceland. The heating of houses began in 1933. The district central heating system in Reykjavík was expanded in the 1930s with the building of the power station at Reykir.[22]

Even a brilliant war leader like Winston Churchill can miss occasional details.[23]

It took a long time before the Icelanders seriously began to exploit their geothermal energy. In the absence of drilling techniques, they had to shiver for centuries in their draughty homes, while the heat in the ground was just under their feet.

The Icelanders of the twentieth century have made up for this in rich measure, eagerly utilizing geothermal energy and hydroelectric power, which are unique riches for a country with a cold and windy climate in the middle of the often storm-tossed Atlantic. In terms of worldwide energy consumption per head, Iceland comes second only to Canada, but before the USA.

Iceland's domestic energy resources—geothermal and hydroelectric—provide over two-thirds of what the country consumes. It is becoming ever less dependent on imported forms of energy (oil and coal). Recent development and a forecast for the year 2000, in terms of oil equivalents, can be seen in the following table, which has been compiled by the National Energy Authority (Orkustofnun):

Type of energy	1980 %	1990 %	2000 %
Geothermal	26.8	31.4	37.7
Hydroelectric	41.0	37.9	37.6
Oil	30.3	28.4	27.4
Coal	1.9	2.3	2.3

Icelandic experts predict that the importance of geothermal energy will grow in the future. At present, as much as 79.2 per cent of the geothermal energy is used for central heating. About 84 per cent of all homes in Iceland are heated from this source. Electricity accounts for 14 per cent and oil for only 2 per cent.

It is also interesting that some of the hot water is pumped up from boreholes in the centre of Reykjavík, right under the houses that it is used to heat. About half of the wastewater is piped back in a closed system. Since the eruption on Heimaey in 1973, the town of Vestmannaeyjar has had some of its cold water heated by the still-glowing lava just under the surface. In 1988, about 40 per cent of heating requirements were still met by the hot lava. The heating of water by lava ceased, however, at the end of 1990.

Geothermal energy is generally easily accessible using modern drills. In addition, it is cheaper than imported oil. It is these advantageous circumstances, combined with rising oil prices, which explain why municipalities in more and more parts of the country (such as Akureyri, Akranes, and some small towns in north-west and south-west Iceland) have turned to geothermal heating instead of oil. The transition has been made despite the high initial costs. Hot water for the district heating plant in Akranes has to be pumped in pipelines from hot springs over 60 kilometres distant.

From the consumer's point of view, heating with natural hot water has only one disadvantage. The hot water sometimes contains silicon, which has to be separated, for example using a pre-heater. The silicon might otherwise clog the valves and corrode the radiators.

Thanks to the occurrence of hot water, most of the municipalities in Iceland have gone to the expense of providing their inhabitants with geothermally heated swimming-pools, where they can enjoy open-air dips all the year round, in water at temperatures of 20–25°C. There are about a hundred such pools in Iceland.

In many ways, Iceland does not deserve its chilly name. Everyone can enjoy heat, both indoors and in swimming-pools. The Icelanders generally have a higher temperature in their rooms than is normal in other countries at the same latitude. In the middle of winter, one can stroll along snow-free pedestrian streets, or park one's car in snow-free driveways.

A decision in principle has been taken in Reykjavík to heat all the streets and pavements in the city centre. This will be done using residual hot water from the surrounding houses.

Energy exploitation also gives an opportunity for new architectural creativity. Hot water for Reykjavík is pumped through six enormous tanks which rise on the crest of a hill, Öskjuhlíð, right in the centre of the capital. Above them towers the city's newest sight, a gigantic glass dome known as Perlan (The Pearl). It contains a rotating restaurant where the visitor can feel that he has been transported to the roof of the world. One can gaze out over infinite expanses of sea, hazy blue mountains, and when visibility is good, the snow-capped peak of

Snæfellsjökull can be seen in the north-west. Perlan by night looks like a shining ball of fire, while in sunshine it glistens like a precious ornament. Perlan is well worth a visit—the crown jewel in the world's northernmost capital.

Since the dawn of the island's history, as described in the sagas, the Icelanders have taken pleasure in bathing in hot springs. Snorralaug in Reykholt, associated with Snorri Sturluson, is a celebrated example. When the country was converted to Christianity, the pagans let themselves be baptized in hot springs. Since the Middle Ages the springs have also been used for more everyday purposes, such as washing clothes and dyeing wool (as von Troil observed), baking rye bread and cooking. During the visit of Christian IX to Iceland in 1874, the hosts entertained the king by showing him a column of water, between fifty and sixty metres high, spouting from Geysir. To the king's delight, they boiled eggs in the steaming hot ground beside the geyser. It is dangerous to enter the enclosed areas around Geysir, where the ground can be treacherously porous.

In modern times—as we shall now see—geothermal energy is used for a wider range of purposes.

Market Gardening, Plant Nurseries, and Fish Farms

Like the nearby valley of Hveradalur, the little town of Hveragerði ('Hot-spring Enclosure'), about 40 kilometres east of Reykjavík, offers remarkable sights. A steaming river that flows from the mountains down to the sea is lined by a landscape with springs issuing billowing clouds and whirls of smoke. One of the springs is called Grýta. At regular intervals of two hours, it spouts up a column of water 12 metres high from its ceaselessly bubbling opening. It is important to stay clear of this hot, sulphurous spray.

The hot springs are very changeable. They sometimes burst out unexpectedly in new places. At Hveragerði they say that it has even happened that a man and wife once received a rude awakening from hot steam under their marital bed.

A large area at Hveragerði, about 75,000 square metres, is covered by glasshouses which are used to grow tomatoes, cucumbers, lettuce, cauliflower, spinach, and other vegetables, and flowers like roses, carnations, and all manner of potted plants. At a latitude of 66° north, sybarites can indulge in bananas, oranges, grapes, and other exotic fruits. The State Horticultural School is situated at Hveragerði; here the visitor can stroll in a large garden with palms and cactuses.

In geothermal areas, including some places in southern Iceland, such as Flúðir near the thousand-year-old episcopal see of Skálholt, Icelandic farmers have started two other interesting innovations. One consists of growing mushrooms indoors. The other is a method for under-soil heating to assist outdoor growth. Large areas (120,000 m² in 1989) are heated by geothermal water transported in plastic pipes a little under the ground surface. In this soil gardeners can produce Chinese cabbage and other tasty early vegetables in the spring.

Would it not be a good idea in a virtually treeless land like Iceland to force saplings on a large scale in glasshouses heated by geothermal water? Or would a plant nursery of this kind be too expensive? Despite the expense, experiments have been made with downy birch (*Betula pubescens*). The method is as follows. During the summer, environmental enthusiasts go out to collect birch seeds. They then sow them in greenhouses, in large vessels with plastic tubes. The seeds quickly germinate and are allowed to burgeon during the winter. When spring approaches, they have grown into small plants, thriving in the heat of the greenhouse. During the summer, the year-old trees are planted in the open by the same enthusiasts who collected the seeds a year before. They can thus see and admire with their own eyes what they have

Snorralaug in Reykholt. Both the pool and the underpass are from the 13th century at least. This ring-shaped open-air pool, filled with natural hot water from a nearby hot spring, takes its name from Snorri Sturluson, Iceland's greatest historian. One might well imagine that Snorri enjoyed his relaxing dip in the Snorralaug.

accomplished. This stimulates their interest in growing things. The passion is spread—like ripples on a pond—to friends and acquaintances, along with a commitment to conservation.

Geothermally heated water of exactly the right temperature is used in fish farms to breed fish fry (salmon, rainbow trout, and so on). The interest in fish farming is growing quickly. This industry has been mentioned earlier in other contexts.[24]

Iceland as a Health Resort

The visitor to Iceland may enjoy the benefits of unpolluted air and water. Bottles with fresh spring water, for example, are a popular Icelandic export article.

In particular, the Nature Cure Sanatorium in Hveragerði, founded in 1955, provides facilities in peaceful surroundings for the treatment of various ailments, such as rheumatism, high blood pressure, and skin diseases. Treatment also includes mud-baths and baths in mineral water direct from the local hot springs. Vegetarian diet, too, is an important part of the treatment. This sanatorium also operates as a convalescent home.

In our times of stress, we all need some relaxation now and again. This need can conveniently be met at Hotel Örk, a luxury hotel and health spa, also located in Hveragerði.

Looking into oneself for a few days, or for a week or even longer, makes a greater difference than many people might realize. On offer during a stay there are, for example, health foods, yoga gymnastics, meditation, swimming, saunas, mud-baths, massage, and relaxation exercises. Alongside the swimming-pool at the hotel there are two hot basins (so-called 'hot pots'), one with pure fountain water, the other with silicon-geothermal water, said to have an especially good influence on certain types of skin disease, as has, for instance, a dip in the Blue Lagoon. Evening activities include lectures by experts on various subjects, concerts by Icelandic artistes, and other interesting events.

On your arrival at Keflavík International Airport it is possible to travel direct to Hveragerði via the afore-mentioned Blue Lagoon. The trip takes the traveller past steep bird-cliffs, one or two fishing stations, and some bubbling hot springs.

Industrial Processes

By lake Mývatn in northern Iceland, not far from the Krafla geothermal power station, the Icelanders have built a diatomite factory. Its production is entirely based on the occurrence of nearby natural resources: diatomite (a deposit composed of the shells of microscopic, single-cell algae with a siliceous cell-wall) on the bed of the lake and geothermal steam emanating from boreholes in the nearby high-temperature area of Bjarnarflag. The raw material is sucked up from the lake, when it naturally contains a large proportion of water. The water is filtered out, and the residue is dried by geothermal steam and then heated. The finished product, which looks like a white powder, is then transported by lorry to Húsavík on a road specially built for the purpose. The 'diatomite road', incidentally, has improved communications in this part of Iceland. From Húsavík the diatomite is shipped mainly to various industries in the European Community which use it in chemical processes, for example, for filtering liquids.

The diatomite factory employs about eighty people. It is also of indirect importance for a number of service companies in this thinly populated part of Iceland, where there is otherwise little employment.

As the reader will no doubt remember, the diatomite factory has long been a thorn in the flesh for Icelandic environmentalists.[25]

Other industrial processes using geothermal energy include drying seaweed, producing carbon dioxide, and washing sheep's wool. Other projects, such as factories for manufacturing paper, sugar, and fish-meal, have as yet only been studied.

The most widely discussed idea is salt production in Reykjanes using geothermal water with a salt content of about 5 per cent. The long-term vision is to use salt as raw material for a future chemicals industry. The most likely products would be caustic soda, chlorine, sodium chlorate, hydrogen gas or hydrochloric acid, and magnesium. For this purpose, a borehole was drilled to a depth of 1,445 metres at Reykjanes on the south-western tip of Iceland in 1983. Water at a temperature of some 300°C spouts out of this hole. It is transformed in part into steam when it emerges from the earth under high pressure. The water contains 5 per cent salt, mostly common salt, which is stored in large evaporation basins.

The long development work at Reykjanes appears to have borne fruit, as a new commercial salt plant started operations there in early 1992.

International Technological Cooperation and Tourism

In the fields of vulcanology, geothermal energy, and general geology, Icelanders have shown themselves able to acquire considerable insight. They have also amassed a great deal of practical experience and made technical progress. This stock of knowledge is of interest for a number of other countries with similar geothermal phenomena.

To carry out the international marketing of know-how in the energy field, Iceland has founded Virkir-Orkint Ltd. This company is owned by a state joint-stock company affiliated to the National Energy Authority, Orkustofnun, and a number of advisory engineering firms with experience of the energy sector. The Reykjavík Municipal District Heating Service has also acquired shares in the company. Countries with which Virkir-Orkint Ltd. has worked include Hungary, Greece, Kenya, Djibouti, China, and Russia (Kamchatka).

Besides this, the National Energy Authority runs the U.N.U. Geothermal Training Programme. Founded in 1979, this school admits 7–12 students each year. The idea is to help Third World countries to develop their geothermal resources. The school is subsidized by the Icelandic state and the United Nations University in Tokyo.

Naturally, it is the many geysers and bubbling springs, the mighty glaciers and slumbering volcanoes, which make Iceland into such an exciting tourist attraction.[26] The flow of tourists to Iceland is generally increasing from year to year, and with them the currency earnings for the country. In 1991 tourism generated 7 per cent of Iceland's total foreign currency revenue.

Hydroelectric Power

We live on top of mines of gold and treasure,
in buried hovels, lacking everything.
In sea and land lie happiness and riches
at the feet of people who are robbed or dead.
Einar Benediktsson, 'Bréf í ljóðum'

Power stations in Iceland are often built on glacier rivers which flow in torrents through volcanic areas. When volcanoes erupt, the power stations and dams can be damaged by flows of lava or showers of ash. However, the energy that is produced by hydroelectric power stations naturally has nothing at all to do with the country's volcanoes. The topic of hydroelectric power is thus, strictly speaking, outside the scope of a chapter entitled 'Volcanoes and Their Effects', but it will be discussed here for the following reason.

Hydroelectric power is one of Iceland's vital energy resources, along with geothermal energy. The two sources complement each other in a significant way. As we have just seen, they combine to make the Icelandic people less dependent on the import of oil. Besides requiring expensive foreign currency, the supply of oil can dry up in times of crisis, as it did in the 1970s. In addition, the Icelanders have no need to build nuclear power plants with their threat to the environment.

Resources and Exploitation

Most of the hydroelectric power which Iceland can potentially use comes from the rivers that flow to the north, the north-east, and the south-west. The northern and north-eastern areas, however, are very sparsely populated. Moreover, they are isolated, especially in winter, since the roads there are mostly substandard and impassable. In these areas where it is difficult to establish industry or to transport electricity over large distances, there would be little economic sense in building large power stations, unless construction costs were particularly low, which they actually are in certain places in the north-east. Considerations of regional policy naturally play a role here.

It is often more economically viable to build power stations along the water-rich rivers—Þjórsá, Tungnaá, and Hvítá—that flow to the south-west from the three glaciers of Vatnajökull, Hofsjökull, and Langjökull. It is easier to harness the force of the water in these rivers, even if power stations on these glacier rivers have to be designed to withstand the effects of ice and sand. Another advantage is that the rivers are near the most densely populated part of the country in the south-west. This area, stretching from Vík í Mýrdal in the east to Snæfellsnes in the west, and with fairly good communications, contains about three-quarters of the population of Iceland.

This area also has most of the hydroelectric power stations operated by Landsvirkjun,[27] which account for over 90 per cent of Iceland's total capacity, expressed in watts (W).[28] The most important of them are the Búrfell I plant (210 MW), Sigalda (150 MW), and Hrauneyjafoss (210 MW).[29] These power stations are located in potentially dangerous areas not far from the volcano Hekla. It has happened that pumice and volcanic ash from Hekla have rained down on Búrfell, with no harm done to the power station. May one surmise that the volcano is displeased with intruders on its land? The newest hydroelectric power station is Blanda (150 MW), which is located in northern Iceland, outside the volcanic zone.

The coming of a high-tension transmission network around the whole country has made it possible to cease operations in the biggest oil-fired power stations, which are now reserved for emergency use.

Iceland is now well provided for electricity. More than 99.9 per cent of the population has access to electricity from the nationwide grid. The remaining 0.1 per cent, who live on about twenty remote farms, have their own generators which receive their power from a nearby waterfall.

Orkustofnun (The National Energy Authority) estimates that 64 TWh can potentially be generated by the Icelandic rivers annually.[30] Earlier in this book we have seen the growing importance attached to environmental and conservational issues in Iceland.[31] At present, it is reckoned that environmental considerations and expected energy prices on the world market will mean that the practical limit for the production of electricity is around 44 TWh per year. Only about 11 per cent of this capacity, or 5 TWh/year, exists at the time of writing.

Utilization

General Consumption and Energy-Intensive Industries

Hydroelectric power provides about 94 per cent of the total electricity production. In 1986, large-scale consumers (the aluminium smelter at Straumsvík just south of Reykjavík, the ferrosilicon plant at Grundartangi by Hvalfjörður, about 100 kilometres by car from Reykjavík, and a fertilizer factory on the outskirts of Reykjavík) accounted for 53 per cent of all electricity consumption. Other major consumers are a cement factory in Akranes north of Reykjavík (to which travellers sail over Faxaflói in the car ferry *Akraborg*) and a rockwool factory in Sauðárkrókur by Skagafjörður in northern Iceland. Public utilities and small private companies accounted for the rest of the electricity consumption.

Five new power stations—all based on hydroelectric power—have been planned, with a view to almost doubling Iceland's electricity production.[32] One of the new stations, Blanda, is already in full operation, using the copious waters of the glacier river Blanda, which is fed by Hofsjökull. It flows north and reaches the sea at Blönduós ('Blanda Estuary'). The additional hydroelectric power from Blanda and the other new power stations will be needed for an expansion of Iceland's energy-intensive industries, such as an increase in aluminium production and the manufacturing that is based on it.

Future Alternatives

Provided that the investment costs are kept to a reasonable level, the unexploited electricity could in theory be used according to three alternatives. The first envisages *the transmission of electricity to other countries*. The idea to do so by satellite, in the same way that television programmes are currently transmitted, sounds like science fiction. It is not technically feasible at present.

Another idea is that Britain could buy Icelandic electricity. Between 500 and 2,000 megawatts could be supplied by conventional hydroelectric power stations, and to some extent geothermal stations. This would be transmitted to Scotland or England via the Faroes in a submarine cable 950 kilometres long or more. This project sounds fantastic, too. According to an article in *The Guardian*, however, it is feasible. Britain is already buying excess electricity from France. This is transmitted in a cable under the English Channel.[33] It is also conceivable that a gigantic investment like this could become a realistic alternative if a new international oil crisis caused prices to soar. We must reckon with the risk of a new oil shock around the year 2000.

A second alternative would be to continue to establish *energy-intensive industries based on foreign raw materials*. One such industry was established in the late 1960s by Alusuisse, Swiss Aluminium Ltd., at Straumsvík (the large aluminium smelter on the road from Reykjavík to Keflavík). The main raw material is bauxite (called after Baux in Provence), which is mined and processed to alumina in Australia and then shipped all the way to Iceland. The companies concerned are considering an expansion of the smelter at Straumsvík and the construction of yet another aluminium smelter and several power stations.

A third alternative which seems natural is to establish *energy-intensive industries based on domestic raw materials*.

From the point of view of the labour market and the national economy, the last two alternatives have two obvious advantages. Increased industrialization would create new jobs and lead to a more varied industrial base. It could thus reduce Iceland's dependence on the fishing industry.

Foreign investors—financially strong companies like Alumax, Gränges Aluminium, and Hoogovens Aluminium—are primarily attracted by the supply of cheap energy in Iceland. Low electricity prices are the main factor. Other advantages are the reliability of the energy supply and the availability of a trained workforce. These companies have conducted negotiations about the joint construction of a new aluminium smelter in Iceland. The idea was to begin operations in the mid-1990s, with an annual capacity of 200,000 tons. Because of the plentiful supply of aluminium on the world market and the consequent low prices, however, the decision to build a new aluminium smelter has been postponed until there is a change in world market prices.

What do the Icelanders themselves think? Many of them are firmly rooted in tradition. Some are suspicious of foreign investors. Many are also opposed to any thought of large-scale industry and Icelandic membership of the European Community.

It is nevertheless clear that a majority in the Althing supports the idea of collaboration with big foreign companies, provided they pledge to give due consideration to environmental interests.

Notes to Chapter 9

1   Uno von Troil, *Letters on Iceland Containing Observations. Made During a Voyage Undertaken in the Year 1772 by Joseph Banks, Esq. F.R.S.* (London, 1780), p. 10.

2   Albert Engström, *Åt Häcklefjäll* (Stockholm: Bonniers, 1911), part II, p. 120.

3   See, for example, Hjalmar Lindroth, *Iceland: A Land of Contrasts* (New York, 1937); Hjálmar R. Bárðarson, *Ice and Fire: Contrasts of Icelandic Nature* (Reykjavík: Hjálmar R. Bárðarson, 1971).

4   Ari Trausti Guðmundsson and Halldór Kjartansson, *Guide to the Geology of Iceland* (Reykjavík: Örn og Örlygur, 1984), p. 34.

5   *Iceland 1986: Handbook Published by the Central Bank of Iceland* (Reykjavík, 1987), pp. 1–6.

6   Páll Imsland, 'Vulkaner, is och kokande vatten—Islands geologiska historia', in *Islänningar om Island,* vols. 16–17 of *Gardar* (1985), p. 11; see also his 'Study Models for Volcanic Hazards in Iceland', *Volcanic Hazards: IAVCEI Proceedings in Volcanology,* vol. 1, ed. J. H. Latter (Berlin: Springer, 1980).

7   See Chapter 2, '*Völuspá*'.

8   See Chapter 1, 'The Æsir and the White Christ'.

9   Iron boats occur in Norwegian folk legends, where they are believed to be used by giants.

10   *The Book of Settlements: Landnámabók,* trans. Hermann Pálsson and Paul Edwards (Winnipeg: University of Manitoba Press, 1972), p. 38. The word *stöðulshlið* used in this account obviously refers to the gate (*hlið*) of a fold (*stöðull*) to which cows were brought for milking on the farm. The Norse word *sel* refers to an enclosure or shieling in the outlands of a farm or in the mountains; livestock was driven there for the summer pasture. These two terms reflect ancient Scandinavian traditions. See *Kulturhistoriskt leksikon for nord-isk middelalder* (Reykjavík: Bókaverzlun Ísafoldar, 1972), s.v. *Sel* and *-støl*. At the site of the eruption there is now a beautiful, well-formed crater known as Eldborg ('Fire Castle'). Icelandic scientists think that the lava at Eldborg was created by two eruptions. The latest probably occurred at the time of the settlement. It is possible that a memory of it could have been preserved in oral tradition. It could also have provided the material for a folk legend. Cf. two legends in Chapter 3: one tells of Sæmundur the priest and the witch in Saxony, the other about Katla, a woman with magical powers and the first eruption of the volcano that bears her name.

11   The original novel was entitled *Voyage au centre de la terre* (Paris, Hertzel, 1867).

12 Paul Gaimard, *Voyage en Islande et au Groënland, exécuté pendant les années 1835 et 1836 sur la corvette* la Recherche, 8 vols. with Atlas (Paris, 1838–52). Compare the illustrations and the notes in Samivel, *L'Or d'Islande* (Grenoble: B. Arthaud, 1963). The English version, *Golden Iceland* (Reykjavík: Almenna bókafélagið, 1967) was translated from the French and adapted by Magnus Magnusson.

13 See Chapter 1, 'Trade Monopoly and Natural Disasters'; *Iceland 1986*, pp. 3–5.

14 See the presentation of this artist in Chapter 4, 'The Cultural Heritage as a Source of Inspiration'.

15 *Safn til sögu Íslands og íslenzkra bókmennta að fornu og nýju* (Copenhagen and Reykjavík: Hið íslenzka bókmenntafélag, 1907–15), vol. 4, p. 410.

16 'Skaftáreldar 1783–1784', *Ritgerðir og heimildir* (Reykjavík: Mál og menning, 1984), p. 36.

17 Markus Båth, *Introduction to Seismology*, 2nd ed. (Stuttgart: Birkhauser, 1979).

18 Ragnar Stefánsson and Páll Halldórsson, 'Strain Release and Strain Build-up in the South Iceland Seismic Zone', *Tectonophysics* 152 (1988), pp. 267–76. See also, for example, Páll Einarsson, 'Jarðskjálftaspár', *Náttúrufræðingurinn* 55:1 (1985), p. 28; Páll Einarsson, 'Seismicity along the Eastern Margin of the North American Plate', chapter 7 of *The Western North Atlantic Region*, vol. M of *The Geology of North America*, ed. Peter R. Vogt and Brian E. Tucholke (Boulder, Colorado: Geological Society of America, 1986); Páll Einarsson and Jón Eiríksson, 'Earthquake Fractures in the Districts Land and Rangárvellir in the South Iceland Seismic Zone, *Jökull* 32 (1982), pp. 113–20.

19 Ragnar Stefánsson, Reynir Böðvarsson, Jörgen Hjelme, *The SIL-Project: The Second General Report* (Reykjavík: Veðurstofa Íslands, May 1989), p. 4.

20 See Chapter 8, 'Jan Mayen'.

21 S. Thorhallsson, 'Combined Generation of Heat and Electricity from a Geothermal Brine at Svartsengi in S.W. Iceland', *Geothermal Resources Council Transactions* 3 (1979), pp. 733–6; G. Björnsson and A. Albertsson, 'The Power-Plant at Svartsengi, Development and Experience', *1985 International Symposium on Geothermal Energy*, 3 vols. (Davis, California: Geothermal Resources Council, 1985), pp. 427–42.

22 *Reykjavík Municipal District Heating Service: Historic Account* (Reykjavík: Hitaveita Reykjavíkur, 1964), p. 5.

23 The epigraph comes from Winston S. Churchill, *The Second World War*, vol. 3, *The Grand Alliance* (London: Cassel, 1950), p. 400. Churchill made a flying visit to Iceland on his way home from a meeting in August 1941 with President Franklin D. Roosevelt.

24 See Chapter 6, 'Ecological Problems' and 'Iceland's Economy and the Surrounding World'.

25 See Chapter 6, 'Ecological Problems'.

26 See Chapter 5, 'Iceland as a Tourist Attraction'.

27 Landsvirkjun, the National Power Company, was founded in 1965. It is divided among the following owners: the Icelandic state (50 per cent), the city of Reykjavík (44.525 per cent), and the town of Akureyri (5.475 per cent).

28   The SI unit of power is called after the Scottish physicist and inventor James Watt (1736–1819). Large units are abbreviated as follows: kW = kilowatt (1,000 watts); MW = megawatt (1,000,000 watts); GW = gigawatt (1,000,000,000 watts); TW = terawatt (1,000,000,000,000 watts).

29   The following power stations existed in Iceland in 1991:
      Hydroelectric power:

      Sog. 89
      Búrfell I. 210
      Sigalda. 150
      Hrauneyjafoss 210
      Blanda 150
      Laxá. 23
      others. 48
      total *880*

      Geothermal energy:

      Krafla. 30
      Svartsengi 11
      Bjarnarflag. 3
      total *44*
      Oil-fired 133
      Grand total. *1057*

30   Haukur Tómasson presented this estimate to an energy conference in Reykjavík in 1991.

31   See Chapter 6, 'Ecological Problems'.

32   Planned power stations, with expected capacity in MW:

      Sultartangi 110
      Fljótsdalur 252
      Vatnsfell. 100
      Búrfell II 100
      Villinganes. 30
      total *592*

      The Búrfell II project includes extending the water reservoir at the large lake of Þórisvatn. This helps to ensure the supply of electricity in a range of situations.

33   'Private Firm Aims to Buy Electricity from Iceland', *The Guardian*, 5 November 1987. Landsvirkjun judges the project to be feasible: 'the possibility of exporting electricity via a DC submarine cable link from the east coast of Iceland to Scotland has become increasingly realistic. A study made by Landsvirkjun indicates that power prices from a converter station in Scotland would be competitive with prices from new coal-fired and nuclear stations in the UK. Such a project could be realised around the turn of the century' (extract from NORDEL report, Reykjavík, 1989).

⊰⊱ Chapter 10 ⊰⊱

Population, Subsistence, and Welfare: Iceland's Present and Future in a Thousand-Year Perspective

Population may permanently increase without a proportional increase in the means of subsistence.

Thomas Robert Malthus, An Essay on the Principle of Population, *1798*

The Malthusian Theory of Population: A Guiding Star

THOMAS ROBERT MALTHUS (1766–1834) was born under a lucky star. Both as a young man and as an adult he lived on the sunny side of life. His childhood home, a manor near the town of Dorking in Surrey, was visited by philosophers like David Hume and Jean-Jacques Rousseau. It is said that Malthus and his father were fond of discussing the ideas of the Enlightenment. Their views often diverged, however. The son's famous theory of population had its roots in these conversations, which were held in the shadow of the American War of Independence and the French Revolution.

After studies (including mathematics) at Jesus College, Cambridge, Malthus took holy orders. Yet he was never to follow a clerical career. He worked for almost thirty years as a well-off professor of history and political economy at the College of the East India Company in Haileybury. It should be said that Malthus was a happily married man, with three children and many friends.

The basic thesis of the Malthusian principle of population[1]—that population growth has a tendency to exceed the means of subsistence—nevertheless does not sound very cheerful. It undoubtedly sounds like a prophecy of doom. Who wants to hear of famine and the destruction of the world? His theory is scarcely made any more attractive by provocative, inhuman sentences such as 'Whoever comes to Nature's table and finds it bare must leave the table.' According to Malthus, population growth can be checked in two ways. One is sexual continence in the form of late marriage. The other is disaster—war, plague, famine, and so on—which brings times of destitution and crime.

Malthus's theory of population provoked controversy and disgust. How could a clergyman be so hard-hearted? And how could a learned professor show such a lack of human compassion? In any case, was he not making a fuss about nothing? With the optimism which characterized the industrialized western world during the long peace that prevailed between the Congress of Vienna and the First World War, many people thought that Malthus was wrong in his main thesis that population levels outgrow the means of subsistence. On this point, however, later development has shown that the visionary Malthus was right.

Demographers in our day have reason to think again. For every day that passes, the world has 238,000 more mouths to feed—almost the same as the population of Iceland. Each year brings 87 million more people. In the past, the population of the world rose at a relatively slow speed. Now it is doubled at intervals of just 35 years. The birth rate in the industrialized west may have dropped, but population in the developing countries is growing many times faster than the supply of food. This is precisely the danger pointed out by Malthus two centuries ago.[2]

Well into the nineteenth century, population growth was held in check by contagious diseases, war, and famine. Nowadays we know that the population explosion, with the threat of world starvation and environmental destruction, is an even more serious problem than it was then. We must curb population growth by peaceful means, within the framework of global cooperation. The means at our disposal are education, birth control, environmental protection, aid to developing countries, and better use of the earth's limited resources.

Three Eras in the Economic History of Iceland

On the basis of a study of a probable relationship between the population of a country and the preconditions for the inhabitants' subsistence and economic prosperity, an Icelandic scholar, Ágúst Valfells, has been able to distinguish three eras in the history of Iceland:

1. a farming era
2. a fishing era
3. a fishing and energy era

Let us take a closer look at this study, for which the Malthusian theory of population provides one angle of approach. It is fruitful to gain an idea of the development of Iceland in the past, the present-day situation, and its economic prospects for the future by examining demographic data and the use of natural resources, and by studying the interaction of these factors.

The work is particularly interesting in that it is based on a study carried out in 1978, Iceland 2000, and a revised version conducted eleven years later by the same author.[3]

The Farming Era (*c.*860–1900)

During the first and longest era, that of farming, there were heavy fluctuations in population. It rose, fell, and finally rose again as follows (the figures are approximate):

year	population
930	23,000
1000	30,000
1095	77,000[4]
1703	34,000
1786	38,400
1901	78,470

When the colonists settled by the deep fiords and in the green valleys of Iceland, they took land that was rich in trees, bushes, herbs, and grass, with rivers abounding in salmon and plenty of fish in the sea. Garðar Svavarsson, according to *Landnámabók,* saw that Iceland was wooded between the mountains and the sea.[5] The settlers' new homeland must have seemed to be flowing with milk and honey. It attracted more and more colonists. The population rose, as did the number of grazing animals. The vegetation cover was quickly depleted.

Historians say that the Icelandic people were on the verge of starvation by the end of the twelfth century. Famine was not widespread, however, until after the Icelanders lost their independence in 1262. In the centuries that followed, adversities accumulated. The plant cover was blown away from ever greater areas. By 1800, only half of the vegetation cover from the days of the discovery and settlement was left. (Today, all that remains is about a third of the original vegetation.) During these grim centuries, the population was halved. It was only around 1900 that it once again reached the levels of 700 years previously.

Contributory factors were—as we have seen—natural disasters, plagues (the Black Death and smallpox epidemics), deterioration in climate (the Little Ice Age around 1600), and the Danish trade monopoly. People fished around the coast in small rowing-boats. This helped them to survive, as long as the government officials permitted them to fish.[6]

The situation became brighter in the nineteenth century. The Icelanders no longer starved to death, with a few exceptions.[7] The trend was unmistakable, although the swing to a more secure supply of food was protracted and seemingly hesitant. In the second half of the nineteenth century, the people of Iceland were still hopelessly caught in the Malthusian population trap.

Many Icelanders, unable to fill their bellies with what the land produced, and discontented with Danish rule during the age of the Governors-General, were enticed by the promises they read in letters from America. They emigrated in large numbers to Canada and the United States.

For a millennium, Iceland was a traditional agrarian society. Agriculture and sheep farming were the main livelihoods, with hunting and fishing as supplementary pursuits. Moreover, for seven whole centuries, the Icelanders wore the strait-jacket of hunger. In the period 1783–6, more than ten thousand people starved to death.[8] The decline during the age of the Sturlungs continued after the fall of the commonwealth and the signing of the treaty (*Gamli sáttmáli*) with the king of Norway in 1262. The upturn was boosted by the success of the struggle for independence and the two partial victories on the way to full independence. In 1874 Iceland received her first written constitution. In 1904 she was granted limited home rule.

The Fishing Era (*c.*1900–1950)

During the fishing era, the population almost doubled. It rose from roughly 80,000 around the turn of the century to some 144,000 in 1950.

The turning-point came with the introduction of modern technology. Thanks to tractors, artificial fertilizer, and more efficient farming methods, a rapidly declining number of farmers were able to produce larger harvests. Most important, however, was the coming of motor-powered trawlers with efficient catching gear. The trawlers revolutionized fishing. They made it profitable. They gave the Icelandic people ever-growing export revenue. This put an end to the ill-fated combination of poor agriculture with recurrent crop failures and a growing population. We have literary testimony to the appalling consequences of this combination in a novel by Halldór Laxness, *Independent People*.[9]

A relevant feature in the picture of this era is that Iceland became an independent republic in 1944.

The Fishing and Energy Era (*c.*1950–)

We are now living in the third era, that of fishing and energy, when the population has continued to grow rapidly. In round figures, it has risen from 144,000 in 1950 to 260,000 at the start of 1992. A forecast made in 1984 estimates that, unless the birth rate suddenly drops, the population will reach around 290,000 by the year 2003.[10]

If full employment and the high standard of living are to be main-tained alongside population growth on this scale, Iceland will need a considerable increase in production, primarily for export, of a kind that can provide more jobs. Experts appear to be in agreement that this can chiefly be expected in the energy sector: the production of energy, energy-intensive industry (aluminium and the like), tourism, and the general export industry. Fish farming and fish processing seem to be particularly attractive areas, along with technical development in the fields of manufacturing and computers.

There is a special interest in fish farming—a combination which exploits the readily available energy and traditional Icelandic know-how.

In addition, studies show that the Icelanders have enormous poten-tial sources of prosperity in their energy resources. With these as a basis, they could build many times the present number of geothermally heated greenhouses. First, however, they should perhaps concentrate on using the resources to establish new chemical industries which require large amounts of energy. In this way they could increase employment and create a more varied industrial base.

Ágúst Valfells has been able to point out three particular factors in his latest study which speak in favour of a new direction for Icelandic industry and employment. First, a long-term trend suggests that catches of cod and other demersal fish will decline. Second, during the period 1978–89—'the lost years'—Iceland invested too little in en-ergy-intensive industries based on both hydroelectric power and geo-thermal heat. Third, population growth in recent years has been quicker than expected.

Ágúst goes on to point out that, in view of the possibility of new international energy crises, it would be a good idea to use domestic energy to produce synthetic fuels. It might be possible in the future to replace imported oil with hydrogen or—using hydrogen and carbon—to produce methanol and other synthetic fuels.

It remains to be seen how such industry and energy policies will succeed. There are several unknowns in the equation. One thing seems clear, however. The Icelanders at present are at the beginning of an energy era which can be an important new phase in the economic history of their country.

Notes to Chapter 10

1   Thomas Robert Malthus, *An Essay on the Principle of Population, Text Sources and Background Criticism,* ed. Philip Appleman (New York: Norton, 1976). The essay was first published anonymously in 1798. In 1803, Malthus issued a second edition, much revised and enlarged, and with his name on the title page. The quotation in the epigraph to this chapter comes from p. 55 of the first edition.

2   Malthus, *Essay on the Principle of Population,* 'Introduction'. The estimates of population growth in 1989 come from *The Economist,* 20 January 1990.

3   Ágúst Valfells, Ph.D., *Iceland 2000: Production, Population and Prosperity* (Reykjavík: Landsvirkjun, 1979); *Back to the Future: Iceland 2000 Revisited* (Reykjavík: Landsvirkjun, 1989).

4   The figure of 77,000 is a highly uncertain estimate. It is based on a register of tithe-paying farmers drawn up on the orders of the Bishop of Skálholt, Gizur Ísleifsson (1082–1118). There are no reliable demographic statistics until the first parish registers, starting in 1735. See *Iceland 1986: Handbook Published by the Central Bank of Iceland* (Reykjavík, 1987), p. 28.

5   See Chapter 6, 'Ecological Problems'.

6   See Chapter 1, 'Trade Monopoly and Natural Disasters'.

7   See Chapter 1, 'The Struggle for Independence (c.1830–1944)', 'The External Framework'.

8   See *Iceland 1986,* p. 29.

9   See Chapter 4, 'Halldór Laxness'.

10   Statistical Abstract of Iceland 1984 (Reykjavík: Statistical Bureau of Iceland, 1984).

❦ Appendix ❦

Indo-European Roots of Norse Mythology by Jacques de Wærn

MANY PRE-CHRISTIAN CULTURES in Europe—and some outside Europe—divided people into three main classes (four if slaves are included), with different functions in society. This division can be found in the ideal state of Plato (*c*.427–348/347 BC) as described in *The Republic* (*Politeia*).[1] According to Plato, the state must be (1) governed, (2) defended, and (3) fed. These functions are exercised by (1) a philosopher-king, (2) warriors or 'guardians', and (3) producers. The virtues associated with each function are (1) wisdom, (2) courage, and (3) temperance. The sins they must avoid are (1) folly, (2) cowardice, and (3) intemperance. We shall not go into Plato's many mythical and historical examples of the virtues and vices on the various levels; we may content ourselves with the observation that the same classification was applied in other major states and cultural areas, such as India, Iran, Rome, Umbria, and northern Europe.

The two most important interpreters of the ideology underlying this tripartite society are both Frenchmen: George Dumézil and Régis Boyer.[2]

Dumézil considered that the Norse gods were the products of a common Indo-European culture. He argued that the division of Norse society into rulers, warriors, and farmers had its counterpart in mythology. Týr and Odin were described by him as the gods of the sovereign function. Thor was the god of the warriors, while Njörður and Freyr were the gods of the farmers and merchants. Dumézil does not mention Plato's *Republic* in his study of Norse mythology (although elsewhere he sees Plato's ideas as a reflection of the tripartite Indo-European ideology), but he receives indirect support from the Athenian philosopher. Plato links the different levels of society with different elements: gold is the attribute of the rulers, iron of the warriors. Plato could not have known that northern Europe had a similar division: Odin (Icelandic *Óðinn*, Old English *Wôden*, Langobardic *Wotan*, Old Saxon *Uuôden*, Common Germanic **Wôdanaz*), god of the sovereign class, has a shining gold helmet, while the chief attribute of Thor (Icelandic *Þór*, Old English *Þunor*, Old Saxon *Thunaer*, Old High German *Donar*, Common Germanic **Þunraz*), god of the warriors, is an iron hammer. According to Plato, alcoholic drinks should be reserved for the upper class. From Snorri's *Edda* we see that Odin lives solely on wine.

According to Dumézil, the sovereign function has two aspects, one exercised by a legislator, the other by a magician-chieftain. These are represented in the ancient Indian pair of Mitra and Varuna and the Roman dyad of Jupiter Optimus and Jupiter Maximus. The Norse equivalents are Týr (Old English *Tiw*, Old High German *Zio*, Common Germanic **Tiwaz*), god of law (as reflected in his alternative name *Thingsus*, showing his connection with the judicial assembly or *thing*), and Odin, whose sphere is magic-mysterious. Here too, Dumézil receives indirect support from Plato's examples of King Rhadamanthys and King Minos.

Other general European and also Indian similarities concern the third function, that of fertility. The gods of this level are often twins or pairs. Rome had Liber and Libera, India had the two Nasatiyas. In the *Elder Edda* we find Freyr and Freyja and Byggvir and Beyla. Perhaps we have a similar pair in the Norse Njörður and Tacitus' Nerthus, if they are not in fact identical. The primeval element of water is significant for this function, as we shall see below.

Dumézil's interpretations can be somewhat strained, leaving some of his conclusions open to objection. It is then salutary to read Régis Boyer's book. Whereas Dumézil has a broad, synchronic approach, Boyer analyses the subject diachronically. He follows the lines of development through time from the Neolithic to the fully personified mythology of the Viking Age, which was well adapted to the Norse people and the natural environment in which they lived.

To a much greater extent than Dumézil, Boyer puts the sacred tree in the centre. We find the tree on Bronze Age rock carvings from Bohuslän in Sweden, and in Adam of Bremen's account of the sacrifice at Uppsala. The gods assembled for their *thing* under the ash Yggdrasill. It was thought that humanity would survive as long as the tree stood. It was the source of all life and destiny, but it was always threatened by the forces of evil.

The world tree, Yggdrasill, is naturally no ordinary tree. It is so contrived that it can only be partly grasped by human thoughts. 'The third root of the ash tree is in the sky,' says Snorri.[3] The tree is beyond the conceptual ability of mankind. The human conception of the tree is necessarily contradictory. It is a tree which cannot be drawn. Many of the world's religions have similar phenomena.

Whereas Dumézil argues too insistently for a hypothetical, uniform Indo-European culture, Boyer's orientation may appear too local. A tree cult was also practised in Lithuania, in honour of the god Perkunas, and among the Frisians, who worshipped Thor. In both these cases the sacred tree was an oak.

The routes followed by religion and mythology can be traced using the methods of comparative linguistics. From an Indo-European root meaning 'sky, heaven' comes the word for 'god', *deiwos*, reflected in Sanskrit *deva*, Latin *deus*, Lithuanian *dievas*, Irish *dia*, and Icelandic plural *tívor* (*Völuspá* 31) or more often *týr*, plural *tívar*. The highest god bears the name 'sky father', *Dyaus pitar* in Sanskrit, *Zeus pater* in Greek, and *Juppiter* in Latin.

The Indo-European goddess of the dawn appears in Sanskrit as *Ushas*. The Greeks knew her as *Eos* and the Romans as *Aurora*. She also found her way to the Germanic peoples: the Venerable Bede derives the name of the feast of *Easter* from an Anglo-Saxon goddess *Eostra* (German *Ostara*). There was a change of sex on the way to Iceland, whether the divinity of the dawn came from the Germans or the Lithuanians (*Aušrà*), resulting in *Austri,* the dwarf of the east and the dawn, who supports the eastern corner of the sky. His comrades *Norðri, Suðri,* and *Vestri* bear up the other corners.

The myth of Baldur the Good is a northern offshoot of the complex of myths about the dying vegetation god. This is found in varying forms in many countries in Europe and Asia. A god dies and nature mourns him by starting to wither; nature does not revive until the god can be found again and brought back to life. The concrete forms taken by the motif depend on the overall religious context in which it appears.

Baldur's son *Forseti*, the god of justice and reconciliation, is considered by modern scholars to be a Norse reinterpretation of the name of a Frisian god *Fosite,* after whom the island of *Fositesland* in the North Sea (now Heligoland) is named. The name *Forseti* means 'he who sits at the fore', in other words, 'he who presides', for example over a court of law.[4] The 'holy land' of Heligoland, which was once the site of a judicial and cultic assembly, could have been where Fosite's mythical court lay. In the Viking Age and Middle Ages, this remarkable island, when seen from the north or south, stood out as two small bumps on the horizon, one red and one white. The former is a red sandstone hill on the main island, while the latter is the chalk summit of the island of Düne. This beautiful sight may have inspired the vision of Glitnir, Forseti's hall, which the Eddic poem of *Grímnismál* describes as shining with pillars of gold and a roof of silver.

Threads of linguistic and contentual similarities, distant influences from the south-east and east, along with chains of archaeological influence, converge in Scandinavia. Examples of this are: (1) *Parjanya*, the Vedic rain-god of ancient India, and *Perkunas*, the Lithuanian god of thunder and mountains, are related to the Norse god *Fjörgynn*, with a feminine counterpart in Gothic *fairguni*, Old English *fyrgen* 'mountain' and Old Norse *Fjörgyn*, being both 'earth' and the mother of Thor. (2) Although the linguistic form and the content may be distant, there is a clear relationship between *Teljavelj*, the divine smith of the Letto-Prussians, and two Scandinavian figures, the Gutnic Þielvar, who brought fire to the island of Gotland, and the Icelandic Þjálfi, a companion of Thor, who could run as fast as lightning. (3) The Slavonic *kvas,* a fermented beverage, appears to be related to Norse *Kvasir*, a wise being who emanated from a beverage made from the saliva of the gods. When Kvasir was killed a mixture of his blood with honey produced a potion of wisdom and poetry from which Odin benefited.[5]

On the amber route that ran north from the Roman trading outpost of Claudia Celeia (Cilli in Styria) and ended in Samland by the Baltic Sea, there are eight places with *Loke* in their name. Prometheus, according to the Greek myth, was bound to a cliff in the Caucasus. Loki was tied to three sharp slabs. It seems clear that Loki's main role is that of the trickster, a sign of oriental influence. The trickster is found throughout the circumpolar area. He rides backwards on a horse, dances in the wrong direction round the camp-fire, is an anti-god and a clown. Odin's shamanistic aspects are likewise of Asian and circumpolar origin. Other influences appear to have reached Iceland from Celtic areas, such as the god Rígur (Old Irish *ríg* means 'king'), the main character in the Eddic poem *Rígsþula*.

Boyer rightly stresses the central position of the heavenly bodies in the myths of the Northmen. They also appear to have been important among the Germanic tribes south of Scandinavia. The first myth in Snorri's *Edda,* after his account of creation and his description of the world, is about the giant who offered to build the stronghold of Ásgarður in one winter, in return for which he would receive Freyja, the sun, and the moon.[6] Odin could not think of giving away three such important divinities. Sun (Sol), Fire (Vulcanus), and Moon (Luna) were worshipped by the Germans in the first century BC, according to Julius Caesar in his *De Bello Gallico.*[7] In a doctoral thesis on medieval and Renaissance views of Caesar, Bo Elthammar recounts a remarkable tale from the thirteenth-century *Sächsische Weltchronik* (ch. 26).[8] It tells how Caesar arrived at a mountain in the moonlight and gave it the name Lüneburg. He hung up a gilded moon on a stone column, an idol worshipped by the inhabitants of that land as well as the Danes and Wends. Moon-worship appears to have continued until the time of Saint Suitbert. He destroyed the idol and built a monastery and chapel on the site in honour of the Virgin Mary. We know of similar happenings in Scandinavia. The Christian missionaries took over pagan sites and Christianized them to make for an easier transition to the new faith.

The moon god and water play a significant role in Snorri's myth of the abduction by the moon of two children, Bil and Hjúki, who had been fetching water from the spring called Byrgir in a pail known as Sægur.[9] The worship of heavenly bodies is suggested by a find from

Bronze Age Sjælland in Denmark, the Trundholm sun-chariot. This is a bronze chariot pulled by a bronze horse. The back axle bears a large circular disc with gold plating. Sun, moon, and fire were thus living divinities for the ancient Scandinavians. According to *Hávamál*, fire and 'the sight of the sun' are among the things that are best for the sons of men.

One of the key texts in our attempts to understand the Norse view of the nature of the world is a stanza that occurs in both Snorri's *Edda* and the *Elder Edda* (in *Grímnismál*). The verse lists three names which are easily assigned to the three functions identified by Dumézil, in the correct order:[10]

Odin says:	*(literal translation)*
Andhrímnir lætr	Andhrímnir lets
í Eldhrímni	in Eldhrímnir
Sæhrímni soðinn	Sæhrímnir seethe

For centuries the stanza has been interpreted as showing that a virtually real cook, Andhrímnir, has a virtually real cauldron, Eldhrímnir, in which he boils a virtually real boar, Sæhrímnir. This misunderstanding, caused by a tendency to think in too concrete terms, has given rise to the story of the boar Sæhrímnir, which is continually slaughtered, cooked, and eaten, only to come back to life afterwards, since Valhalla is an eternal paradise which—somewhat inconsistently—will be destroyed in the distant future, in Ragnarök. This is the last great battle, which annihilates almost all of the old world with its gods and mortals.

Yet this verse is actually deeply symbolic, with an archaic meaning. It comes from the doctrine of the elements, which was imported to Scandinavia from the south and the east, but which was fostered throughout Europe and Asia in pre-Christian times. It was, for example, taught by philosophers of the seventh and sixth centuries BC in the Greek city of Miletus. Only a small proportion of the ideas in Norse mythology can be traced back before the birth of Christ, but here we have an example: the Greek philosopher Empedocles of Agrigentum (fifth century BC) described four variants of a fundamental element of which he claimed that the world consisted, namely, fire, water, air, and earth. These four elements are successive stages in the transformation of the primeval element. This doctrine appeared roughly simultaneously in different parts of Asia, presumably independent of Greek speculation, as the Swedish philosopher Anders Wedberg has pointed out.[11] As we have seen, Odin (or at least important elements of his personality) was of shamanistic origin. Shamanism was practised throughout the circumpolar area, and also at an early stage among more southerly peoples in Asia and Europe. If one goes back far enough in time, it was found everywhere.

Of course, the Greek pre-Christian philosophers—like Odin in the shape of Grímnir—were ignorant of what we know now. With their theory of the primeval elements, they and the Asian thinkers were trying to find a method for understanding the world. Its inner nature had to be described using the available store of words and concepts. Applying this interpretation to the three names in the Eddic stanza, we see that when we remove the element *hrímnir* (etymologically related to 'rime' frost), we are left with three elements: (1) *And*, representing Icelandic *andi* 'air', Odin's level; (2) *Eld*, Icelandic *eldur* 'fire', Thor's level; (3) *Sæ*, Icelandic *sær* 'sea', the level of Njörður and Freyr, that is, the function of transport, sailing, and fertility. Freyr owned the ship Skíðblaðnir and the boar Gullinbursti (Golden-bristle), which glistened as it moved. He was the god who ensured plenty. Air, fire, and water are transformations of the same element, of which the whole of creation was built.

If the Milesian philosophers had been able to hear *Grímnismál* and Odin's verse about the nature of the world, they might have objected that 'earth' was missing. But the primeval element could probably be transformed in time to this valuable element. Perhaps this was considered too self-evident. Alternatively, earth may have been lost as the theory wandered through the centuries.

The crux of what was eaten by the fallen warriors who came to Valhalla is indeed a difficult one. We may conclude by emphasizing that the world of the gods, as seen by the ancient Scandinavians, was much more abstract than the mortals and their earth-disc, and more abstract than we usually conceive it. Snorri writes in the same passage as the stanza we have quoted, 'But as for the question you are putting now, it seems to me that not many people would know enough to give you the correct answer.' Moreover, the stanza ends with the following lines: 'but few men know on what Valhalla's champions feed'.[12]

Notes to the Appendix

1   Plato, *The Republic*, trans. H. D. P. Lee (Harmondsworth: Penguin, 1955).

2   Georges Dumézil, *Les Dieux des Germains: Essais sur la formation de la religion scandinave*, 2nd ed. (Paris: Presses Universitaires de France, 1959); this has been translated by Einar Haugen as *Gods of the Ancient Northmen* (Berkeley: University of California Press, 1973). Régis Boyer, *Yggdrasil: La Religion des anciens Scandinaves* (Paris: Payot, 1982).

3   *The Prose Edda of Snorri Sturluson: Tales from Norse Mythology*, trans. Jean I. Young (Berkeley: University of California Press, 1975), p. 43.

4   H. R. Ellis Davidson, *Gods and Myths of Northern Europe* (Harmondsworth: Penguin, 1964), pp. 171–2.

5   Ulf Drobin, 'Mjödet och offersymboliken i fornnordisk religion', in *Studier i religionshistoria tillägnade Åke Hultkrantz professor emeritus den 1 juli 1986*, ed. Louise Bäckman, Ulf Drobin, and Per-Arne Berglie, pp. 97–141 (Löberöd: Plus Ultra, 1991).

6   See Chapter 2, 'Snorri's *Edda*'.

7   Caesar, *The Conquest of Gaul*, trans. S. A. Handford (Harmondsworth: Penguin, 1951), p. 35 (VI, 21, 2).

8   Bo Elthammar, *Julius Caesar inför eftervärlden: Studier i Caesaruppfattningen under medeltid och italiensk renässans* (Stockholm, 1976), p. 24.

9   *The Prose Edda of Snorri Sturluson*, p. 38.

10 Finnur Jónsson, *Edda Snorra Sturlusonar* (Copenhagen, 1931), p. 42; the same stanza occurs in *Grímnismál* 18 in the *Elder Edda*.

11 Anders Wedberg, *A History of Philosophy*, vol. 1. *Antiquity and the Middle Ages* (Oxford: Clarendon, 1982).

12 *The Prose Edda of Snorri Sturluson*, p. 63.

❧ Literature, Opera, and Film: A Guide ❧

Select Bibliography

General

Björn Rúriksson. *Iceland from Above*. Photographs and text. Translated by Dr. Georg Douglas. Seltjarnarnes: Geoscan Publishing, 1990.

Haraldur Sigurðsson. *Writings of Foreigners Relating to the Nature and People of Iceland: A Bibliography*. Reykjavík: Landsbókasafn Íslands, 1991.

Hjálmar R. Bárðarson. *Iceland: A Portrait of Its Land and People*. Reykjavík: Hjálmar R. Bárðarson, 1982.

Horton, John J. *Iceland*. World Bibliographical Series 37. Oxford and Santa Barbara: Clio Press, 1983.

Iceland 1986: Handbook Published by the Central Bank of Iceland. Reykjavík, 1987.

Jón Aðalsteinsson Jónsson. *One Hundred Years of Icelandic Stamps, 1873–1973*. Translated by Peter Kidson. Reykjavík: Post and Telecommunications Administration, 1977.

Lindroth, Hjalmar. *Iceland: A Land of Contrasts*. Translated by Adolph B. Benson. New York, 1937.

Magnusson, Magnus. *Iceland Saga*. London: Bodley Head, 1987.

Roberts, David (text), and Jon Krakauer (photographs). *Iceland: Land of the Sagas*. New York: Harry N. Abrams, 1990.

Sigurður A. Magnússon. *Northern Sphinx: Iceland and the Icelanders from the Settlement to the Present*. London: Hurst, 1977.

200 Years of Icelandic Periodicals. A Bibliography of Icelandic Periodicals, Newspapers, and Other Serial Publications, 1773–1973. Compiled by Böðvar Kvaran and Einar Sigurðsson. Reykjavík, 1991.

Language

Cleasby, Richard, and Gudbrand Vigfusson. *An Icelandic–English Diction-ary.* 2nd ed. with a supplement by Sir Wiliam A. Craigie. Oxford: Claren-don Press, 1957. (A comprehensive dictionary of Old Icelandic/Old Norse.)

Geipel, John. *The Viking Legacy: The Scandinavian Influence on the English and Gaelic Languages.* Newton Abbot: David & Charles, 1971.

Haugen, Einar. *The Scandinavian Languages: An Introduction to Their History.* London: Faber, 1976.

Jón Friðjónsson. *A Course in Modern Icelandic.* Reykjavík: Tímaritið Skák, 1978.

Stefán Einarsson. *Icelandic: Grammar, Texts, Glossary.* Baltimore: Johns Hopkins Press, 1945.

Sverrir Hólmarsson, Christopher Sanders, and John Tucker. *Concise Ice-landic–English Dictionary: Íslensk–ensk orðabók.* Reykjavík: Iðunn, 1989.

Sören Sörensson. *Ensk–íslensk orðabók með alfræðilegu ívafi.* Reykjavík: Örn og Örlygur, 1984. (Modern English–Icelandic dictionary.)

Valfells, Sigrid, and James E. Cathay. *Old Icelandic: An Introductory Course.* Oxford: Oxford University Press, 1981.

Old Icelandic Literature; Mythology and Folklore

Auden, W. H., and Paul B. Taylor. Norse Poems. London: Athlone Press, 1981.

Bekker-Nielsen, Hans, and Ole Widding. *Arne Magnusson: The Manuscript Collector.* Translated by Robert W. Mattila. Odense: Odense University Press, 1972.

The Book of Settlements: Landnámabók. Translated by Hermann Pálsson and Paul Edwards. Winnipeg: University of Manitoba Press, 1972.

The Book of the Icelanders (Íslendingabók) by Ari Þorgilsson. Translated by Halldór Hermannsson. Ithaca: Cornell University Press, 1930.

Boucher, Alan. *Adventures, Outlaws and Past Events.* Reykjavík: Iceland Review, 1977.

———. *Elves, Trolls and Elemental Beings.* Reykjavík: Iceland Review, 1977.

———. *Ghosts, Witchcraft and the Other World.* Reykjavík: Iceland Review, 1977.

Boyer, Régis. *Yggdrasil: La Religion des anciens Scandinaves.* Paris: Payot, 1982.

Davidson, H. R. Ellis. *Gods and Myths of Northern Europe.* Harmondsworth: Penguin, 1964.

Dumézil, Georges. *Gods of the Ancient Northmen.* Edited by Einar Haugen. Berkeley: University of California Press, 1973.

Egil's Saga. Translated by Hermann Pálsson and Paul Edwards. Harmondsworth: Penguin, 1976.

Eyrbyggja Saga. Translated by Hermann Pálsson and Paul Edwards. Harmondsworth: Penguin, 1989.

Eysteinn Ásgrímsson. *Lilja (The Lily): An Icelandic Religious Poem of the Fourteenth Century.* Edited and translated by Eiríkr Magnússon. London: William & Norgate, 1870.

The Faroese Saga. Translated by G. V. C. Young and Cynthia R. Clewer. Belfast, 1973.

Gísli Sigurðsson. *Gaelic Influence in Iceland: Historical and Literary Contacts: A Survey of Research.* Studia Islandica 46. Reykjavík: Bókaútgáfa Menningarsjóðs, 1988.

Grettir's Saga. Translated by Denton Fox and Hermann Pálsson. Toronto: University of Toronto Press, 1974.

Gudbrand Vigfusson and F. York Powell. *Origines Islandicae: A Collection of the More Important Sagas and Other Native Writings Relating to the Settlement and Early History of Iceland.* Oxford: Clarendon Press, 1905.

Hallberg, Peter. *The Icelandic Saga.* Translated by Paul Schach. Lincoln: University of Nebraska Press, 1962.

Hollander, Lee M. *The Sagas of Kormák and The Sworn Brothers.* Princeton: Princeton University Press, 1949.

————. *The Skalds: A Selection of their Poems, with Introduction and Notes.* Ann Arbor: University of Michigan Press, 1968.

Hrafnkel's Saga and Other Icelandic Stories. Translated by Hermann Pálsson. Harmondsworth: Penguin, 1971.

Icelandic Legends. Translated by George E. J. Powell and Eiríkur Magnússon. London: Bentley, 1864–6. Reprinted New York: AMS Press, 1980.

Icelandic Sagas, Eddas, and Art: Treasures Illustrating the Greatest Mediaeval Literary Heritage of Northern Europe. New York: The Pierpont Morgan Library, 1982.

Jónas Kristjánsson, *Icelandic Sagas and Manuscripts.* Translated by Alan Boucher. Reykjavík: Iceland Review, 1980.

————. *Eddas and Sagas: Iceland's Medieval Literature.* Translated by Peter Foote. Reykjavík: Hið íslenzka bókmenntafélag, 1992.

The King's Mirror. Translated and edited by Laurence Marcellus Larson. New York: Twayne, 1917.

Laws of Early Iceland: Grágás. Translated by Andrew Dennis, Peter Foote, and Richard Perkins. Icelandic Studies 3. Winnipeg: University of Manitoba Press, 1980.

Laxdæla Saga. Translated by Magnus Magnusson and Hermann Pálsson. Harmondsworth: Penguin, 1969.

Martin, John Stanley. *Ragnarök: An Investigation into Old Norse Concepts of the Fate of the Gods.* Melbourne Monographs in Germanic Studies 3. Assen: Van Gorcum, 1972.

Njal's Saga. Translated by Magnus Magnusson and Hermann Pálsson. Harmondsworth: Penguin, 1960.

Poems of the Vikings: The Elder Edda. Translated by Patricia Terry. Indianapolis: Bobbs-Merrill, 1969.

The Poetic Edda. Translated with an introduction and notes by Henry Adams Bellows. Scandinavian Classics 21 and 22, 2 vols. in 1. New York: American-Scandinavian Foundation, 1923. Reprinted New York: Biblio & Tannen, 1969.

The Prose Edda of Snorri Sturluson: Tales from Norse Mythology. Translated by Jean I. Young. Cambridge: Bowes & Bowes, 1954. Reprinted Berkeley: University of California Press, 1973.

The Saga of Gisli. Translated by George Johnston. London: Dent, 1963.

The Saga of Tristram and Ísönd. Translated by Paul Schach. Lincoln: University of Nebraska Press, 1973.

Seven Viking Romances. Translated by Hermann Pálsson and Paul Edwards. Harmondsworth: Penguin, 1985.

Simpson, Jacqueline. *Icelandic Folktales and Legends.* London: Batsford, 1972.

———. *Legends of Icelandic Magicians.* Cambridge: Brewer, 1975.

———. *The Northmen Talk: A Choice of Tales from Iceland.* London: Phoenix House, 1965.

Snorri Sturluson. *Heimskringla: History of the Kings of Norway.* Translated with introduction and notes by Lee M. Hollander. Austin: University of Texas Press, 1964.

Sturlunga Saga. Translated by Julia H. McGrew and R. George Thomas. Library of Scandinavian Literature 9–10. New York: Twayne, 1970–4.

The Vinland Sagas: The Norse Discovery of America: Grænlendinga Saga and Eirik's Saga. Translated by Magnus Magnusson and Hermann Pálsson. Harmondsworth: Penguin, 1965.

Modern Icelandic Literature

Arts and Culture in Iceland: Literature. Booklet published by the Icelandic Ministry of Culture and Education, Reykjavík, 1989.

Beck, Richard. *History of Icelandic Poets, 1800–1940.* Islandica 34. Ithaca: Cornell University Press, 1950.

Bibliography of Modern Icelandic Literature in Translation, Including Works Written by Icelanders in Other Languages. Compiled by P. M. Mitchell and Kenneth H. Ober. Ithaca: Cornell University Press, 1975.

Fire and Ice: Three Icelandic Plays. Edited by Einar Haugen. Madison: University of Wisconsin Press, 1967. (Includes Jóhann Sigurjónsson's *Galdra-Loftur* [*The Wish*], Davíð Stefánsson's *Gullna hliðið* [*The Golden Gate*], and Agnar Þórðarson's *Kjarnorka og kvenhylli* [*Atoms and Maidens*].)

Guðmundur Kamban. *Hadda Padda: A Drama in Four Acts.* Translated by Sadie Louise Peller. New York: Knopf, 1917.

———. *The Virgin of Skalholt.* Translated by Evelyn Ramsden. Boston: Little, Brown, 1935.

Gunnar Gunnarsson. *The Black Cliffs: Svartfugl.* Translated by Cecil Wood. Madison: University of Wisconsin Press, 1967.

———. *Guest the One-Eyed.* Translated by W. W. Worster. London: Gyldendal, 1920.

———. *The Night and the Dream.* Translated by Evelyn Ramsden. New York: Bobbs-Merrill, 1938.

———. *Seven Days' Darkness.* Translated by Roberts Tapley. New York: Macmillan, 1930.

———. *Ships in the Sky: Compiled from Uggi Greipsson's Notes.* Translated by Evelyn Ramsden. Indianapolis: Bobbs-Merrill, 1938.

———. *The Sworn Brothers: A Tale of the Early Days of Iceland.* Translated by C. Field and W. Emmé. London: Gyldendal, 1920.

Hallberg, Peter. *Halldór Laxness.* Translated by Rory McTurk. Twayne's World Authors Series 89. New York: Twayne, 1971.

Halldór Kiljan Laxness. *The Atom Station.* Translated by Magnus Magnusson. London: Methuen, 1961.

———. *Christianity at Glacier.* Translated by Magnus Magnusson. Reykjavík: Helgafell, 1972.

———. *La Cloche d'Islande.* Translated by Régis Boyer. Paris: Aubier Montagne, 1979.

————. *The Happy Warriors*. Translated by Katherine John. London: Methuen, 1958.

————. *Independent People: An Epic*. Translated by J. A. Thompson. London: Allen & Unwin, 1945.

————. *Paradise Reclaimed*. Translated by Magnus Magnusson. London: Methuen, 1962.

————. *Salka Valka*. Translated by F. H. Lyon. London: Allen and Unwin, 1963.

————. *The Fish Can Sing*. Translated by Magnus Magnusson. London: Methuen, 1966.

————. *World Light*. Translated by Magnus Magnusson. Madison: University of Wisconsin Press, 1969.

Icelandic Lyrics: Originals and Translations. Edited by Richard Beck. Reykjavík: Þórhallur Bjarnarson, 1930. Reprinted Reykjavík: Litbrá, 1956.

Icelandic Poems and Stories: Translations from Modern Icelandic Literature. Edited by Richard Beck. Princeton: Princeton University Press for the American-Scandinavian Foundation, 1943.

Icelandic Short Stories. Translated and edited by Evelyn Firchow Scherabon. New York: Twayne, 1975.

Jóhann Sigurjónsson. *Eyvindur of the Mountains*. Translated by Francis P. Magoun. Reykjavík: Helgafell, 1961.

Magnús Á. Árnason. *An Anthology of Icelandic Poetry*. Edited by Eiríkur Benedikz. Reykjavík: Ministry of Education, 1969.

Northern Lights: Icelandic Poems. Translated by Jakobina Johnson. Reykjavík: Bókaútgáfa Menningarsjóðs, 1959.

The Postwar Poetry of Iceland. Translated with introduction by Sigurður A. Magnússon. Iowa City: University of Iowa Press, 1982.

Stefán Einarsson. *A History of Icelandic Literature*. Baltimore: Johns Hopkins Press, 1969.

Three Modern Icelandic Poets: Selected Poems of Steinn Steinarr, Jón úr Vör and Matthías Johannessen. Translated by Marshall Brement. Reykjavík: Iceland Review, 1985.

Þorbergur Þórðarson. *In Search of My Beloved*. Translated by Kenneth G. Chapman. New York: Twayne & American Scandinavian Foundation, 1967. (Partial translation of *Íslenzkur aðall*.)

Art and Culture

Aðalsteinn Ingólfsson and Matthías Johannessen. *Kjarval: A Painter of*

Iceland. Translated by Haukur Böðvarsson. Reykjavík: Iceland Review, 1981.

Árni Björnsson. *Icelandic Feasts and Holidays: Celebrations Past and Present*. Translated by May Hallmundsson and Hallberg Hallmundsson. Reykjavík: Iceland Review, 1980.

Arts and Culture in Iceland: Arts, Architecture and Crafts. Booklet published by the Icelandic Ministry of Culture and Education, Reykjavík, 1990.

Arts and Culture in Iceland: Music. Booklet published by the Icelandic Ministry of Culture and Education, Reykjavík, 1990.

Arts and Culture in Iceland: Theatre, Films and Ballet. Booklet published by the Icelandic Ministry of Culture and Education, Reykjavík, 1990.

Bergendahl, Göran. *New Music in Iceland*. Translated by Peter Lyne. Reykjavík: Iceland Music Information Centre, 1991.

Elín Kristjánsson, *Some Icelandic Recipes*. Translated by Hólmfríður Jónsdóttir. Reykjavík: Örn og Örlygur, 1975.

Elsa E. Guðjónsson, *National Costume of Women in Iceland*. Reykjavík: National Museum of Iceland, 1970.

————. *Traditional Icelandic Embroidery*. Reykjavík: Icleand Review, 1985.

Fiske, Willard. *Chess in Iceland and in Icelandic Literature with Historical Notes on Other Table-games*. Florence, 1905.

Kristján Eldjárn. *Icelandic Art*. London: Thames and Hudson, 1961.

Matthías Johannessen. *Erró: An Icelandic Artist*. Reykjavík: Iceland Review, 1978.

————. *Sculptor Ásmundur Sveinsson: An Edda in Shapes and Symbols*. Translated by May and Hallberg Hallmundsson. Reykjavík: Iceland Review Books, 1974.

Nordisk Tidskrift. 1925–1935. Published by the Letterstedska Society (Letterstedska föreningen). Stockholm.

Sigurður A. Magnússon. *Iceland Crucible: A Modern Artistic Renaissance*. Reykjavík: Vaka Helgafell, 1985.

Sveinn Einarsson, *The Reykjavík Theatre Company*. Reykjavík: Leikfélag Reykjavíkur, 1972.

Thór Magnússon. *A Showcase of Icelandic National Treasures*. Translated by May and Hallberg Hallmundsson. Reykjavík: Iceland Review, 1987.

History and Society

Ágúst Valfells. *Iceland 2000: Production, Population and Prosperity.* Reykjavík: Landsvirkjun, 1979.

———. *Back to the Future: Iceland 2000 Revisited.* Reykjavík: Landsvirkjun, 1989.

Albert Jónsson. *Iceland, NATO and the Keflavík Base.* Reykjavík: Icelandic Commission on Security and International Affairs, 1989.

Ari Trausti Guðmundsson and Halldór Kjartansson. *Guide to the Geology of Iceland.* Reykjavík: Örn og Örlygur, 1984.

Benedikt Gröndal. *Iceland from Neutrality to NATO Membership.* Oslo: Universitetsforlaget, 1971.

Björn Þorsteinsson. 'Henry VIII and Iceland'. *Saga-Book* 15 (1957–61), pp. 67–101.

———. *Thingvellir: Iceland's National Shrine.* Reykjavík: Örn & Örlygur, 1987.

Brent, Peter. *The Viking Saga.* London: Weidenfeld and Nicolson, 1975.

Davis, Morris. *Iceland Extends its Fisheries Limits: A Political Analysis.* Oslo: Universitetsforlaget, 1963.

Einar Ól. Sveinsson. *The Age of the Sturlungs: Icelandic Civilization in the Thirteenth Century.* Islandica 36. Ithaca: Cornell University Press, 1953. Reprinted Kraus, 1966.

Fenton, Alexander, and Hermann Pálsson, eds. *The Northern and Western Isles in the Viking World.* Edinburgh: John Donald, 1984.

Gilchrist, Sir Andrew. *Cod Wars and How to Lose Them.* Edinburgh: Q Press, 1978.

Gjerset, Knut. *History of Iceland.* New York: Macmillan, 1924.

Gunnar Gunnarsson. *The Keflavík Base: Plans and Projects.* Reykjavík: Icelandic Commission on Security and International Affairs, 1986.

Gunnlaugur Thordarson. *Les Eaux territoriales d'Islande en ce qui concerne la pêche.* Reykjavík: Hlaðbúð, 1958.

Gylfi Þ. Gíslason. *The Problem of Being an Icelander Past, Present and Future.* Translated by Pétur Kidson Karlsson. Reykjavík: Almenna bókafélagið, 1973.

Halldór Hermannsson. *Sir Joseph Banks and Iceland.* Islandica 18. New York: Cornell University Library, 1928.

Hannes Jónsson. *Friends in Conflict: The Anglo-Icelandic Cod Wars and the Law of the Sea.* London: Hurst, 1982.

Hood, John C. F. *Icelandic Church Saga*. London: Society for Promoting Christian Knowledge, 1946. Reprinted Westport: Greenwood Press, 1981.

Ingstad, Helge. *Westward to Vinland: The Discovery of Pre-Columbian Norse House-sites in North America*. Translated by Erik J. Friis. London: Jonathan Cape, 1969.

Jón Hnefill Aðalsteinsson. *Under the Cloak: The Acceptance of Christianity in Iceland with Particular Reference to the Religious Attitudes Prevailing at the Time*. Uppsala, 1978.

Jón Jóhannesson. *A History of the Old Icelandic Commonwealth: Íslendinga Saga*. Translated by Haraldur Bessason. Winnipeg: University of Manitoba Press, 1974.

Jones, Gwyn. *A History of the Vikings*. Revised edition. Oxford: Oxford University Press, 1984.

——. *The Norse Atlantic Saga*. Revised edition. Oxford: Oxford University Press, 1986.

Kendrick, T. D. *A History of the Vikings*. London: Methuen, 1930.

Magnusson, Magnus. *Viking Expansion Westwards* (London: Bodley Head, 1973).

——. *Vikings!* London: Bodley Head, 1980.

Njörður P. Njarðvík. *Birth of a Nation: The Story of the Icelandic Commonwealth*. Reykjavík: Iceland Review, 1978.

Nordahl, Else. *Reykjavík from the Archaeological Point of View*. Aun 12. Uppsala, 1988.

Wahlgren, Erik. *The Vikings and America*. London: Thames and Hudson, 1986.

Travel in Iceland, Past and Present

Auden, W. H., and Louis MacNeice. *Letters from Iceland*. London: Faber, 1937.

Coles, John. *Summer Travelling in Iceland; Being the Narrative of Two Journeys across the Island by Unfrequented Routes*. London: Murray, 1882.

Dufferin, Lord. *Letters from High Latitudes*. London: Murray, 1857.

Eggert Ólafsson and Bjarni Pálsson. *Travels in Iceland Performed 1752–1757 by Order of His Danish Majesty*. Translated from the Danish. Revised English edition (Reykjavík: Örn og Örlygur, 1975).

Escritt, Tony. *Iceland: A Handbook for Expeditions*. Harrow: Iceland Information Centre, 1990.

Gaimard, Paul. *Voyage en Islande et au Groënland, exécuté pendant les années 1835 et 1836 sur la corvette* la Recherche. 8 vols. with Atlas. Paris, 1838–52.

Henderson, Ebenezer. *Iceland, or the Journal of a Residence in that Island during the Years 1814–1815.* 2 vols. Edinburgh: Waugh & Innes, 1818.

Hooker, William Jackson. *Journal of a Tour in Iceland in the Summer of 1809.* 2 vols. London: Longman, 1813.

Kidson, Peter. *Iceland in a Nutshell.* Reykjavík: Iceland Travel Books, 1974.

Mackenzie, Sir George Steuart. *Travels in the Island of Iceland during the Summer of the Year MDCCCX.* Edinburgh, 1811.

Morris, William. *Journal of Travels in Iceland.* In *The Collected Works of William Morris*, vol. 8. London: Longman, 1911.

Philpott, Don. *The Visitor's Guide to Iceland.* Ashbourne, Derbyshire: Moorland, 1989.

Troil, Uno von. *Letters on Iceland Containing Observations . . . Made During a Voyage Undertaken in the Year 1772 by Joseph Banks, Esq. F.R.S.* London: Richardson, 1780.

Williams, David. *Iceland: The Visitor's Guide.* London: Stacey International, 1986.

Nature

Carwardine, Mark. *Iceland: Nature's Meeting Place.* Reykjavík: Iceland Review, 1986.

Hjálmar R. Bárðarson. *Ice and Fire: Contrasts of Icelandic Nature.* Translated by Sölvi Eysteinsson. Third edition. Reykjavík: Hjálmar R. Bárðarson, 1980.

———. *Birds of Iceland.* Reykjavík: Hjálmar R. Bárðarson, 1986.

Hörður Kristinsson. *A Guide to the Flowering Plants and Ferns of Iceland.* Reykjavík: Örn og Örlygur, 1987.

Jón Eyþórsson and Hlynur Sigtryggsson. 'The Climate and Weather of Iceland.' *Zoology of Iceland*, vol. 1, part 3. Copenhagen: Munksgaard, 1971.

Kristján Sæmundsson. 'Outline of the Geology of Iceland.' *Jökull* 29 (1980), pp. 7–28.

Maizels, J. K., and C. Caseldine. *Environmental Change in Iceland: Past and Present.* London: Kluwer Academic Publication, 1991.

Pétur M. Jónasson. 'Ecology of Oligotrophic, Subarctic Thingvallavatn.' *Oikos* 64 (1992), pp. 1–437.

Preusser, Hubertus. *The Landscapes of Iceland: Types and Regions.* The Hague: Junk, 1976.

Sigurður A. Magnússon. *Stallion of the North: The Unique Story of the Iceland Horse*. Reykjavík: Iceland Review, 1978.

Thorleifur Einarsson. *The Heimaey Eruption in Words and Pictures*. Reykjavík: Heimskringla, 1974.

Thorleifur Einarsson and Kristinn Albertsson. 'The Glacial History of Iceland during the Past Three Million Years.' *Philosophical Transactions of the Royal Society of London*, series B 318 (1988), pp. 637–44.

Williams, David. *Mývatn: A Paradise for Nature Lovers*. Reykjavík: Örn og Örlygur, 1988.

Opera

Operas by three Icelandic composers have been staged to date. They are:

Atli Heimir Sveinsson. *Silkitromman* (*The Silk Drum*). Premièred in Reykjavík in 1982. Also performed in Caracas.

————. *Vikivaki*. Nordic television production. First shown at Easter 1990.

Jón Ásgeirsson. *Þrymskviða* (*The Lay of Thrym*). Premièred in Reykjavík in 1974. Jón has composed another opera, *Galdra-Loftur* (*Loftur the Wizard*), based on some of Jóhann Sigurjónsson's poems and chiefly on his play of the same name, which uses a motif from an Icelandic folktale; not yet performed.

Karolína Eiríksdóttir. *Någon har jag sett* (*Someone I Have Seen*). Written for the Vadstena Academy in Sweden, premièred at Vadstena Castle, 1988. Also performed in Reykjavík.

Films

Examples of Icelandic feature films and foreign feature films with Icelandic connections, listed in chronological order:

Silent Films

Berg-Ejvind och hans hustru (*The Outlaw and His Wife*). Sweden, 1918. Directed by Victor Sjöström. The film is based on the play *Fjalla-Eyvindur* (*Eyvindur of the Mountains*) by Jóhann Sigurjónsson.

Hadda Padda. Denmark/Iceland, 1924. Directed by Gunnar Róbert Hansen and Guðmundur Kamban. Based on the play by Guðmundur Kamban.

Borgsläktens historia (*The History of the Borg Family*). Denmark, 1926.

Directed by Gunnar Sommerfelt. Based on the novel by Gunnar Gunnarsson. The main role is played by the Icelandic painter Muggur (Guðmundur Thorsteinsson).

Talking Films

Salka Valka. Sweden/Iceland, 1954. Directed by Arne Mattsson. Cinematographer: Sven Nykvist. Based on the novel by Halldór Laxness.

Land og synir (*Land and Sons*). Iceland, 1980. Directed by Ágúst Guðmundsson. Based on a novel by Indriði G. Þorsteinsson about the flight of people from the countryside during the crisis years of the 1930s.

Óðal feðranna (*Fathers' Estate*). Iceland, 1980. Directed by Hrafn Gunnlaugsson.

Útlaginn (*Outlaw: The Saga of Gísli*). Iceland, 1981. Directed by Ágúst Guðmundsson. Based on the Icelandic saga *Gísla saga Súrssonar*.

Hrafninn flýgur (*When the Raven Flies*). Iceland, 1984. Directed by Hrafn Gunnlaugsson.

Atómstöðin (*Atomic Station*). Iceland, 1984. Directed by Þorsteinn Jónsson. Based on the novel by Halldór Laxness.

Skytturnar (*White Whales*). Iceland, 1987. Directed by Friðrik Þór Friðriksson. Screenplay by Einar Kárason and Friðrik Þór Friðriksson.

Í skugga hrafnsins (*In the Shadow of the Raven*). Iceland, 1988. Directed by Hrafn Gunnlaugsson. Based on the chivalrous saga of Tristan and Isolde.

Kristnihald undir jökli (*Under the Glacier*). Iceland, 1989. Directed by Guðný Halldórsdóttir. Based on the novel by her father, Halldór Laxness.

Magnús. Iceland, 1989. Directed by Þráinn Bertelsson.

Films Produced 1990–1992

Pappírs Pési (*Paper Peter*). Iceland, 1990. Directed by Ari Kristinsson. Screenplay by Ari Kristinsson, based on an idea by Herdís Egilsdóttir.

Ryð (*Rust*). Iceland, 1990. Directed by Lárus Ýmir Óskarsson. Screenplay by Ólafur Haukur Símonarson, based on his play *Bílaverkstæði Badda*.

Hvíti víkingurinn (*The White Viking*). Iceland, 1991. Directed by Hrafn Gunnlaugsson.

Börn náttúrunnar (*Children of Nature*). Iceland, 1991. Directed by Friðrik Þór Friðriksson. Screenplay by Friðrik Þór Friðriksson and Einar Már Guðmundsson.

Ingaló. Iceland, 1992. Direction and screenplay by Ásdís Thoroddsen.

Svo á jörðu sem á himni (On Earth As in Heaven). Nordic co-production, 1992. Direction and screenplay by Kristín Jóhannesdóttir.

Veggfóður (Wallpaper). Iceland, 1992. Directed by Júlíus Kemp. Screenplay by Júlíus Kemp and Jóhann Sigmarsson.

Sódóma, Reykjavík. Iceland, 1992. Direction and screenplay by Óskar Jónasson.

Karlakórinn Hekla (Hekla, The Men's Choir). Iceland, 1992. Direction and screenplay by Guðný Halldórsdóttir.

Films in Production 1993

Hin helgu vé (The Sacred Mound). Directed by Hrafn Gunnlaugsson. Screenplay by Hrafn Gunnlaugsson and Bo Jonsson. Scheduled release date 1993.

Stuttur Frakki (Behind Schedule). Directed by Gísli Snær Erlingsson. Screenplay by Friðrik Erlingsson. Scheduled release date 1993.

Bíódagar (Movie Days). Directed by Friðrik Þór Friðriksson. Screenplay by Einar Már Guðmundsson and Friðrik Þór Friðriksson. Scheduled release date 1994.

Vita er Mors. Directed by Hilmar Oddsson. Screenplay by Hjálmar H. Ragnarsson and Hilmar Oddsson. Scheduled release date 1994.

❧ Index ❧